Washington Territory's Grand Lady

The Story of Matilda (Glover) Koontz Jackson

Julie McDonald Zander

Copyright © 2019
Julie McDonald Zander

Chapters of Life
Toledo, Washington
www.chaptersoflife.com
chaptersoflife1999@gmail.com

Library of Congress Control Number: 2019913513

ISBN 978-1-939685-42-1

Printed by Lightning Source

Cover design by Kathy Campbell

No part of this publication may be reproduced or transmitted in any form or by any means, electronic or mechanical, including photocopy, recording, or any information storage or retrieval system, without permission in writing from the author.

Cover photo of Matilda Jackson, C2016.0.185 Washington State Historical Society, Tacoma, Washington. Map from the Washington State Parks Department. Author photo of Jackson Courthouse.

Dedication

To the pioneer women
who endured hardship and heartache
to tame the wild land in the Northwest,
and to the pioneer women in my life,
especially my mother,
Nora Charline (Sheehan) McDonald.

Author's Note

Readers today may find the word Indian objectionable when referring to Native Americans, but in a history about a nineteenth-century pioneer, using modern, inclusive terms would be distracting and historically inaccurate, suggesting a racial tolerance not practiced at the time.

Acknowledgments

This book could not have been compiled without the letters, articles, diaries, and other files at the Washington State Library, the Lewis County Historical Museum, and the Oregon Historical Society. I also relied on access to historical records at Ancestry.com.

I appreciate the help from the late Margaret Shields, volunteer research librarian at the museum for nearly four decades.

Two of Matilda's granddaughters, Anna Koontz and Nettie Beiries, and stepgranddaughter Dr. Kate Gregg did a terrific job preserving her legacy as much as possible. Her daughter, Louisa (Jackson) Ware, set aside land dedicated as a state park honoring her mother.

Many earlier historians wrote about Matilda (Glover) Koontz Jackson, among them Noah B. Coffman and Charles Miles, who coauthored a column called Claquato Landmarks; Mabel Glover Root, whose family history is preserved at the Oregon Historical Society; and Trudy R. Hannon, author of *John R. Jackson: Washington's First American Pioneer*.

I am grateful to fellow historians and authors who reviewed this draft of the book before publication. Among those who provided corrections and suggestions are:

- Sandra Crowell, author of *The Land Called Lewis: A History of Lewis County, Washington*;
- Lewis County Commissioner Edna Fund;
- Fellow *Chronicle* columnist Brian Mittge and Kerry MacGregor Serl, coauthors of *George Washington of Centralia*;
- Vic Kucera, author of local history books *Onalaska: From Kansas to Washington…via Wisconsin, Arkansas, Minnesota, and Texas, 1886-1942*, and *Alpha: The classic hills of Alpha Prairie, Washington*;
- John Martin, former editor of *The Daily Chronicle* and a fellow historian.

I am forever grateful to my husband, Larry Zander, my personal editor, who reviews everything I write without complaint, year after year, saving me from countless embarrassing errors, and to my children, Paul and Nora, who spent years hearing about Matilda as I juggled research trips, writing, and parenting.

Contents

Prologue	9
The Coontz Family	11
The Glovers in Missouri	15
Nicholas and Matilda Coonse	17
Westward Bound	25
June and the Platte River	37
Oregon Trail Landmarks in July	53
Reaching the Rocky Mountains	63
Tragedy on the Snake River	67
Whitman Mission to Oregon City	81
John Robinson Jackson	93
Quick Courtship and a Wedding	107
Building a Courthouse	123
Trying to Create a Territory	137
Life at Highland Farm	153
Flying the First Flag	159
A Post Office and a Diary	169
Indian Wars and Grievous Loss	183
More Tragedy and Heartache	201
End of a Deadly Decade	207
Life and a Girl's Diary	209
Death of a Gentleman Farmer	251
A Widow Living with Her Son	283
Preserving Pioneer History	287
Legacy of a Great Lady	293
Endnotes	325
Bibliography	347

Prologue

Long braids flapping in the soft breeze, Matilda Glover tossed an egg into the Port Tobacco River. The white orb plunged beneath the surface. The next egg cracked and surfaced again in a streak of yellow floating downstream like a golden vein in a liquid serpent.

Eggs were plentiful on the Maryland farm of John Philpott and Matilda (Nettle) Glover, and little Matilda, the youngest of their eight children, enjoyed creating fun for herself like any other child.[1]

Nine slaves toiled on the farm where the Glovers raised their family, property handed down through the generations over the previous 150 years.[2] Matilda's ancestors were given the land in what became Maryland after sailing to the New World from England with Lord Baltimore in 1634. King Charles I gave the land east of the Potomac River to Lord Baltimore and it was named Maryland after the queen consort, Henrietta Maria.[3] Matilda's mother's mother, Edith Dutton Nettle, was a famous lace maker in England.[4]

Early settlers lived in a time of religious conflict between Roman Catholics and Puritans who sought freedom from persecution in the New World. Tensions over colonial rule increased during the 1700s, culminating in the American Revolution, the war for independence from England. Both young Matilda's grandfather and great-grandfather fought in the war to gain independence from British rule, and two of her brothers—James and Philip—faced fierce battles during the War of 1812 against the British.[5] She and her family loved this nation they called home.

Although her father owned slaves to help farm his land, he didn't like slavery. Quakers and Methodists, who opposed slavery on Christian grounds, together formed the Maryland Society for Promoting the Abolition of Slavery in the 1790s, and the Protection Society of Maryland in 1816. Their anti-slavery message fell on fertile ears. More plantation owners freed their slaves, and Matilda's father was among them.

He disliked slavery so much he wanted to move his family west to a state that outlawed the enslavement of humans as workhorses. The Cumberland Road, the nation's first federal highway, led from

Cumberland, Maryland, west and north to Illinois, a free state in what was then referred to as the Northwest Territory.[6]

By 1818, the Glovers had freed their slaves and sold their plantation. They packed all their belongings into a Conestoga wagon, hitched a six-horse team to it, and rumbled over the new Cumberland Road. They traveled nearly nine hundred miles by wagon and floated downriver on a raft. They wintered in Kentucky.

At seven years old, Matilda left behind everything familiar to her in Maryland.

But Matilda's uncle, her father's brother, thwarted their intended plans when he gave to his nephew and namesake, Philip Glover, a surprise parting gift of twenty-one slaves. That meant the family couldn't settle in Illinois, but instead veered south to Missouri, a state that still allowed slavery.

It also became the launching point for emigrants traveling two thousand miles west to Oregon Territory, a journey Matilda would take nearly three decades later as the pregnant wife of Nicholas Coonse* and mother of their four young sons. She would crack eggs again in a small cabin on a rise in the densely forested Pacific Northwest, where she entertained the first territorial governor of Washington as well as Generals Ulysses S. Grant, George B. McClellan, and Philip H. Sheridan, and hundreds of pioneers.

The surname of Nicholas was spelled many ways—Coons, Coonse, Coontz, Koontz, and even Kountz. A fort named for Nicholas's father and uncle was spelled Coontz, although Nicholas signed his one-page diary as Nicholas Coonse. After she married the youngest son of Nicholas and Matilda (Glover) Coonse, Charlotte (Simmons) Koontz finally changed the spelling of the surname to Koontz in 1876.

Chapter One

The Coontz Family

ALONG THE THIRTY-MILE ROUTE from St. Louis to St. Charles, Missouri, sat a trading post, tavern, and stagecoach station run by Nicholas Coontz, who kept trappers and fur traders entertained with tales of life on the wild frontier. His grandfather, John Coontz, a Dutchman, ventured west from New York to Pennsylvania and raised his family in Bedford County. It was in Pennsylvania where Nicholas grew up with his parents, Nicholas and Mary, and two brothers, John and Jacob.[1]

Family lore says that in 1780, during an attack by natives, eleven-year-old Nicholas Sr. fought with such courage the tribe spared his life, instead raising him as one of their own. At fifteen, while rounding up stolen cattle near a white village, Nicholas escaped. Others in the family insist that Nicholas was scalped and left for dead, but it's more likely he simply fled. He later mended relations with the tribe, which referred to him as their "white brother."[2]

Even after he married Rebecca McConnell, the Indians considered his house their own; in fact, one time the couple returned home to find a dozen or so Indians stretched out and sleeping on their cabin floor.

In the late 1780s, the Coontz family moved southwest and settled in Missouri. Together, Nicholas and his brothers, John and Jacob, owned nearly fifteen hundred acres of what was then the western frontier, an untamed land with few white people. They also owned slaves. Their land fell under Spanish ownership until 1800, and then under French rule

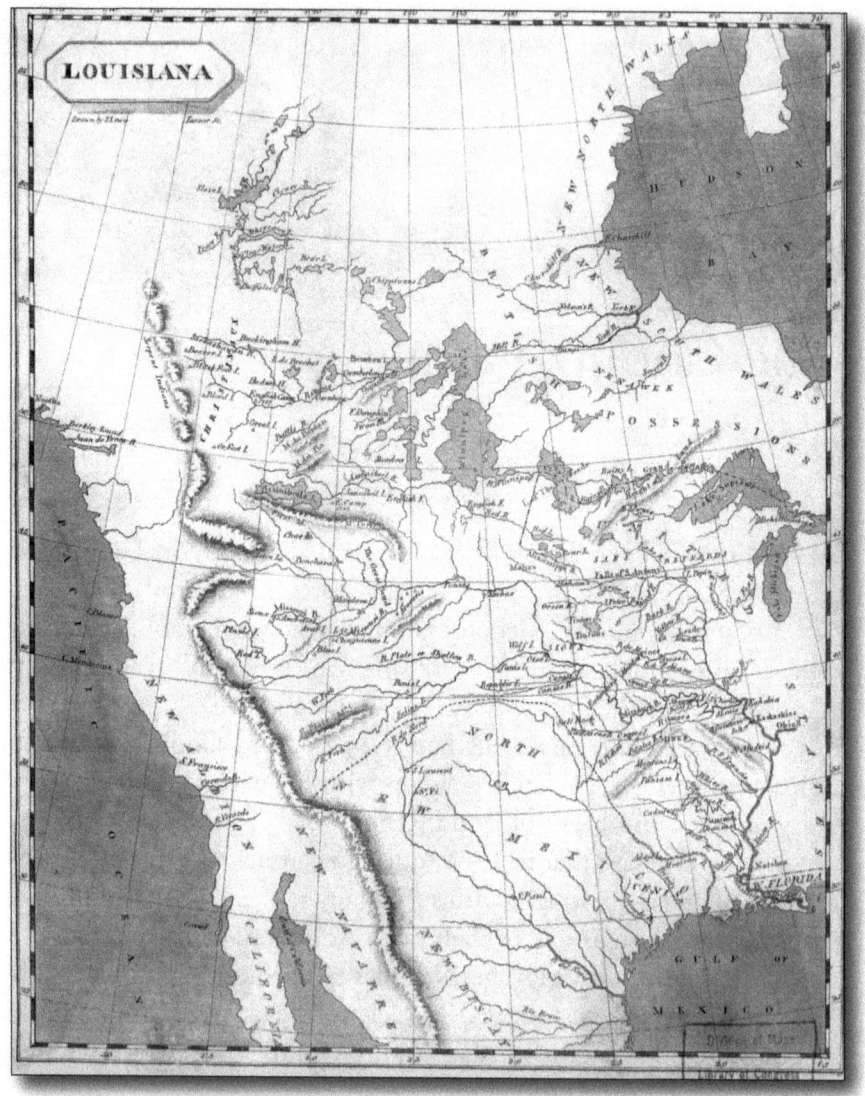

LIBRARY OF CONGRESS GEOGRAPHY AND MAP DIVISION

"Louisiana" Arrowsmith & Lewis New and Elegant General Atlas, 1804 by Aaron Arrowsmith and Samuel Lewis.

for three years. When Robert Livingston, James Monroe, and François Barbé-Marbois signed the Louisiana Purchase April 30, 1803, their property became part of the United States of America (although Missouri didn't become a state until 1821, and then only after a vigorous debate over the morality of slavery).[3]

Chapter One: The Coontz Family

The Coontz family left a legacy of protection in early-day Missouri. To offer protection from Indians in the early 1800s, rangers built Coontz Fort, close to a pond on 320 acres in Dardenne Township near Cottleville, on the old Indian trail between St. Louis and St. Charles.[4] The log building about eight miles west of St. Charles had holes in the upper story for aiming muskets at approaching enemies. It was named after Colonel John and Nicholas Coontz.[5] In 1808, Nicholas helped build Fort Osage and accompanied General William Clark of the Lewis and Clark Expedition fame to that site to sign a treaty while a member of Lt. William Mackey Wherry's St. Charles dragoons.[6]

After the War of 1812 ended in 1815, Nicholas converted the fort into a tavern and trading post along the main route linking east to west. Emigrants and missionaries traveled west along the Boone's LickBoon Road and often stopped at the Coontz place.[7] The Rev. John Mason referred to Nicholas Coontz as "rough, wicked and yet hospitable" after a visit in December 1818.[8]

At the trading post, Nicholas and Rebecca catered to passengers on as many as five westbound stages that passed daily leaving from St. Charles. Hundreds of wagons, carriages, and carts passed by their establishment, carrying emigrants west from Kentucky and Tennessee—at least 271 during October 1818 bound for the Boone's Lick country, according to the April 23, 1819, edition of the *Old Franklin Intelligencer*.[9] Twenty wagons a week, thousands of people, all headed west from St. Louis, following routes forged by explorers like Meriwether Lewis and Captain William Clark's Corps of Discovery, who traveled overland to Oregon in 1804, and General Zebulon Pike's explorations in 1810.

This land, granted to Nicholas Sr. by Spanish authorities in 1789, and confirmed by United States officials in 1818, today serves as home to Lindenwood University.

In this location Nicholas and Rebecca raised a family of six children, only a few miles from where the famous frontiersman Daniel Boone lived in his later years.[10] Their children—Sarah, Abraham, William, Felix, Maria, and Nicholas Jr., born in 1812—grew up hearing adventure stories woven by frontiersmen, trappers, and traders, tales about the lush, green land in the west. They witnessed the eagerness in the faces of emigrant families venturing toward Oregon country.

ST. CHARLES HISTORICAL SOCIETY

WAYMARKING.COM

The Coontz house built on the site of Louis Blanchette's property in St. Charles County, Missouri, in 1769. At left is the old historical marker for the Boone's Lick Road erected in 1913 by the Daughters of the American Revolution, and the newer marker at lower left mentioning Kountz Fort (1800). Below is the plat map showing John Coontz's property in 1817.

1920 PHOTO BY RUDOLPH GOEBEL POSTED ON WAYMARKING.COM

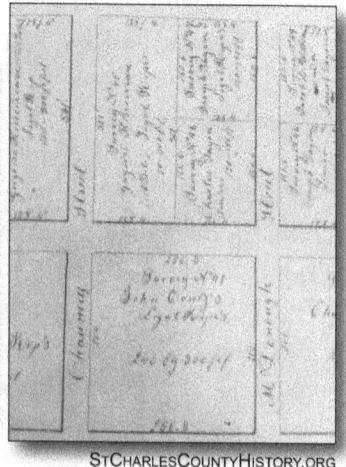

STCHARLESCOUNTYHISTORY.ORG

Chapter Two

The Glovers in Missouri

THE GLOVERS, who traveled from Charles County, Maryland, settled in 1818 on a farm outside of St. Charles, Missouri. They would have encountered members of the Coontz family, who operated the tavern and trading post eight miles from St. Charles. At the time, the population of the Territory of Missouri was less than seventy thousand people with fifteen percent of those slaves.

Within two years of the Glovers's arrival in Missouri Territory, a wedding joined the two families. Matilda's big brother Philip Glover, who was twenty-four, married Sarah "Sally" Coontz on November 12, 1819. She was sixteen.

At the time of the wedding, Matilda Glover was eight years old, having been born January 29, 1811. Sally's little brother, Nicholas, was seven. The two youngsters might have played together, but it's doubtful either one envisioned sharing a life and children in the future.

Three years later, Missouri marked a milestone August 10, 1821, when it became the twenty-fourth state admitted to the United States of America. The battle for statehood had bogged down for several years as abolitionists and slaveholders in Congress battled over whether Missouri would be a slave or a free state. The Missouri Territorial Legislature petitioned for admission as a slave state in 1819, but congressmen opposed to slavery feared upsetting the delicate balance between slave and free states and fought admission. To maintain that balance, the Missouri Compromise in 1820 granted Missouri admission as a slave state and Maine as a free state. The compromise also established the boundary between free and slave regions.[1] The capital was established temporarily at St. Charles and moved in 1826 to Jefferson City.[2]

The Glover and Coontz families likely joined in the statehood celebrations, although that's the year when Nicholas lost his larger-than-life father. The elder Nicholas Coontz fell from a horse and died of his injuries. At the time, Nicholas was only ten. A decade later, when he was twenty, his mother died in April 1831.

When she was eighteen, Matilda met a handsome young man named Marcus and they courted. He lived in St. Charles, which had been Missouri's capital city from 1821 to 1826. They even became engaged, according to one of Matilda's granddaughters. But distance hampered the relationship. Eventually, Marcus married another woman and broke Matilda's heart.[3]

She continued to live at home with her parents, John Philpott and Matilda (Nettle) Glover, the youngest child with four older brothers and three older sisters. Matilda did attend a few dances in St. Charles—in fact, an invitation to a dinner ball dated June 18, 1835, remained in the family's possession—but as the years passed, she likely worried about becoming a spinster. At the time, most women married by the time they were twenty and most men by twenty-six.[4]

While attending Marion College in Alabama, Matilda's brother Matthew, who was only a year older, wrote a letter to his eldest brother, Philip. At the time, Philip and Sally lived near Troy, Missouri. The postscript on Matthew's May 9, 1837, letter stated: "Give respects to all the pretty girls you see for girls are as scarce here as hens' teeth."

Matilda, described by a territorial governor's wife years later as "a handsome woman," might have spurned early romantic overtures from the young boy she'd known as a child, Nicholas Coontz, who spelled his surname Coonse. But at the age of twenty-six, she agreed to marry him. They wed in May 1837.

The following year, Matilda gave birth to Henry, followed two years later by Alonzo Barton in 1840, then Felix "Grundy" a year later, and, finally, John Nicholas April 6, 1844.

In 1843, Matilda's father, John Philpott Glover, died of apoplexy, likely a cerebral hemorrhage or a stroke.

Chapter Three

Nicholas and Matilda Coonse

NICHOLAS AND MATILDA COONSE lived on a farm near St. Charles. But with farming comes risks, as crops and cattle depend on the grace of Mother Nature for growth. The Panic of 1837 didn't help.

The year they married, a financial crisis in the United States plunged the nation into a recession that lowered profits, prices, and wages. Unemployment increased. Land values plummeted. Gold and silver prices rose as the value of paper money fell. Banks, factories, and businesses closed. Farmers received little for their crops. Many blamed the crisis on the economic policies of the administration of President Andrew Jackson, who served from 1829 to 1837, and his refusal to charter the Second Bank of the United States. He paid off the national debt in 1835 using federal money from land sales, but the following year, Congress decreed that such money should be distributed to the states. President Jackson, in turn, declared in a Specie Circular, or an executive order, that payment for federal land must be made only in gold or silver. When President Martin Van Buren assumed office in 1837, he inherited a major economic crisis.[1]

Finally, in 1843, the national economy started to recover, but by then struggling farmers like the Coonse family had been forced to sell land at low prices. Nicholas sold property to John Spencer in 1841 for eight hundred thirty-five dollars.[2]

Just as they tried to recover from the panic, disaster struck again when the Missouri River flooded in June 1844.

"The greatest calamity has befallen the inhabitants residing in the Missouri bottoms, by the most unprecedented rise in the Missouri River within the recollection of the oldest settlers," *The Boon's Lick Times* of Fayette, Missouri, reported June 22, 1844.[3] The Missouri River joins the Mississippi River about ten miles north of St. Louis, near St. Charles.

"The amount of property swept away by the flood is incalculable. Farms are entirely inundated and a great many houses have been carried away, together with stock and property of every description. The water is deep enough in the streets of Rocheport, Old Franklin, Brunswick and Chariton to make them navigable for the largest class of Steamboats and a great many families have narrowly escaped with their lives. So much distress has never been known in this country. Thousands are now without a home, every thing they possessed in the world having been carried away by the flood."

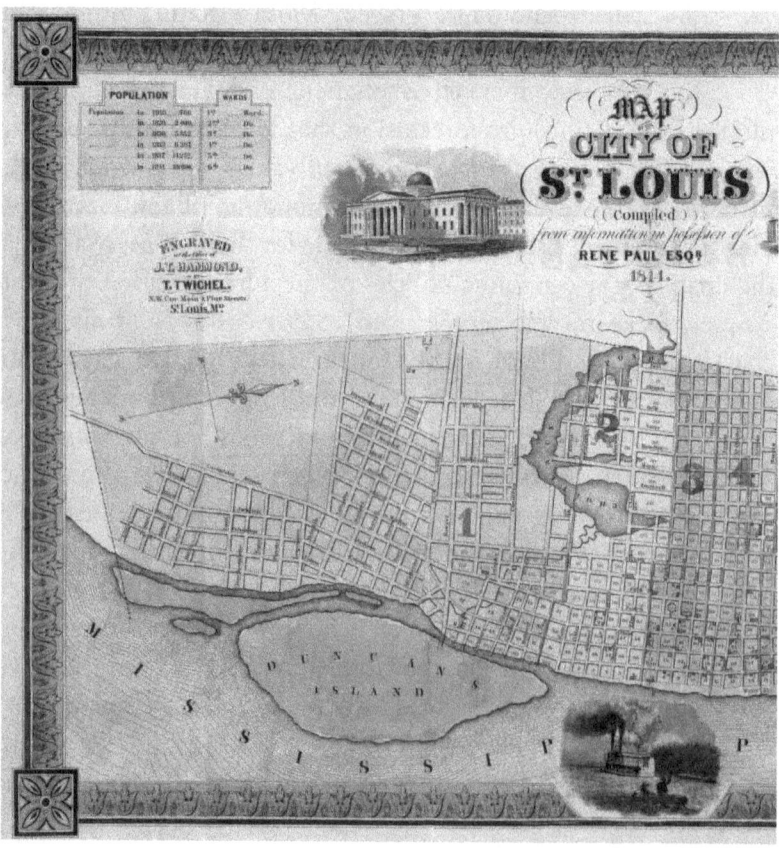

Meanwhile, a cholera epidemic claimed the lives of healthy men and women in Illinois, Missouri, and elsewhere during the 1830s and 1840s, reaching a peak in 1849.[4] Nobody knew for sure how to treat the severe and often fatal disease, although doctors tried bleeding, purging, opium, and sometimes rinsing with salt solutions. Panic spread as fast as the disease.

In nearby St. Louis, five hundred people died from cholera in 1832, and that number increased tenfold to nearly five thousand by 1850, claiming between five and ten percent of the population. John Snow pinpointed drinking water as the culprit in a cholera epidemic in London in 1849.

In addition, political friction between the slave states and the free states continued to increase, and war loomed on the horizon.

But the combination of the economic crisis, flooding, and disease prompted many to seek a better future out west by following the

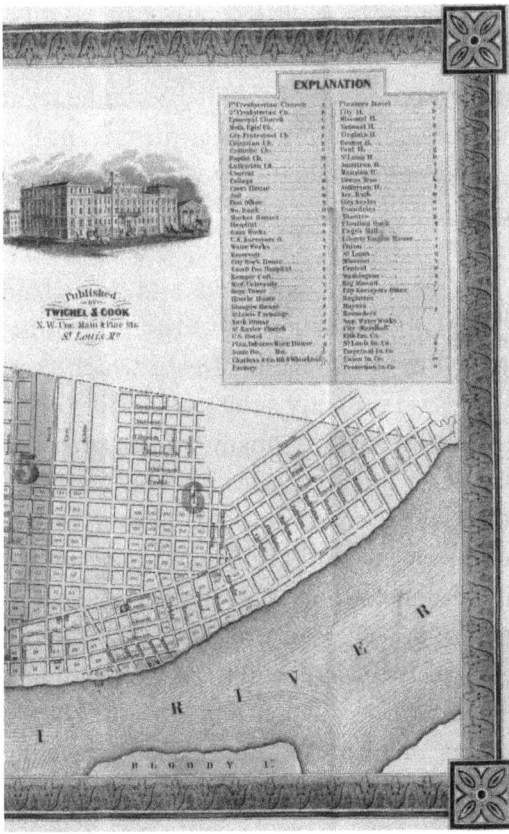

The map at left shows St. Louis in 1844 and the city streets flooded when the Missouri River rose.

Oregon Trail. Hundreds of people gathered in May 1843 at Independence, Missouri, as one of the first waves of emigrants with dreams of Oregon headed west. The 1844 floods prompted more to follow the trail, and the westward migration soared, drawing more than 315,000 settlers to California, Oregon, and Washington by 1860, according to John D. Unruh Jr., author of *The Plains Across: The Overland Emigrants and the Trans-Mississippi West, 1840–1860*. Most of those traveled west after the 1849 Gold Rush in California. Between 1840 and 1848, the number of emigrants traveling west totaled 18,847, Unruh said.

The intrepid emigrants received encouragement from President James Knox Polk, a Tennessee Democrat who campaigned for office insisting that it was the nation's "manifest destiny" to settle the land all the way west to the Pacific and south into Texas.[5] God had ordained that the United States expand west, including California and the entire Oregon Territory, wresting the land north of the Columbia River from the British Empire. Patriotic Americans needed to claim the land for the United States. The presidential campaign slogan, "Fifty-four forty or fight!" urged that the northern border of the United States be set at a latitude line of fifty-four degrees, forty minutes near the present-day southern border of Alaska.[6] A compromise at latitude forty-nine degrees established the boundary between the United States and Canada in the Treaty of Oregon signed June 15, 1846.

Most emigrants sought free fertile farmland and forestland promised in the untamed Willamette Valley of Oregon Territory. Congress had passed the Pre-Emption Act of 1841, which gave newcomers the opportunity to claim property simply by settling on it.

Despite turmoil facing them in Missouri, many women preferred to stay near family and friends rather than venturing into the unknown. Husbands often persuaded their wives to accompany them west, or they simply made the decision to uproot the family and go. Other men left to follow the Oregon Trail and promised to send for their families when they settled. Sometimes they did; others created new families.

Whether Nicholas had to persuade Matilda to travel west with him in 1847 is unknown, but it's likely. She was a mother of four boys—nine, seven, six, and three—and pregnant before they left. Traveling west meant leaving her widowed mother, Matilda (Nettle) Glover, saying a final goodbye as nobody could fathom traveling two thousand miles and five months for a visit.

But Nicholas possessed a yearning for adventure nurtured by tales of trappers, traders, and mountain men coupled with a desire for fertile farmland in the Willamette Valley. Fathers needed to provide a place where their sons could grow and flourish, a place with abundant land where they could raise families of their own. He might have tried to reassure Matilda with the news that the president had approved establishing military posts along the trail to Oregon.

Before they left, most men sought advice on what to take with them from those who had previously traveled west and returned to write about their adventures.

One of those was Francis Parkman, an American historian whose sketches of life on the Oregon Trail and in the Rocky Mountains appeared as serialized installments in *The Knickerbocker* magazine between 1847 and 1849.[7]

Many relied on *The Emigrants' Guide to Oregon and California*, written by Lansford W. Hastings and published in 1845.[8] He wrote about his journey westward and misfortunes such as disease and death. People died of accidents and illnesses.

He also spoke of the blessings found in Oregon Territory south of the Columbia River.

"It is a very beautiful and productive valley, and as it is well timbered, well watered, and as it yields a superabundance of all the grasses, and the various other kinds of vegetation, it is admirably suited to agricultural and grazing purposes," the book stated.

In his book, Hastings identified "the equipment, supplies, and the method of traveling."

They needed a solid four- by nine-foot wagon, narrow enough to turn corners on the trail but long and sturdy to haul their supplies. Men plastered the wagon beds with layers of tar to keep them watertight at river crossings.

Oxen—castrated male cattle trained as draft animals—were better than horses or mules, Hastings said. "Oxen endure the fatigue and heat, much better than either horses or mules; and they also, subsist much better, upon vegetation alone." They're also less likely to be stolen by Indians since they move so slowly, he said, and they don't wander far

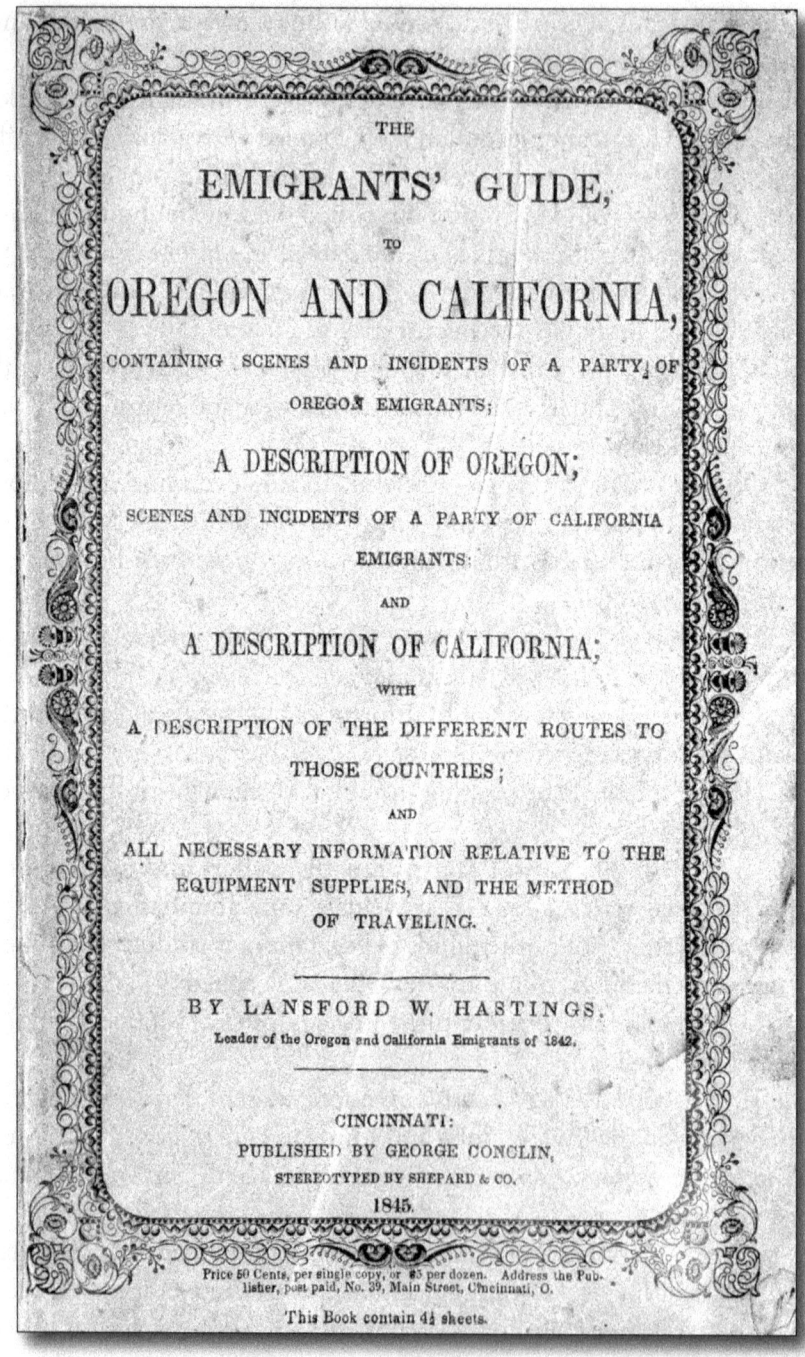

The front page of The Emigrants' Guide to Oregon and California *written by Lansford W. Hastings, published in 1845.*

from camp. However, he urged emigrants to bring oxen older than five but younger than ten so they could endure the long trip without their hooves wearing out.

As for supplies, Hastings said, each emigrant needed at least two hundred pounds of flour, 150 pounds of bacon, ten pounds of coffee, twenty pounds of sugar, and ten pounds of salt. For a family of six, that amounted to a lot of food.

"… Children as well as adults, require, about twice the quantity of provisions which they would, at home, for the same length of time," Hastings wrote. "This is attributable to their being deprived of vegetables, and other sauce, and their being confined to meat and bread alone; as well as the fact, of their being subjected to continued and regular exercise, in the open air, which gives additional vigor and strength, which, greatly improves the health, and therefore, gives an additional demand for food."

Anyone who depends on buffalo for meat will starve, he said, as they'd have little time to hunt, and when they did, it would be in the company of others. "Then it would seem, that, although the buffalo are vastly numerous, they cannot be relied upon," Hastings said.

The book recommended emigrants carry a good gun with at least five pounds of powder, and more ammunition if they brought pistols. Cooking utensils needed were "a baking-kettle, frying-pan, tea-kettle, tea-pot, and coffee-pot" along with a coffee mill, knives, forks, spoons, and tin plates and cups.

For sleeping, they'd need only blankets, sheets, coverlets, and pillows, since many emigrants who took feather beds discarded them along the way to ease the burden on oxen. They also needed "good wagon covers and tents, tent poles, axes, spades, and hoes, as well as strong ropes, of about sixty feet in length, for each horse or mule, with a supply of stakes."

Hastings recommended bringing tobacco, beads, handkerchiefs, blankets, butcher knives, fishhooks, and ready-made clothing such as shirts, vests, and pantaloons to trade with Indians. They would each need extra shoes since they'd be walking most of the two thousand miles to Oregon Territory. Nicholas planned to use oxen to pull the wagon, and the supplies, furniture, and utensils would make it heavy enough without the added weight of passengers.

They also needed money to pay for ferries and to replenish food supplies at forts along the trail. Nicholas planned to sell his farm, but it hadn't sold by the time he was ready to leave in the spring of 1847. His brother-in-law and sister, Philip and Sarah "Sally" (Koontz) Glover, gave him cash and promised to the sell the farm for him.[9]

"Emigrants should, invariably, arrive at Independence, Mo., on, or before, the fifteenth day of April, so as to be in readiness, to enter upon their journey, on or before, the first day of May," Hastings wrote.

Chapter Four

Westward Bound

MATILDA AND NICHOLAS SOLD almost everything they owned. They gave keepsakes to family members and culled their belongings down to only a few. Packed with food, gunpowder, and other supplies for the journey, the four-foot-wide wagon didn't leave much room for keepsakes.

On April 20, 1847, the couple and their four sons headed west from St. Charles to Montgomery County[1], where they stopped to visit their older siblings—Matilda's older brother Philip and Nicholas's sister Sarah (Coontz) Glover. The Glovers lived in a white, flint-rock farmhouse surrounded by fertile fields, bountiful orchards, and outbuildings where their Negro slaves lived. Nicholas and Matilda wanted to say goodbye and let their boys bid farewell to their cousins.

Philip and Sarah's eldest son, William, and his wife, Jane, were accompanying them to Oregon. William, twenty-four, and Jane, nearly twenty, had been married since October 1843.

Since they were spending the night, Sarah and Matilda rolled out beds on the floor upstairs where the boys would sleep, then proceeded back downstairs to discuss the upcoming trip. Philip and Sarah wanted to move west too, but they weren't ready to go yet. He intended to free his slaves and sell both his farm and Nicholas's since he had given them money to purchase supplies. Nicholas promised to keep a journal of the trip to let them know about the trail.

The Old Oregon Trail as published by Ezra Meeker in 1907.

When noise from upstairs interrupted the discussion, Matilda climbed the steps, dressing down her boys in her gentle voice, telling them to keep quiet—a trip she repeated several times before her excited young ones finally fell asleep.

Saying goodbye to her mother proved difficult. She had lived with her mother for twenty-six years. They promised to write, but each knew they'd likely never see each other again in this life. Matilda embraced her mother but her religious upbringing told her she must cleave to her husband.

They left the first of May to join a wagon train heading into the unknown country. They trudged beside the heavily laden wagon rather than adding to the burden pulled by their team of six oxen. A double-folded white canvas, treated with linseed oil to make it more waterproof, covered bowed strips of wood evenly spaced over the nine-foot wagon bed. Following the guidelines in Hastings' book, they crammed the wagon with wooden crates and barrels filled with blankets, clothing, flour, sugar, rice, coffee, bacon in brine, and dried peas, beans, and fruit.

Chapter Four: Westward Bound

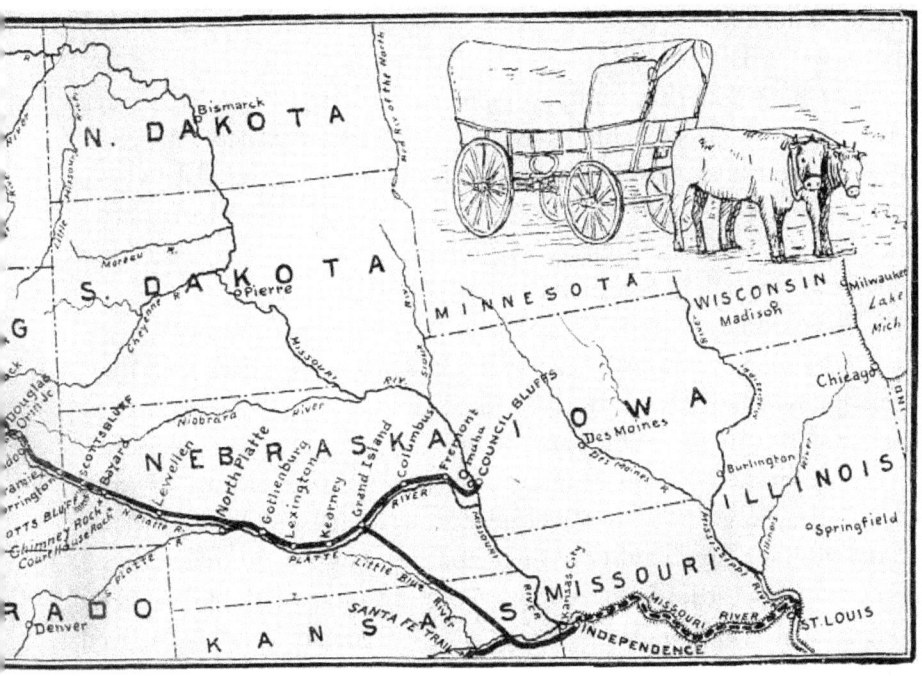

WIKIPEDIA COMMONS

A box contained cakes of soap, another held saleratus [powder for baking], and a third, candles. Kitchen utensils dangled from overhead hooks in the bowed wooden ribs. Barrels of gunpowder, tucked in the wagon, remained ready for use at a moment's notice. A heavy chest with the family's most precious belongings took up a section of the wagon over the wheels, with items piled on top and farming tools tucked underneath. Matilda stowed her cloth bag containing needles, thimble, and thread behind the seat along with a medicine kit for emergencies.

This was it! They were in their mid-thirties with four sons, leaving the land where they grew up for a new home in the fertile Willamette Valley, two thousand miles away.

"Giddyap!" Nicholas shouted, slapping the reins on the hindquarters of the six oxen pulling the wagon, which weighed nearly two thousand pounds. The oxen were Pet, Baul, Browny, Duke, Old Buck, and Jerry.[2]

They headed northwest toward Independence, known as the "jumping off" point for the Oregon Trail. Traveling between fifteen and twenty miles each day, the trip from St. Charles to Independence took about twelve days.

On May 12, they camped eight miles west of the McKinney pasture at Elm Grove, which was twelve miles from Independence. It was the gathering place for emigrants traveling west, the place where they formed into wagon trains and elected a captain to lead them across the plains. Those with mules left before the slower plodding oxen, and men on horseback herded hundreds of head of livestock.

The Coonses and the Glovers joined a company of eighty wagons and more than a thousand head of stock. To elect a captain, men from a company usually lined up behind the man they supported for the position. But in their company, such maneuvering wasn't necessary. Everyone backed Joseph Magone, a twenty-six-year-old miller from New York who seemed a natural leader.[3] In fact, he later became a major in the military. The handsome single man seeking adventure had hired on to work the cattle but agreed to serve as captain instead. He promised to remain alert and vigilant and do his best to see that everyone arrived safely in the Willamette Valley.

Shortly after leaving Kansas City, they traveled past several farms without fences, rumbling along the pleasantly rolling treeless plains.

Each day, Matilda and the other women wearing ankle-length calico dresses unpacked cooking utensils, gathered wood, and cooked meals over an open fire, morning and night, using a cast iron skillet and Dutch oven secured above the flames by a tripod. They ground coffee beans, drew water from a keg attached to the wagon's side, and boiled it in kettles over the flames. At midday, they often ate a cold meal of leftover biscuits and bacon. The women washed the dishes, repacked the cooking utensils, and kept an eye on their children as they all walked beside the wagons. Occasionally, they found a creek to wash clothes.

The two older boys helped their pa by wiping out the dirt clogging the nostrils of their hardworking oxen. They covered a stick with a cloth and swiped inside each nostril, pulling out any debris collected inside during that day's travel. They also counted the revolutions of the front wagon wheels to keep track of how far they had traveled.[4]

Travel grew tedious and women had to keep their children entertained with games or stories or even singing of Bible hymns. They identified birds, flowers, and plants along the route, and gathered twigs

Chapter Four: Westward Bound

The diary of Nicholas Coonse started in May 1847.

(Washington State Library's collection of the Jackson, Koontz, Glover family papers, 1837–1952.)

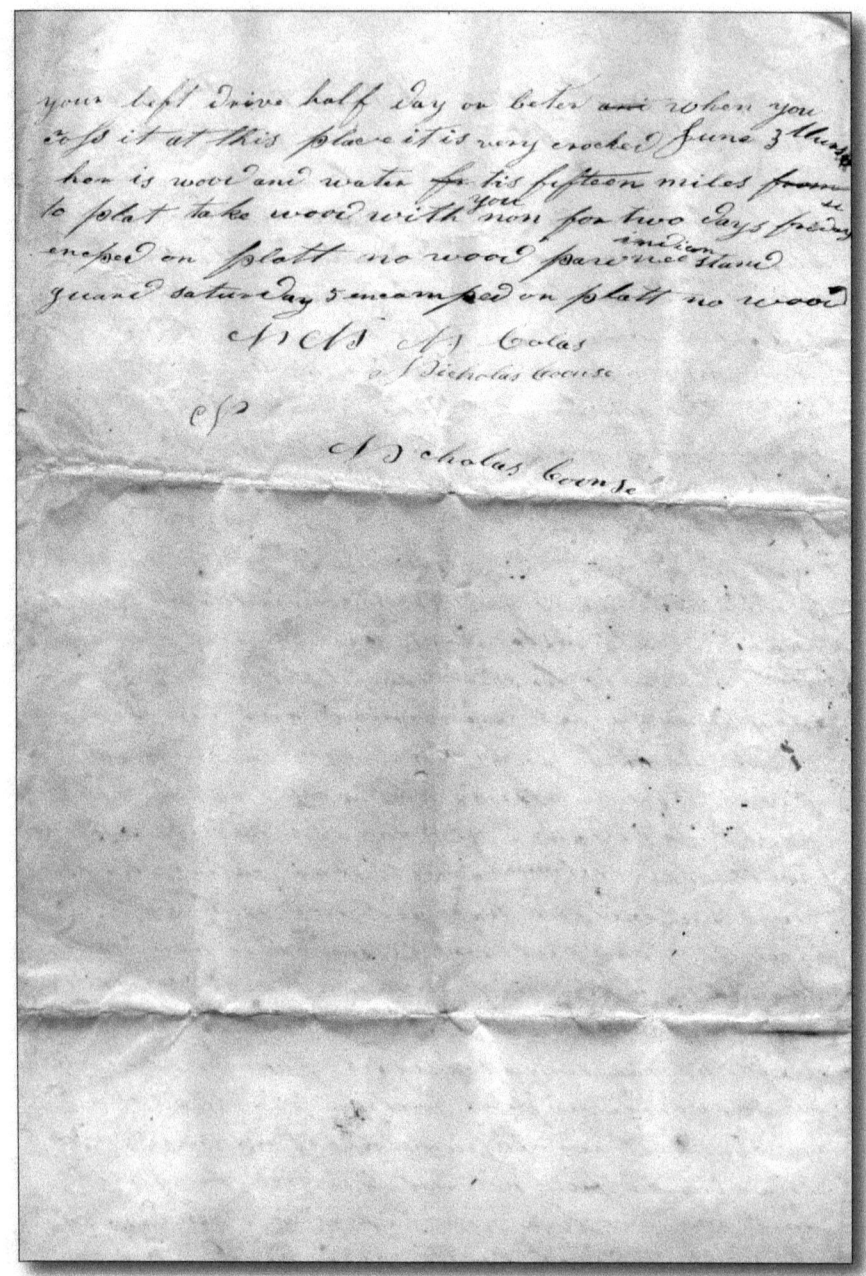

WASHINGTON STATE LIBRARY'S COLLECTION OF THE JACKSON, KOONTZ, GLOVER FAMILY PAPERS, 1837–1952.

The back side of the one-page diary written and signed by Nicholas Coonse.

and dried grasses for fires as they walked. Matilda often had to yank on her skirt to pull her petticoats free from clinging weeds, grasses, thorns, and thistles.

At night, after pitching the tent where they'd sleep, they gathered around the campfire and Nicholas shared stories with the boys, usually about his fearless father, their grandfather. Captured by Indians as a boy, he had learned to hunt and often crawled into hollow trees and dens to feel whether the bears inside were fat enough to kill.[5]

When he remembered and found time to do it, Nicholas jotted short notes about the trip on a sheet of paper.

On May 18, a Monday, Nicholas cryptically wrote in his journal, "Crossed Cow [Kaw or Kansas River] river. Drove four miles and encamped wood and water. This creek is bad. Drove out five miles oxen."[6] Two days later, he wrote that the company drove twelve miles before camping. "This place is worse than the other one," he said.

On Saturday, May 22, the Coonse wagon broke an axletree, and the following day, the company had two coupling poles break. "Make your coupling pole stout and your axletree four inches at the big end of the hub," Nicholas wrote. "Have your timbers of the best and well-seasoned wood."

Nicholas described the road in Missouri from Columbia to Independence as good, except for a sixty-mile stretch. "The road from tharon is first-rate except sum places they are very bad," he stated. "We organized and divided and subdivided; went through this operation twice."

Organizing nearly a hundred wagons each day proved unwieldy so the company broke into smaller groups, with twenty-seven wagons led by Captain John McKinney and sixteen by Captain Elijah Patterson, with Captain Joseph Magone in charge of the remaining thirty-seven. The Coonses remained with Magone's train and slowly became acquainted with other people in their company.

After erecting the tent and spreading blankets on the ground beneath it, boys gathered near the center of the camp or found a spot to shoot marbles with other children who had finished their chores. They returned with stories of boys like thirteen-year-old James Gibson, who with his younger brother Humphrey helped Phineas Carruthers herd sixty head of cattle while their family traveled in one of the wagons.[7]

The Coonse family and other emigrants loaded all their worldly goods into wagons like the one above for their trips west on the Oregon Trail.

Mrs. James Jory, known as Sarah Budd before she married a young Englishman, was already with child as they began the trip. So were several other women. Matilda scarcely showed although another was growing in her womb.

Tramping on foot, the emigrants had plenty of time to admire the scenery around them—whip-poor-wills singing in a hickory tree; strawberries growing wild along the trail, ripe for the eating; shrubby timber providing twigs and limbs for firewood.

As long as she had her family close, Matilda could endure the hardships of a trip west, sleeping on the ground in a tent, sweeping dust daily from inside the wagon, kneading dough outside, baking bread and cooking meals over open fires.

Nicholas, a jovial man who liked most people, greeted the other emigrants like old friends—at least most of them. At times he found himself frustrated with a few of the folks, such as on Sunday, May 23, when he wrote about a "great uproar about calves and horses all because

Chapter Four: Westward Bound

Jim Loflin [sic]. He is grumbling with the women about their calves."⁸ The women wanted the calves kept inside the circle of wagons to protect them, rather than left in the field with the larger animals.

James Laughlin and his brother, Samuel, were among the eleven Laughlins traveling with Captain Magone.⁹

Each morning the men scoured the nearby hillsides rounding up their oxen and cattle for the day's journey, which is what Nicholas was doing when fire damaged his wagon.

"My wagon sheet caught fire but was discovered when first flaming and put out," Nicholas wrote in his journal May 23. "My powder and provisions was in it. I was hunting the oxen at the time. It caught fire on the inside of the circle. No fire was made on the inside that morning. Whether it was an accident by smoking or not I can't tell. Jim Laughlin and me has had some difference."

Although he suspected the accident might have been something more, Nicholas probably didn't speak those suspicions aloud. He did write them in his journal, though, and shared them with his wife. She may have reminded him of what the Bible said in Ephesians. "Be ye angry, and sin not: let not the sun go down upon your wrath."

It was just as well that Nicholas left his worries of the previous day behind, as the next day the wagon broke a wheel, which required the Coonse family to stay behind in camp near a creek to repair it.

"When you get here, take notice of this creek by its timber," Nicholas wrote on Tuesday, May 26. "The timber is generally cotton[wood]. We'll make up this better than two days [delay]."

In his journal, Nicholas described the stream as quite crooked where his wagon crossed onto a picturesque prairie.

The Coonse family, as well as many other emigrants on the Oregon Trail in 1847, heard about Henderson Luelling, a bearded Quaker man from Iowa with a long face and a green thumb who left Missouri only a few days after Magone's company. He was taunted at times for

WIKIMEDIA COMMONS

Henderson Luelling hauled fruit trees west on the trail.

hauling a heavy second wagon west filled with seven hundred grafted fruit trees, with up to sixty different varieties of apples, pears, plums, peaches, currants, gooseberries, grapes, hickory nuts, and black walnut. To create his traveling nursery, he filled the long sturdy wagon bed with charcoal, soil, and manure as compost and planted seedlings inside. He traveled with his wife, Elizabeth, and eight children, and a couple of other Quaker families, the Hockettes and the Fishers.[10]

When the Coonses caught up with their wagon train, the family discovered that a French-Canadian bishop and seven Roman Catholic priests had joined the company at Captain Magone's invitation. Augustin Magloire Alexandre Blanchet, who was traveling west to serve as bishop of Walla Walla in Oregon Territory, kept an extensive diary of his journey. He traveled with an older brother and several missionaries. The priests had hired a guide to hunt for them and lead the animals as far as Fort Hall.[11] The priests and others who had joined the company brought the total number of rigs under Magone's supervision to forty-four.

The wagons rumbled over the rough prairie, bouncing and shifting from side to side, the oxen plodding along at two or three miles an hour hauling such heavy loads. Setting up camp near the Big Blue River, they saw a grave at the foot of a tree, with a marker at one end: "Mrs. Sara Keyes, 70, deceased May 1846."[12]

A grave alongside the trail dampened the spirits of men, women and even children, reminding each that they were traveling a trail fraught with danger that could kill any one of them, any time. Illness. Accidents. Many likely paused

This image is available from Bibliothèque et Archives nationales du Québec under the reference number P560,S2,D1,P95

Augustin Magloire Alexandre Blanchet, who joined the Magone train, circa 1870.

to pray and ask God to safely see them across the plains, over the rivers, and through the mountains to Oregon Territory.

James Jory, the husband of Sarah (Budd) Jory, left Illinois to travel west because he feared for the safety of his young bride with the cholera running rampant. His father and brothers planned to join him along the trail. He recorded his recollections of their time on the trail.[13]

He noted that a family named Wilcox had started west but perished early on the trip when they contracted measles. They had spent many hours in the rain looking after cattle. All except two girls and a little boy died. How heartbreaking to hear of such a tragedy!

The wagons spread out on the open prairie, a long line of white canvasses flapping in the breeze as far as the eye could see, sometimes creating new paths, other times following the ruts of earlier wagons. They met companies that started from St. Joseph in Missouri as well as from Council Bluffs in Iowa. Usually they traveled between eight and eighteen miles a day. They left about seven each morning, rising early to eat breakfast and round up the cattle, then stopped for lunch at midday and set up camp around five o'clock each evening.

Matilda and the boys scoured the nearby land for wood to stockpile for use in campfires when they reached the open prairie. On May 29, as they rolled near what Blanchet referred to as the Little Sandy before noon, they spotted a freshly dug grave on the right bank. A marker identified it as the final resting place of six-year-old R. Young, who had died only eight days earlier, on May 21, 1847.[14]

A child's death prompted mothers to hold their babies tighter as they imagined the pain that ripped through the heart of Mrs. Young when she left her little one buried beside a river.

The wagons followed the old road to the left, which was shorter by up to eight miles, according to guidebooks, even though it had flooded in the past.

As they traveled, the landscape changed with limestone bluffs visible in all directions and new shrubs and flowers growing in the sandy soil. As they approached the Big Sandy River, Captain Magone stopped the wagons before they crossed.

Reaching down to ruffle the fur of his dog, Ring, the captain ordered, "Dash in, Ring!" The canine careened into the water, his master following on horseback with a long pole in hand, measuring the depth as he rode. He then turned back to order the lead wagon to follow. This became Captain Magone's routine at every river.[15] After crossing the Big Sandy, the company traveled another four miles before camping.

That night, rain pelted the tents and wagons, punctuated by clapping of thunder and flashes of lightning in the black clouds. A violent wind drove the rain into the canvas, drenching everyone and everything inside. The next morning, after a cold wet night, the emigrants packed up the soggy blankets and tents.

The rain poured from the skies during the day, with the first sighting of an antelope the only break in the travel routine. The loose sandy soil morphed into an uneven muck that slowed the oxen's progress. The company reached the Little Blue River, which they followed for three days as they passed over grassy hills with granite boulders toward the landmark Platte River. The wagon train covered more than twenty miles May 31, ending the rather wet month on a weary but satisfied note, knowing they were hundreds of miles closer to their goal.

Despite occasional conflicts, Magone didn't have to break up any major fistfights, unlike in another company that crossed the Oregon Trail in 1847, where quarrels erupted into fights and men drew guns, women joined in, and a fellow pulled a knife. That occasion resulted in the expulsion of one family from the wagon train.

Chapter Five

June and the Platte River

IN EARLY JUNE, the Coonse wagon rolled over bumpy prairie grass toward the Platte River, which would guide the emigrants through much of what later became Nebraska. In the hot sun, mirage-like visions of lakes or pools of water appeared at the bottom of high rocky bluffs dotted with brushy thickets. Despite the hordes of people who had already traveled west, most of the campsites provided ample vegetation for the cattle. Five additional wagons joined Magone's company.

After finishing breakfast and cleaning the dishes, Matilda packed everything tightly into the wagon and held little John's hand as they walked alongside the wagon rumbling across the prairie. Grundy and the other boys scampered ahead but steered clear of the wagons as they helped their mother gather twigs and branches for kindling, tossing them into a basket attached to the wagon.

The wagons left the Blue River and approached the wide Platte. The wind blew and rain drenched the canvas tops covering the wagons. Many hunkered inside the wagons as the oxen plunged dutifully forward, hauling their heavy loads. The company forged ahead another eight miles after crossing the river. Men checked the wet yokes to avoid harming the oxen's necks. The company had planned to remain near the Blue River an extra day to gather wood for axles, yokes, and campfires, but since the guide hired by the Catholic priests had gone hunting for antelope, the wagons kept moving. The travelers knew it would be tough to find wood before reaching Fort Laramie.

On Thursday, June 3, Captain Magone organized the men into six groups of ten, each supervised by a sergeant, to stand guard during half the night to prevent the theft of horses and cattle.

"Don't pull the trigger during the night without seeing imminent danger," he told the men.[1]

He exempted the bishop and priests because of their religious status and the fact that their hired guide provided services to the entire company. With more rain pouring from the skies, the company rested for the day to relieve their oxen. Women took advantage of the time to wash clothes in rivers or creeks using soap and a washboard.

The following day, the company traveled eighteen miles to the Platte River—320 miles from Independence. The smooth road in the white clay and sandy soil enabled the wagons to move more quickly. Although they could see wood on the many islands in the middle of the river, the water was too high for even the most adventurous men to swim for fuel. Instead, for the first time, the men, women, and children gathered the sun-dried dung of buffalo to feed the fire, fuel often referred to as "buffalo chips."

At night the wagons often created a circle, with men taking shifts as guards to watch for any threats to the animals or the people. Inside the circled wagons, a few men played the flute or violin or clarinet, while couples danced to the music or relaxed after a long day of walking across the vast prairie before turning in. Children played together, creating clever games of catch using buffalo chips or anything else they could find.

Meals most often consisted of fried bacon for breakfast, along with hardtack or soda biscuits, cornmeal mush, or rice sweetened with milk, butter, and sugar. Sometimes the women whipped together pancakes or johnnycakes using cornmeal. For lunch and dinner, they often ate beans and biscuits with fresh butter churned along the trail by the wagon's motion. Occasionally they enjoyed a molasses pudding, apple dumpling soup, or berry pie.

Like other mothers, Matilda kept her boys close, fearing accidents or injuries. They spotted black-tailed prairie dogs, little squirrel-like critters, but their mother quickly called her boys back to avoid the possibility of being bitten by poisonous snakes or losing sight of the wagon train if they darted off. She wanted her entire family to arrive safely in Oregon.

Chapter Five: June and the Platte River

They spotted wagon trains ahead and behind them, crossing the prairie in search of a new home. Some raced ahead, but most traveled at a steady rate, knowing the western territory offered plenty of land for emigrants willing to farm it.

Often after rains, the oxen slogged through mud, pulling wagons through muck that covered the axles. Unlike horses, the oxen were sturdy, strong, and much less prone to injury. Yet the occasional white skulls of dead animals alongside the trail proved that even the mighty oxen weren't invincible.

By June 4, the Coonses and their wagon train were camped along the Platte River. Two days later, they passed seventy wagons camped alongside the trail. By June 10, Magone's company was made up of 172 people.[2]

Matilda and other mothers cleaned their children's scrapes and scratches to prevent infections that could prove fatal. They made sure their children slept to restore their energy for the next day's walking. Before they lost the light, the women mended tears in clothing and cleaned dust from wagons. As wolves howled nearby, they gathered their children closer.

Rough and rutted trails caused wagons to sink into soggy ground up to the wheel hubs, but the caravan continued, traveling eighteen miles most days, although rain forced a late start at times. One company of forty wagons stayed put until after the burial of one of their men, John W. Fisher, who was only thirty-one.[3] He had been unwell on the trail and died of an illness referred to as the mountain fever or sometimes the black fever, because the patient's teeth turned black. He was buried near willows on the north side of the road nine miles from where his company first arrived at the Platte River. They covered the grave with sod but couldn't find a stone, so they carved his name and age onto a post pounded into the ground at the head of the grave. Fisher's wife and little girl had to fend for themselves and survive on what others could give, according to William A. Hockett, who traveled with the Fishers.

Captain Magone helped anyone needing an extra push to move their wagons out of the mire. The company camped near Plum Creek, where the water was high, and crossed a canyon the next day, covering thirteen miles before camping at 5:30 in the evening. Traveling along the prairie, they learned that the soil they walked and rolled their wagons over was deposited there by floodwaters from the now placid Platte. With riverbanks only about four feet high, heavy rains easily flooded nearby land. The grass covering it was fertilized each year as buffalo roamed the prairies. Only on islands in the river could emigrants find wood—scrubby cottonwood and stunted willow.

On June 9, before reaching Scotts Bluff, Captain Magone spotted a big cloud of dust in the black hills to the left. He rode ahead and pulled out his spyglass to check for danger. He discovered a herd of four thousand buffalo heading their way. The company hadn't seen any buffalo as they crossed the plains because most were farther north that early in the summer. Magone halted the wagon train to let the animals rush past, their thundering hooves so loud nobody could hear anything else. They passed so close that Magone shot one of the beasts, a year-old heifer.[4]

Returning to the wagons, he ordered the company to set up camp although they had traveled only fourteen miles. Then, with three pairs of oxen, he dragged the buffalo he had killed nearly two miles to the camp. The captain then told the men gathered in a circle to take a piece of the buffalo's meat. Even though each wanted to try it, nobody wanted to look greedy.

"Come, come," Magone said. "Don't be bashful; the best-looking man start first."

Still nobody moved.

"Well, then," the captain said, "the man with the best-looking wife come first."

Nicholas and the other men rushed forward, each carving a chunk of the buffalo's meat for their wives to cook. James Jory Jr. later described that first buffalo as "the best meat tasted on the trip." When he ate the meat the next day, Bishop Blanchet likened its flavor to that of Canadian beef.

The Coonse family became acquainted with the Jorys during the journey. Although Nicholas was outgoing and jovial, James Jory was among the most quiet men in the company. The Jorys had planned to travel west with his parents, her sister, and their families. However, they never connected at Independence. They hoped to meet them on the trail. The Jorys, a family of carpenters and mechanics, had emigrated from England to New Brunswick in Canada and then traveled to New

York, where a man persuaded them that Missouri offered great land for farming. However, upon arriving in the frontier town of St. Louis, they discovered that slavery, which the patriarch of the Jory family found detestable, was legal in Missouri. So after a winter of working on a large plantation, they moved northeast across the Mississippi River into Illinois, a free state, where they paid an affordable price for land that they farmed for a decade.

But after marrying Sarah Budd on March 12, 1846, James Jory Jr. began to worry about the cholera sweeping the Illinois prairies, striking young married women particularly hard. For the safety of his young bride, he wanted to move to a healthier climate free from the disease, so he discussed moving west to Oregon Territory with his wife, father, and brothers. They decided to leave in the spring of 1847 and he and Sarah joined Captain Magone's wagon train.

Delays occurred regularly on the trail. One morning after three pair of missing cattle delayed resumption of the journey, the captain called a meeting at noon. Each morning, he said, the company spent much time searching for stray cattle. Starting late caused the entire caravan to travel too slowly, which could be deadly if they didn't cross the Blue Mountains before snowfall began in October.

Magone asked for suggestions to prevent such delays searching for stray cattle.

The captain recommended the men who liked a particular suggestion should line up behind the man who offered it so majority opinion would prevail. After several ideas had been rejected, James Jory Jr. proposed that each stock owner count his cattle at night after reaching camp and before setting them free to graze. Then they should count the animals again early the next morning.[5] The company would search for any animals missing in the morning that had been there the previous night, but they wouldn't waste time searching for animals that might have been missing for days. The majority of the men lined up behind Jory, approving of the quiet Englishman's practical plan. It worked admirably after the first few days.

At one campsite, the company saw a board on the side of the road where the wagon train captains who had passed by since June 1 had written their names. Captain Magone added his name to the eight already there.

Visitors to their camp often shared news of happenings elsewhere on the trail, such as the report that several men who ventured too far from their camp were robbed and stripped of even their clothing. A company behind Magone's lost twenty animals, and a man had his wrist broken by his gun. Antelope provided tasty meat whenever the bishop's guide or hunters shot one of the deer-like animals.

After a dozen days of trekking along the Platte River through present-day Nebraska, the company camped above the junction of the Platte and its South Fork. The next day, June 13, they forded the two-foot-deep South Fork with its sandy bottom. The oxen then pulled the wagons across several creeks. They traveled twenty miles the next day to reach the Platte again. They saw small roses on a bush growing on an island, where they searched for wood.

The wagons crossed the river in the morning, followed by herdsmen shepherding the livestock through the water, which was only a couple of feet deep. Crossing the rivers with their sandy bottoms took a toll on the oxen, which dragged two-thousand-pound wagons through the muck at each river crossing. Ten miles one day, followed by eighteen miles the next, brought the emigrants closer to their destination, but after more than a month on the trail, both the animals and the emigrants grew weary.

Traveling through Nebraska, the company halted for a day when Mrs. Nelson's labor pains began. The women who had already given birth to children gathered near her wagon to assist as needed. She gave birth to a son.

Despite occasional thunderstorms, the weather remained dry, cool and pleasant for most of the trip. Morale remained high, at least until the group passed another grave along the trail. The sight of a freshly dug grave put a damper on spirits as emigrants wondered whether they might have to leave loved ones behind before reaching their journey's end.

It became harder to ignore their fears when a six-year-old girl in their company died June 16. Sara Brown, the daughter of J. Brown, died before she had been baptized by the Catholic priests, so the next day the bishop refused her father's request to say words over his daughter's grave, dug on the right side of the trail near the camp.[6] To avoid the difficult decision they faced that morning, the priests set about urging parents to have their children baptized.

Chapter Five: June and the Platte River

AUTHOR PHOTOS

Emigrants crossed the wide Platte River, seen above, and many Nebraska prairies like the one below as they traveled the plains west toward Oregon.

That day, which started with the heartbreaking burial of a child, proved even more difficult in the afternoon when they reached Ash Hollow, a steep bluff they needed to descend. Before them lay broken hills, high sandbanks, and ragged rocks that seemed to sprout ancient cedars. Although the descent appeared daunting, Nicholas and the other men chained the back wheels of their wagons and unyoked two pairs of oxen, leaving only one to lead the rig downhill. To prevent the wagon from running into the oxen, Nicholas placed his feet on the chained wheels, acting as a brake that kept the wagon on the ground and slowed its descent while another man led the oxen.

After the arduous descent, the company found freshwater springs. They delighted in drinking the cool water and filled their barrels. After lunch the company crossed soft sand into which the wagons sunk to the hubs, exhausting the already tired oxen. They camped at seven that evening, falling into exhausted sleep after an emotional and taxing day.

As a Christian, Matilda tried to trust God for her family's safety, relying on words in the gospel of Matthew, chapter six, verse thirty-four: "Take therefore no thought for the morrow: for the morrow shall take thought for the things of itself. Sufficient unto the day is the evil thereof."

Catching up with another company of fifty-two wagons June 18, Captain Magone halted his train to prevent the mixing of animals from several different companies. Because wood was scarce, people picked up buffalo chips for fuel. It took about three bushels of chips to make a good fire, but the emigrants began using the dried dung more sparingly to ensure they could continue building fires. One wagon broke an axle, which was quickly repaired.

After covering twenty miles, the weary group spotted a landmark that bolstered even the most flagging spirits. In the distance, Captain Magone and his group spotted a lonely tower of rock protruding from the ground: Courthouse Rock, also known as Castle Rock. They crossed the Lawrence Fork, drank heavily of the cool water, and gazed up at the huge sunbaked rock resembling a large building. It appeared only a mile or two away, but the distance was five or six miles.

The company stayed in place June 19 as Mrs. Knighton's time to give birth arrived. Again, Matilda and other women who had given birth

Chapter Five: June and the Platte River

AUTHOR PHOTOS

Courthouse Rock is visible in the distance, above, and Chimney Rock can be seen at center and Scotts Bluff below. Emigrants often camped near landmarks.

tended to her during her labor. They boiled water and soaked cloths to wipe her brow as she toiled to give birth inside a tent. Finally her son arrived; they named him Sagarlin Columbia.

The company moved out the next day and stopped for lunch June 21 across from Chimney Rock, a rounded hill of sunbaked clay with a rock spire nearly three hundred feet tall pointing toward the sky. From a distance it had looked like a small stub on the landscape, but as they drew nearer, they saw the bank of clay and rock rising from the ground like an ancient round castle with a large flagstaff on top.

Many of the men left camp to carve their names with a knife in the soft limestone, marking their passage alongside the names of all those who had traveled the route before. They all knew the rock meant they had traveled more than six hundred miles from Independence, but they still had 1,570 miles to go.

The following day, the company approached Scotts Bluff rising from a level plain with the meandering river at its side among sparse pine trees. The eight-hundred-foot sandstone rock towered above the North Platte River with only a few trees or shrubs marring the smooth light brown surface. They found sparse grass for their oxen and cattle because they followed behind several other companies. Their livestock wandered off in the night seeking fodder. Blackened areas showed where fires sparked by lightning had devoured the turf and scorched the earth. Wild currants and choke cherries grew in a nearby ravine.

Frequently the emigrants spotted antelope grazing on whatever grass they could find, often in gullies shaded from the brutal sun beating down on hot summer days. Sometimes the travelers awoke to find a horse or two had been stolen.

On June 23, the train rested at Horse Creek shortly after noon. After oppressive heat during the morning, the emigrants welcomed the small storm that brought "hail as big as hazelnuts," according to Bishop Blanchet, making for "an agreeable afternoon." The next day, amid barking prairie dogs, the train passed yet another grave.

Finally, June 25, the wagon train members took time to groom themselves in anticipation of a visit to Fort Laramie with its whitewashed mud walls. They pitched tents and circled the wagons on the bank of the Laramie River about a mile from its confluence with the North Platte River.

Fort Laramie, started by William Sublette in 1834 as a fur trading post, became known first as Fort William and later, after the American Fur Company bought it, as Fort John.[7] As the fur trade dwindled, the fort catered to the needs of westward-bound emigrants. The trail from Fort Laramie led gradually uphill toward South Pass, where wagon trains crossed the continental divide before dropping into the Snake River Valley, crossing the Blue Mountains, and descending into the valleys of Oregon Territory.

The fort was a good place to refresh animals, repair axles, and stockpile goods for the rest of the trip. Some people found their exhausted oxen dead on the prairie; others traded worn-out animals for well-rested beasts, adding goods or money to make the trade more even. Emigrants could hire guides or drivers. They could replenish supplies, but only at exorbitant prices. Sugar cost two dollars a cup and flour a dollar a pint. The women took advantage of the short break in traveling to wash clothes.[8]

Sioux Indians, camped outside the fort with their ponies and half-wolf dogs, brought beads, furs, and moccasins to trade with emigrants for shirts, bacon, and other wares. Matilda and the women turned their eyes away from Indian men who wore little more than loincloths, exposing most of their naked bodies to full view. Most of the Indian women wore dresses of hide or cloth; some of the men wore cloth pants or leather leggings.

At the fort, Indians watched a man greasing his wagon, Jory recalled. When he noticed the wagon hammer gone, and an Indian scurrying away with a blanket drawn tightly around his body, the emigrant stood and bellowed: "Bring back that wagon hammer!"[9] The Indian stopped, turned around and shook his head, denying he had stolen anything. To prove his point, he spread his blanket wide and shook it, then turned and hurried away. The man walked to where the Indian had stood and found the hammer on the ground.

After two days at Fort Laramie, which gave the emigrants and their animals a well-needed rest, Captain Magone ordered the train to move again over the parched and rolling hills with occasional pine and cedars growing in the dry soil. On June 26, shortly after leaving Fort Laramie, they saw a herd of three thousand buffalo. They killed three of the beasts to provide fresh meat for everyone.[10]

AUTHOR PHOTOS

These pictures taken at Fort Laramie in 2017 show the Laramie River where women washed clothes during their stay at the fort and trading post.

Chapter Five: June and the Platte River

"Their flesh is generally coarser and dryer than beef, but a fat buffalo heifer is as good meat as I would wish to taste of," Elizabeth Dixon Smith wrote in her diary June 26. The next day, she noted, "A buffalo gallops and rolls like a horse."

The train passed Register Cliff, a sandstone landmark that drew more westward-bound emigrants who chiseled their names in the rock with axes, knives, or other sharp utensils. Some skipped the trip to the landmark, continuing west toward a river known as the Bitter Fork, named for the bitter black poplars growing there. Animal carcasses were strewn along the trail, some eaten by wolves, others simply white bones drying in the sun. The train headed toward Laramie Mountain, also known as Ice Peak, passing another herd of buffalo and capturing two calves from it. One ran away quickly but herdsmen drove the other with the cattle for a few miles before it veered off.

The bitter and thorny sage each person trudged through snagged and stained clothing, but at times it served as the only source of fuel for fires. Most people learned quickly to avoid going barefoot if they didn't want to suffer after treading on prickly pear cactus.

With no doctor in their train, the women took care of their family's wounds themselves, cleaning scrapes and cuts, removing splinters from hands and feet, and placing poultices and salves on rashes.

They passed Indian villages along the route but didn't stop. One evening as the emigrants prepared to set up camp, a band of five hundred Sioux approached.[11] Captain Magone ordered everyone to create a half-circle of the wagons, with women and children inside, protected. They clustered the animals near the opening of the half circle, then seventy-five armed men—Nicholas among them—lined up on the other side to guard the animals, wagons, women, and children.

As the natives approached, Magone signaled the chief to halt and gestured for him to dismount and sit. When he did, Magone lit a "peace pipe," which he puffed and then handed to the chief. Behind the wagons, the women prepared bread and other food to share with the Sioux as a gesture of friendship. When it was ready, Magone presented the food to the chief to share with his tribe. After eating, the men smoked the pipe again and the Indians left. Whenever the train encountered Indians, the emigrants provided bread, shirts, flour, or

AUTHOR PHOTO OF DISPLAY AT FORT LARAMIE NATIONAL HISTORIC SITE

The drawing above at Fort Laramie Historic Site depicts Fort John, 1841–1849, as the fort was called when Captain Magone's train stopped there. The photo below shows the interior of the fort in the 1840s.

AUTHOR PHOTO OF DISPLAY AT FORT LARAMIE NATIONAL HISTORIC SITE

other "gifts" or "treats" as gestures of goodwill. Sometimes the Indians spread out blankets for the emigrants to fill with flour and cornmeal.

Matilda likely whispered her fears to Nicholas at night, while he pointed out that the captain knew what he was doing. Her belly was now protruding slightly as the baby in her womb grew. Matilda prayed often to God for protection, finding solace in Isaiah 41:10: "Fear thou not; for I am with thee: be not dismayed; for I am thy God: I will strengthen thee; yea, I will help thee; yea, I will uphold thee with the right hand of my righteousness."

Grass for the livestock grew scarce as they traveled west, often along a rocky trail. Some of them became sick; others died. Those who started with six or eight oxen made do with fewer, which put even greater strain on the animals who survived. But all eight of the Coonses' oxen lived. Emigrants lightened the wagonloads as much as possible as they rumbled along the rough, uneven terrain.

Along the trail, Nicholas and Matilda heard tales from visitors of other companies rife with friction and quarrels, much worse than any animosity between Nicholas and Jim Laughlin. Sometimes they watched wagons roll past in the morning as they packed up camp or in the evening as they set up tents. Even though they passed through pristine and often uninhabited land, they saw many others along the trail.

Emigrants often carved their names in the soft sandstone of Register Cliff.

Chapter Six

Oregon Trail Landmarks in July

BY EARLY JULY, Nicholas and Matilda had traveled nearly eight hundred miles and looked forward to seeing Independence Rock, the next milestone along the trail. The boys, although occasionally complaining about all the walking, still looked upon the journey west as a grand adventure.

With each passing day, Matilda felt the new life inside her growing, despite the rather monotonous diet of biscuits, beans, and bacon, and occasionally fresh antelope or buffalo. Most distracting was trying to sleep at night, with a weary body and mind but an active babe in the womb who had slept most of the day, lulled by her mother's walking and riding.

News arrived of a man in another company who had been hunting with others when he shot and killed himself accidentally, leaving a wife and six young children to find a way west without the support of a husband and father.[1] Matilda prayed for the widow of Smith Dunlap and her children, heartbroken as they must have been by the tragedy.

The nation's Independence Day fell on a Sunday, so the company gathered in the morning to determine whether to stay in camp for a day. The majority decided to stay, which was a relief as they had rested only four days since they embarked on their journey. The men drove the cattle to the southern bank of the Platte where they could graze on rich pastureland.

Since the Fourth of July fell on the Sabbath, the company waited until early the following morning to celebrate the Declaration of Independence that led to freedom from British rule. Gunshots rang out early and everyone enjoyed a morning feast. One emigrant played a clarinet as others sang patriotic songs. After reading the Declaration of Independence, Captain Magone gave a speech greeted by toasts and hurrahs.[2]

Then everyone repacked the wagons and hit the trail by eight in the morning. Along the route, they met eight people riding east on horseback, accompanied by mules carrying their provisions. They had left Oregon City May 5 and followed the new Barlow Road, which they described as horrible and 150 miles longer than the river route to Walla Walla. Before meeting Magone's company of now forty-four wagons, they had seen 789 prairie schooners destined for Oregon. Their desire to reach Oregon fueled, the Magone company traveled fourteen miles before camping.

The next day, the company arrived at the spot where they needed to cross the Platte again, about a hundred miles west of Fort Laramie. They found Mormons had erected a blacksmith shop for wagon repairs and a ferry to help wagons cross to the north side of the river. Men of the company debated whether to pay a toll of a dollar per wagon for the ferry or ford the river themselves. Most crossed on the Mormon Ferry, while a few suggested building their own rafts. The Mormons ferried thirty-six wagons while eight men took their wagons upstream to ford the river themselves. Captain Magone told the ferry operators that, when he arrived in Oregon City, he would publish the names of wagon train captains who passed and the number of people who traveled with them.

A few wagons crossed on the ferry that evening. The others began crossing in the morning, but while they awaited their turn, Nicholas and Matilda greeted a handful of travelers from Oregon who shared disturbing news. Emigrants in the Donner party heading to California the previous fall starved to death and, before that, some had resorted to eating the bodies of dead companions. Eating human flesh! Oh, what an abhorrent and unimaginable sin. The news filled everyone with disgust and fear as they tried to understand the incomprehensible.

A subdued group traveled away from the familiar North Platte River for the final time, stocked with filled barrels to water the animals and quench the travelers' thirst over the next several days until they reached the Sweetwater River more than fifty miles away. Some of the cattle grew lame from traveling over alkaline and rocky ground bordered by red cliffs.

Chapter Six: Oregon Trail Landmarks in July

FILE ID 65653621 © PHILCOLD DREAMSTIME.COM STOCK PHOTOGRAPHY

Most of the encounters between the emigrants and Native Americans proved peaceful. The depiction above shows two Native Americans on rocks watching a wagon train moving below.

The company discussed dividing once again into smaller, more manageable groups, with those who wished to leave early each morning in one group of fifteen wagons (among them the archbishop) and Captain Magone in charge of twenty-nine wagons, including the Coonses and the Jorys.

The next day, before leaving, the company met Jim Bridger. He was a mountain man, fur trapper, scout, and early explorer of the western territory who in 1843 established a fort named after himself nearly four hundred miles west of Fort Laramie. He had not yet heard of the fate of the Donner party, most of whom had perished en route to California.[3]

Finally, upon reaching the Sweetwater River, the emigrants spied what looked like a giant beached whale in the distance—Independence Rock. The granite rock, nearly two thousand feet in length, seven hundred feet wide, and 128 feet high, was named by fur trappers who celebrated Independence Day there in 1830. Once again some of the

AUTHOR PHOTOS

The emigrants couldn't mistake Independence Rock because they hoped to reach that landmark by the Fourth of July. Many carved their names into the rounded stone.

men rode to the rock and climbed it, taking along chisels to carve their names into the stone, letting all who passed by later know that they had gone ahead to Oregon Territory. Others smeared their names with axle grease onto the rock among the hundreds of names already there.[4]

The next day the train passed by yet another grave, this one carved with the name "Fred Rich Fulkerson, 18 years old, died July 1, 1847."[5] It might have been the measles, a disease infecting many of the emigrants in trains heading to Oregon, the same disease that killed the Wilcox family two months earlier and wreaked havoc in the Bydenhour wagon, where both the parents and several of the children were ill, feverish with hacking coughs and itchy rashes. The dust rising behind the wagons didn't help, particularly those already struggling to breathe. It coated everything inside and outside of the wagons.

They met a few people from Oregon, but far fewer traveled east than west. Sometimes they heard stories about the great pioneer lives of earlier emigrants; others told about hardships, horses stolen by Indians, and deaths. A colonel described the high cost of goods in Oregon Territory: for a dollar one could purchase a bushel of wheat or ten pounds of sugar or a ready-made shirt. Coffee cost two dollars for ten pounds, and salt was seventy-five cents a bushel. (A dollar in 1847 was equivalent to twenty-seven dollars today; two dollars more than fifty-four dollars today.) Salmon and speckled trout abounded.[6]

Several mentioned that Indians at Walla Walla didn't want more white people settling on their lands. They even objected to Dr. Marcus Whitman, a missionary, fencing his field, even though he had been in the region for a dozen years.[7]

While stockpiling water for the long, dry trip to the Green River from the Sweetwater, Mr. Jory noticed a couple of Indians standing near his wagon and suspected them of mischief. He kept one eye on the pair as he filled his keg, and finally decided to intervene. He noticed one man had removed a screw that held down the wagon cover, so he demanded its return. The culprit opened his palm to show the screw, but Jory gestured that he should screw it back in. The Indian tried to screw it in using his butcher knife; Jory finally used the knife to do it himself. The other Indian laughed heartily over his companion's bungled attempt at theft.[8]

Along the Sweetwater River the company passed an elderly woman from the Snake tribe who had been abandoned to wait for death in a hut cobbled together of branches.[9] Although emigrants provided her with food, they had little extra to spare. Matilda couldn't imagine a culture that left elderly women alone to die … of course, she had left her mother in Missouri. However, she had siblings to care for her mother there.

As they traveled farther west, massive granite rocks with smatterings of gray-green wild sage and pine trees towered on either side of the narrow pass. Oppressive heat beat down on them most days, with relief provided occasionally by light rain.

They passed shortcuts along the way, but after careful consideration opted for the old route, which they knew had carried earlier emigrants safely to Oregon.

At one point, they met a family heading east along the trail, away from the Promised Land. Nicholas joined the men who gathered around the Grants, listening as the eldest once again explained what he had told emigrants all along the trail, words recounted by Ralph C. Greer, who was in a train ahead of the Coonses.[10]

"In the first place," Grant told Greer, "they have no bees there; and in the second place, they can't raise corn, and whar they can't raise corn, they can't raise hogs, and whar they can't raise hogs, they can't have bacon, and I'm going back to old Missouri whar I can have corn bread, bacon, and honey."

By mid-July, Captain Magone's company had reached the foot of South Pass, where Matilda found gooseberries that tasted like wild fox grapes. With help from her sons, she gathered enough to bake a pie on the edges of the fire. It was a special day July 16, even on the prairie, as her oldest son turned nine.

As they traveled gradually higher, temperatures dropped. They found patches of snow on shaded ground. Snow covered the peaks, even in July. Temperatures dipped so low at night that water froze. They passed a small mountain lake surrounded by pine trees and crossed several streams that emptied into the Sweetwater.

They navigated over the Sweetwater itself nine times before crossing the continental divide, where the emigrants beheld the wonder of watching water flow west toward the Pacific Ocean instead of east toward the Atlantic. Shortly thereafter, they reached the banks of the Sandy River.

Later, they saw the beautiful mountain-fed Blacks Fork of the Green River, west of the Sandy River, which offered good pasture for the stock. Before fording the Blacks Fork, Nicholas and Matilda rolled past a campsite where they saw the grave of W. Powell, a man who traveled with them in Magone's group before it divided at Independence Rock.[11] He was only twenty-six when he died July 26. It might have been the measles, which killed all the Bydenhours except for one son.

Some campsites offered good springs for water, plenty of wood, and grass for the oxen. Others were devoid of all three essentials. Occasionally the company's cattle mixed with those of other wagon trains, which created problems as they needed to be sorted before the trains moved forward. They left the Blacks Fork River and traveled fifty miles without

Chapter Six: Oregon Trail Landmarks in July

WIKIMEDIA COMMONS

AUTHOR PHOTOS OF FORT BRIDGER DISPLAYS

Above is Fort Bridger in 1850 as seen in a lithograph by James Ackerman. At left is the famed mountain man, Jim Bridger, 1804 to 1881. Below is Fort Bridger drawn by Frederick Piercy in 1853, as seen on a placard at Fort Bridger State Historic Site and Museum.

AUTHOR PHOTOS OF FORT BRIDGER DISPLAYS

The Fort Bridger State Historic Site and Museum has reconstructed the original trading post, as seen in these photos.

water and pasture for the animals along well-traveled paths. Soon the company reached the swift and clear waters of the beautiful Green River, bordered by quaking aspen. Here they met Captain Hopper from California, who had stopped for four days on his journey east.

Finally, nearly four hundred miles west of Fort Laramie, the weary travelers reached Fort Bridger, where they could repair damaged axles, restock supplies, and purchase oxen to replace those that had been lost. The fort consisted of only two fifty-foot houses surrounded by several smaller dwellings in the grassy valley inhabited by mountain men, Canadians, and Creoles from St. Louis. They swapped stories with other emigrants, including those from their original group. Emigrants who took a cutoff trimmed seventy miles from their trip but lost quite a few animals.[12]

From the fort, the Mormon travelers took a southern trail to the Great Salt Lake Valley, where they settled. Those heading to Oregon and California rumbled north over a rough and hilly route from Fort Bridger to the Muddy Creek, Bear River Mountains, and the green grasses of Bear River Valley, surrounded by steep ridges.

By the end of July, even Matilda's rambunctious boys began to tire of the continuous travel, asking every day how much longer it would take to reach the Willamette Valley. Nicholas assured his sons that they were nearer to Oregon every day, but even his words sounded hollow as the dust swirled. They appreciated rivers with drinkable water as well as edible grasses for the cattle near their banks. The route, which followed the Bear River through hills and valleys, was relatively good, passing through a beautiful stand of trees amid the barren land. They passed by mountains spotted with green grass and flowers with cool, clear water gurgling from springs and flowing from waterfalls. When it rained occasionally, emigrants walking beside their wagons relished the fresh water as it washed weeks of dust from their faces and clothes.

As they approached Soda Springs (in present-day Idaho), the emigrants knew they faced a parting of the ways, as those heading to California would follow a trail to the south.[13]

AUTHOR PHOTOS

As more emigrants followed the Oregon Trail, their wagons carved deep ruts in the soft sandstone, as seen here near Register Cliff in Wyoming.

Chapter Seven

Reaching the Rocky Mountains

ALTHOUGH MANY FELL ILL during the trip west, Matilda praised God for keeping her family healthy and safe. At times she tended women who were sick, or the children they couldn't watch. Everyone worked together on the Oregon Trail.

The going was slow as the oxen pulled the Coonse wagon through the Rocky Mountains, but descents always followed ascents, with the trail leading into yet another beautiful valley with cool mountain streams and grassland upon which the cattle could graze.

Occasionally the train encountered mountain men—hunters and trappers—and Indians who shared tales of the country and its wildlife and discussed the route with the men. Some emigrants traded with them.

After traveling nearly 1,155 miles, the tired emigrants finally arrived in what today is known as Idaho. At Steamboat Springs, they saw mounds of stone about forty feet wide and ten feet high with a three-foot hole in the middle.[1] They watched in amazement as blood-warm bubbly water spewed a foot to eighteen inches above the ground at regular intervals. Finding warm water proved delightful to the women, who could finally wash the dirt from their clothes and bodies with hot water as they had done back in Missouri before they began this journey.

At Soda Springs, a mile or so away, they tasted mineral water with the flavor of soda but drinkable if sugar was added.[2] But it couldn't compare with the cool, clear mountain water they had tasted earlier! Scrubby cedars and pine grew in the thin layer of a white salty substance that covered some of the ground, which the cattle enjoyed licking.[3]

Three miles past Soda Springs the emigrants spied a long rock about eight feet high and thirty feet long, which looked hollow.[4]

People traveling east from Oregon stopped occasionally to share news of the trail ahead. They heard of two wagons left behind by their company when the occupants fell ill with camp fever, or mountain fever, today known as typhus. A day or so later, though, they resumed their journey west after joining another company.

The dust kicked up by the oxen as they traveled the barren land even clouded the sight of the oxen's horns, not to mention the trail ahead, and drifted down to land on everything—clothes, bonnets, barrels, and the canvas of the wagon itself.

Near the confluence of Raft Creek and the Snake River, the emigrants going to California took the southern route after Soda Springs, while travelers to the Oregon Territory continued westward.[5]

Finally the company reached Fort Hall, a British-owned Hudson's Bay Company trading post north of the Snake River and about two hundred miles northwest of Fort Bridger. The fort was a large square building made of sunbaked clay bricks. Although friendly to French-Canadians, proprietor Captain Grant wasn't quite as cordial to the Americans who stopped to purchase supplies at high prices.[6] They camped a little past the fort but fought constant attacks by large mosquitos, feasting on both man and beast the entire time. Everyone rose early, eager to leave behind that miserable location with its hungry pests. Temperatures occasionally dropped below freezing at night even though it was August. Although they often shivered with cold at night, the sun beat down mercilessly during the day as they rumbled along the trail, drying the bloody mosquito bites on their animals.

Arriving at the Portneuf River, a tributary of the Snake River, they continued a mile farther to find a better place to ford. They met Nez Perce Indians who greeted the emigrants without begging from them.[7] The oxen plodded uphill again, hauling the heavy wagons to the summit of the Portneuf Range and then descending along a rather treacherous trail onto yet another plain.

They could hear the roar of American Falls on the Snake River in the distance, prompting grins as they marked off another landmark on the long journey west. Five miles farther on they stood in awe, feeling the spray from the roaring river as it splashed and tumbled over rocks,

Chapter Seven: Reaching the Rocky Mountains

foaming and sending spray skyward. Lush green trees on either side of the river created a gorgeous backdrop to the powerful force of the river. The hum of the falls lulled them to sleep.

The westward trail followed the south side of the Snake River, though the emigrants traveled above the stream most of the time as it wound its way through deep canyons and ravines, twisting and turning like a snake slithering around the rock formations. The emigrants often used sage as fuel for fires; they had left the bulk of the buffalo chips far behind on the prairies to their east.

Near the Bear River, they picked small grape-like currants to nibble on as they traveled but not enough for a pie. By mid-August they reached more waterfalls, where the roaring and foaming Snake River plunged two hundred feet over rocks into a deep green pool. Oh, what a magnificent sight! The river splashed over a smaller lava rock formation first and then plunged into the deep pool, also fed by a falls to the side of the larger one. Matilda wanted to plunge into that cool mountain water and rinse all the dust of the trail from her body. But reaching it entailed descending a steep, stony and treacherous path, so it was out of the question. She took solace in the rain that fell in the evening to wash away dirt from the trail.

A short detour took the company to a mountain spring where they could fill barrels with water. They would have no access to water for the next twenty miles, until they reached the Malad River, deemed unhealthy after trappers grew sick when they ate beavers that feasted on false morel mushrooms. The nearby Camas Mountain took its name from the onion-like bulbs found in its meadows.

Yet again poor Captain Magone, a bachelor, was required to halt the forward progress as the time drew near for Mrs. Watts to give birth.[8] With help from the women, she greeted a healthy baby boy and named him Lewis, perhaps after Meriwether Lewis, who first explored this western land that everyone in the company planned to call home. Rubbing her hand over her abdomen, Matilda thanked God she wouldn't be giving birth to her baby until after they had settled in the Willamette Valley.

At times salmon leapt to the surface and rippled the smooth water of the Snake River before diving below. The natives knew well how to catch those slippery fish, so the emigrants traded with them for smoked salmon whenever they could.

LIBRARY OF CONGRESS

This photograph of Shoshone Falls on the Snake River was taken in 1874 by Timothy H. O'Sullivan. It is approximately three miles northeast of present-day Twin Falls, Idaho.

Chapter Eight

Tragedy on the Snake River

SEPTEMBER ARRIVED with Captain Magone and his company of wagons still rolling west on steep rocks alongside the Snake River. Each passing mile brought them closer to the country they would claim as home. They measured their progress by landmarks and looked forward to Fort Boise and then the Blue Mountains, from which they would drop into the Columbia River Valley and float downstream to the Willamette Valley.

While excited by the long-term goal, the emigrants quickly grew accustomed to the daily routine. They passed fresh gravesites that reminded them of the journey's inherent dangers. At Salmon Falls, fish sprang from the water into the air and Indians with nets caught as many as they could. The natives traded fish to the emigrants for shirts, bacon, or other goods. Some of the travelers caught their own salmon at the falls rather than trading for fresh fish.

The emigrants left the Snake River for thirty miles and rolled across the desert without water for two days. Then they reached one of the few spots where the Snake River left the canyons and spread out enough for wagons and cattle to cross. Good grassland and water sources on the river's north side enticed them to cross, although it was treacherous. But the northern route also trimmed a few miles from the journey. They would then travel about one hundred thirty miles to Fort Boise.

Captain Magone called the men together to discuss the route. The majority decided to ford the river to the north side when they arrived at Three Island Crossing, near what today is Glenns Ferry in Idaho.[1] The crossing had gained a reputation as treacherous, with deep holes on the bottom of the fast-moving river and strong whirlpools that could suck under a flailing oxen or topple a heavy wagon.

They caulked the wagon beds to prevent water from penetrating and used them as ferries to cross the river. Men swam to the other side with ropes to pull their wagons across while their animals swam in the water, which was six to eight feet deep. Others preferred to remain on the Snake's south side rather than brave the treacherous waters.

Courageous drivers maneuvered oxen and wagons into the river, across sandbars and two islands. Though the water looked calm, the strong current and pockmarked river bottom frequently overturned wagons and carts, spewing treasured belongings into the river to float downstream.

On Tuesday, September 7, the Coonses and the Jorys were among the last to ford the river as their heavy wagons caused them to lag behind. Jory, who described Nicholas as "a jovial man," recalled the events of that fateful day.[2]

Nicholas urged his cattle into the water and then spotted an oxen with its horns caught in the ferry cable stretched across the river. When he started forward on his saddle horse to free the beast, Matilda cautioned him to be careful. He laughed as he reassured her.

"If I was born to be drowned I won't be hanged," he said, "and if born to be hanged, I'll never be drowned."[3]

As Matilda and their four sons watched, Nicholas left his horse and swam toward the struggling ox. "But miscalculating the current, [he] was carried below, and was caught in a whirlpool and went down," Jory said. Some accounts say his horse kicked him in the head, which knocked him unconscious before he was sucked below by a whirlpool.

When her husband disappeared, Matilda held her breath, scanned the water, and waited anxiously for him to resurface. Her boys began to call for their pa. Matilda prayed fervently that her husband would surface downstream and walk back to them, laughing as he calmed her fears.

A rider rushed ahead to give the news to Captain Magone, who searched the water for Nicholas, but nearly suffered a similar fate.

"Persons from the Mississippi Valley were very much deceived in the waters of the Columbia or Snake, which are very much lighter than those

Chapter Eight: Tragedy on the Snake River

DREAMSTIME_XXL_17378546 CREDIT LINE ID 17378546 © PHILCOLD DREAMSTIME.COM

By the time they reached Three Island Crossing on the Snake River, emigrants had crossed many rivers, as depicted above. But the Three Island Crossing had a reputation for being dangerous.

PHOTO COURTESY OF IDAHO DEPARTMENT OF PARKS AND RECREATION

to which they are accustomed, and also colder, and with stronger currents and more dangerous eddies," Jory said.[4] "Magone himself was nearly drawn down into a whirlpool of the Snake, and only was saved by resting for a time on the edge until he recovered strength to break away."

Shock gripped Matilda when her husband failed to surface. They searched the shores and downstream for several miles but never found his body. She tried to console her sons, but the emotional trauma and shock doubled her over in pain. She inhaled deeply, but the pain ripped her abdomen. It was too soon for the baby to come! She knew it, yet she could do nothing to stop the spasms. No, oh, no!

Other women in the camp hastily moved items in the wagon to create a makeshift bed for Matilda. Shock engulfed her as tears of grief mingled with the pangs of childbirth tore at her petite body.

Her nephew, William, rushed to the Coonses' wagon while his wife, Jane, gathered the boys together and hugged them as they cried … or tried not to. William assured his aunt that after they arrived in Oregon and spent the winter, he would take her and the boys back to Missouri in the spring. Eventually darkness swallowed her, a blessed unconsciousness.

A couple of hours later, a traveler heading east stopped by the Magone wagon train, where he learned of the horrific tragedy that had occurred that day. He spoke with William Glover and promised to share the news with the family when he arrived in Missouri.

The next day, Matilda pushed forth a new life, her fifth child, a tiny baby girl.[5] The women cleaned the baby and wrapped her in warm cloths, but grief over the loss of her husband, the man pledged to her for life, numbed Matilda's joy. Not death. Not this early. Not this young. He was only thirty-five.

The train remained in camp a day to give Matilda time to recover her strength, but the loss of blood during the birthing of her baby and the emotional shock proved traumatic. Her tiny daughter, born a few months early, struggled to breathe, gasping, too small and weak.

Matilda's sons lingered outside the wagon, peering in occasionally to see their mother, their only surviving parent, their link to the life they'd left behind in Missouri. They saw the tiny bundled baby, who scarcely even moved. William and Jane Glover tried to assure the boys that they were not alone in this wilderness.

Chapter Eight: Tragedy on the Snake River

AUTHOR PHOTOS AT THREE ISLAND CROSSING STATE PARK

Brush still lines the Snake River's banks at Three Island Crossing, where Nicholas Coonse drowned and Matilda lost the baby she delivered prematurely.

Matilda's daughter quit breathing altogether, following her father in death by two days.[6] They buried the infant along the trail, not far from the river that had claimed her father's life.

Captain Magone checked on Matilda, who was scarcely conscious. He promised to see her and the boys safely to Oregon City. She could only nod, acknowledging his kindness as tears pricked her eyes before blessed darkness engulfed her again.

With help, Henry, as the eldest boy at nine, harnessed the oxen to the wagon and guided them along the trail. Seven-year-old Barton, the next eldest, watched his younger brothers, Grundy and John, as the wagons resumed their journey west. William and Jane fed them meals, but nobody could answer the boys' questions about their uncertain future in Oregon Territory, now that their pa had died.

The Magone train climbed out of the Snake River Valley onto a dusty desert. Small streams provided cool water to thirsty emigrants, but Matilda remained weak and unable to walk as the wagon rumbled over the rough trail. They traveled along a narrow ridge only wide enough for the wagons, with steep drop-offs on either side. Occasionally oxen perished along the route.

The boys did the chores their father used to perform and shared with their mother at night stories of what they had seen that day. They had heard about a woman in another company who was so angry with her husband, Mr. Marcum, she refused to leave the camp or let her children go.[7] The husband hitched the oxen and pleaded with her, but she wouldn't budge. Three other families took the children with them in their wagons, and eventually the husband drove off and left his wife sitting, an incident recounted in vivid detail by Elizabeth Dixon Smith.

"She got up, took the back track, and traveled out of sight. Cut across and overtook her husband. Meantime, he sent his boy back to camp after a horse he had left, and when she came up, her husband said, 'Did you meet John?' 'Yes,' was the reply, 'and I picked up a stone and knocked out his brains.' Her husband went back to ascertain the truth and while he was gone, she set fire to one of the wagons that was loaded with store goods. The cover burnt off with some valuable articles. He saw the flames and came running and put it out, and then mustered up spunk enough to give her a good flogging."[8]

Matilda could never show her husband such disrespect. But then she remembered she no longer had a husband. She tried to be strong for her sons, but her body felt weak.

During the middle of September, they dropped into the lush, green valley surrounding Fort Boise, which like Fort Hall three hundred miles away, had been constructed of sunbaked bricks.[9] It sat near the confluence of the Snake and Boise Rivers, offering a brief respite for weary travelers. Captain Magone's party camped near the fort and forded the cold, waist-deep Snake River the next day. This time, after crossing the river without incident, Captain Magone led his wagon train across Keeney Pass to Vale on the Malheur River, where they camped near warm springs in a large dry valley covered in coarse grass and small willows.

After having followed the Snake River more than three hundred miles, the company arrived at Farewell Bend, where the river turned north and the emigrants continued northwest toward the Blue Mountains. That's where the Coonse boys saw their last glimpse of their father's watery grave, where Matilda bid a final farewell to her husband of ten years.

She wasn't alone in her heartache as emigrants in other trains dug graves to bury loved ones who had died of diseases, such as Omar J. Kimball, who suffered from typhus and died along the Oregon Trail September 26, 1847.[10] The boy, who had just turned fourteen in August, was buried near the Burnt River, a small creek bordered by steep limestone mountains.

The wagons crossed the Burnt River, a tributary of the Snake, six times during the next week as they slowly climbed out of the steep canyon onto a dry barren prairie with short grasses, sagebrush, and occasionally willow, alder, and birch trees. They were along the Burnt River when Mrs. Jory's time arrived, so Captain Magone ordered the company to lay over a day while she gave birth to her daughter, Phoebe. Matilda's physical weakness prevented her from helping with the birth.

"It was considered something of a joke on Magone, being a bachelor, that no less than five times he was obliged to give the order to halt the train a day on account of the birth of a child," James Jory Jr. said.[11] "These were in the families of Mr. Watts, Nelson, one of the Knightens, and of Mr. Jory."

The fifth stop—the name not mentioned in Jory's list—was for the premature birth of the Coonse baby, Nicholas and Matilda's infant girl, buried on the trail near Three Island Crossing.

Like many emigrants, Captain Magone's group encountered Nez Perce Indians who traded with the weary travelers. They provided salmon, beef, peas, squash and camas bulbs, which looked like onions but tasted more like potatoes, in exchange for clothing or other goods. Many scattered and weakened emigrant trains owed their lives to the friendliness and helpfulness of these natives, Jory noted.

Finally they reached a valley with abundant grass, wood, and water. After climbing more hills, they spotted the Grand Ronde Valley. They crossed the Grand Ronde River, where Cayuse and Walla Walla Indians lived in longhouses, although Snake Indians claimed ownership of the land. Black trees and the stench of smoke testified to recent forest fires in the region, adding one more cause for concern.

From there the emigrants ascended into the Blue Mountains, weaving among tall pine and spruce trees and changing oxen often as they hauled heavy loads uphill. They stopped to camp after only four or five miles each day to rest their animals. Temperatures plummeted at night. They stopped at the summit to wait for others. At one point, Mr. Jory recalled a visit from Indians. A curious native peered inside the Nelson wagon and the irate patriarch lashed the embarrassed young brave with an ox whip to the laughter of both his fellow Indians and the emigrants. "Such punishment is regarded by the Indians as a great joke; but killing an Indian is, or was, a very serious matter," Jory recalled.[12]

Descending from the Blue Mountains into the Umatilla River Valley could be treacherous. Wagons accelerated on the steep downhill slope and at times careened off the trail and tumbled down the mountainside. Men steadied the wagons while most of the women carried their children or walked beside them. Although it was risky to ride in the wagon, Matilda had no choice, too weak physically to walk. The captain maneuvered the wagon down the mountainside.

After reaching the Umatilla Valley in late September, the emigrants camped for several days to rest and encountered their first Cayuse Indians. When one of the Cayuse saw a Catholic priest among their group, he approached the black-robed man and motioned toward a crucifix hanging

Chapter Eight: Tragedy on the Snake River

from his belt. He spoke long and loud, wringing his hands as if tearing the cross into pieces and tossing it to the ground in rage, punctuating his speech with reference to Doctor Whitman. Jory understood it to mean the doctor who established the Whitman Mission had little use for Catholics. The emigrants posted a guard to watch for Indian attacks, which hadn't been a necessity while traveling through Nez Perce land.

While encamped along the Umatilla River, which flowed from the Blue Mountains into the Columbia, riders who had traveled ahead of their own wagon train stopped and informed James Jory that his father and brothers were en route. Jory and his wife and newborn daughter stayed behind and waited for their arrival. While there, Jory recalled losing a couple of his oxen one morning, only to spot them in the bottoms. As he rushed after them, he saw an Indian driving the animals.

"Are you stealing my cattle?" Jory demanded.[13]

"Heap water," the Cayuse replied. He indicated he was only watering the beasts for Jory. He then demanded a shirt in payment for his services. Jory refused to pay, stating that he could water his animals himself, and noted that one animal was missing. "No one ox," the Indian said.

After driving his animals back to camp and searching, Jory found the missing ox. But the same Indian reappeared the next day and demanded a shirt. Jory said he grew belligerent and threatened to kill Jory. To calm the man, Jory offered him half the powder in his horn, but the Cayuse rejected it. Finally, Jory emptied the entire powder horn, which satisfied the Indian, who left, perhaps assuming Jory was now defenseless. But Jory simply returned to his wagon and refilled his powder horn from a hidden keg. He packed powder into his rifle while he was at it.

Many trains on the Oregon Trail received a visit from Doctor Marcus Whitman, a medium-sized man who provided the emigrants with fresh beef, killed and dressed and divided among the company. He spoke in a direct way to the emigrants, explaining that snow in the Cascade mountains would make it difficult for the wagons to travel on the new Barlow Road. He preached a sermon to the exhausted emigrants and renewed them spiritually after their long, arduous overland journey.[14]

Dr. Whitman recommended they follow a route through the foothills above the Columbia River's sandy shore to reach Wascopam Mission at The Dalles. He invited anyone who wanted to rest for the winter to stay with him and his wife at the Whitman Mission.

"When a party has been traveling five or six months through dust and sagebrush, with their teams tired out, their clothes worn out, their pocketbooks rubbed very thin, and their patience about exhausted, a few words of encouragement and cheer from one they know they can trust is like 'oil poured on troubled waters.' It seems to give us new life," wrote J.Q.A. Young, who traveled west with Captain John William Bewley's company in 1847 and appreciated Dr. Whitman's words.[15]

Although exhausted, most of the emigrants opted to keep moving west. But Matilda and her boys joined the Jorys and other emigrants who traveled to Whitman's mission so she could regain her strength.* She remained weak and exhausted. She couldn't physically do much. She reduced what remained in the wagon to essentials that fit inside a large chest she took with her. Captain Magone promised to see her rig safely to Oregon City, where she would go after regaining her strength. She said goodbye to her nephew and his wife.

The Whitman Mission, known as Waiilatpu (near present-day Walla Walla), consisted of several buildings surrounded by dry grassland fenced to keep in stock. Matilda and her boys were greeted by Narcissa Whitman, who helped them settle into temporary quarters and explained how she and her husband, the good doctor, had started the Methodist mission in 1836. They were teaching the nearby Cayuse Indians about God, Jesus, and the Bible. The doctor also provided medical care to the natives when they needed it.

Among those staying at the mission during that time was Elizabeth Ann Fenn. Both her mother, who died, and her stepmother were sisters of James Jory Jr. He had waited for his father to catch up and then spent three weeks at Waiilatpu while Matilda and her boys were there.

[*Matilda's granddaughter Kate Gregg contended that Matilda and the boys stayed at the Whitman Mission, but another granddaughter, Anna Koontz, said they traveled on the south side of the river to The Dalles Mission, which had fallen into disrepair and was sold to the Whitmans in 1847. Matilda told a writer for* The Weekly Oregonian *in 1899 that she heard Doctor Whitman preach at Fort Walla Walla, which was near the Whitman Mission. Lewis County banker and historian Noah B. Coffman also reported in 1926 that Matilda stopped at the Whitman Mission.]*

Chapter Eight: Tragedy on the Snake River

The Whitman Mission (also known as Waiilatpu) near Fort Walla Walla in 1843. At right are portraits of Doctor Marcus and Narcissa Whitman, who were killed in November 1847 shortly after Matilda Coonse left. Below is a sketch of the mission done by Paul Kane in 1846.

"Before reaching the mission, a considerable amount of property was stolen from the emigrants' camp by the Indians," recalled Elizabeth (Fenn) Coonc, who married a man named David M. Coonc, no relation to Matilda or Nicholas. When they reported their losses to Dr. Whitman, she said, he called the Indians together. They gathered in a half circle and faced the doctor, wrapped in blankets, many with their faces painted. He began to harangue them about the thefts.

"I looked on, standing beside Father and holding his hand," she said. "As the Doctor proceeded, and the guilty consciences of the Indians were awakened, from time to time a knife, fork, or frying pan would be dropped by an Indian from beneath his blanket, and when Dr. Whitman finished, most of the stolen property was lying about on the ground at the feet of the Indians. One of the Indians threw down a skillet with considerable force, and, as I thought, threw it at the Doctor, but Father said, 'No, they are mad.'"

Matilda visited Fort Walla Walla, built in 1842 of clay brick baked in the sun.[17] The square fort, which faced the river a hundred yards away, included several houses, an armory, and a warehouse. Native families camped nearby. The fort's chief clerk was Mr. McBean, a Hudson's Bay Company employee.

Dr. Whitman encouraged the emigrants to remain through the winter, but they were eager to reach Oregon City and find land to begin their new lives.

In late October, they left the mission aboard flat-bottomed barges and canoes. Floating down the Columbia River didn't prove taxing until the emigrants reached Celilo Falls, a series of dangerous cascades and waterfalls where the river dropped more than sixty feet over a dozen miles. The natives called it Wyam, which meant "echo of falling water" or "sound of water upon the rocks."[18] Indians fished below the falls, and lived nearby, but with drops between three and fifteen feet, the strong currents and dangerous waterfalls easily claimed the lives of many emigrants.

Aware of the dangers, about a quarter mile above the falls the boats pulled to the shore so that the passengers could portage around the waterfalls. Men and women carried their precious possessions with them along a narrow and somewhat slippery path. They allowed their flat-bottomed barges, some carrying wagons, to churn through the rapids.

Chapter Eight: Tragedy on the Snake River

WIKIMEDIA COMMONS PHOTOS

Celilo Falls as it was before construction of The Dalles Dam. Most emigrants portaged around the falls, but Matilda was too weak to walk so she passed over the falls in a canoe. Native Americans fished at the falls for centuries.

Captain Magone, who may have gone to the Whitman Mission from The Dalles to help Matilda, and Mr. Jory carried Matilda's chest of goods around the falls, "slung on a pole between the two," Jory said.[19]

Although her boys could trudge around the falls, Matilda's weakened body couldn't manage the trek. She asked to float over the falls on a raft, but emigrants and Indians alike cautioned her of the dangers. What about a canoe? It was dangerous, they said. But if she lay flat in the bottom and held tight, perhaps she could survive as the canoe plunged through foaming water, slammed against rocks and ledges, twisted around a bend, and raged through a one-hundred-fifty-yard-wide chute before it spewed into the wider more placid water below.[20]

She had no choice. Not without a few tears, her boys said goodbye to their mother before they portaged around the falls. She put her trust in God as she climbed into a canoe and held tight as it rocked gently before it was let loose to shoot through the rapids. The canoe struck first one rock, and then another, spinning as it swept through the whitewater, plunged over the rocks, and dropped up to fifteen feet. Matilda gripped the edges tightly with hands and feet, praying the entire time. Finally, the canoe slowed, the rapid whitewater replaced by a gentle lull. A man swam into the water to capture the canoe and haul it to shore.

At the bottom of the falls, emigrants boarded rafts again, passing the Wascopam Mission at The Dalles, established in 1838 by Methodist Henry Perkins.[21] Wagons couldn't continue past The Dalles because steep cliffs lined the Columbia River. So just beyond the mission, at Emigrant Bottom, travelers set up camp so the men could topple a dozen pine trees and build flat-bottomed rafts from forty-foot-long logs to float their wagons downstream. Some built canoes. Others rented boats.

The Hudson's Bay Company operated bateau boats that carried families downriver to Fort Vancouver near the river's confluence with the Willamette, a tributary, at a cost of eight dollars. As they floated downstream, emigrants could see the majestic snow-covered peak of Mount Hood to the southwest.

Although Captain Magone had asked the single young men to promise they would stay with the families to the end of the trail, some left, eager to establish new homes in the promised land of Oregon. Other men herded a thousand head of cattle over the mountains while their families floated downstream on the Columbia River.

Chapter Nine

Whitman Mission to Oregon City

AFTER LEAVING FORT VANCOUVER, emigrants paddled south up the Willamette River to Oregon City, the end of the Oregon Trail, at the base of the forty-foot-high Willamette Falls. It was November 18, 1847, when Matilda and her boys climbed ashore to gaze upon the town they'd call home, at least temporarily.[1] Oregon City, more than two thousand miles from their farm in St. Charles, Missouri, consisted of dozens of wooden buildings nestled along the river, some with whitewashed walls, others with bare wood planks. A main street ran through the town's center and wooden fences kept animals close to homes. A church with a belfry sat near a mill along the water.[2]

The community was started by Dr. John McLoughlin, chief factor of the Hudson's Bay Company at Fort Vancouver, which the British opened in 1825. He had built three houses near the falls in 1829 for employees of the fort and set up a small fur trading post. A decade later the settlement, called Willamette Falls, had grown. During early 1840, when Methodist Reverend Alvin F. Waller and George Abernethy arrived, Dr. McLoughlin donated land for construction of a church as well as a store, which Abernethy managed. The doctor, who stood six-foot-four with blue eyes and long white hair, even allowed them to use timber his employees had already cut. Some people referred to him as the Great White Eagle.

Reverend Waller also set up a sawmill to make lumber and a gristmill to grind wheat into flour. McLoughlin platted the town and,

NATIONAL PARK SERVICE

The sketch above shows the Wascopam Mission at The Dalles in 1849. The Methodist Mission operated from 1838 to 1847 but fell into disrepair before it was purchased by the Presbyterians in September 1847 and left in the care of Perrin Whitman, Doctor Marcus Whitman's nephew. Below is Willamette Falls looking south in 1867, with Canemah, Oregon, in the background on the right.

WIKIMEDIA COMMONS

in 1842, dubbed it Oregon City. The church opened in 1843 and, a year later, the town incorporated with about five hundred people living and working in seventy-five buildings. McLoughlin, criticized by his British colleagues for loaning exhausted Americans supplies to survive their first winter, resigned as chief factor in 1845. The following spring, at sixty-two, he moved to Oregon City, where he lived the rest of his life. He built a two-story rectangular home over a stone foundation with chimneys at each end, nine windows in the front and six on the side.

Most wagon train emigrants pitched tents on Abernethy Green, a large meadow near the home of George Abernethy, a storekeeper who became governor of the Oregon Provisional Government. Matilda may have found help from the Rev. John McKinney, who had started out with Magone but led wagons himself after the company divided. He had traveled west with his adult son, William, and daughter-in-law Matilda. The McKinneys arrived in Oregon City before Magone, who had stayed at The Dalles but assured Matilda that someone would bring her rig, oxen, and other things. However, they never arrived.

Despite their heartache, Matilda likely praised God for keeping her sons safe on the journey west. She had no way of answering their questions about the future in Oregon, now that their father had drowned. She might have quoted Jeremiah Chapter 29, verse eleven: "For I know the thoughts that I think toward you, saith the Lord, thoughts of peace and not of evil, to give you an expected end." Their lives, she probably told them, were in God's hands.

When she heard that Mr. McMillan would be traveling from Oregon City to The Dalles, she prepared and sent food and other items with him for Captain Magone to thank him for his assistance after Nicholas died. Magone later thanked her in a letter.[3]

In Oregon City, Matilda, still struggling to recover her health, tended to a sick son as three-year-old Johnny had contracted the measles. In the dark of night, when the rest of the boys were asleep, Matilda likely found her mind contemplating what she and her four boys would do alone in Oregon, without a husband and father, two thousand miles from her home and family.

Since the ratio of men to women in Oregon Territory was about twenty to one, Matilda quickly found herself in demand as a bride, even with four sons. It was too soon, but what choices did she have?

Picture above shows Oregon City in 1845 as drawn by Henry Warre.

Although she and her sons needed to grieve for Nicholas and recover their health, the options for a penniless widow in Oregon were few.

Shocking news swept Oregon City in early December: Angry Indians had slaughtered Doctor Marcus Whitman and his wife, Narcissa Prentiss Whitman. She and Eliza Spaulding had been the first white women to travel overland to Oregon Territory.

Indians also killed a dozen other men, including John and Frank Sager. The two teenage boys had traveled alone along the Oregon Trail with their five younger siblings after the deaths of both their parents.

The Whitmans had established their Waiilatpu mission near the Walla Walla River in 1836, providing the Walla Walla and Cayuse Indians with food and medical attention while attempting to convert them to Christianity.[4] As fur trading decreased and more white emigrants traveled west, tensions increased between the missionaries and the neighboring tribes, especially the Cayuse. When emigrant trains brought a measles epidemic west with them, many Cayuse men, women, and children died from the disease. Believing the Whitmans had poisoned hundreds of their people, several men carrying tomahawks and guns stopped at the mission, pretending to need medical help.[5] On

Chapter Nine: Whitman Mission to Oregon City

November 29, 1847, sixty Cayuse and Umatilla Indians murdered the Whitmans and eleven men, battering Marcus Whitman and shooting Narcissa. They took fifty-three people hostage. One man drowned while trying to escape. Two children—six-year-old Louise Sager and ten-year-old Helen Mar Meek—died of measles while held captive. If they had stayed, Matilda and her sons could have been among the victims.

The news rocked the community. Men volunteered to create a militia to chase those responsible for the massacre. Joe Meek, whose daughter had died, traveled east to Washington, D.C., to share news of the massacre and lobby for creation of Oregon as a U.S. Territory worthy of military protection. [Congress created the territory on August 14, 1848. Two years later, on June 3, 1850, Cayuse Chief Tilaukait and five other men were convicted of murder and hanged by Meek.[6] The Army moved troops west to exact justice for the murders, spawning the Cayuse War of 1848 to 1850.]

In late January 1848 Matilda received a letter from Captain Magone, who addressed her as "respected friend."[7] He thanked her for the things she had sent to him and explained that her rig and some of her oxen had been stolen.[8]

> Mr. McKinney, who you are aware has returned to this place, informed me that Mr. [Alanson] Hinman would not stop at Park Rose, notwithstanding he had pledged his word and honour to me to do so; and consequently they did not get the articles that I wrote you they would bring. This you are aware is not the first time that these gentlemen (if such they may be called) betrayed the confidence that I supposed in them; and what looks worse than anything else, is the fact of Mr. Hinman carrying off your Rig which I charged him so particular to send you by Mr. McKinney, who it was known was going direct to the City, but if reports are true, it is not the only thing that has found itself adrift in the same channel.
>
> Wilson wrote me that your little Boy was sick with the measles, but as friend Tompkins wrote me you were

> Dalls Mission Jan. 20th 1848
>
> Respected Friend
>
> I rec'd of Mr. Mc-
> Meller some things which you sent
> me, & for the taste and good order in
> which they were done up, (aside from
> the presents for which I cannot express my
> gratitude) I return you my heartfelt
> and sincere thanks. Mr. McKinney
> who, you are aware has returned
> to this place, informed me that Mr.
> Finney would not stop at Parker's
> Notwithstanding he had pledged his word
> and honor to me to do so; and conseq-
> uently they did not get the articles
> that I wrote you they would bring.
> this you are aware is not the first
> time that these Gentlemen (if such they
> may be called) betrayed the confidence
> that I reposed in them; and what looks
> worse than anything else, is the fact
> of Mr. Finney carrying off your keg
> which I charged him so particular
> to send you by Mr. McKinney, who it
> was known was going direct to the city:
> but if reports are true, it is not the only
> thing that has found itself adrift in
> the same channel. The poor Indians, &
> soldiers must stand responsible to the
> Emegrants for many little notions which
> have some how or other stepped out very
> mysteriously. but time and opportunities can
> more fully develop this part of the story.
>
> Your friend
> J. Magone
>
> P.S. Remember me to the Gentle-
> manly Mr. Wallace, and Family, and all
> others who may enquire after me
> J.M.

This letter from Joseph Magone dated January 20, 1848, was addressed to "Mrs. Coonse, Oregon City, OT."

WASHINGTON STATE LIBRARY'S COLLECTION OF THE JACKSON, KOONTZ, GLOVER FAMILY PAPERS, 1837–1952.

all well, I take it for granted that He has recovered. I hope so at last. I have seen some but not all of your cattle. Among those seen were Pet and Baul, Duke and the Heifer. I have not seen Browny or old Buck. I have seen William's Ned and Berry, but not Duke or Jerry. His Racer is also here, but I have not as yet seen either of yours. But my word for it, you shall have them or others in stead as good if not better than they dare be. Mr. McKinney has not found all of his cattle and his horses are among the missing. Himself, Gaffne and Hinman are at loggerheads, and the way that hurts my feelings you may imagine.

I have but little time to write now, and little to write about, but more from me hereafter. My best respects to William and his family if you have an opportunity to send to them. I have enjoyed first rate health since I left and I am now in first rate spirits."

After signing off as "ever your friend," Magone added a postscript: "Remember me to the gentlemanly Mr. Wallace, and family, and all others who may enquire after me."

[Magone married Miss Mary Ann Tomlinson, whom he met on the plains, on July 4, 1850. She died in 1859. He served in the Cayuse War and was promoted to major. He worked in the California gold mines. Years later, Magone walked back to Chicago, retracing his journey on the Oregon Trail, even though trains by then carried most people across the country.[9]]

Matilda and her boys were among nearly five thousand emigrants who traveled west along the Oregon Trail in 1847, increasing Oregon Territory's population to more than twelve thousand. Oregon City, the capital of the Provisional Government, had three stores, three churches, two blacksmith shops, and two flour mills. *The Oregon Spectator* published news and advertisements once a week. A post office opened in March 1848. Mailing a letter cost ten cents for each half ounce.

Although she wrote a letter to her family in Missouri, news of Nicholas's death reached Matilda's mother, Mrs. Matilda Nettle Glover,

Matthew D. Glover sent this letter to his sister addressed to "Mrs. Coonse, Oregon City," dated April 2, 1848.

WASHINGTON STATE LIBRARY'S COLLECTION OF THE JACKSON, KOONTZ, GLOVER FAMILY PAPERS, 1837–1952.

Chapter Nine: Whitman Mission to Oregon City

by way of a traveler heading east who met the emigrant train west of the Snake River and learned the news. He passed it on upon arriving in Missouri, according to Matilda's brother, Matthew, who mailed a letter to her April 2, 1848.[10] An excerpt is below.

> Dear sister there is a report in sirculation here that Nicholas got drowned in Snake River on your way out and you are left a destitute widow in a wild frontier country, if this is your situation it is a deplorable one indeed. I spend many anxious thoughts about you, but I cannot fully believe the report although it appears to have come strait. A man Felix Coons saw a man named Berdie who came from Oregon last fall and winter. He states that he met you and company in about three hours travel from the place where the accident should have happened and that he conversed with William Glover about it himself. He states further that William was going to move you back this spring, if this is the case. God grant that you all may get back safe is my prear. If this report be false and Nicholas is yet alive, give my best love to him and best to remember me to all your children, this is the reason I do not write no more to Nicholas. Polly sends her love and good wishes to you all and would rejoice to see you back again. Elizaann talks frequently about you and all your children and sends her love to you and Grundy.

Matilda's nephew, William Glover, and his wife, Jane, settled in Champoeg, about halfway between Oregon City and Salem. He wrote to Matilda in April 1848.[11]

> Dear Aunt,
> I have neglected writing to [you] thinking I would come down soon but matters and things have turned out so I have not come. I would have been down some time

ago had it not a been fore the Indian fuss kicked up on the Abacora between the Clammoths and whites which dotless you have heard of before this, I was in the battle if it deserves to be named, we killed some seven or eight of them and drove the balance off. A good many of the people up hear are pretty badly scart, thinking that the clammath will come on in the summer but as to my own part I apprehend no danger. Thomas Fine informed me that you had concluded to remain at the fawls until after harvest which I think best myself if you can get along well for there is no getting nothing hear without the money but if you are not doing well write to me and I will come after you immediately. I can get something to eat until harvest then I am not afraid but what we will have plenty dear aunt. I am ready and willing at any time to do any thing in my power that I can without money. Money is a thing I can't get. It is my calculation for you to live with me and I want you to. I will do everything in my power to make you comfortable and it will be my delight to do so. I have been in the woods ever cinse I have been hear. Until now I have just cacpt [set] out to also make garden. I am going to make a big one here.

 All of us I have got as good a garden spot as can be and we are going to try for a pretty big one. I can answer you. John Edmunson is gone up the river. I supposed I haven't heard from him for better than two months. When he left my house he said he would be back in fore or five days, and I have been looking for him ever cince so I could come down for my wagon. We are all well and have bin wel during the winter. Jane sends her best love to [you] and children and wants to see you all very bad. I want you to be sure to write to me all about how you are getting a long and doing. I got a letter from Joseph Magone not long cince and I intend to write to

Chapter Nine: Whitman Mission to Oregon City

William Glover offered to take his aunt and her sons back to Missouri in this letter dated April 9, 1848.

Champoeick county April 9th 1848

Dear aunt I have neglected writing to thinking I would come down soon but matters and things have turned out so I have not come I would have been down some time ago had it not a been fore the indian fuss kicked up on the Abacawthe Cammoths and which doubtless you have heard of before this I war in the battle if it deserves the name we kiled some seven or eight of them and drove the balance off a good many of the people up hear are pretty badly scart thinking that the Cammoths will come in on us in the summer but as to my own part I apprehend no danger Thomas fine informed me that you had concluded to remain at the fawls until after harvest which I think best my self if you can get along well for thare is no getting nothing hear without the money but if you are not doing well write to me and I will come after you immediateately I can get something to eat until harvest then I am not afraid but whot we will have plenty dear aunt I am ready and willing at any time to do any thing in my power that I can with out money money is a thing I cant get it is my caculation for you to live with me and I want you to I will do every thing in my power to make you comfortable and it will be my delight to do so I have binn in the woods ever cinse I have been hear until now I have just crept out to make a garden I am going to make a big one...

he is very well and has bin ever cinse he has bin out he sends his best love to you I must come to a close and shall ever remain your affectionate nephew

Mrs Matilda Coonz
Wm Glover

Washington State Library's collection of the Jackson, Koontz, Glover family papers, 1837–1952.

him to day. He is very well and has been ever cince he has ben out. He sends his best love to you. I must come to a close and shall ever remain your affectionate nephew.

She appreciated the invitation from her nephew. But about that time, she was introduced to a handsome, intelligent Englishman with bushy sideburns and a bad eye who had traveled south to Oregon City for supplies.

Chapter Ten

John Robinson Jackson

OREGON CITY SERVED as the principal place for emigrants who needed to purchase supplies, so most pioneers traveled to town at least once or twice a year. John Robinson Jackson, a British native who settled on high ground north of the Cowlitz River, was no exception.

The pioneer who first settled Lewis County arrived in the world January 13, 1800, at Ingleton in the Staindrop parish of Durham County, England. Some census records list his birth year as 1802, and a baptismal record from Staindrop parish says 1804, but the notation on his gravestone at Fern Hill Cemetery in Chehalis states, "John R. Jackson, born Jan.13, 1800, died May 23, 1873, aged 73 yrs. 4 mos. 10 dys. Pioneer of 1844."

Jackson's father, Michael Jackson, was a farmer near Raby Castle, home of Charles Nevil, the sixth earl of Westmoreland. His mother, Mary Robinson, named him after her father, John Robinson. He had two brothers—William and Anthony Calvert—and four sisters, Catherine, Mary, Anne, and Susannah. He learned to read and write, and his father taught him to farm. Some records indicate John was apprenticed as a butcher and traveled a bit in Scotland.[1]

John R. Jackson.

OFFICE OF

THE COUNTY CLERK OF DUTCHESS COUNTY

POUGHKEEPSIE, N. Y.

FREDERIC A. SMITH
COUNTY CLERK

March 28, 1952

Mr. Walter H. Twiss
5001-8th Ave. N.E.
Seattle 5, Washington

Dear Mr. Twiss,

    In respect to your inquiry about the naturalization of John R. Jackson, I find an entry in an old index which would indicate that John Jackson was naturalized in the Court of Common Pleas, October 27, 1834. Reference is made to the minutes of common pleas for that date and a search of those ancient records fails to show Jackson's name as having been naturalized within three months of that date. It probably will take considerable research to find the entry but doubtless it is in that minute book somewhere, or it would not be shown in the index.

    If you require certification or a copy of these proceedings, it seems to me you should write to the Department of Naturalization & Immigration, 70 Columbus Ave., New York City and ask their advice. We are forbidden by law to make copies of present day naturalization records but there might not be any objection to making a copy of a record as ancient as that. If you were to require us to search through that whole minute book, I would estimate that our search fees would be in the neighborhood of $5.00 and a copy of the proceeding if we were able to find it would not cost more than $1.25, in addition. Of course, there is no guarantee that we will be able to find it.

              Very truly yours,

               FREDERIC A. SMITH
               Dutchess County Clerk

FAS/rr

WASHINGTON STATE LIBRARY'S COLLECTION OF THE JACKSON, KOONTZ, GLOVER FAMILY PAPERS, 1837–1952.

Walter H. Twiss, a friend of Anna Koontz, sent her the letter above with a note that explained he had made inquiries about John R. Jackson while researching his family history. He received the letter above showing that Jackson was indeed naturalized October 24, 1834, in Dutchess County, Poughkeepsie, New York.

In his late twenties or early thirties, depending on which birth year is used, John, who stood more than six feet tall, boarded a ship in England headed for a new land and a new life on the American frontier. He landed in New York September 27, 1833, where he lived for a time.

The congenial Brit applied for American citizenship October 27, 1834, after filling out naturalization paperwork in the Court of Common Pleas in Poughkeepsie, in Dutchess County, New York, about eighty miles north of New York City.[2] He traveled west to Illinois, living near Griggsville and Pittsfield in Pike County, where he boarded with different families and plowed their fields.

In Illinois, where he lived for ten years, Jackson purchased property and later sold it, but not everyone paid what was due, so he tried to recover the money owed in court, according to a descendant, Walter Twiss, who researched the records. More often than not, the judgment remained unsatisfied.

Throughout his life, Jackson kept meticulous records of what he spent and what he earned. For example, May 28, 1836, his diary notes that he paid William Ridgeway $1.87½ for three yards of jeans, a dollar and fifty cents for a pair of shoes, and one dollar for five pounds of coffee. He hired Morrison Boring to work in April that year for eight dollars per month until fall. He bought a wagon and yoke of oxen for $120, then purchased two more yoke of oxen (forty-nine dollars and forty-five dollars) as well as a bay mare for seventy-five dollars, a chestnut with saddle and bridle for sixty-eight dollars, and another bay for fifty-six dollars.[3]

In Illinois, he plowed land, bought lumber, and built fences. One July he received eighteen dollars from Lorenzo Hitchcock for four days of hauling with five yoke of cattle but also paid him nine dollars for lumber.

He also bought and sold land frequently. In November 1835, he received a patent from the state of Illinois for 41.9 acres of government school land purchased for $303.77. That same month, he and another man, Thomas Limpkin, took out a mortgage at 12 percent interest to buy 87.71 acres. Two years later, he paid six hundred dollars to Henry and Sally Brown for 120 acres, although in March 1838, he gave the Browns a large ox wagon and four yoke of work cattle between five and six years old, and promised to saw rails for fencing of forty acres and break eighty acres of land in consideration of $240 he owed.[4]

In October 1837, Jackson sold land to Peter L. Coughenour under a real estate contract to be paid off in three years. For land priced at $320, Jackson would receive $362.50, with 5 percent interest calculated. In January 1840, he transferred another warranty deed to Coughenour for $350.

Interestingly, the paperwork says it was signed by Jackson and his wife before John McCallister, justice of the peace. McCallister wrote that "having been by me made acquainted with the contents of said Deed and being by me examined separate and apart from her said husband acknowledged that she had executed the same and relinquished her right of dower in and to the premises therein conveyed."

This is the only reference to Jackson ever being married. No other details are available. Perhaps it referred to another John Jackson as records show men by that name married Rachel Boosinger of Ray County, Missouri, March 16, 1838; Patsey Taylor February 19, 1835; Rebecca South May 7, 1834; Mariah Thompson March 16, 1837; Jane Nichols December 12, 1839; Keziah Welch on December 5, 1839; and possibly a relative, Martha Jackson, February 15, 1838. Those women all married men named John Jackson.

The land transactions continued. In September 1838, Jackson sold his mortgage for $247 to David Baldwin, issuing a mortgage for $276.66 in January 1840, which was satisfied January 27, 1845.[6]

In October of 1838, Jackson turned over his warranty deed to John Coughenour for $400, but that same month he was awarded a judgment against James Coughenour for $25.50, plus costs. It was appealed to the Circuit Court, and by October 24, 1838, the costs were $51, but the outcome was never recorded.[7]

On November 14, 1838, acting on behalf of Richard C. Robertson, Jackson was awarded a judgment against John M. McConnell for $49.29 in the Justice of the Peace office at Griggsville, Illinois. McConnell appealed the case and lost September 2, 1839, but the judgment went unsatisfied because McConnell had no property to confiscate.

In September 1839, Jackson gave a mortgage to Usler Shad for $600 as interest for a dozen yoke of oxen, four to eight years old, "which constitutes my Prairie Teams, together with my Prairie Plough and six ox chains and ox wagon and horse saddle and bridle, and sow and five pigs, also seventeen acres of corn growing on the south west eighty of

Chapter Ten: John Robinson Jackson

WASHINGTON STATE LIBRARY'S COLLECTION OF THE JACKSON, KOONTZ, GLOVER FAMILY PAPERS, 1837–1952.

In 1952, Walter H. Twiss sent Anna Koontz the map at right where he marked the property owned by John R. Jackson near Griggsville, Illinois. He also sent photos he took from the center of the farms owned by Jackson while living in Illinois.

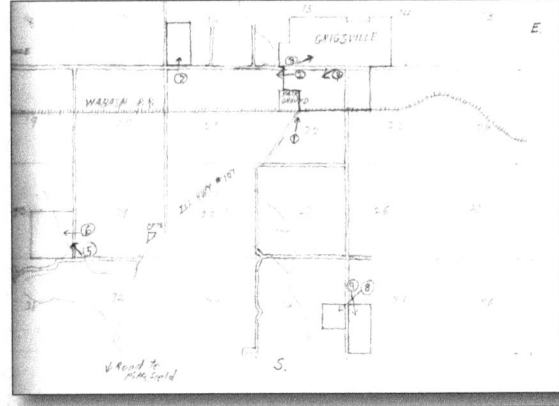

land....property to remain in the possession of John R. Jackson. Mortgage due on or before October 1, 1840."[8]

On September 21, 1839, Jackson was awarded a judgment against John Peerson and John A. Windsor for $40 and costs, a ruling appealed from John McCallister's Justice of the Peace court to the Circuit Court. Andrew Philips, who held the note, later stated in writing that it had been mislaid and couldn't be found, so the suit was dismissed March 20, 1840.[9]

Jackson held a promissory note of Richard Windsor for $16.52 and received a judgment for it March 27, 1839, but the sheriff noted in writing July 2, 1839, that no property could be found to levy for the judgment.[10]

Finally, Jackson was awarded a judgment September 14, 1839, in the justice court at Griggsville against John P. Gordon, but the case was appealed to the Circuit Court. On April 15, 1840, Jackson won a judgment for $18.30, but the sheriff again returned unsatisfied, failing to find property upon which to levy the execution.[11]

Perhaps after the final judgment, Jackson decided to move to Missouri, where he established a prosperous farm raising cattle and crops. Records from 1843 show he purchased six pounds of coffee for one dollar; bacon at six-and-a-half cents per pound; pantaloons material at thirty-seven cents per yard; a gallon of whiskey for a dollar; pair of shoes for $1.50; hauled a load of plank for twenty-five cents, two loads of rock for a dollar, three-fourths cord of wood for seventy-five cents, and a half-cord of wood for fifty cents. He also hired people to help him on the farm, including D. Ray.[12]

In the spring of 1844, three years before the Coonses left Missouri, torrential rains brought heavy flooding. Jackson saved his livestock by moving them to higher ground but his crops were destroyed. Devastated by the loss of his hard work, Jackson decided to start over in a mild climate where the rains would never destroy his crops again. He sold his farm and herded his cattle west. On May 1, 1844, he paid George Bronk $31.30 for ten bushels of wheat, seven bushels of peas, three bushels of oats, and pork.[13]

That same day in 1844, Jackson joined Colonel Nathaniel Ford's company of about a hundred wagons and five hundred people and left Missouri for Oregon.[14] So did James Clyman, who kept a diary of their travels.[15] For the most part, the emigrants of 1844 didn't suffer from mountain fever, smallpox, or cholera as their counterparts did later.

One thousand five hundred emigrants traveled west in 1844. During the first two months, they traveled amid thunder, lightning, and torrents of rain that gushed from darkened skies and muddied the trail. Oxen slogged through the muck and pulled their heavy wagonloads. The emigrants experienced only eight days in the first two months without precipitation. Wind blew down tents and tore at the canvas covering wagons. Three of the five companies that headed west in 1844 traveled to Oregon—those under the leadership of Nathaniel Ford, Cornelius Gilliam, and John Thorp.

Ford's company, which left May 14, employed Major Moses (Black) Harris, an old mountain man with a great sense of humor, as a guide. He also worked for Gilliam, who left two weeks after Ford with three hundred people but overtook the other train. Among those traveling with Gilliam were Michael T. Simmons, who established the first American settlement near the Puget Sound, and Henry Sager, who died near the Green River, followed a few weeks later by his wife. That left their seven children as orphans. Captain Shaw, who worked for Gilliam, and his family cared for the orphans en route to Waiilatpu near Walla Walla, where they were adopted by Dr. Marcus and Narcissa Whitman. Two of them were killed with the Whitmans in 1847.

Another traveling companion was William Packwood, a native of Patrick County, Virginia, who explored Oregon and Washington. Dr. Kate L. Gregg of Chehalis, Matilda's stepgranddaughter, described her "Old Uncle Billy" as an explorer, prospector, miner, and "a spirit in whatever community he lived."[16] She recalled as a child seeing him ride across Jackson Prairie leading a packhorse behind him. "And my mother would say; 'There goes old Packwood. He's off to the Upper Country again.'" After two years in what became Yamhill County, Oregon, Packwood sold out and, with his wife, Rhoda Bell Prothro, and their four children, moved north in 1847 and, after stops at Cowlitz, Jackson and Newaukum Prairies as well as Centralia, settled in a log cabin on the Nisqually River Flats. He was described as "the first bona fide American settler north of Olympia."[17] In the mid-1850s, along with James Longmire, Packwood charted a low pass across the Cascade Mountains under the direction of the Washington Territorial Legislature The town of Packwood in eastern Lewis County is named for him, but the charted pass, called Packwood Saddle, remains unused today with the Cascades crossed instead at nearby White Pass.

Jackson, described as a man with a quick wit, herded his cattle and pack mules to prevent them from straying too far. A forty-three-year-old bachelor, he likely met many fine-looking young ladies in the wagon train but remained single.

Occasionally, horses and mules disappeared at night, stolen by Indians from the look of the moccasin tracks, Clyman said. The company established rotating guard duties to prevent the theft of livestock, although Clyman said men without horses grumbled a great deal about the chore. Among those traveling with John R. Jackson and Clyman was another man named John Jackson, only his middle initials were H.P. and he settled in California. Both Jackson men herded livestock and each had animals stolen during the trip. They both owed the wagon train captain $3.50, the sum he paid to a chief for the return of their lost horses June 25.[18]

After its slow and soggy start, the pace picked up and they reached Fort Laramie in seventy-eight days. The emigrants and their animals suffered from the heat and dust as they journeyed across South Pass to the arid western side of the Rockies. The company buried a Mr. Barnett, who died of typhus fever in August, near a bed of green willows along the Sweetwater River.

After more than 150 days of travel, the emigrants arrived at The Dalles. While most of the company skipped the forty-mile trail to Waiilatpu, the Sager children were taken to the Whitman Mission, where they found a new (but not safe) home. Those with wagons built rafts to float down the Columbia River, or paid up to a hundred dollars per wagon for transport downriver, while men herding livestock followed a narrow trail alongside the river.

They arrived at Fort Vancouver, a wooden stockade with a company store and offices of the Hudson's Bay Company, as well as a row of buildings for servants and workers. They met the chief factor for the company, Dr. John McLoughlin, a Canadian native who had crossed the Rocky Mountains in 1824 and established Fort Vancouver for the British-owned Hudson's Bay Company the following year. He greeted them hospitably and shared information about the territory, the Indians, Oregon City, and settlers. He encouraged Americans to settle south of the Columbia River since Great Britain hoped to retain ownership of the land to the north, which he described as poor land of little use except to fur traders.

Chapter Ten: John Robinson Jackson

WIKIMEDIA COMMONS

Fort Vancouver in 1845 as depicted by Lieutenant Henry Warre.

McLoughlin told of the wheat, flour, beef, pork and lumber exported to the Sandwich Islands [now the Hawaiian Islands] and north to Russian Alaska. The fort purchased imported manufactured items from Britain, China, and East Coast communities, as well as molasses, coffee, sugar, and rice. Timber, both white and red fir, split easily for building neat rail fences. Trees of oak, maple, willow, boxwood, hazel, alder, and large evergreens were plentiful. Bogs, underbrush, and ferns covered much of the land, he said.

Jackson, whose accent told of his English roots, was welcomed heartily by Dr. McLoughlin, even when he expressed interest in exploring land north of the Columbia near Tumwater Falls and the Deschutes River. Given that Jackson clearly hailed from England, McLoughlin probably didn't object. It's likely that Jackson failed to mention he had applied to become a naturalized American in 1834.

Initially, Jackson settled in Clackamas Bottom in Oregon November 5, 1844.[19] But in March, 1845, he traveled north to Cowlitz Prairie, where he met Simon Plamondon, a giant of a man who had first visited the region two decades earlier. Plamondon, a native of Quebec who stood six feet two inches tall, traveled west to the Oregon land in 1818 as a fur trader with the Northwest Trading Company, headquartered in Montreal.[20]

In the 1820s, after Northwest merged with its rival, the Hudson's Bay Company, Plamondon canoed up the Cowlitz River and disembarked at Cowlitz Landing, near present-day Toledo. Cowlitz Indians, a Salish tribe that lived primarily off fish, berries, and roots, had erected longhouses on both sides of the river. According to local lore, they captured Plamondon, a white man they feared would be like the British fur trappers who, accompanied by Iroquois, had raped a party of Cowlitz women. But the tall young man knew enough Chinook jargon to communicate with them. He carried no weapons. They let him go.

But Plamondon returned with gifts for the chief, Scanewa, who let him marry one of his daughters, Thasemuth, who was baptized as Veronica. When Chief Scanewa was murdered in 1828 by a Klallam Indian, oral tradition says his son, Richard, was too young to serve as chief so his son-in-law, Plamondon, became the leader until Richard could rule.

In 1833, Plamondon staked out a claim to 640 acres on the Cowlitz River. Five years later, the Hudson's Bay Company's affiliate Puget Sound Agricultural Company began operations on four thousand acres known as the Cowlitz

Simon Plamondon, first white settler in what became Washington state.

Farm, on which the company grew oats, wheat, peas, potatoes, and barley as well as livestock.[21] French-Canadian employees of the Hudson's Bay Company worked at the farm and established homes in the community. Among those was Marcel Bernier, whose farm Jackson had visited during his first trip north of the Columbia.

Plamondon accompanied Jackson as far as Bernier's cabin on the

Newaukum River.[22] Jackson returned south to Oregon City for the winter, having selected the spot where he wanted to live, and retrieved his personal property and cattle he had brought overland from Missouri. He frequently visited the Hudson's Bay Company's Fort Vancouver and developed a close friendship with George Roberts, who later managed the Cowlitz Farm.

In April 1845, Jackson ventured north again and found the land he wanted to claim as his own—640 acres of highland prairie where floodwaters wouldn't destroy his crops, about nine miles up the Cowlitz Trail from Cowlitz Landing. The land was close enough to the meandering Lacamas Creek and natural springs for water but elevated enough to protect it from flooding. He called his new home "The Highlands" or "Highland Farm."

Jackson built a one-room cabin, which measured eighteen by twenty-four feet, with a split cedar door. He pounded the logs in place while gazing at the gorgeous views of Mount Rainier to the northeast, looming 14,000 feet above sea level, and Mount St. Helens to the southeast, which soared 9,700 feet above sea level. The Cowlitz called Mount St. Helens "Loowit," which means "fire mountain," or "Lavelatla," translated as "smoking mountain."

At the Cowlitz Farm, Jackson and George Roberts, who had arrived from Fort Vancouver in 1838 to help manage the agriculture and livestock, became fast friends.

While building his cabin, Jackson met Michael T. Simmons and his party as they explored the northern land. Debate has raged over which of these two men was the first American to settle north of the Columbia River—Jackson or Simmons.

But renowned historian Edmond S. Meany, an early twentieth century University of Washington professor, said neither was. He noted that two American missionaries, Dr. J.P. Richmond and W.H. Wilson, settled at Fort Nisqually in 1840, before either Jackson or Simmons arrived in Oregon Territory.[23] "They stayed only two years and their cabin was burned on their departure in 1842," Meany wrote.[24]

Simmons, one of ten children born in Kentucky, had camped with his group during their first winter on the north bank of the Washougal River, where they had cut trees for logs and crafted cedar shingles for Dr. McLoughlin. Simmons' wife gave birth to a son in April 1845; they named him Christopher Columbus Simmons.²⁵ Then they were ready to find land.

However, racist Oregon laws prevented one of their members—a man of mixed race named George Bush of Clay County, Missouri, and his family—from settling south of the Columbia River.²⁶ The Oregon Provisional Government in June 1844, while declaring slavery illegal, passed the "Lash Law," which required blacks to be whipped twice a year "until he or she shall quit the territory."²⁷ Although deemed too harsh by December 1844, it allowed for forced labor of blacks and prohibited them from owning land south of the Columbia.

In April 1845, Simmons, Bush, German native George Waunch and a handful of other men canoed up the Columbia to the Cowlitz and upriver to an Indian village. They stopped first at the home of Simon Plamondon, who told them that John R. Jackson was building a cabin just north of Cowlitz Prairie. They stopped at his cabin before going north toward Puget Sound, where they arrived in August.

As they returned south, Waunch left the small group to establish his farm near the Skookumchuck River south of the Puget Sound but north of Highland Prairie and Marcel Bernier's place.²⁸

The Simmons group left Washougal with their families in October and returned to the Puget Sound, guided by Peter Bercier. Simmons, who had seven members in his family, established New Market (today known as Tumwater), while Bush settled on a prairie a mile south, not far from the Deschutes River. The high ground still bears his name—Bush Prairie. Others in the group included the McAllisters, Joneses, Kindreds, and Sam Crockett and Jesse Ferguson.²⁹

In September of 1845, Jackson had watched a plume of black smoke and ash curl into the sky as Mount St. Helens erupted in the distance. The black hovered like a canopy over the snow-capped peak, a stark contrast to the blue skies.³⁰

A month later, Jackson purchased supplies from Simon Plamondon, whose name he wrote as "Pernondo," including eleven pounds of pork at ten cents per pound, one bushel of potatoes at fifty cents, a half-bushel of peas for fifty cents, and five bushels of wheat for three dollars.³¹

That's the same year Simon Plamondon made the first brick on his farm above the Cowlitz Landing.

The Oregon Provisional Government in 1845 carved the territory into four districts, including the huge Vancouver district north of the Columbia River. On December 19, 1845, the Vancouver district was divided in two, with the bulk of it called Lewis County, named to honor the famous explorer, Meriwether Lewis.[32] The county ran from about the Cowlitz River north as far as Russian Alaska. The government named Jacob Wooley, S.B. Crockett, and John Jackson to serve as the "judges of the county court" and appointed James Birnie as treasurer, Alonzo M. Poe as clerk, and R. Brock as sheriff, assessor, and collector.

American settlers north of the Columbia River received good news after Congress signed the Oregon Treaty with the United Kingdom in Washington, D.C., June 15, 1846. The treaty established the northern boundary of the United States of America at the 49th parallel of north latitude. Under the treaty, the Puget Sound Agricultural Company retained its right to property north of the Columbia River, both at Cowlitz Farm and Nisqually. It also stated that property rights of the Hudson's Bay Company and British subjects south of the new boundary would be respected. The Hudson's Bay Company moved its headquarters north to Victoria in British Columbia.[33]

In June 1846, Lewis County voters picked Hudson's Bay Company Chief Factor Dr. William F. Tolmie to represent them in the Oregon Provisional Government's Legislature. The governor was George Abernethy, who had been serving in that role since the 1845 election, when he took over from a governing commission of three. In 1846, Abernethy sought re-election but was opposed by A.L. Lovejoy, who received 518 votes in the old part of the region compared to only 477 for Abernethy. However, the returns from Lewis County—sixty-one votes for Abernethy and only two for Lovejoy, gave the victory to Abernethy, 538 to 520.

In 1846, as Lewis County assessor, John R. Jackson recorded the county's produce (most of it grown at the Cowlitz and Nisqually farms by the Puget Sound Agricultural Company): Oats, 9,250 bushels; peas, 4,475 bushels; and potatoes, 5,760 bushels.

Jackson's records show that on April 6, 1846, George Waunch paid him $7.70 toward a new plow, and on July 16, 1846, he hired Joseph Borst to work for a month. On September 14 he paid Borst for seventeen days of work with twenty-seven dollars Oregon currency and $13.25 in trade. On July 23, 1846, Jackson hired "Tom the Indian" to work for two months at two blankets per month.[34]

On August 25, 1846, he sold items to Paul Moore, including a shirt and a kettle for a dollar each, a wedge for two dollars, two planes for six dollars, and a jack for a dollar. He also assessed him $2.44¾ for his 1846 tax, for a total of $13.44¾, plus a saddle for five dollars, a debt settled May 10, 1847.

In the spring of 1847, Mount St. Helens twice again belched white smoke. On March 26, 1847, as artist Paul Kane sketched the mountain on a clear day under blue skies, he said, "suddenly a stream of white smoke shot up from the crater of the mountain, and hovered a short time over its summit; it then settled down like a cap. This shape it retained for about an hour and a half, and then gradually disappeared." Four days later, while visiting the Cowlitz Farm, Kane saw the volcano emit "a long column of dark smoke."[35]

Later that year, Simon Plamondon built the first flour mill, with burrs and a water wheel, on Drew's Creek.[36]

By July 1847, when Jackson was elected justice of the peace, Lewis County had three voting precincts—Jackson's home at Highland Farm, Michael T. Simmons' home at New Market, and Dr. Tolmie's home at Nisqually. That summer, in a letter to *The Oregon Spectator*, Lewis County settlers voiced their opinion supporting resolutions passed at a May 14 meeting in Oregon City. The letter was signed by Jackson, Tolmie, Simmons, Bush, Bercier, Plamondon, Waunch, Bernier, Roberts, Crockett, and forty-four other men.[37]

The county's first meeting of commissioners took place in Jackson's cabin October 4, 1847.[38] At the time, Jackson presented an invoice for $66.28 for services rendered as sheriff. Dr. Tolmie, who oversaw the Hudson's Bay Company's farm near Steilacoom, asked for $1.92 for county stationery. Jackson presented his Lewis County census that showed 285 white inhabitants, with ninety-two of them female, but most of those under the age of twelve. He listed 102 taxpayers, a valuation of $30,406.12, and taxes collected of $488.32, including a fifty-cent per person poll tax and assessment on livestock, wagons, town lots, and merchandise. Cattle were assessed at twenty cents a head and hogs at ten cents. Commissioners also discussed building a road from New Market to Plamondon's Cowlitz Landing.[39]

Chapter Eleven

Quick Courtship and a Wedding

BY 1848, A THOUSAND WHITE RESIDENTS lived in the community of Oregon City, served by Catholic, Methodist and Baptist churches, two flour mills and two sawmills. Most pioneers traveled to the city for supplies at least once or twice a year.

John R. Jackson was no exception. He had hired carpenter Leander Wallace in the fall of 1847 to help build his home, and once it was completed, he left for Oregon City for supplies and perhaps to find a wife. [Wallace was killed May 1, 1849, at Fort Nisqually in an altercation with Snoqualmie and Suquamish Indians. Five men were tried during a special court session at Steilacoom in October 1849 and two were executed.[1]]

During Jackson's visit, he might have stopped by to visit Dr. McLoughlin, and it may be from him that he heard about the handsome widow with four boys who lost her husband in the Snake River at Three Island Crossing.

In any event, during his trip to Oregon City, Jackson, by then a prosperous and well-established pioneer, met Matilda Coonse. A quick courtship followed.

Matilda, facing an uncertain future, considered the security offered to herself and her four boys if she married Jackson, a tall man with dark hair and mutton-chop sideburns. As a child, a horse threw him and he landed in hawthorn bushes, which punctured one eye and blinded it. For his part, Jackson likely welcomed the companionship offered by the

THE OREGON SPECTATOR, MAY 4, 1848

The Oregon Spectator *published a brief notice about J.R. Jackson's marriage to Mrs. Matilda N. Coonse May 4, 1848.*

handsome Matilda, a devout Christian woman, and saw her four fine young lads as hard workers for his farm.

Whatever their reasons, when Jackson proposed marriage to Matilda, rather than risk her sons' lives on an arduous journey back across the country to Missouri, she accepted. They were married by the Reverend Hezekiah Johnson, a Baptist minister who had traveled west in 1845, according to a report on the wedding of John R. Jackson of Lewis County to Mrs. Matilda N. Coonse of Oregon City in the May 4 edition of *The Oregon Spectator*.[2] It must have been difficult for the boys, especially Henry, the eldest, to accept another man in the role of Matilda's husband not eight months after their father's death.

During their courtship, Jackson likely shared with Matilda the finer attributes of Highland Farm and the rest of the country between the Columbia River and the Puget Sound. Perhaps his recitation of the region's qualities to her prompted him to accede to editor George Law Curry's request to write about the region for *The Oregon Spectator*. It was published May 18, 1848.[3]

For the Oregon Spectator

Mr. Editor—Sir, according to your request, I communicate a brief description of that portion of the Territory lying between the Columbia river, and Puget Sound, and the country immediately adjoining. The Cowlitz settlement is in a prairie district, situate on the Cowlitz river, about thirty miles, by way of the river, from its mouth. The settlement is small as yet, and composed principally of

Chapter Eleven: Quick Courtship and a Wedding

Canadians, who are excellent citizens, and for industry, not surpassed by any citizens of the Territory.

The soil in the neighborhood of the Cowlitz river, is extremely rich, and covered with timber up to the settlement. In passing up the Cowlitz river, twenty miles from its mouth, strong signs of lead and iron ore appear, which continue as you proceed up the river. Stone-coal is found here in great abundance, and from the usual indications, and the question of intelligent men who have been conversant with iron districts, it is supposed that Iron Ore exists here in abundance, and of an excellent quality. The river is now navigated by bateau, from its mouth to the settlement, and it is said by more experienced watermen than myself, that it may be navigated by steamboats for the same distance, six or eight months in the year. The distance from the settlement to the Columbia river, is estimated at twenty miles, over which a wagon road is practicable. The settlement has a saw and flouring mill.

To the East of the settlement, and also to the West, in the direction of the mouth of the Columbia river, the country is diversified with timber and prairie—the plains are small but beautiful, and the soil excellent. Ten miles North from the settlement the road leading to Puget Sound reaches the waters of the Chehalis, and five miles still farther, reaches the main river—thus far, the soil is similar to the soil of the Cowlitz, and the country conveniently interspersed with beautiful plains. Down the Chehalis, upon said road, for fifteen miles, the character of the country and soil are admirably adapted to agriculture, and grazing purposes; at the expiration of this distance, the plains expand, and the soil is composed of sand and gravel intermixed with clay. The Chehalis river is about 150 miles long; Gray's Harbor is within its mouth, its banks are smooth and beautiful, and altogether, it is one of the most safe and easy streams in Oregon for navigation. In passing from Chehalis to Puget Sound, fifteen miles, the soil for the first ten miles is composed of sand and gravel, and the last five miles of sand and black loam. There is a small American settlement at the head of the Sound, which also has a saw and flouring mill. The settlement is called New Market, and I have seen as good vegetables growing there as I ever saw on the continent of America. Probably, the prairie land in the vicinity of the Sound is nowhere excelled, in those qualities which are peculiarly adapted to the great growth, and rare perfection of vegetables. The growing crops of wheat there, look well. Ten miles from New Market, is another small American settlement, on the Nisqually bottom, formed in 1847; the soil here is equal to the soil in the Cowlitz settlement, and three miles beyond it is Fort Nisqually. The distance from New Market to Fort Nisqually, by Water, is about thirty miles. The soil about Nisqually is a gravel, but gravelly as it is, I have seen it produce 20 bushels of wheat to the acre, and of as good a quality as any in the Territory.

The timbered land in the vicinity of the Sound, is strongly impregnated with clay, and the timber is very fine. North from the Fort there is much land of an excellent quality: to the East towards the mountain is the most beautiful landscape I have seen in the Territory, and near the mountain the soil is principally clay, and produces camas plentifully. The soil of Whitby's [Whidbey] Island, laying off the mouth of the Snohomas river is very good, and this island will afford a fine settlement. There are several other smaller islands in the South promising soil of excellent quality. Water privileges for mechanical purposes, in the vicinity of the Sound, are as good as can be found in the world. Puget Sound is a beautiful sheet of water, more than one hundred miles in length, which, with its numberless bays and harbors, will admit of the settlement of one thousand families, on a section each, and each having ship navigation at their own door.

J.R. Jackson

Jackson never saw his article in print until much later, as the newlyweds and Matilda's boys left Oregon City only a week after the wedding to journey north up the Cowlitz River. Their honeymoon trip, accompanied by four small boys and the Indians paddling them upstream, took three full days. They left the canoes at Cowlitz Landing, climbed onto ponies, and rode along the Cowlitz Trail to the little cabin on what Jackson called Highland Farm. They arrived May 14, 1848. The tiny one-room cabin with a chimney of sticks and mud, constructed

Chapter Eleven: Quick Courtship and a Wedding

in the previous autumn by Jackson and hired carpenter Leander Wallace, had no windows.[4] Light came through the chimney hole or door until they added a window later. The door fastened with wooden pegs rather than nails. Wooden wisps served as hinges.

Matilda, who probably hadn't expected a mansion, quickly set to cleaning the cabin and cooking excellent meals for her new husband and her sons. If she needed fresh air or sunlight, she opened the door.

Jackson found chores for the boys to do. He gave the older boys more responsibility than Grundy and John. They often worked alongside Cowlitz Indians who lived near the cabin. Jackson paid them in blankets, clothing, and manufactured items rather than money, which meant little to them. As an excellent seamstress, Matilda found herself cutting material and sewing shirts to use in payment for the natives' labor. The Cowlitz liked Jackson. He was British, after all, rather than a pushy "Boston," their term for American settlers, according to Trudy Hannon, author of *John R. Jackson, Washington's First American Pioneer*.[5] Jackson erected a cross on a fir tree in front of the cabin, which might have fostered friendliness among natives who had been exposed to the teachings of French-Canadian priests since establishment of the Cowlitz Mission in 1838.

The little family settled into a routine. Matilda cooked and cleaned and tended a garden. Henry and Barton farmed. Jackson worked outside but primarily kept the accounts and delegated the manual labor to others. He raised crops and butchered livestock, which he sold. At times he helped Matilda around the house, especially when guests arrived. She prepared meals while he visited with the travelers and offered them whiskey or other beverages as they settled near the fireplace.

Among their neighbors were George Roberts at the Hudson's Bay Company's Cowlitz Farm and Thomas Cunningham, who ran a flour mill at Drew's Prairie. Also living nearby were French-Canadians Simon Plamondon, perhaps the earliest white settler in the region, and Julien Bernier who arrived in 1841 and settled on Newaukum Prairie.

Shortly after she married Jackson, Matilda received a news-filled letter from her brother Matthew, who lived in Montgomery County, Missouri. Dated April 2, 1848, it was addressed to Mrs. Matilda Coons, Oregon Territory. It was the last letter she would receive from him.

AUTHOR PHOTO

It's hard to imagine Matilda's thoughts when she first glimpsed the cabin nestled in the woods that she would call home. That cabin, unlike the one above built in 1850, had no windows.

Dear Sister,

I take this opportunity of addressing you a few lines. My family is in common health. Polly is still affected [by] rheumatism ever since last Christmas. She has been a little worse so that she has to use her crutches again. Our connection as far as I know are in good health and not many changes amongst them. Mother is about as well as when you left, but has left Mr. Duncans and is living now at Philip Glovers because Duncan charged her board. Sarahann Hancock was married to Lewis Armstrong in January. James Dutton died last fall in St. Louis. The rest are about like they were when you left. Philip still trying to sell to go to Oregon. Several persons have been to look at his farm and liked it very well but something or other turned up that he has not sold

Chapter Eleven: Quick Courtship and a Wedding

yet nor won't shortly that I know of. He bargained off your place once but the man flew from the contract. John Glover thought that he had sold and bought his wagons and some oxen to move but the man disappointed him and I don't know but he will give it out altogether he sais that he will determon this year. That report that was in sirculation when you left about James Glover and his wife was false, his family and Thomas Eltons were all well and doing well the last I heard from them …

Give my love to William and Jane. I wish I could see them but I never expect to go to Oregon to do it for I am further out of the notion of Oregon if possible than was. I want him though to write to me if he don't come back as well as yourself and tell me all about Oregon. We can write to one another if we cannot see each other. Therefore we ought to imbrace every opportunity of conversing in this way,

The war with Mexico is thought to be about over and Old Gen. Taylor is expected to be President, our Election comes on this year. We had fine crops of corn, hay, and oats last year. Our wheat was thin but excellent grain and also, good most las[t] fall so that you may know we have plenty of corn and bacon in Missouri. There is no settled price for corn, wheat is worth 85 to 90 cents per bushel, oats from 12 to 18 cents, bacon very low from 2 to 3 cents per pound. Stall fed beef cattle 2 to 4 dollars per hundred weight, good horse mules bear the best prices of any thing. Horses are worth from forty to seventy-five dollars and mules in proportion. We have had a … moderate winter…not much plowing done yet… Now my dear sister let us remembrance another in love and do the best we can for ourselves and those around us and try through all discouraging circumstances not to give way to dispare though you should meet with loses and croses, ups and downs, you should not be discouraged but hoap for better times, I feel axious to hear from your correctly and fear to hoap that you are in a better situation than I fear you are, when I think of your every feature of you appears plain. In my mind I think of you often but can hear from you but seldom. I must conclude, my love to you and all your family, your affectionate brother til death, farewell

    Matilda N Coons ~ Matthew D. Glover

Travelers often brought news, or copies of *The Oregon Spectator*, which Jackson devoured eagerly as he had a keen interest in politics. He welcomed news during the summer that, after lobbying by former fur trader Joseph Meek, and contentious battles among members over slavery, Congress voted August 13, 1848, to create the new Oregon Territory, which was to be free of slaves. President Polk signed the bill in August, making it official. Meek, a delegate to Congress, was appointed U.S. Marshal for Oregon, a task he relished in his desire to track down the Cayuse who had massacred the Whitmans and kidnapped his daughter, Helen, who died of measles while in captivity. Meek and a detachment of soldiers escorted Joseph Lane, who was appointed governor of the new Oregon Territory, from Washington, D.C., to Oregon City.

Jackson also enjoyed hearing that the first United States flag flew in Oregon City during the Fourth of July celebration, which featured a parade, picnic, and speeches as well as a thirty-one-gun salute to honor each state in the Union.[7]

In Lewis County, Jackson hosted official government meetings at his cabin. So did Sidney S. Ford, who settled twenty miles north of Highland Farm on what became Ford's Prairie in Centralia. Ford hosted a two-day session November 21 and 22, 1848, but Jackson didn't attend. The county assessed no property for tax purposes, and the court determined only property not assessed the previous year needed to be assessed. The sheriff, who served as assessor, at that time was Antonio B. Rabbeson. The court appointed administrators for the estates of settlers who had died.[8]

It's unclear whether the court met at all during 1849. That winter, while Matilda was expecting a child, Jackson partnered with four men, including Isaac N. Ebey, to buy a freighter called the *Orbit*, which arrived in Olympia January 1, 1850. Workers loaded the brig with cargo bound for San Francisco. Later, Jackson sold his interest in the freighter to Michael T. Simmons.

John and Matilda welcomed a baby girl to their family July 9, 1849. They named her Mary Elizabeth. As she gazed at her infant daughter, did she think of the little girl buried along the Oregon Trail near the Snake River?

Letter from Mother Matilda

Matilda received the following letter, dated April 1, 1849, from her mother in Lincoln County, Missouri, sharing news from home, prayers for her daughter, and grief over the fact that her children were moving away and she'd never see them again.[9] Two of Matilda's older brothers—Phillip and John P. Glover, were preparing to follow the Oregon Trail west when the letter was written. Philip and Sarah (Coontz) Glover settled in Salem, while John took up a claim at Eagle Creek.

> *My dear child, Matilda,*
>
> *I make use of the present favourable opportunity of sending you a few lines, wishing they may find you and children well, and in comfortable circumstances. With respect to myself, I can say that I am yet alive and at present, in tolerable health, but have, and do not yet see many troubles. I sometimes, my dear child, mourn over my desolate situation. My children moving off from me, at a distance that I can have no hope of ever seeing of them again in this life, but I cerish the hope of meeting them all in a better World, where there will be no more parting, nor troubling scenes, and where I hope we will all meet and shake hands again together on the fair banks of Eternal Deliverance. I often feel like that I must soon go home; where I hope to rest under the protection of my blessed Redeemer, in whom I trust. May God bless you my dear child, to give you becoming fortitude to act well your part in this life, with a right spirit*

and direct you in the ways of peace is the sincere wish of your dear Mother. Your poor brother Matthew is gone from me, is now Dead, but hope he is better off, about which he left us some evidence, and that he was not afraid to Die. Polly, his widow, was married on the 29th day of March 1849 to William Brunk. I saw them married at Hiram Duncan's where I am living and expect to live my other few days, if they both survive and continue to attend to me, as formerly, where I have formerly and continue to see more peace and quietness than at the other places where I have sometimes lived. They are now apparently the only friends I have. And I trust them, that they will administer to my necessities, so far as they are able. Do not understand me as accusing of my own children of ungratefulness towards me.

(Neither do I wish to hurt the feelings of any living mortal, but do freely forgive all.) I have just received a letter from James Glover, he writes that they are all well. Since you left he has had two more in family, a son and a daughter, but has but little help to work, and represents his circumstances as being rather unflattering. Thomas T. Elson and family, he writes are also well and living near him. Clarissa Buriess has another son. Poor child, she lives about 10 miles from me (near Troy yet) but I get to see her only about once in two years. I sent to you by James Cannon last spring fifteen dollars, feeling for you, in your desolate situation, and hoping that you might get it, and that it mite relieve in some measure your sufferings, and if it should have that effect, I shall feel well gratified, in that particular. As to myself, the Lord knoweth how long my stay is to be here in this world, But trust him for protection, and Help in my time of Knead. The little money that I now have at my command is about $100.00. I think it to be sufficient for me to defray my expenses several years. (Should I live that long) and if in case of future adversity, or want befall me, I hope

Chapter Eleven: Quick Courtship and a Wedding

Matilda's mother sent her a letter April 1, 1849, informing her of the death of her brother, Matthew, and lamenting her children living so far away from her.

> County of Lincoln & State of M. April 1st 1849
> My Dear child, Matilda.
>   I make use of the present favourable opportunity of sending you a few lines, wishing they may find you and children well, and in comfortable circumstances. With respect to myself, I can say that I am yet alive and at present, in tolerable Health, but have, and do yet see many troubles. I sometimes, my dear child mourn over my desolate Situation, my children moving off from me, at a distance that I can have no hope of ever seeing of them again in this life, but I cherrish the hope of meeting them all in a better World, where there will be no more parting, nor troubling Scenes, and where, I hope, we will all meet and Shake hands again together on the fair banks of Eternal Deliverance. I often feel like that I must soon go home; where I hope to rest, under the protection of my blessed Redeemer, in whom I trust. May God bless you my dear child, to give you becoming fortitude to act well your part in this life, with a right Spirit and direct you in the ways of peace is the Sincere wish of your dear Mother. Your poor brother Matthew is gone from me, is now Dead, but hope he is better off, about which he left us some evidence, and that he was not afraid to Die. Polly his widow was Married on the 29th day of March 1849 to William Brunk. I was there Married at Hiram Duncans where I am living and expect to live my other few days, if they both Survive and continues to attend to me, as formerly, where I have and continue to see more peace and quietness than at the other places where I have sometimes lived. They are now apparently the only friends I have. And I trust they will administer to my necessities, So far as they are able. do not understand me as accusing of my own children of ungratefulness towards me
>
> and peace, and during my stay here in this World I now feel like that I Spend them many an hour of it in Meditating and thinking about my poor children that are Scattered abroad. No more of importance to relate to you, but with all of my tenderest feelings, and best wishes towards you, and towards my grand Children, and to all enquiring friends, do ever hope to remain, yours &c. Hiram, Duncan and Senth both sends their love to you, relations and friends, with their best wishes &c. Eliza, Laura, Hancock wishes

... of living mortal ... received a letter ... are all well ... a Son and ... work, and rep— ... unflattering ... do well and ... another Son ... me (nearTroy yet) ... years. I sent ... Dollars feeling for ... you might ... measure your ... dust, I shall feel ... myself. The Lord ... in this World ... of Bread ... my command is ... for me to obey ... long) and if in ... me. I hope my ... will administer ... of my days I ... (illegible) Sustenance

WASHINGTON STATE LIBRARY'S COLLECTION OF THE JACKSON, KOONTZ, GLOVER FAMILY PAPERS, 1837–1952.

my children though far from me may and will administer to my relief. For during the remainder of my days I expect to kneel but little, and that mainly sustenance and peace, and during my stay here in this World I now feel like that I shall spend many an hour of it in Meditating and thinking about my poor children that are scattered abroad. No more of importance to relate to you, but with all of my tenderest feelings, and best wishes towards you, and towards my grand children, and to all enquiring friends, do ever hope to remain yours. Hiram Duncan and Jenett both sends their love to you, relations and friends, with their best wishes. Eliza Laura Hancock wishes her love to be given to her aunt Matilda and to be remembered by her. I want you to write to me by the first opportunity telling me know if you got the money that I sent to you and how you are doing and about whatever you think I would like to hear about while I remain yours until death.

Matilda Glover

Upsetting News

Only a year after arriving at her new home, Matilda learned the horrific news of an attack on Fort Nisqually by Snoqualmie Indians on May 1, 1849. Could that happen here, where they lived so far from any cities or towns, surrounded by Cowlitz and Chehalis Indians? At the time, she was seven months pregnant with the Jacksons' first child.

Much worse, though, was the effect the news had on John Jackson when he learned that Leander C. Wallace, a young man he had hired to help on his farm, was killed in the attack. Wallace was twenty-six, single, and working for the Simmons Mill in Tumwater at the time. A man named Lewis was injured in the attack, instigated by an accidental shot by a guard.[10] One Snoqualmie was killed and another injured.

The fort's clerk, Walter Ross, wrote that the attack occurred after dinner about noon near the water gate, when a large party of about one hundred Snoqualmie and "Skewahamish" arrived. When asked what they wanted, one said that Lahalet, who had married one of their chiefs' daughters, was treating her brutally so they wanted to see about it. They said they hadn't come with the intention of harming whites.

Chief Patkanim was invited into the fort and the others given tobacco to smoke the pipe of peace—after first smoking it to assure the Indians it wasn't poisoned. Ross said he heard gunfire and rushed outside, where "four or five of the worst Snoqualmies came rushing to the gate." When he confronted one, the Indian cocked his gun and drew his dagger, thrusting toward Ross, who ordered the gate to be closed. Shots were fired by both Indians and whites, and the Snoqualmies fled, followed by their chief, who was escorted out after young Lahalet closed the gate.

"Wallace and Lewis were outside when the affray commenced, and did not respond to the call of 'all hands come in and shut the gate,'" Ross wrote. "Cussass is said to have shot poor Wallace. Lewis had a wonderfully narrow escape; one ball went through his vest and trousers, and another grazed his left arm.

"S'Geass, an Indian, was wounded in the neck, and a medicine man (a Skewhamish) was killed; also a Snoqualmie was wounded in the shoulder. We do not suppose that the war party came here with the intent of attacking us, but think they had some other object in view besides the affair with Lahalet."

Some believe the Snoqualmies intended to capture the fort, Ross said, and massacre the whites on the Puget Sound, a victory that might unite all the tribes in a move to exterminate the settlers. The settlers anticipated war and built blockhouses at Tumwater and Cowlitz and notified Governor Lane of the threat. Lane, who was superintendent of Indian Affairs, headed north with arms and ammunition, escorted by a lieutenant and five soldiers with the Mounted Rifle Regiment. He asked Dr. Tolmie of the Hudson's Bay Company to refrain from selling guns to the Indians. By July Captain Bennett H. Hill of the U.S. Army's First Artillery Regiment was stationed at Fort Steilacoom.

At the first territorial legislative assembly in Oregon City July 16, 1849, Lane demanded that the Snoqualmies deliver the murderers for trial. With no judge assigned to Lewis County at the time, the Legislature passed a special act allowing for court to be held at Fort Steilacoom to try six Indians. They were surrendered September 5 by Patkanim, who was promised eighty blankets by a subagent. (That agent resigned afterward when Lane objected to his bartering for justice.) The Indians were Quallawowt, a brother of Snoqualmie Chief Patkanim; Kussass (or Cussass), a Skykomish chief; Sturharnai (Stulharrier), Talatarn (Tantam), Whyesk (Whyerk) and Quatthlinkyne (Qualthlinkyne).

Three weeks later, Chief Justice William P. Bryant opened the first session of the territorial court in the Puget Sound country in a log cabin at Fort Steilacoom on the first Monday in October. It lasted three days.

John R. Jackson was appointed grand jury foreman. He served with David Chambers Jr., Marcel Bernier, Benjamin LaRamer, Michel Cottonier, John Batise Charloafter, Gabriel Jones, John Bradley, Simon Plamondon, J. Batise Real, Samuel Hancock, George Brill, Isam Carrier, Oliver Duffany, and Michael T. Simmons. The grand jury, which completed its work the first day, indicted the six Indians for murder. As foreman, Jackson issued a subpoena for Chief Whayguaylalkit to testify.

The trial jury included Thomas M. Chambers as foreman, Peter G. Stuart, John Sexton, Hiram Stuart, David Kindred, Jonathan Burbee, John Ellenberge, Sidney Ford, Lewis Plamondon, William Craig, James Porter and Nathaniel Hamlin. They convicted Cussass and Quallawowt but found the other four not guilty—one of the men not having even been present at the time of the attack. Cussass and Quallawowt were then executed in the presence of most of the tribe. Territorial Marshal Joseph Meek and District Attorney Alonzo A. Skinner were officers of the court.

Court clerk was Leander's brother, William Wallace of Whidbey Island, and defense counsel was thirty-seven-year-old David Stone, who had settled along the Cowlitz River near Monticello [present-day Longview], where he later served as postmaster.

The trial, which included the price of the eighty blankets, cost the territory $2,379.54.

Court at Plamondons

In 1850, according to early records, the court met September 2 at the home of Simon Plamondon on Cowlitz Prairie. Jonathan Burbee and Samuel Gill were "justices of said court," while Andrew J. Simmons served as sheriff and John R. Jackson as clerk. The court ordered Antonio

Chapter Eleven: Quick Courtship and a Wedding

B. Rabbeson, former sheriff, to appear at the next court term. Isaac N. Ebey and others asked for a county road from Plamondon's landing on the Cowlitz River to the town of Olympia, and the court appointed three men—Michael T. Simmons, Sidney S. Ford, and Peter Schalle—to investigate and report at the next meeting. Ebey and others also petitioned for a road "from the town of Olympia in said county to the Mountain plain." The court appointed John Edgar, Charles Obrits, and Ebey to investigate. The board disapproved the bonds of Simon Plamondon, county treasurer, and Jackson, who were ordered to furnish new ones at the next court term.

The court established several "townships."

- Pacific took in all of Pacific County and extended north and east of the present county borders;
- Washington extended north of the Cowlitz River, northwest of Chehalis to the mouth of the Skookumchuck River and east toward Clark County, and then to the southwest corner of Lewis County;
- Olympia extended south to the Chehalis and Skookumchuck rivers, west to the Pacific Ocean, north to along the Strait of Juan de Fuca, and east to a point opposite the mouth of the Nisqually River;
- Nisqually covered the land east of Olympia township and north and east to the far ends of the massive Lewis County.

At the time, only a few settlers lived along the east side of Puget Sound at Tacoma, Seattle, and Bellingham. Although not specified, Cowlitz township covered the region around Cowlitz Landing.

Assessor Alonzo M. Poe presented the tax roll for 1850 as well as his bill for ninety dollars for doing the work. The court levied a tax of 2.5 mills and a poll tax on everyone between twenty-one and fifty. It also levied a school tax of two mills, and another half-mill tax for an unspecified purpose. Merchants had to pay a special tax of ten dollars on every four thousand dollars of capital or less, and $2.50 for every added one thousand dollars of working capital.

Jonathan Burbee was appointed president of the court, which was scheduled to be held at Jackson's home December 5, 1850. However, he didn't show up when court convened. Only three people did—Isaac N. Ebey, judge of probate; Andrew J. Simmons, sheriff; and John R. Jackson, clerk. Without a quorum, the court adjourned until the next day, when Commissioner Simon Gill arrived and Ebey was appointed president pro tem. The board approved the treasurer's bond. George B. Roberts was appointed justice of the peace for Cowlitz Township, and H.A. Goldsborough for Olympia Township. The court appointed William L. Fraser county surveyor and A.J. Simmons as administrator of the Israel Brashears estate, with Goldsborough and Samuel B. Crockett as witnesses. The following day, the court appointed Seth Catlin justice of the peace for Washington Township, appropriated one hundred dollars to buy books and stationery for the probate court, and accepted Jackson's bond as clerk of the probate court. Treasurer Plamondon filed his statement balanced to December 7, 1850.

LEWIS COUNTY HISTORICAL MUSEUM

The Jackson Courthouse, built north of John R. Jackson's first cabin, served as a home for the family as well as the place where men gathered for jury trials and county business. Above is the reconstructed cabin, which volunteers rebuilt after it fell into disrepair.

Chapter Twelve

Building a Courthouse

AFTER BRINGING HIS NEW WIFE and four stepsons to Highland Farm, Jackson resumed his normal business operations, selling butchered meat from livestock raised on his farm to settlers throughout the region. He also raised crops and sold them. For example, on April 30, 1850, he sold potatoes for two dollars and twenty pounds of bacon for six dollars to Schuyler S. Saunders, who had just settled above a swampy area in the Chehalis River drainage twelve miles north of the Highlands.[1]

Their home, especially with the graciousness, hospitality, and tasty meals provided by Matilda, became a frequent stopover for weary travelers, located as it was on the Cowlitz Trail, the main route from the Columbia River to the Puget Sound. Jackson greeted everyone to his home, a genial host always eager to meet new people and chat over drinks about the news of the day, especially politics. He was an ardent Democrat.[2] Matilda's reputation for hospitality extended all along the West Coast; her kindness and good cooking even graced the conversations in drawing rooms in the nation's capital. Eventually John and Matilda expanded their home, added buildings and, by September 1862, operated a wayside hotel and trading post.

Junior military officers, who traveled the Cowlitz Trail between Fort Vancouver and Fort Steilacoom, also stopped at the Jackson home. Several of their visiting soldiers gained fame for their military service and rose to the rank of general, including Ulysses S. Grant, George B. McClellan, and Philip H. Sheridan.[3]

Matilda's days took on a familiar routine.[4]

Each morning Matilda rose early to prepare breakfast for her family, stirring coals from the previous evening's fire, stacking kindling, and adding wood to warm the house. She stepped outside to draw fresh water from the well, feed the chickens, and gather fresh eggs from the hens. She boiled water for coffee and sliced slabs of bacon into a cast-iron fry pan. Cracking eggs into the pan, she watched them carefully sizzle in bacon grease as she greeted her husband and each of the boys. She added coffee to the hot water and poured a cup for Jackson as he and the boys sat at the table, where Matilda set plates, cups, and silverware.

After breakfast she cleared the table, poured boiling water into a basin to wash the dishes, and then pulled out flour, lard, salt, and yeast to make bread. She added honey when she had it. Sometimes she whipped together buttermilk biscuits and boiled eggs for breakfast or noonday meals. Until 1853, when Jackson bought her a stove, she baked bread and biscuits in a Dutch oven, much as she had on the Oregon Trail.

Matilda kept the house clean and tidy, as noted by the many visitors who stopped by, and tended a large garden outside the cabin that always required weeding and later harvesting of corn, peas, onions, beans, and other fresh produce. She preserved food to tide the family over during the winter. She and her younger sons gathered berries from wild blackberry vines growing nearby. Jackson planted an orchard behind the cabin to provide more fruit for the family. After she or the boys milked the dairy cows, she would strain the milk through a clean cloth and skim off the cream to churn for butter and to make cheese.

From milk she had set aside to sour, she heated yellow curds of whey over a low fire until the mixture hardened, separating into clumps she strained with a cloth to remove liquid whey. The drying curds, sprinkled with salt and moistened with cream to stick together, created cheese. Sometimes she made a more intricate cheddar cheese that took six weeks before it was ready.

They stored milk, cheese, and butter in a spring house in the woods to keep it cool.

Matilda created sausage and head cheese from butchered pigs, and Jackson built a smokehouse for curing ham, bacon, beef, and sometimes venison shot in the surrounding woods. She hung sausage and head cheese

Chapter Twelve: Building a Courthouse

Matilda cooked in the brick fireplace and spun wool using the spinning wheel below. These photos were taken inside the cabin in the 2000s.

there as well as bacon often sold to settlers. They stored the animal fat so Matilda could make tallow candles and lye soap, mixing ash leached from the fireplace into the lard and heating it in a large iron kettle outside.

Sometimes Matilda milked the cows, but most days Henry or Barton did it. The older boys also chopped firewood, cleaned the barn, fed and watered the animals, built fences, and worked in the fields as they grew older. If hens were hatching chicks, they'd bring the fuzzy yellow creatures inside in a box to keep them warm until they were hardier.

During the day, Matilda often washed clothes, bedding and blankets outside in a basin, wringing out the water before lifting them high to dry on a cable strung between two buildings. With babies in the house, she did laundry daily, rinsing and cleaning cloth diapers she wrapped around her infants' bottom. She dug and peeled potatoes, shucked corn, snipped beans, and baked pies or cakes. If she had enough berries and sugar, she'd make jam and jelly preserves.

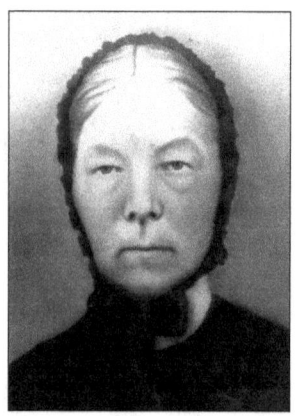

LEWIS COUNTY HISTORICAL MUSEUM

Matilda Coonse Jackson.

Evening meals most often consisted of meat, potatoes and gravy, vegetables, bread, and a dessert. After cleaning the dishes and sweeping the floor, Matilda settled down near the fireplace to read her Bible or a prayer book, often picking up a needle and thread to mend clothes or sew more shirts for trading with Indians for labor. At times she sat in front of the spinning wheel, carding wool and spinning it into yarn that could be used to make blankets, caps, mittens, and sweaters. After settling her children into bed for the night, thanking God for His tender mercies to all of them, she crawled into bed beside her husband and blew out the candle.

Matilda preferred to stay home during her husband's trips to Cowlitz Landing or neighboring farms. She was a gracious hostess whenever anyone stopped by, welcoming them with food, drink, and any other comforts they required. She was a quiet woman, perhaps even a little shy.

She grew to know Simon Plamondon, the French-Canadian who settled on the Cowlitz Prairie. He had married his third wife, Louise

Henriette Pell, the niece of Bishop Francis Norbert Blanchet, in 1848, the same year she and John had wed. His first two wives had been Cowlitz Indian women. Each of his wives bore him children and he raised three families.[5]

Meanwhile, Jackson purchased additional land whenever he could, expanding his farm from 640 acres to more than 2,200. He raised cattle, horses, sheep, and hogs, pastured on the green fertile prairie that he had fenced, and grew crops of wheat, oats, and peas.[6]

A Courthouse

During the fall of 1850, Jackson and his stepsons began constructing a new log cabin as a residence just north of their home. As Henry and Bart lay shakes on the roof, a man on a horse stopped by, according to Anna Koontz, Matilda's late granddaughter.

"Hurry up with that roof!" Judge William Strong told the boys. "I need it for my courthouse."[7]

Assisted by Matilda's nephew, Joe Glover, and his relative, Joseph Manning, within a week they erected the peeled log cabin measuring sixteen by twenty-six feet, with openings for windows and a door. Hard-packed dirt served as the building's floor. Similar to the fashion used by Cowlitz and other natives in building longhouses, Jackson put a fireplace in the center of the ground and an opening in the roof above so that smoke could curl up and out. A steep stairway led to the second-floor loft.

"Civil court was held one week after it was built, before the windows or foundation floor was in. Cuts of logs were used for seats," wrote Matilda's son Barton Coonse. The first regular Federal District Court convened there November 12, 1850.

The man on the horse was William Strong, the first federal judge in Oregon Territory. He was appointed September 17, 1849, by President Zachary Taylor to serve as associate judge of the supreme court of Oregon. He arrived in Oregon in 1849, and lived in Vancouver during the winter of 1850 to 1851.[8] His jurisdiction covered all of what today is Washington, Idaho, and Montana as well as Clatsop County in Oregon. His salary was two thousand dollars a year, and the judge noted that "it was slow in coming," according to his records at the Oregon State Library in Salem, unearthed by Anna Koontz.[9]

"But I never had anything charged me for stopping overnight in any place when I traveled in Oregon territory," Strong wrote in his notes. "I always found the people ready to give me what I wanted and to help me along."

Twenty men attended that first court session. Some traveled as far as seventy miles. Strong presided as judge, and his brother, James, served as clerk.

In his notes, Strong said he presided over few commercial cases but "a good many homicides."

"I think I tried some eighteen homicidal cases and most of them arose from disputes about land under the D.L.C. laws," he wrote, referring to the Donation Land Claim Act of 1850, which promoted homesteading in the Pacific Northwest. "There were also some cases of assault. I cannot recall ever foreclosing a mortgage."

Edward Huggins' Travels

Edward Huggins, overseer of the Hudson's Bay Company's affiliate, the Puget Sound Agricultural Company at Nisqually, wrote a first-person account of his travels south to the Cowlitz Farm near present-day Toledo in the early 1850s. Originally published in *The Oregonian* in 1900, it was republished in *The Chehalis Bee-Nugget* April 7, 1922.[10]

Like Jackson, Huggins, an Englishman, became a naturalized American citizen. He wrote about the almost impassable Saunders Bottom, "in many places little better than a lake," and told of people stuck in the mud.

One horseback rider, leading another horse, found a fellow stuck up to his middle in mud and offered him the horse he was leading.

"The bemuddled man thanked him, declining his kind offer, and informed him that he 'had a much better horse under him.' How the man got out of the hole with his horse the story does not say."

Another time he met John Sutherland in Pierce County with an overturned wagon in a mudhole with the legs and shoulders of four horses flailing and sides of bacon scattered everywhere. He was hauling the bacon for Jackson. He declined Huggins' offer to help. Later, corduroyed planks covered the worst mudholes, although they floated away during high water.

Huggins described arriving at Chehalis founders Schuyler and Eliza Saunders' homestead around 4 p.m.

"I was feeling tired and so did my old horse, and I obtained permission from Saunders to remain there all night. The place was very primitive, a small log house and a very small log barn. Saunders lived there with his wife, and I think there were no children. He was a man of about forty years of age, I should think, stout and strongly built and not at all a bad looking man. He was a wonderful talker, and it struck me that from the manner of his behavior and style of talk that he was either half drunk or nearly crazy. I had a scant supper there, and before dark I told 'Saunders' I would like to sleep, being very tired and stiff from the effects of the unusually long ride. He led me to the log barn and, pointing to a heap of pea straw, said that was the only spare bedroom the establishment boasted. I think I settled my bill before parting with him, as I intended leaving that unsavory place very early the next morning. I made a hole in the straw and crept in, feeling certain that tired nature would soon assert itself and sleep possess me. But, alas! I reckoned falsely, for above my head, upon a beam, slept or roosted some of the chickens of the place, and I found it impossible to get any sleep during the night."

FINDAGRAVE.COM

Edward Huggins.

Leaving the rather inhospitable barn of Schuyler and Eliza Saunders, Huggins saddled up "old Garcon" to travel south from Chehalis.

"After riding several miles through a rich-looking country, I came to a small prairie containing about 500 or 600 acres," Huggins wrote. He saw a fence and uninhabited log house and learned it had been the claim of a Canadian Frenchman named "Summatooh," an ex-Hudson's Bay Company employee who later moved to Pierce County and died near Steilacoom.

"I now rode quietly along, feeling quite hungry. I had no breakfast and my supper last night was of a very light character. I next came to a good-sized river, easy to ford. This was the Newaukum River, which emptied into the Chehalis. Across the Newaukum is the prairie of that name, the soil of which is very good, being a clay loam of great fertility. Two or three settlers were living on this plain—an old French Canadian, whose name I have forgotten, a Red River half-breed named Marcel Bernier and an Englishman named George Roberts. The latter was an old clerk, who came to Fort Vancouver in 1832 or 1833."

At the time of Huggins's journey, Roberts, who had traveled to England in the 1840s and returned with a wife, was in charge of Hudson's Bay's Cowlitz Farm. Huggins described Roberts as "an intelligent and kind-hearted man."

"I proceeded, and in a short time got into a fine, rather large prairie, upon which was a good deal of the usual zigzag fencing and two or three houses," Huggins wrote. "The first place was the home of an old Canadian, and at the far end of the prairie was the well-known farm of John R. Jackson, who owned a full section of what looked to me to be the finest kind of land. It was fairly well improved. On it were several log houses. The dwelling was large and the main room was very much like an English farm kitchen. Jackson was an Englishman, and had been a farmer in Yorkshire. He was never in the service of the Hudson's Bay Company, but was a genuine emigrant, arriving at the site of his home early in the '40s.

"Jackson's was, in 1850, the best-known place in the country, and was the stopping place for almost all people traveling between Portland and Puget Sound. Jackson had provided ample accommodation for the exigencies of those times. When this country was part of Oregon Territory and Thurston was the only county on the Sound, District Court was held at Jackson's and that gentleman built a palatial building of large peeled logs which was used as a courthouse," Huggins said.

It's hard to imagine anyone driving past the old Jackson Courthouse today describing it as "palatial."

Judge William Strong, at that time Oregon's most prominent lawyer, held District Court at Jackson's new courthouse in November 1850. Huggins noted that anyone born on foreign soil who wanted to claim 320 or 640 acres under the Donation Land Claim Act of

1850 visited the courthouse to declare intentions of becoming an American citizen.

"To my personal knowledge, many a chap that couldn't tell you who Washington was, the name of the president of the United States, nor even the name of the territory in which he was residing, was admitted to citizenship," Huggins wrote. Most were uneducated foreigners—many ex-company employees—who voted the Democratic ticket when they did vote, he said. "But sometimes a few of them on election day would become so drunk on free whiskey as to be totally unfit to vote."

Huggins described Jackson as "a big, lusty man, and, as usual with Yorkshire men, sharp and smart at a trade." He said Jackson, a good farmer who owned many fine horses and cattle, was married to an American woman and the father of a family.

Huggins described Matilda as "per necessity, a hard-working, motherly kind of woman, as were most of the American women, farmers' wives, I met in those days."

Writing about this trip in 1900, Huggins stated, "I have no doubt that the old fellows now alive that traveled that road, nearly fifty years ago, still recollect the savory, well-cooked meals the kind-hearted Mrs. Jackson would prepare for them."

When he arrived at the farm, Huggins said, John R. Jackson "was doing justice to a toothsome meal of Yorkshire bacon and eggs, cooked in inimitable style."

Famished, Huggins enjoyed a meal and "a long chat with the worthy farmer," later walking over his farm, impressed by the extent of his improvements.

"He showed me, with a great deal of pride, the new courthouse and pointed out to me its architectural beauties, which, I admit, I failed to see, having so recently come from a land wherein fine buildings were common. I took care not to let the old gentleman know this and towards evening bade the worthy couple a kindly good bye and slowly plodded on through a clay-soiled country of woods and openings, for about six miles, when I came into a large rolling prairie country, with fences and buildings here and there."

He saw the Cowlitz Mission, a Roman Catholic church with an adjacent cemetery, with crosses erected to mark the graves, and knew he was on "the much-talked-of Cowlitz Prairie."

"The reality far exceeded my imagination," Huggins wrote. "It was a rolling, undulating country, all open and comprising I should think about 16,000 or more acres. The soil was a clay loam and to my unpracticed eye appeared to be of great fertility. I rode through an 80-acre field of red clover, which was many years old and was as thick as it could stand upon the ground and stood two feet in height."

He saw Mount Rainier to the east and to the south, across the prairie, Mount St. Helens "of sugarloaf shape and so regular and smooth in its outline as to look as if artificially made instead of a wild product of nature."

"I rode slowly along full of admiration until I got within a short distance of a large dwelling, granary, and outbuildings, all bearing the mark of Hudson's Bay Company construction and I knew this must be the Cowlitz farm of which I had heard so much. As I approached near to the house, I espied an old gray-haired gentleman approaching and whom I soon recognized to be George Roberts, then in charge of the farm. I had met him before at Fort Nisqually, so was immediately made at home and was kindly received. He had not very long ago buried his English wife and was left with three motherless children."

He named retired company employees who owned claims on the prairie—French-Canadians such as Simon Plamondon Sr., Xavier Catman, Jean Baptiste Bouchard, Joseph Brulez, Cottonier, Marcel Bernier, Joseph Legard, Jean Chaulifoux, Peter Bercier, Elie Sareault. He also mentioned Edward Warbass, who filed a donation land claim in 1850 and laid out a townsite adjacent to Cowlitz Landing, which he called Warbassport, and Captain Drew, who owned a little water-powered sawmill on a stream at the prairie's west end. Warbassport later merged with Cowlitz Landing.

After resting, Huggins and a colleague named Puss, who had arrived earlier and bagged wheat for packing, lashed three bushels totaling 180 pounds on each horse's pack saddle, and they headed back to Nisqually, camping first at Jackson's place.

The return trip proved uneventful until they arrived just south of Chehalis, on the prairie where Summatah lived.

"We heard the music of a horn blowing and soon saw emerging from the woods a strange figure upon horseback. It was a man dressed in a skin coat, painted in red stripes, a curiously shaped and marked cocked hat, and with a painted face. It was poor Saunders as mad as a March hare. He stopped us and after blowing a loud blast upon his trumpet proclaimed himself the angel Gabriel and predicted soon the end of the world and talked a lot of wretched stuff, poor fellow!

"Not long afterwards he was arrested by the sheriff and taken to Fort Steilacoom and kept there in the guardhouse, there being no other place to keep him and he being the only insane person in the territory. The poor chap remained there some time and his behavior at times was so annoying to the soldiers that they did not treat him very delicately. I do not know what became of him, but never heard that he returned to his claim."

Huggins died January 24, 1907, in Tacoma.

Donation Land Claims

The Donation Land Claim Act of 1850 was designed to encourage settlement of the Oregon Territory.[11] It was patterned after similar attempts at colonizing untamed land. In 1842, Congress had passed an act donating 160 acres of public lands to all able-bodied adults who settled and established homes in East Florida. Attempts to encourage settlement in Oregon Country began in 1821 with Representative John Floyd of Virginia, according to an October 24, 1939, Claquato Landmarks article, one of a series of weekly historical pieces written by pioneer Chehalis banker N.B. Coffman and Northwest historian Charles Miles published in *The Chehalis Bee-Nugget* in the 1930s. Later, Senator Lewis F. Linn of Missouri championed similar bills. In 1839, Methodist missionary Jason Lee petitioned Congress to take action to encourage settlement in the Oregon Country. He asked for a guarantee that the settlers would own the land they worked and receive protection from the United States.

"It may be thought that Oregon is of little importance; but rely upon it, there is the germ of a great state," Lee's petition stated.[12]

While Congress continued debating the issue, the Oregon Provisional Government passed a law granting 640 acres to a settler and his wife. Americans wanted to encourage colonization to ensure the land belonged to the United States rather than Great Britain as a treaty of joint occupancy remained in effect. The boundary between Canada and the United States was finally established along the 49th parallel in 1846, which spurred action on offering land grants to settlers in the Oregon region. But debate over slavery delayed the bill, as the provisional government had banned slavery in Oregon and the slave states lined up in opposition to the land act and territorial organization. Finally, August 14, 1848, Oregon became a territory of the United States, and two years later, on September 27, 1850, the Donation Land Claim Act of 1850 was enacted.[13]

After its passage, emigrants flooded the Pacific Northwest to claim free land. The act, designed to promote homesteading, gave single men 320 acres and married couples 640, a section, if they settled the land and improved the property within five years. It worked well for Americans, but as a Canadian, Dr. McLoughlin in Oregon City lost his rights. Americans staked claims on his property but let him keep his home and business.

On November 20, 1850, John R. Jackson once again applied for naturalization as an American so he could file a claim under the act. Sidney S. Ford and Michael T. Simmons acted as witnesses.

Donation Land Claims in Lewis County were filed in geographic areas—Adna, Boistfort, Centralia, Chehalis, Claquato, Ethel, Mossyrock, Napavine, Pe Ell, Winlock, and Toledo.[14]

Not everyone appreciated the Donation Land Claim Act, particularly George B. Roberts, who was overseer at British-owned Puget Sound Agricultural Company's Cowlitz Farm.[15] In letters responding to questions from Mrs. F.F. Victor between 1878 and 1883, shortly before his death, Roberts railed against the American "squatters" who claimed company land as their own under the act. He expressed bitterness over the loss of his property on the Cowlitz Farm to Americans. "I let them have it, giving up the graves of my wife and family," he wrote.[16]

Roberts and William F. Tolmie, who oversaw the Nisqually Farm, estimated that American settlers killed thousands of the farm's cattle between 1853 and 1856. Their protests were ignored and injunctions filed against the culprits were dismissed.

Roberts, who moved to the Cowlitz Farm in 1846, said he was "undoubtedly very harshly if not cruelly treated at the Cowlitz." However, some of the old-time residents including John Jackson aided him and urged newcomers to leave him in peace.

"This did me more service than all the law administered by a democratic Judge," Roberts said.[17]

Jackson never interfered with the company's rights, Roberts said.

"John R. Jackson was in youth an English Butcher from Yorkshire—he kept a way side house for which his fine farm furnished good cheer to many a hungry traveler," Roberts said.[18] "He was universally known—his bane the love of drink."

Bitterness laced Roberts' letters.

"It fairly ruined me," Roberts said. "The squatters took my crops year after year—the records of WT [Washington Territory] are a curiosity in my case. I had no end of injunctions issued only to be rescinded."

He described Judge C.C. Hewitt, who heard the cases, as a "poor man, a mere apology for a Judge."

"Think of the wrongs done me from '59 to '71 at the Cowlitz farm," Roberts wrote. "The old carcass of the Company brought every wolf and vulture to the banquet and the government rewarded the wrong doers by giving them the lands. The voting power did it all."

He spoke to Judge Strong about his concerns in 1859, but the judge was noncommittal. Years later he told Roberts he knew what would happen but couldn't acknowledge it publicly.

Roberts named some of the worst, the squatters of 1854 and 1855: Jackson Barton, Thomas Pearson, J.L. Finch, Horace Howe, and James Galloway. He claimed they shot at him and his son.

"Old Howe is still there," Roberts wrote. "He was offered lately $10,000 for his ill gotten property."

He scoffed at the idea that they were "hardy pioneers" when they simply took over the company's beautiful farm. Battling them in court did him no good.

"At length the people took the matter in hand peremptorily told Howe ad hoc to leave me in peace or put up at once with the consequences," Roberts said.

Finally, in 1869, the United States government agreed to compensate the Hudson's Bay Company for its losses by offering $450,000.[19] Hudson's Bay received only a third of that amount, with the final payment made in 1871, the year Roberts moved from the Cowlitz Farm to Cathlamet. The Puget Sound Agricultural Company received no compensation.[20]

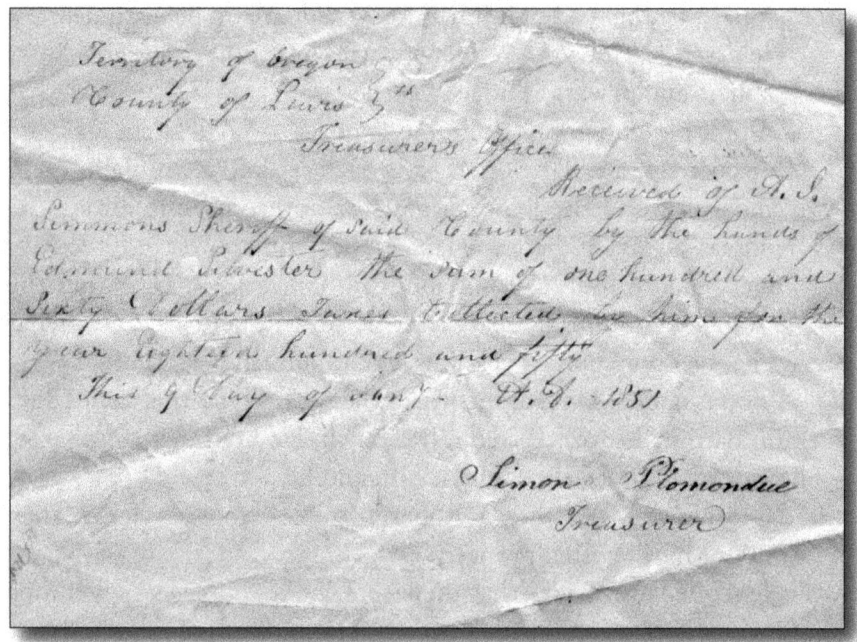

WASHINGTON STATE LIBRARY'S COLLECTION OF THE JACKSON, KOONTZ, GLOVER FAMILY PAPERS, 1837–1952.

Simon Bonaparte Plamondon served as treasurer for Lewis County in Oregon Territory in 1851, but on the paper above his surname is spelled differently.

Chapter Thirteen

Trying to Create a Territory

THE YEAR 1851 proved eventful for the Jacksons and the territory where they lived as the first settlers built homes in Seattle. That year Matilda gave birth to their second child, a son they named Andrew. She was now the proud mother of five sons and a daughter.

A receipt from Simon Plamondon, the Lewis County treasurer, dated January 9, 1851, shows that Sheriff A.J. Simmons collected $160 in taxes for the year 1850.[1]

When Jackson performed a marriage ceremony at the courthouse, his wife prepared the celebration dinner. When Robert W. Brown married Mary Jane Mills at the courthouse in 1851, Matilda cooked and served their wedding supper, according to Esther (Brown) Grant, a Lewis County native living in Seaside, Oregon, in 1939.[2] She told *The Chehalis Advocate* that their bridal suite was a loft above the courthouse. The bride's father and her maternal grandfather, Cain Mills, both served on the first jury in the courthouse, she said, and her father served as postmaster at Skookumchuck.[3]

John Robinson Jackson became one of the Northwest's best-known farmers and businessmen. He owned and farmed, with the help of his stepsons and support of his wife, hundreds of acres of rich prairie land. He raised cattle, horses, sheep, and hogs. He bought and sold produce and kept meticulous records. For example, April 12, 1851, he sold Captain George Drew five bushels of potatoes for $7.50, ten chickens for ten dollars, and forty-two pounds of bacon for $12.60.[4]

During one long, cold winter, when Cowlitz Indians struggled to survive near Ethel, Jackson gave them blankets, food, and other help.

Some travelers kept in touch after stopping at the Jacksons' hotel.

"I know you always manifested the greatest interest in my welfare," one man wrote. "I suppose you have heard before this that I took the mumps the night after we left your house. We stayed with Mr. Cochran and then I found I had got the mumps. Went on next day took breakfast at Mr. Ford's. I found Mrs. Ford a very pleasant woman indeed."

He noted that they arrived home with jaws swollen and their daughter Bell also had it. He also noted he had left some items at their house when he left and asked Mrs. Jackson to send them to him.[5]

Among those taking shelter at the Jacksons' was the Cutting family, who emigrated from England to the United States and later settled in Napavine. The parents with their son and two daughters sailed from London on the *Emma R. Hunt* in January 1851 for San Francisco, arriving 205 days later after the captain thwarted an attack by pirates. After seven months in San Francisco, the family sailed to Astoria, Oregon, and then to Rainier, Oregon, in a small river steamer. Indian canoes carried them across the Columbia River and up the Cowlitz River to the Cowlitz Landing, where they were met by George B. Roberts, Hudson's Bay Company agent at the Cowlitz Farm and J.B. Cutting's uncle. He also was a good friend of the Jacksons. They stayed at the Jackson place that night before traveling to Roberts' home on Newaukum Prairie, where they arrived August 10, 1852, and remained for the winter before staking a Donation Land Claim.

In the early 1850s, J.B. Cutting said, settlers bought groceries at the Cowlitz Prairie store and packed them on a horse or their own backs. Each man had to use a shovel and ax to help open roads. For flour, they packed sacks of wheat on a horse or in wagons and hauled it to Drew's Station, a mill that produced a barrel of flower a day.

Jackson enjoyed politics and held positions as sheriff, assessor, justice of the peace, clerk of the court, and tax collector. He served as a territorial representative to gatherings where men shaped the region's future. He wallpapered the rooms with newspapers, recalled his stepgranddaughter, Anna Koontz.

County commissioners met April 7, 1851, at Jackson Courthouse, with the Honorable I.N. Ebey and G. Gill as judges, Sheriff A.J.

Simmons, and Jackson as clerk.[6] They approved a petition from Michael T. Simmons and others for a road to Olympia from Plamondon's Landing on the Cowlitz River.

The 1851 election for the Cowlitz precinct occurred at Jackson's place and George Drew, I.B. Chapman, and Edward D. Warbass were appointed judges. In Olympia it took place at the house of Simmons and Smith, and in the Nisqually township at Fort Steilacoom. The commissioners cut Skagit precinct from Nisqually and Olympia, which included "all that portion of the above mentioned townships lying north of a parallel of latitude passing through the mouth of the Duwamish." The election there took place at the home of Clements Sumner.

The following day, April 8, the commissioners refused to create Chinook and Pacific City precincts, saying they didn't have jurisdiction. The treasurer filed a statement showing $2,160 received and $380 disbursed.

The Washington township's election took place at the schoolhouse with Henry D. Huntington, Seth Catlin and L.P. Smith as judges.

David Smith and others petitioned to lay a road on the west side of the Cowlitz River from the mouth to intersect with the road from Plamondon's Landing to Jackson's Courthouse and the Puget Sound. Roberts and Warbass viewed a county road from Cathlamet to the Boistfort Plain and then to join the Olympia-Cowlitz Landing road. Court-appointed viewers of that road were James Burney, Thomas Lowe, and S.S. Ford, who were to meet at the Schuyler Saunders' home. Viewers were appointed to determine a road's location and review the work when completed.

On July 7, 1851, the commissioners court met at Jackson's with President Jonathan Burbee, Judge Simon Gill, Jackson as clerk, and Andrew Jackson Simmons as sheriff. They allowed bills submitted by James C. Strong, "clerk of the district court of the territory for said county," for $100 "for services as said clerk the past year," and $24.50 was allowed "for half a dozen chairs and half a dozen stools purchased and for use of court."

John R. Jackson, Michael T. Simmons, and Sidney S. Ford were appointed to view the road from Olympia to Plamondon's Landing since the earlier appointees had failed to do so.

David S. Maynard, who was appointed assessor, posted a five hundred dollar bond. He was ordered to take a census of inhabitants.

Edward Warbass took over as treasurer from Plamondon, who retired, and presented a bond in the names of Jackson, Plamondon, and Simmons. The treasurer's statement showed revenue in 1850 totaled $1,579.67 and $557.03 in spending. That left a general fund balance of $1,022.64. Taxes collected in 1850 for schools totaled $825.32, but nothing was spent.

Cowlitz Convention

People living north of the Columbia River grew tired of traveling to Oregon City for public meetings regarding the Oregon Territory. Attorney John B. Chapman urged creation of a territory separate from Oregon during a July Fourth address in Olympia in 1851.

Three days later, when the superior court met at the Jacksons' farm at Highland, the men decided to call a convention to create the Territory of Columbia out of Oregon. They scheduled the convention for late the following month.

On August 29, 1851, Jackson joined twenty-five other delegates at Cowlitz Landing for what became known as the Cowlitz Convention. In a "memorial to Congress," drafted by attorney John Chapman, the convention sought to separate the land north of the Columbia River into a separate territory.[7] They noted that Oregon Territory's seat of government was three hundred miles from the north's principle settlements, leaving citizens "neglected" and with "no benefit or convenience whatever" from the government. It noted that traveling to the clerk's office in Oregon City cost more and took longer than a trip from St. Louis, Missouri, to Boston. They also asked for construction of military roads from the Columbia River to Puget Sound and east to Walla Walla.

The memorial and the full proceedings of the Cowlitz Convention were published in *The Oregonian* September 20, 1851, and *The Oregon Spectator* three days later.[8]

After submitting the memorial, the pioneers simply had to wait for Congress to act.

Courthouse Battle

On September 1, 1851, the Commissioners Court opened at Jackson's with Burbee and John B. Chapman as judges, A.M. Poe as clerk, and A.J. Simmons as sheriff. The board levied a tax of 3½ mills. Viewers of the road from Olympia to Steilacoom were appointed—James McAllister, David Chambers and Daniel Brownfield.[9]

At the meeting, Brownfield presented a petition from Michael T. Simmons and others asking that the seat of justice and place for holding court be fixed at Olympia. William Packwood asked for establishment of a ferry across the Nisqually River. And Olympia residents asked for an additional justice of the peace. The board took all three petitions under advisement.

M.T. Simmons and Jackson presented a plat for the road between Cowlitz Landing and Olympia. Hugh A. Goldsborough was appointed by the board to survey the road between Olympia and Steilacoom.

Twenty-five students were in the Washington township and the district received $208.65.

The next day, the board established the Newaukum township with Sidney S. Ford as justice, appointed D.S. Maynard justice of the peace for Olympia township, and appointed grand and petit jurors for November.

A special commissioners' term at the house of John R. Jackson October 6, 1851, brought together attorney John B. Chapman, who drew the three-year term, and W.P. Daugherty, who received the two-year term, as judges, A.M. Poe as clerk, and A.J. Simmons as sheriff.

The board granted a license for William Packwood to operate a ferry across the Nisqually River and fixed the rates. He filed a bond.

The following day, the board refused to pay claims from retiring commissioners Simon Gill and J. Burbee for attendance at the October term, and H.A. Goldsborough's claim for services at a special election in August 1850. The court appointed men as supervisors directing the opening of the road from Plamondon's Landing to Olympia. They were Simon Plamondon, George B. Roberts, E. Mills, Joseph Borst, and Michael T. Simmons. John M. Swan, James McAllister and J. Brashears were appointed supervisors of the Olympia-Steilacoom road. The court appointed three men justice of the peace—Thomas M. Chambers for the Steilacoom township, Hugh A. Goldsborough for Olympia, John R. Jackson for Cowlitz, and George B. Roberts for Newaukum.

But as more people settled north of Highland Farm near the Puget Sound and Steilacoom, tension increased to move the county court north from Jackson's courthouse, in part so jurors wouldn't need to go through the muddy swamp known as Saunders Bottom to reach the

LEWIS COUNTY HISTORICAL MUSEUM

A battle over the location of the Lewis County courthouse ensued when people north of Chehalis wanted to meet at the home of Sidney S. Ford, above, rather than at John R. Jackson's.

court or cross the turbulent Skookumchuck River near Centralia. John B. Chapman, an attorney who was elected county commissioner in 1851 and platted Steilacoom on claims he and his son staked, led the fight to hold court in Sidney S. Ford's two-story home northwest of present-day Centralia instead of at Jackson's.

Chapman and one of two new commissioners, William P. Daugherty, who also lived on the Sound, met at Ford's home October 27, 1851, for a special session of the commissioners' court, where Ford served as clerk pro tem. Edmund Sylvester, coroner, was appointed as sheriff.[10]

During that session, they ordered that Ford's place "be received as the courthouse in which the several courts of Lewis County are to sit and hold their terms of court." They asked Ford to set aside a second-floor room with writing table, stove, and safe place for papers and records of the court. In short, they declared Ford's home as the county seat.

The board ordered the clerk to issue notice of a special election to fill the offices of probate judge, sheriff, and one commissioner.

The following day, the board changed supervisor appointments, replacing M.T. Simmons with Benjamin Gordon, James McAllister with William Packwood, and John Swan with Edmund Sylvester. The men were ordered to open roads in their districts.

The board confirmed the road between Olympia and Steilacoom. The board received a petition from Thomas Glasgow for a road from Steilacoom to the Cowlitz River by way of Yelm and Nisqually.

The special session took place on the same date court was scheduled to open at Jackson's Courthouse.

When Judge Strong traveled from Cathlamet to Jackson's October 28 for Federal District Court, he discovered only nine of the sixteen men called for a grand jury had shown up and only four of twenty-three petit jurors were there. Two cases were scheduled to be heard, but neither of the defendants appeared.

The judge, irked by the disrespect for the court, called a second grand jury and signed a warrant for George Shazeer of Nisqually, a defendant accused of assault. Two days later, when he convened court, five jurors still failed to appear so it was called off. Sheriff A.J. Simmons told Judge Strong that Chapman and others prevented him from serving the warrant. The judge issued another warrant. He also ordered Chapman to show why his law license shouldn't be revoked for malfeasance and obstructing the sheriff.

Meanwhile, the northern faction held court at Ford's place twenty miles away and censured Judge Strong for "pretending" to hold court at Jackson's and charged him with "nonattendance at the legal county seat." Chapman wrote a letter about the meeting published in *The Oregonian Statesman*, a Democrat newspaper. A committee cited James Strong, the judge's brother and clerk of the Federal District Court, for "failure and refusal to maintain an office in the county."[11]

The committee also objected to the judge's orders, as related by the sheriff, that jurors show up at court.

"They have come down here to the Courthouse and in the preemptory and authoritative tone of a slave driver and (in their own words) ordered 'every hoof of you right off to the judge'," Chapman wrote in his letter.

"Your committee, with all due regard to the dignity of a court of law, cannot help expressing their astonishment and surprise at the conduct and their great indignation at the attempt of a judicial officer to trifle with the sanctity of a court of justice and make it the instrument of a revengeful spirit and with bloodhounds and whiplashes trample upon the rights and privileges of free men."

Chapman suggested the citizens might seek relief from Congress "for correction of the evil."

Within days, *The Oregon Spectator* printed communications from Judge Strong. One letter signed by Chapman, Michael T. Simmons, and D.F. Brownfield, who attended court at Ford's, excused the judge's behavior.

"We are now fully satisfied that you were not aware that the county commissioners had made any change in the place of holding the courts and that you went to Jackson's in pursuance of what you deemed your duty."

Judge Strong asked to be served with official notice changing the courthouse location, which Dr. R.H. Lansdale, clerk of the Commissioner's Court, provided.

On December 1, 1851, the court was held at Sidney Ford's home with Commissioners John B. Chapman and William P. Daugherty attending. Andrew J. Simmons returned as sheriff, and R.H. Lansdale, deputy clerk, filled in for A.M. Poe as clerk.[12]

The board wanted to know why the records of the court hadn't been turned over for keeping in the upstairs of Ford's house, as decreed earlier. The board appointed John Bradley, Adam Benson, and L.M. Collins as viewers of a road from Steilacoom to the Duwamish River.

The following day, the board appointed James Hall as justice of the peace for Steilacoom township, John Bradley as a supervisor in place of Joseph Brashears, and Richard H. Lansdale as a justice of the peace for Olympia.

The road between Olympia and Steilacoom was ordered opened.

The board ordered that the District Court be notified that the clerk's office is ready at Ford's for the clerk to hold his office there and must hold his office there. Jackson, ex-clerk of the board, was ordered to work with Poe in transferring records before January 1852, when the next court was scheduled to convene at Ford's.

Chapter Thirteen: Trying to Create a Territory

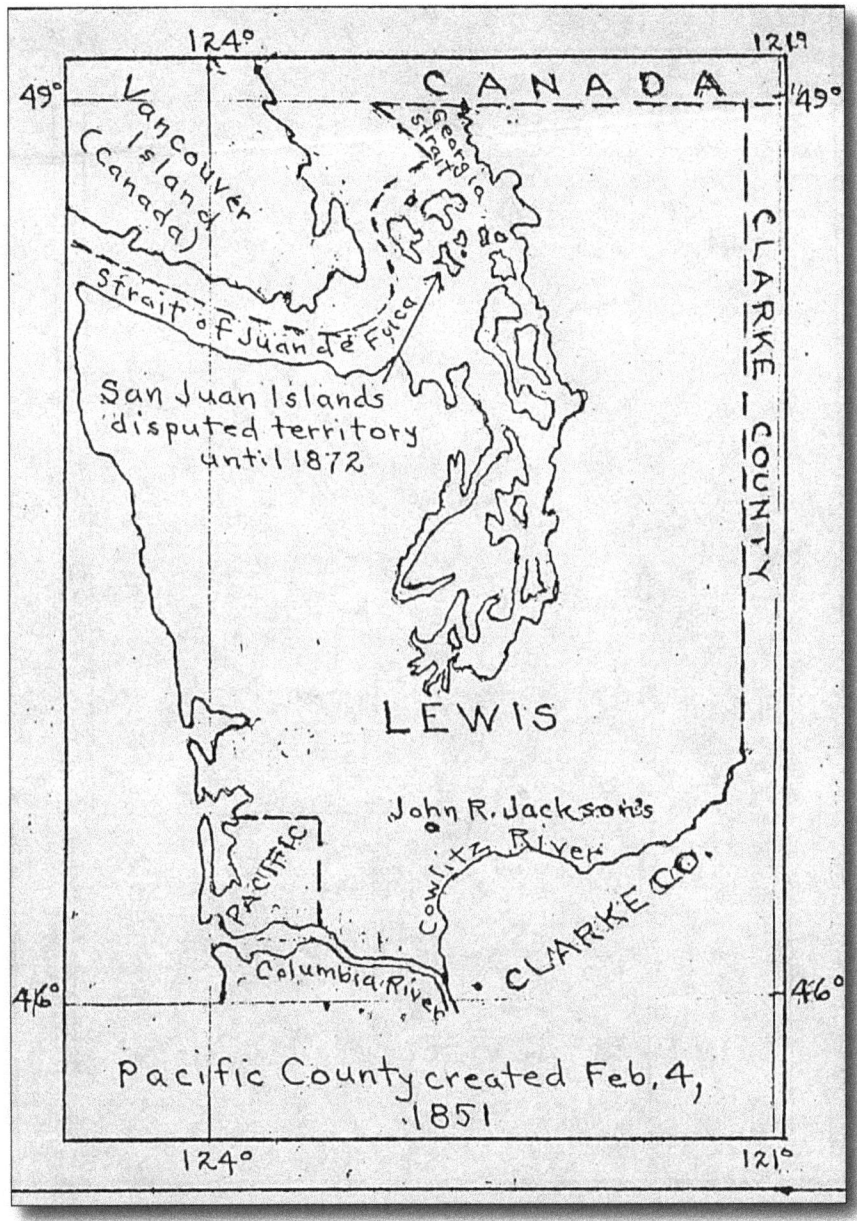

LEWIS COUNTY COURT RECORDS

The map above shows Lewis County in 1851, with the home of John R. Jackson marked above the Cowlitz River.

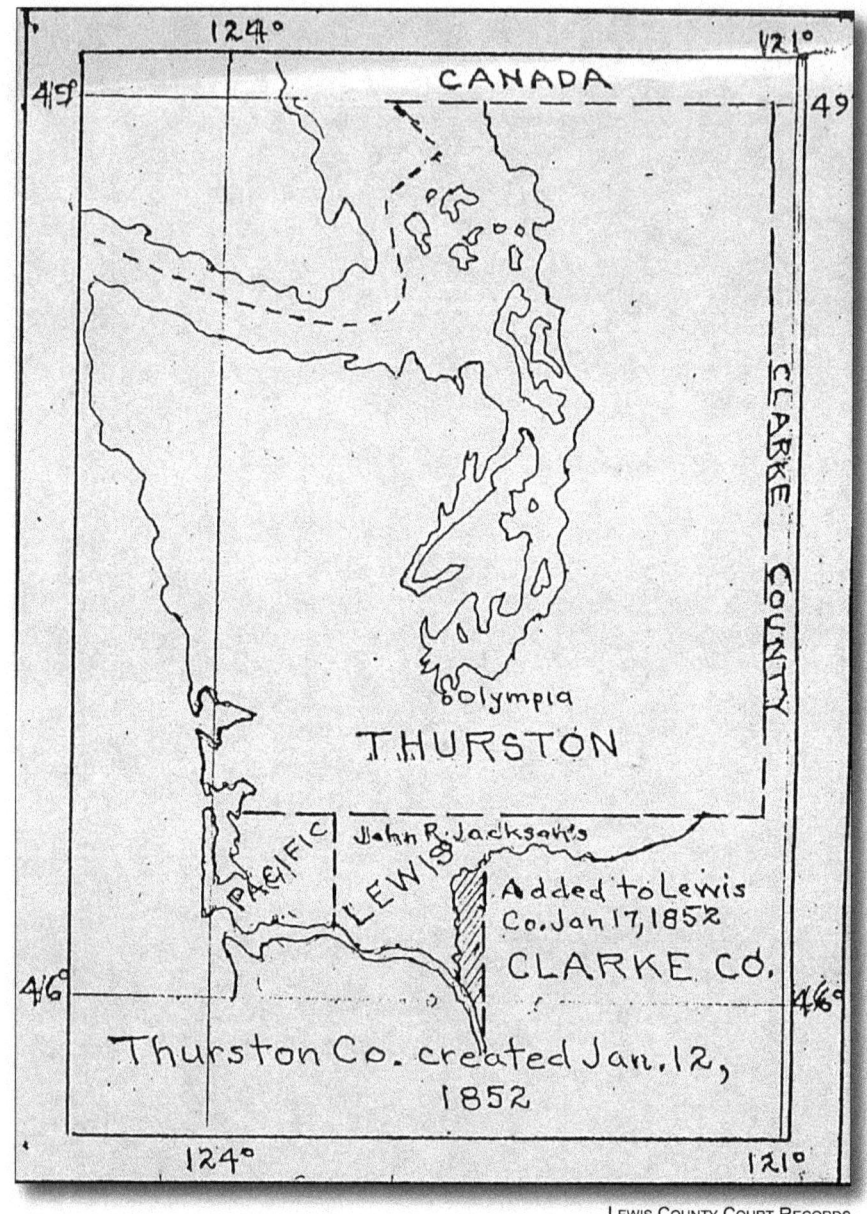

The map above shows Lewis County and Thurston County, after it was created January 12, 1852. Jackson's home is still marked prominently on the map.

Chapter Thirteen: Trying to Create a Territory

Commissioners granted Sheriff A.J. Simmons twenty dollars for hauling Schuyler Saunders as a prisoner from Cowlitz to Steilacoom.

The Federal Court convened again May 24, 1852, at Ford's home, and a contempt order against Chapman was dismissed. Absentee jurors who had been cited paid ten dollar fines and costs, or, in hardship cases, just costs.

The dissension led to creation of Thurston County, with Olympia as its county seat, January 12, 1852.[13]

Judge Strong, who owned property at times in Toledo and Cathlamet, served from 1850 to 1854 as district judge in the third district of Oregon Territory and as a territorial judge until 1861.

The Jackson courthouse was converted to a family residence in November 1851, and later Jackson used it as an office. He hired drivers to haul freight in his wagons pulled by four-horse teams from the Cowlitz River to Tumwater and back.

With mixed emotions, Matilda read another letter from her mother in Lincoln County, Missouri, dated November 17, 1851.[14]

> My Dear Matilda,
> I feel much gratified to hear from you once more, my Dear Child, in this life. Your first letter to me has just come to hand, and I am truly glad to hear that you are well and doing so very well; yes, I rejoice at it, but often times since you left me have I reflected upon and felt sorrowful for your desolate and disagreeable situation that you were left in after the death of poor Nicholas. Often have I felt for you and for your poor children fearing some mischief and distress to befall you, but now how favorably changed is your condition from what it was then. You ought to feel thankful to kind Providence for such blessings, and remember now the Creator before it be too late. I rejoice to hear that you have found a friend there in that distant Land, a dear friend to accompany you so long as you both live. May you love each other and be Happy in time and Eternity is accompanied with my best wishes. I am yet living with Janette and Mr. Duncan and enjoy about as good

Health as I have for several years past. Their family are well. They do the best they can in administering to my necessary wants, for he himself is rather weakly and has to hire help about the most of his work. He is in rather poor circumstances. Thomas D. Hancock left this fall for Texas intending to return in the spring. He has bad Health. They have now all left but Eliza. Thomas is a fine steady youth and he was Captain and joined the Church last spring. Mr. Burress is yet living in the neighbourhood of Troy. I have not seen poor Clarissa since the year before Philip left. Her circumstances is about the same as when you left but has another son born since. Weston is yet living and is still afflicted. I have lately heard from my children in Wisconsin and they were all well. Samuel, Elton, Thomas Glover and Dely ann Glover is all married, poor Elvira is Dead. She left three children under the care of her mother in law, Mrs. Bainbridge. You wrote to me to inform you what was done with your Land. Philip sold it just before he left to James J. Cravens, a tanner by trade for the sum of $250.00—cash, out of which Philip offered to return to me fifteen dollars that I had previously sent to you by James Casnon, but I did not receive it, the reason of this was that I learned from a letter from William Glover to his Father, how that Nicholas Coonse got drowned and that you was left on the rout somewhere among strangers without the necessary means for continuing on your Journey till certain arrangements could be made.

 This news was so distressing to me that I sent you $15 of my little mite hoping that you might get it in time of your kneed. I want you to inform me whether or not you got it and what became of it if you did not get it (if you can). Dear Matilda, I have seen much trouble since you left me, if I could see you, I could tell you many things that you would be surprised to hear, but I now only have but one of my children to look upon and converse with about these things, the one I ever find helpful and con-

Chapter Thirteen: Trying to Create a Territory

Matilda Glover wrote a letter to daughter Matilda Jackson November 17, 1851.

WASHINGTON STATE LIBRARY'S COLLECTION OF THE JACKSON, KOONTZ, GLOVER FAMILY PAPERS, 1837–1952.

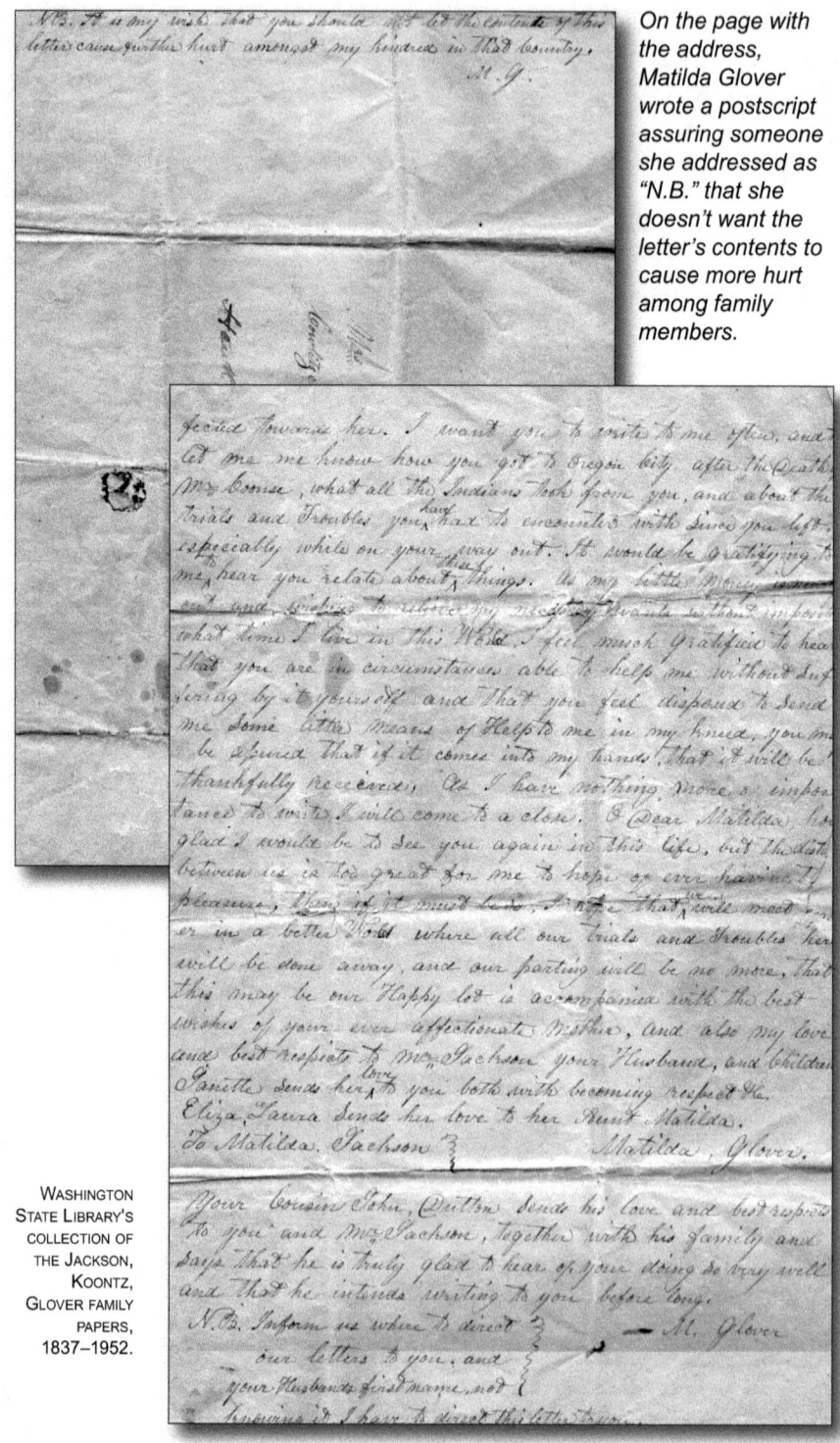

On the page with the address, Matilda Glover wrote a postscript assuring someone she addressed as "N.B." that she doesn't want the letter's contents to cause more hurt among family members.

Washington State Library's collection of the Jackson, Koontz, Glover family papers, 1837–1952.

Chapter Thirteen: Trying to Create a Territory

soling unto me, and her Husband has ever been willing to supply my necessary wants; I lived a short time at Philip's, as long as I could stay there, for I was as good as turned out of doors, but not by himself. I was then treated unwelcome to what I stood in kneed of and abused. None of my children that have left me, except you left me the least present whatever, knowing that I had but small means in hand for my support. As to my being disagreeable to live with I leave that for you to judge. Janette seems to feel a little hurt with you, for not mentioning of her name in your letter inasmuch as I am living with her, and after having had the care of me so long, she is in hopes that you have not forgotten her in that distant country, nor become disaffected towards her. I want you to write to me often, and to let me know how you got to Oregon City after the Death of Mr. Coonse, what all the Indians took from you, and about the trials and Troubles you have had to encounter with since you left, especially while on your way out. It would be gratifying to me to hear you relate about these things. As my little money is nearly out and wishing to relieve my necessary wants without imposition what time I live in this World. I feel much gratified to hear that you are in circumstances able to help me without suffering by it yourself and that you feel disposed to send me some little means of help to me in my kneed. You may be assured that if it comes into my hands, that it will be thankfully received. As I have nothing more of importance to write, I will come to a close.

 Dear Matilda, how glad I would be to see you again in this life, but the distance between us is too great for me to hope of ever having the pleasure, then if it must be so, I hope that we will meet each other in a better World where all our trials and troubles here will be done away and our parting will be no more. That this may be our Happy lot is accompanied with the best wishes of your ever affectionate Mother. And also my love and best respects to Mr. Jackson, your Husband, and children. Janette sends her love to you both with becoming respect.

Eliza Laura sends her love to her Aunt Matilda.

Matilda Glover
To Matilda Jackson

Your cousin, John Dutton, sends his love and best respects to you and Mr. Jackson, together with his family and says that he is truly glad to hear of your doing so very well and that he intends writing to you before long.

—M. Glover

N.B. Inform us where to direct our letters to you and your Husband's first name, not knowing it, I have to direct this letter to you.

Chapter Fourteen
Life at Highland Farm

LIFE AT THE HIGHLANDS proved difficult in many respects. When Matilda's older brother, Philip Glover, first visited the Highlands, he complained that Jackson "worked the boys too hard."[1] However, the boys thrived and knew that someday the farm would belong to them. Jackson also hired a teacher for Matilda's sons, and later for his own children he had with her.

Furnishings in the old home included a settee, bookcase, and handmade chairs with rawhide seats built with wooden pegs. There were benches, a speaker's chair, a desk, a spinning wheel, the original grate in the fireplace, a cradle, scythe, tanning boards, flaxseed and coffee grinders, and a water bucket neck yoke for hauling water.

Jackson continued to keep meticulous records of purchases and sales. In December he paid four dollars for two gallons of whiskey and $1.75 for a pair of small boots.

January 29, 1852, he paid six dollars for twenty yards of furniture cotton, twelve cents for a skein of black silk, $1.25 for two chisels, $3.50 for a dozen spoons, $1.50 for three knives, fifty cents for a bottle of mustard, a dollar for four bars of soap, twenty-five cents for paper, fifty cents for two combs, $5.76 for thirty-six yards of calico, and more items, including a shower of some sort.[2]

On February 17, he paid fifty cents for four spools of thread, $1.25 for five caps, thirteen cents for needles, four dollars for a white blanket, nine dollars for a case of tea, eight dollars for a looking glass, $12.60 for eighty-four pounds of sugar, and three dollars for four yards of flannel.

On May 4, he paid two dollars for twenty-four yards of lace, a dollar for two knives and another dollar for four papers of garden seeds, seventy-five cents for a box of cigars, two dollars for two bottles of brandy, and $1.25 for two yards of lace for caps.

On June 2, he paid three dollars for a pair of boots, two dollars for a pair of pants for someone named Miller, $1.50 for 1½ gallons of vinegar, thirty-eight cents for a comb, a dollar for a bottle of brandy, $1.35 for nine pounds of coffee, forty-four cents for tallow, twenty-five cents for a pound of saleratus, and seventy-five cents for a box of cigars.

On August 30, he paid twenty-five cents again for a pound of saleratus and thirty-six dollars for two kegs of nails.

On October 13, he spent twenty dollars for a churn, $4.50 for a dozen brooms, fifty cents for two salmon, $1.50 for two plugs of tobacco, fifty cents for two pounds of saleratus, $175 for five head of cattle, twelve dollars for two dozen sacks, thirty-five dollars for a plow, and other items.

He also tracked money brought into Highland Farm from sales of its produce, livestock, and other goods.

For example, on February 8, Jackson received $2.50 for four-and-a-half pounds of butter and thirty dollars for thirty bushels of oats. A month later, on March 9, he brought in $285 from the sale of oats at a dollar a bushel, thirty dollars for thirty dozen eggs, $63.65 for 128 pounds of butter, $29 for four dozen fowl, $26.60 for eighty-nine pounds of bacon, $18.90 for sixty-three pounds of lamb, $32.70 for 304 pounds of fresh beef, $8.50 for chickens, eighty cents for sixteen pounds of salt, and other produce.

The year 1852 marked a milestone for Jackson as he was admitted to citizenship in the United States. He had applied in 1834, and Professor Edmond S. Meany wrote that he had been naturalized in 1835,[3] but Judd Bush, editor of *The Chehalis Bee-Nugget*, asked for clarification in 1922.[4] He knew court records showed Jackson's naturalization occurred in 1852, so he wondered whether the Englishman had been naturalized twice. The renowned University of Washington history professor responded that Jackson himself answered the question when he testified in the settlement case with the Hudson's Bay Company and the Puget Sound Agricultural Company. In his deposition, recorded on page 15 of the "Evidence

Chapter Fourteen: Life at Highland Farm

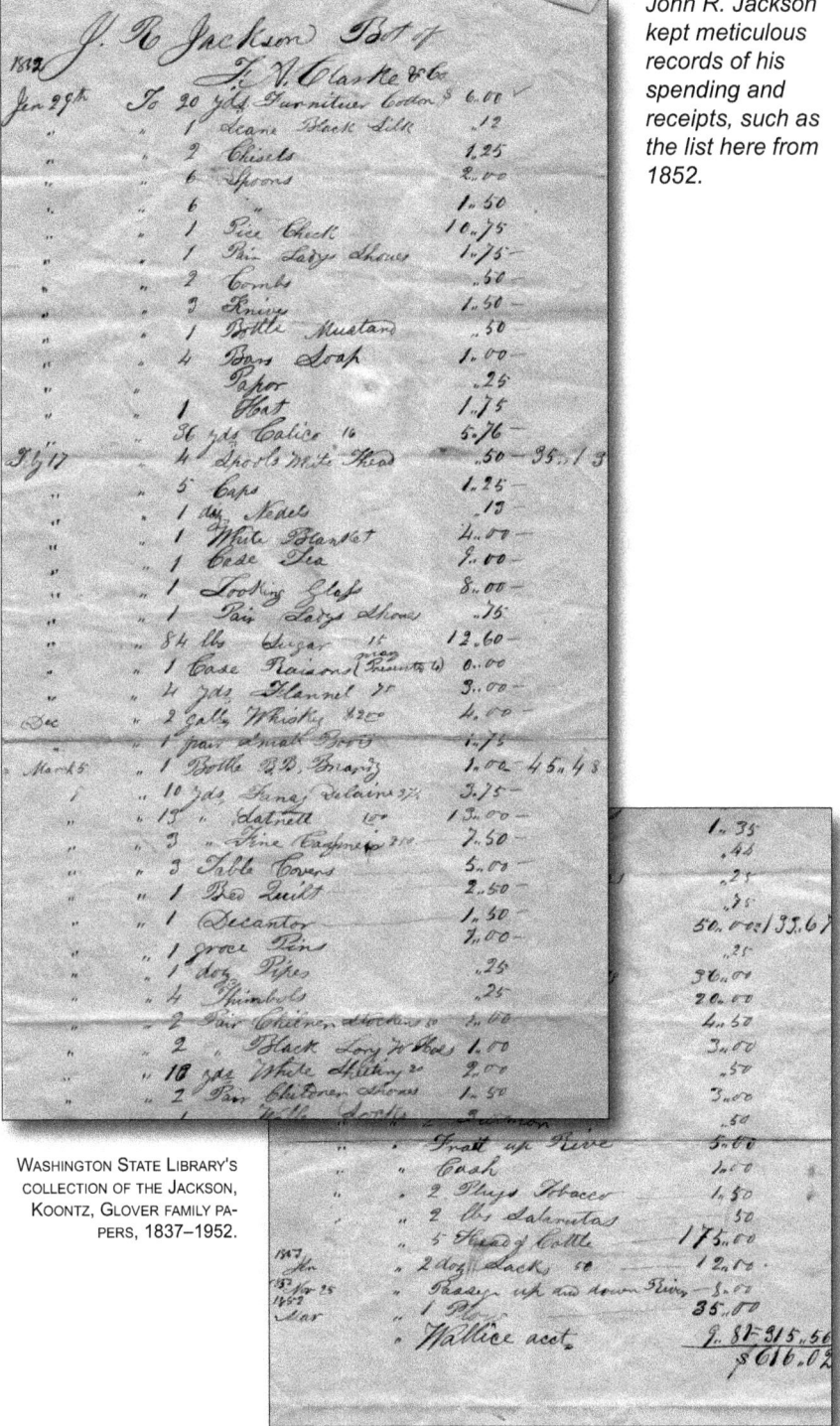

John R. Jackson kept meticulous records of his spending and receipts, such as the list here from 1852.

WASHINGTON STATE LIBRARY'S COLLECTION OF THE JACKSON, KOONTZ, GLOVER FAMILY PAPERS, 1837–1952.

for the Puget Sound Agricultural Company pending before the British and American Joint Commission," Jackson testified that he became a naturalized American citizen in 1835. Meany considered it firsthand evidence. It's not clear why Jackson applied twice.

On May 25, 1852, Lewis County court records show Jackson became naturalized after having proved to the court's satisfaction that he had declared his intention two years earlier.[5] Both Michael T. Simmons and Senator Sidney S. Ford testified he had lived within Oregon Territory for the previous five years and "he has behaved," according to William P. Bonney, secretary of the Washington State Historical Society in Tacoma. Judge William Strong approved the paperwork, filed by court clerk James C. Strong.

"The record shows that Simon Plamondon took out his papers the same day," Bonney wrote in 1922.

The first marriage at the Jackson courthouse took place in 1852 when fourteen-year-old Mary Jane Mills married Robert Brown, her father's best friend, according to Donna Tisdale.[6] She was the daughter of Elkanah Mills. Tisdale said Brown and the elder Mills helped build the courthouse and served as jurors at the first trial.

County commissioners met at Sidney Ford's place in January, with Commissioners John B. Chapman and William P. Daugherty in attendance as well as Sheriff A.J. Simmons, Clerk A.M. Poe, and Deputy R.H. Lansdale. They created the Duwamish township.

But afterward, most court sessions took place at Jackson's home through 1854, when the Washington Territorial Legislature first met. By that time, Lewis County was carved into smaller jurisdictions and Thurston County's creation resolved concerns over the location of the courthouse.

The court established bounties for killing wild animals—ten dollars for killing a panther, five for a big wolf, and three for a small wolf. A peddler's license cost a hundred dollars annually.

In July 1852, James Cochran, who lived at Cowlitz Landing but homesteaded property in Centralia for his foster son, a black man named George Washington, was sworn in as a county commissioner, Richard J. White court clerk, and Jackson justice of the peace. M. Davis of Claquato was also sworn in as commissioner. Their predecessors were ordered to turn over all documents by August 9.[7]

The board met at Jackson's with Commissioners Cochran and Davis attending, as well as Clerk White and Sheriff A.B. Dillenbaugh. Poe, the former clerk, delivered the records. The sheriff called twenty-three people to serve as grand jurors and twenty-six as petit jurors. E.D. Warbass, county treasurer, gave a report August 10 and former Sheriff Simmons was ordered to settle all balances with the treasurer.

The court met again September 6 at Jackson's. Warbass asked commissioners for seventy-one dollars for books needed by the county. The county ran short of money the previous year by $101.20, which was less than in some preceding years. The court selected grand and petit jurors. Cochran tendered his resignation so a new commissioner needed to be elected.

On December 7, 1852, the commissioners met at Jackson's with the newest commissioner, George B. Roberts. In addition to Davis and Sheriff Dillenbaugh, Jackson served as deputy clerk. Commissioners granted F.A. Clark's petition to establish a ferry over the Cowlitz at Cowlitz Landing and fixed the toll. The clerk was ordered to provide a book to record stock brands in the county at a charge of a dollar a brand.

Monticello Convention

On October 27, 1852, citizens living in the northern part of Oregon Territory gathered at the courthouse on Jackson Prairie.[8] The men appointed delegates to attend a convention November 25 at Monticello, on the west bank of the Cowlitz River in what today is Longview, to petition Congress again for a separate territory north of the Columbia River. John Jackson was among the forty-four delegates who signed the Monticello Convention Memorial seeking creation of the new Territory of Columbia.[9]

The memorial noted that the territory of Oregon contained an area of 341,000 square miles, and was entirely too large an extent of territory to be embraced within the limits of one state. The Honorable Quincy A. Brooks of Port Townsend pointed out that Oregon's size is five times as large as Missouri, six times as large as Virginia, and seven times as large as New York.[10]

"I venture the assertion that there is no state in the Union of equal extent of territory capable of supporting as large a population," he said.

At the time, it took six weeks for word to reach national lawmakers in what at that time was called Washington City. But eleven days after the Monticello Convention, on December 6, 1852, Oregon's territorial delegate, Joseph Lane, introduced the petition—perhaps the version approved at the Cowlitz Convention—to Congress. It was referred to the committee on territories and debated in February 1853, by which time Lane would have received the Monticello memorial. The House of Representatives passed it in February 1853, but changed the name from Columbia to Washington Territory. President Millard Fillmore signed the measure March 2, 1853. Congress established Olympia as the capital and appointed Isaac Stevens as the first governor.

Communication was slow in those days, and word didn't reach the citizens of the new territory until the end of April.

However, those at the Monticello convention say that's what created the new territory.

Fifty years later, Brooks wrote a letter for the sesquicentennial offering regrets for his inability to attend, but stating, "It was the Monticello convention of November 25, 1852, that secured the separation of Washington from Oregon, and I don't forget that I was a delegate to that convention from the County of Thurston. I remember also that in going to the convention I traveled on the hurricane deck of a cayuse from Olympia to the Cowlitz landing, and from there I went in a canoe down the Cowlitz River to Monticello."

Chapter Fifteen

Flying the First Flag

MATILDA SELDOM SAT except when spinning wool, sewing, or reading the Bible. She worked from dawn to dusk. She cooked. She cleaned. She weeded the garden. She tended to her toddlers, Mary and Andrew, while pregnant yet again.

On May 11, 1853, at the age of forty-two, Matilda gave birth to her last child, a daughter they named Louisa Matilda Jackson. She had five sons, two daughters, and a little baby lost along the Oregon Trail.

Blessings abounded, despite the loss and heartache following the death of Nicholas.

True to his word, John provided well for his family. He ordered a cookstove brought around Cape Horn for Matilda. It arrived in 1853.[1]

The boys worked hard on the farm. They planted and harvested crops. They herded cattle. They rode horses to the Cowlitz Landing, where they rented them to travelers.

In 1853, Jackson hired a teacher to instruct his stepsons. They conducted school in the Jackson home. The teacher, a Mr. Robins, lived with them.[2] He also worked on the farm and taught Matilda's sons in the evenings. Most of the region's children learned the Chinook jargon to communicate with local Indians, who primarily belonged to the Cowlitz or Chehalis tribes.

The Jacksons' younger children later attended school at the home of George Roberts on Newaukum Prairie, where a law student named Daniel Dodge taught them. Other students attending the school were three or four Urquharts, three Moores, and Frank and Peter Bernier, according to Louisa (Jackson) Ware.

"We used to drive an old pony back and forth to school, but sometimes he got away from us and then we had to walk home," she said. "George Roberts, the senior, lived on Cowlitz prairie after living on Newaukum prairie. Our second school was about a half-mile farther out on the prairie and we had about the same pupils. The teacher of that school was Mr. Hennessey, but we didn't like the school so well."

In his later writings, Roberts noted that Matilda Jackson's fame as a grand housekeeper and cook spread. She held a reputation as a gentle but heroic hostess who provided a mecca for hungry and weary travelers.

The First Flag

After the success of the Monticello convention, and the creation of Washington Territory March 2, 1853, Jackson ordered material from San Francisco so that several people could work together to sew a United States flag to fly over the courthouse during the Fourth of July celebration.[3]

When the red, white, and blue bunting arrived, Matilda and women and men from twenty miles around convened with needle and thread to sew the flag in June 1853. Among those helping were the families of John MacDonald and Captain George Drew.[4]

The flag, patterned after the nation's first banner, measured six feet by fifteen feet. It contains thirteen white muslin stars but only eight stripes because they ran out of material to create more, according to a July 4, 1958, article in *The Tacoma News Tribune* by Pat Winkler.[5]

Beside his peeled log cabin home, Jackson erected a tall flagpole to fly the nation's banner, first unfurled for the Independence Day celebration July 4, 1853.

During the celebration, Jackson said, "The rising generation of Washington Territory—May they grow up like the cedars of our forest, unequaled in the world and never surpassed by our sister States, kindred or tongue."

Later in the day, Jackson served as master of ceremonies at a celebration at Cowlitz Landing. An article in *The Columbian* newspaper in Olympia July 16, 1853, described "The Cowlitz Celebration."[6]

Matilda Jackson and others stitched together the flag above, which was flown at the Jackson Courthouse in 1853.

"Having no guns, we put powder into thirteen of the large fir logs and touched them off at sunrise," wrote the settler who submitted the report. "The people gathered quite early and raised a Liberty pole. At twelve o'clock a procession of thirty couples formed and marched, with music, to the dinner table on the bank of the river. The table was canopied with boughs and spread with an abundance of good cheer."

Jackson served as president of the day, and his family likely accompanied him to the festivities. He introduced R.S. Robinson, the reader of the Declaration of Independence. The crowd cheered and played music when he finished reading. The Reverend J.W. Goodell, orator of the day, "delivered one of those appropriate addresses, instructive and gratifying to every American citizen."

They toasted Independence Day, Washington Territory, and the president of the United States. The crowd responded to the toasts with "huzzas."

Hospitality and Politics

The Highlands sat along the old Cowlitz Trail that led from the Cowlitz Farm to Fort Nisqually, and it remained a prominent route to the Puget Sound as more pioneers settled the land to the north. Many stopped at the Highlands for food and rest along the way.

Among the military men who sought shelter overnight at the Highlands was George McClellan, who had graduated second in his class from West Point in 1846. He was stationed at Fort Vancouver in 1853, where he was ordered to find the best railroad route from the east. In 1857, he left the military to serve as a railroad executive, but returned to the Army during the Civil War. He served in the Union Army and ran for president as a Democrat in 1864, but Abraham Lincoln defeated him. He later served as New Jersey's governor.

Ulysses S. Grant, who arrived at the Columbia Barracks near Fort Vancouver in September 1852, stayed overnight at the Highlands during his fifteen months as regimental quartermaster. He was transferred in early 1854 to Fort Humboldt in California and later fought as a Union Army general in the Civil War and ran successfully for president in 1868 and 1872.[8]

As a lieutenant, Grant stopped at the Jackson home during a rainstorm in the summer of 1853 to buy provender, or animal feed,

Chapter Fourteen: Life at Highland Farm

for the soldiers to use at the fort. He had been traveling to Steilacoom from Vancouver.[9]

"Grandmother told me about the visit," recalled Anna Koontz, Matilda's granddaughter, who often sat before her grandparents' fireplace and read aloud the Bible.[10] If she erred, Matilda corrected her without referring to the book. "Lt. Grant stood before the fireplace to dry himself. My oldest uncle [that would be Henry] saw U.S. in gilt on Grant's army belt. He thought it stood for Uncle Sam."

When the Army officers stopped, Jackson enjoyed discussing current events and politics of the day with them. He was a strong Democrat who liked to stay informed of the nation's happenings, although his daughter, Louisa, said he didn't go to school as a child. Witnesses recalled he would discuss politics with visitors late into the night.

In 1852, Jackson hired an eighteen-year-old newcomer, Edward Yates, to work with him on the ranch. Seventy years later, Judd C. Bush, editor of *The Chehalis Bee-Nugget*, interviewed Yates about his recollections of Jackson and published his account March 17, 1922.

"In the spring of 1853, I worked three or four months for him and put in the crop on the place," recalled Yates, eighty-eight at the time of the interview.[11] "We planted wheat and oats that year as the principal crop. There were also potatoes and a garden and as the land was new the crops were fine. Mr. Jackson did not do farm work himself. I never knew him to work a single day on the farm."

Instead of doing a lot of the physical labor himself, Jackson hired help, kept the books, and operated his hotel.

"He attended to business, as he kept a stopping place for travelers, and helped Mrs. Jackson a great deal in the house," Yates said. "He kept a four-horse team and a driver busy hauling people from the landing near Toledo to Olympia. Passengers were usually hauled from the Cowlitz Landing to Jackson's, where they spent the night and continued on to Olympia the next day. He filled various county offices and when not holding a county office was usually a justice of the peace. I heard him claim once that he had performed more marriage ceremonies than any other justice in Lewis County, but I do not think that was many.

"Once I heard him say that he had settled on the Missouri and the high water had washed him out. He determined then that when he settled again it would be on the highest place he could find and he made good the resolution by settling on Highland Prairie, the highest point between the Cowlitz River and Olympia.

"John R. Jackson was a good-looking man. He must have been six feet tall and well proportioned. He wore side whiskers, a style common among Englishmen in those days, and would have been noticed in any crowd. He was an educated man, a fine talker, and talked on all subjects. Army officers and other travelers who stopped at his place often argued with Jackson and talked until late in the night. He was a strong Democrat and one night he and Mr. Wallace, who was once a candidate for Congress, argued politics all night.

"There was as much as thirty acres of crops the year I worked on the place. The land in crop was all natural prairie and there was enough of it on the Jackson claim that he did not need to clear up any land. I do not know of him ever clearing or slashing land. We used both cattle and horses with which to do farm work. We had a plow and harrow, and a roller made of a log. The crop was cut with hand reapers, not the little one-hand affairs but heavy reapers with wooden guards that helped bunch the grain in piles so it could be the more easily bound. It was afterwards threshed out with a hand flail. 'Flailing' out grain was one of the first jobs I did when I worked for Mr. Jackson. He had a lot of the 1852 crop that had not been threshed. The wheat was taken to Captain Drew's mill to be ground. Mr. Jackson was always pleased with what I did. He never said I didn't do things right or didn't do enough work.

"There were cattle, horses, hogs and chickens at Highland, but I do not think there were any sheep there at that time. It was a nice, pleasant place to live and I enjoyed working there."

Yates described Matilda's sons with Nicholas as "all of them nice boys."

"I hardly think you would ever find four as good brothers, always willing to do their part," he said.

He noted that Matilda worked hard.

"I often wondered how Mrs. Jackson kept up with all the work that was to be done in the house. There was no female help. But Mr. Jackson helped as did the boys—and they were very good boys. There were no conveniences like there are now in modern houses," Yates told Bush in 1922. "Water had to be drawn from a well. Mrs. Jackson didn't

Chapter Fourteen: Life at Highland Farm

AUTHOR PHOTO TAKEN AT AURORA COLONY MUSEUM IN OREGON

Washington Governor Isaac Stevens, left, and George McClellan, later a general in the Civil War, were among the prominent leaders who stayed at the home of John and Matilda Jackson, where she was known for her gracious hospitality.

stand and look when she had things to do but kept going. She was a great woman to work.

"What was known and referred to as the 'courthouse' was used for storage and a good many people slept there. It was the custom then for travelers to carry their blankets. They could get meals and sit about the fire in the Jackson house, but they had to sleep in the courthouse or in the barn."

He noted that Jackson himself often traveled on horseback and slept under a blanket in the woods.

Bush also interviewed the Jacksons' daughter Louisa Ware and published her recollections in *The Chehalis Bee-Nugget* in 1922.

"My father was an Englishman by birth and a butcher by trade," Louisa Ware said.[12] "He never went to school a day although he wrote a good hand and was educated. He read a great deal and was interested in politics."

As a boy, which is when he lost his right eye in a hawthorn thicket, Jackson traveled in Scotland and spoke Scottish. Louisa said he "tried to teach me but I couldn't learn it and he would laugh.

"I was out of doors a great deal with father ... He had lots of horses and cattle and some good ones and I used when a little girl to ride frequently with him. In later days we had a two-horse buggy which father used, as he was badly crippled with rheumatism."

Louisa recalled the original cabin stood twenty feet south of the rebuilt courthouse.

"I have heard father say there were lots of Indians about when he first settled and they were sometimes rude," she recalled. "He put a cross up in one of the fir trees that stood almost in front of the house and that seemed to have a good effect on them. Once an Indian came in to beg and on being refused drew a knife. Father took a club and the Indian got out."

The original chimney where the courthouse stands didn't draw well, she said. They added onto the building, a sawed-board addition with a kitchen and large fireplace, dining room, and big bedroom.

"A short distance south of the house was what I remember as 'the office,' a pole house perhaps fifteen by twenty feet in size in which father kept his books and transacted business. There was a big 'Franklin' stove in there and beds for travelers who slept there but sat in the sitting room of the main house and ate in the dining room."

She recalled her father's political discussions.

"Father was a very strong Democrat and couldn't see any other light. He hated to see anyone turn. Mother was a wonderful worker. Sometimes women stopped and helped her sew. Sometimes we had a man cook. I remember one named Gus Gangloff who was particularly handy. We had Indians to help in the fields but not in the house.

"I remember seeing Governor Stevens, Mrs. Huggins, and Doctor Tolmie. They brought me some little books. Brother Barton remembered seeing General Grant. There were many travelers who stopped at the place.

"Father didn't clean up much land in the early days. There was plenty of open prairie. In later days he had Indians clear some land."

Louisa's older sister, Mary, attended school in Olympia and lived there, while Louisa went to Claquato and then Chehalis. She owned an old desk made of cherry wood grown on Jackson's property in Illinois.

"He brought the desk across the plains with him and used it in his office here," she recalled.

Prices in 1853

Army officers left their families back East because of the high cost of living in the West. One of Jackson's old accounting books gives a good indication of the prices in the period from November 1853 to July 1855.[13]

A gallon of syrup cost two dollars; two gallons of whiskey six dollars; and three plugs of tobacco a dollar. He paid twelve dollars to have four bushels of wheat ground at Drew's mill. Although Matilda sewed clothes, evidenced by the purchase of four thimbles for twenty-five cents each, the Jacksons also purchased store-bought items in 1853: six pairs of woolen socks for three dollars; a coat for five dollars, three tables covers for five dollars, and ten yards of white sheeting for two dollars. Jackson spent four dollars for twenty-five pounds of sugar, two dollars for two pounds of tea, and a hefty price of sixty dollars for Matilda's cookstove.

During the years 1852 and 1853, workers improved the Cowlitz Road to Olympia. During the same time, seven school districts were established in Lewis County.

County Commissioners

Lewis County commissioners met in April 1853 at Jackson's house with Commissioners L.H. Davis and George Roberts present, A.B. Dillenbaugh as sheriff, and Jackson as deputy clerk. At that meeting, the commissioners established the Cowlitz township as well as Jackson, Chehalis, and Boistfort. Jackson was appointed surveyor of the township bearing his name, while Schuyler Saunders had that role in Saundersville and J.C. Davis in the Cowlitz township.[14]

In early September they met at the Cowlitz Hotel, operated by Thomas Carter and C.C. Pagett at Cowlitz Landing, who also ran a store and bar. Commissioners appointed J.P. Manning as county assessor for collection of taxes. They met again in October "at the county seat," which would have been Jackson's at that time. Jackson arrived the following day after finishing his business away from home. Manning listed the amount of taxable Lewis County property as $155,116, with $180 in poll tax collected.

In early December, the commissioners met at the Cowlitz Hotel at Cowlitz Landing, with Davis and Roberts as commissioners, Jackson as clerk, and Dillenbaugh as sheriff.

The commissioners granted John Moore permission to operate a ferry on the Newaukum River for a year. The license fee was one dollar. The commissioners fixed the prices that could be charged: twenty-five cents per footman; a dollar for a wagon and span of horses or yoke of cattle; twenty-five cents for each extra horse or head of cattle, and five cents a head for sheep and swine. The fee for a man on horseback was fifty cents.

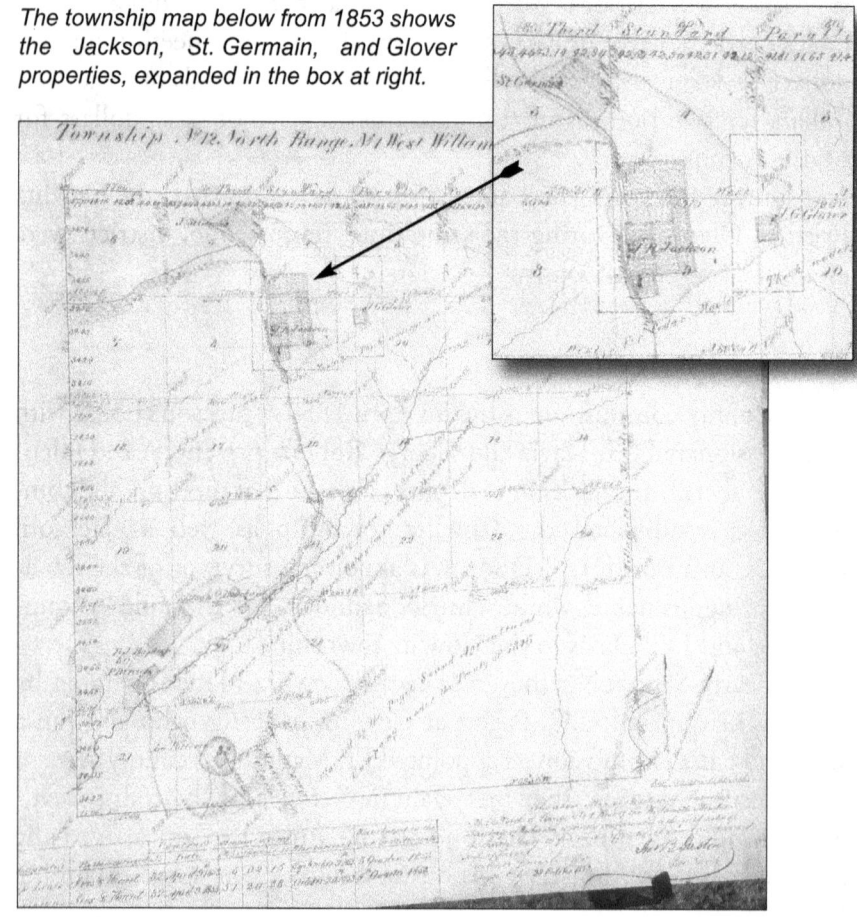

The township map below from 1853 shows the Jackson, St. Germain, and Glover properties, expanded in the box at right.

Chapter Sixteen

A Post Office and a Diary

MATILDA'S ELDEST SON, HENRY, kept a diary during his fifteenth year. He jotted items in a book previously used by Andrew Levitt, who may have worked for the Jacksons, according to a July 11, 1954, article in *The Seattle Times*. In 1851, Levitt kept a diary of his time living near Willapa Bay at what later became Westport.

Matilda's son usually referred to himself as Henry Coonse, but at times he was mentioned as Henry Jackson.

On January 1, 1854, he wrote "Henry's Journal" at the top of a clean page. He mentioned visitors who stopped at their place, including T.S. Clendenin, the territorial district attorney, and other men involved in the court proceedings at Cowlitz Landing.[2]

He spoke often about the work he did. He retrieved Jackson's horses from Cowlitz Landing that were rented to travelers heading north, and sometimes rode to the Puget Sound to bring back horses left there.

Henry traveled to Cowlitz Landing for writing paper. When school at the Jacksons' home closed February 6 after probably only three months, Mr. Robinson, the teacher, continued to work on the farm.

Then the hard labor began. Henry drove hogs, hauled rails, fixed fences, cleaned wheat, worked around the barn, and chopped cordwood. He worked with his brother Barton and a Mr. Glen to erect fences and kill hogs, that is, until Mr. Glen quit and left for the Puget Sound.

Then Henry and Barton did the work of building fences. Their stepfather hired another man, Mr. Bowseth. They threshed grain and Henry hauled their neighbors' rye, wheat, and oats to the mill.

"I took 770 pounds of flour to Cowlitz landing," he wrote February 20, 1854.

They opened and tended a charcoal pit in which they burned wood slowly in a shallow pit covered with soil to create charcoal used as fuel in blacksmithing.

In March they plowed the land and threshed oats and peas.

He knew Washington's first territorial governor, Isaac Stevens, who traveled between the territory and the city of the same name on the East Coast. On March 26, Henry wrote, "I went down to the Landing with the governor and his men to bring the horses back."

The following month, Henry and Popliseth, an Indian friend, hunted for deer, but didn't find any. He hauled stakes and rails for fences, and then grafted apple trees. He made yokes and helped in the garden. He mentioned going for purchases to the "French store" operated by Crumlin Ladu on the Cowlitz.

He and Barton spent May plowing, harrowing, and planting potatoes. After the Territorial Legislature ended its first session in Olympia, Henry traveled to the Cowlitz Landing five times to bring home horses the Jacksons had rented to travelers.

June brought more plowing, trips to retrieve horses, visits to the mill for grist, and pitching straw. They enjoyed a rare day off on the Fourth of July, when they celebrated the nation's independence. Barton was in Olympia July 23.

They cut, peeled and hauled timbers for rafters. They cleared a road to build a new barn, which they wanted ready for the harvest in August.

They worked every day except the Sabbath as they cut grain and harvested it through the hot days of early September.

On October 8, Henry broke a bit of bad news regarding the farm. "Warm day. Holy Sabbath. Blacksmith shop was burned up."

They harrowed, dug potatoes, plowed, sowed, and chopped firewood. They killed a pig, gutted fattened hogs, hauled potatoes, and cleaned oats. On cold days they thrashed peas.

In October they plowed, sowed, and dug potatoes. They hauled firewood and worked in the barn. November brought more work around the barn and chimney repairs.

In December they did more threshing of wheat and oats. They dug holes for the apple trees and set out cherry trees.

Henry's last entry, December 16, read, "I and Joseph went ... Mr. Small's to get some oak timber."

The Post Office

In the 1850s, riders carried the mail across the country on horseback and followed old Indian trails from the Columbia River to Steilacoom, dropping off letters and parcels at post offices along the way.

In 1854, the region's first post office opened in Jackson's home, Highland Farm, and Jackson was appointed postmaster April 18, 1854.[3] He is listed in the 1855 edition of *Post Offices in the United States* as postmaster of Highland, Lewis County, Washington Territory. He operated the post office there for a decade. A December 10, 1862, order directed Jackson, as postmaster at Highland, Lewis County, W.T., to pay the contractor who carried the mail on the route, F. Chable, at the end of each quarter "the whole amount due from you to the United States."[4]

Highland Post Office was discontinued December 5, 1864, and merged with the Cowlitz Post Office on Cowlitz Prairie, according to Matilda's son, Barton Koontz.

The Cowlitz Post Office was established April 29, 1854, with Edward D. Warbass serving as postmaster until he left the region for Whatcom County during the Fraser River Gold Rush in 1858.

Travelers

Many of the people passing through stopped at the Jacksons, approaching the homestead on a broad grassy lane that widened onto a natural prairie with stands of fir trees. Those arriving on horseback tied their animals to the long cedar hitching rack near the entrance, which was enclosed with a whitewashed picket fence.[5] The front gate fastened with a chain and weight. Foxgloves flourished along the picket fence with clumps of yellow-blossomed tansy planted alongside the gate. Rose bushes, pink and dark red with tight blossoms, grew along the front fence.

A cedar puncheon driveway led into the property, while pedestrians followed a brick walk, lined with red and white daisies, from the front gate to the front porch. Periwinkle grew on the east side of the courthouse, a laburnum tree on the south, and a purple lilac on the north. A white rambler rose framed the porch entrance to the log courthouse while a fragrant honeysuckle on the building's south end attracted hummingbirds. Roses also grew on the south side of the building near the big bedroom, including the Hudson's Bay Rose, a deep pink single bloom that was a gift from the company's Cowlitz Farm headquarters. A white rambler also grew over the gate to the backyard. Wild raspberries and large clumps of pink sweetbriar grew on the north side of the house where catnip and horehound flourished. The sweet fragrance of flowers greeted visitors to the home.

Just south of the home was Jackson's office, a building of fir poles measuring fifteen by twenty feet. It had a large Franklin stove and beds for travelers. The farm contained a woodshed, barns and pens for livestock, and other sheds for storing crops and produce.

A carpet covered the floor in the house, which featured chairs, a center table, and a lounge.

In November 1854, Isaac Stevens, Washington's first territorial governor, and his family traveled upriver sitting on mats in a canoe and trudged through ankle-deep mud to a small log house at Cowlitz Landing, just south of present-day Toledo.

"Here we found a number of dirty-looking men with pantaloons tucked inside their boots and so much hair upon their heads and faces they all looked alike," Mrs. Stevens wrote.[6] "After tea we were shown a room to sleep in, full of beds, which were for the women."

She lay on a narrow strip of bed, fully dressed, with her family beside her on the same bed. Her husband sat on a nearby stool and slept.

"He had been shown his bed through a hole on top of the shanty," she wrote. "He said one look was sufficient. Men were strewn as thick as possible on the floor in their blankets. The steam generated from their wet clothes, boots and blankets was stifling. One small hole cut through the roof was the only ventilation."

The next day, the Stevens family rode in a wagon north and stopped at the Jacksons' Highland home overnight. Mrs. Stevens wrote about the Jacksons' hospitality in her diary.

"After another long day's tiresome travel, we stopped at a big log house for the night, upon entering from the porch, we found a big room with a wood fire filling up one side, blazing and crackling, low chairs in front; in the center of the room was a table with a clean cloth on it,

NATIONAL REGISTER OF HISTORIC PLACES APPLICATION

Despite its small size, the Jackson home, considered almost palatial at the time, offered weary travelers a great place to rest. The photo below shows the steep staircase in the far right corner.

and a repast of well cooked food, relishing and abundant was placed upon it, to which we all did ample justice," she wrote.

"Our host was an Englishman farmer who was getting on well, a genial hospitable man; his wife was a superior woman, she was a fine-looking woman and a thorough housekeeper. At night she took us across the yard into another log house and where we found a bright fire burning on the hearth, and nice clean beds; I felt like staying in this comfortable shelter, hearing the rain patter on the roof until the rainy season was over, at least."

The hospitality was, she said, "much superior to that received elsewhere." She described Jackson as a "stalwart pioneer" and said Matilda's "fine housekeeping, delicious cookery and graciousness endeared her to the passing travelers.

"She was a very superior woman, but with such a sad, sad face," she wrote.[7]

Territorial Legislature

The first Washington Territorial Legislature met in early 1854, and the boundaries of Lewis County shrunk as lawmakers carved out more specific counties. The lawmakers carved out Pierce, Pacific, and other counties.

While Jackson served as a representative in Olympia at the Territorial Legislature, he sent letters home to Matilda.

On March 1, 1854, Jackson wrote to let her know he had arrived safely.[7]

> Dear Wife—
> When I arrived at Olympia on Monday the legislators had settled about the election and yesterday morning I took the oath of office, and shall have to remain here for some time. I want to hear from you every day if I can. By this time you will have received Mrs. Keyser's letter. Give my love to all the children, and accept the same for yourself. Your ever affectionate husband, John R. Jackson.
> This gentleman [bearing the letter] will leave Jim (the horse) with you, and let him have another to ride to the Cowlitz. Tell Grundy that he must write me his jour-

Chapter Sixteen: A Post Office and a Diary

WASHINGTON STATE LIBRARY'S COLLECTION OF THE JACKSON, KOONTZ, GLOVER FAMILY PAPERS, 1837–1952.

While serving in the Territorial Legislature, John R. Jackson sent letters home to his wife, who oversaw life at the Highlands.

nal every day. I want Henry and Barton to be sure and look over and after the cows and calves. I have had Jim well shod and the boys can thresh what oats they want and take good care of Bill. I shall want to have him sent over here before long, to ride over to see all of you. It will not be many days now before the ground will be dry enough to commence ploughing.

 Your ever affection Husband
 John R. Jackson

On March 2, 1854, Jackson wrote the following letter to his wife from Olympia.[8]

 My Dear Wife,
 As I have an opportunity of sending you a few lines by the man who rode Bob over I embrace the chance.
 I send by the bearer Staffords pans and your shoes.
 I expect that the ground is getting almost fit for the plough. When dry enough I want the bohoys to plough the field on the other side of the Barn and be sure and do it well. The Garden to you want to put your early Potatoes and other thing in tell the Boys to be sure and look well after the Cowes & Calfs. I should like to have them sent down to where Stafford took his Claim but be sure and not take any that is a little weak and let Barton go and see them every day. He might Take some of the poorest Horses to the same place.
 I see Mrs. Keyser and Bel @ going to the sewing society yesterday. I expect to get a letter from you to day and @ Long epistle from Grundy. The town is chock full of Gents.
 Give my kind love to all and except the same from
  "Your affectionate
   Old man
  John R. Jackson
  (swirly underline)

He sent another one April 25, 1854.⁹

> *Mrs. John R. Jackson*
> *Please pay Edward Hartford or bearer the sum of one hundred dollars.*

He signed off with "Oblige your Husband, John R. Jackson."

In another letter, Jackson asked Matilda to give a man named Hume another ride to the Cowlitz.

Jackson noted that the boys should take good care of Bite. "I shall want to have him sent over here a' for long to ride over to see you all," he wrote. "It will not be many days now befor the ground will be dry enough to commence ploughing."

Shrinking County

On June 5, 1854, Lewis County commissioners met in the courthouse of what was now Washington Territory. They were sworn into office, including Commissioners Henry R. Stillman and J.C. Davis, Sheriff J.L. Mitchele, and John R. Jackson as clerk.

The following day, the court appointed people to oversee roads from Cowlitz Landing and Eden Prairie. Township elections were scheduled for Cowlitz, Jackson, and Chehalis. The assessor was Martin S. Prudhomme.

The meeting lasted two more days. Jackson was appointed justice of the peace. E.D. Warbass, former treasurer, handed over records to C.C. Pagett, incoming treasurer. County commissioner Henry Stillman received fifteen dollars for his services, and J.C. Davis received $13.20 while Jackson received twelve dollars for services as sheriff. Henry Miles was appointed Lewis County's superintendent of common schools.

The commissioners met again in early July with Stillman, Davis, and a third commissioner, William Metcalf. Commissioners appointed Edward D. Warbass to replace Jackson as county auditor.

The assessment roll for 1854 was $141,663 with a charge of four mills on the dollar for the county, two for the school tax, and one for the territorial tax. That brought more than five hundred dollars into county coffers, $283.32 for schools, and $141.66 for a territorial tax and a poll tax of a dollar for 115 people.

The county treasurer, C.C. Pagett, noted that money received and expended totaled $102.40. The cost of stationery and services was $3.50.

Bills allowed for four days at the July session and mileage: To William Metcalf, $15.60; J.C. Davis, $13.20; H.R. Stillman, $15.00; E.D. Warbass (3 days clerk), $9.00; J.L. Michele, $6.00; Joseph P. Manning, $6.00.

The commissioners held an extra session later in July with Stillman and Davis in attendance.

Letter from Home

Matilda received a letter from her sister, Jane, and brother-in-law, Hiram Duncan, in Lincoln County, Missouri. It was addressed to Philip, Matilda, and John, the three Glovers who had emigrated west along the Oregon Trail. The letter was dated May 15, 1854. Philip and his family had settled in Marion County, Oregon Territory. John T. Glover lived in Clackamas County, Oregon Territory.[10]

The letter was sent to Philip and forwarded to John, who sent it to Matilda September 8, 1854, with the following note:

> Dear Matilda
>
> According to request I have sent you Hiram Duncan's letter to read and consider. You will see Mother's helpless condition. He thinks it is the duty of all her Children to bear an equal part in taking care of her. I think it is right that we should contribute something and not have any reflection on our part. Philip says he has made arrangement to send them $25 dollars and I intend to send them something as soon as I can attend to it. I am sorry James Glover has acted as he has. I think he had done very wrong. He told me when I saw him last that he would pay that money when Mother stood in need of it.
>
> This leaves us all in as good health as common. My respects and well wishes to Mr. Jackson. I have not forgotten his promise in paying us a visit this fall and we would be delighted to see with him if it is convenient. Come to see us as soon as you can. Write to us soon.
>
> Mr. Jackson will please write also and give me the

news from that side. Rachel and the children join me in love to you all. I remain your affectionate brother.

John P. Glover

Tell Joseph I think it is time we had a hearing from him. Tell him to write and let us know how he is getting along. We have had considerable rain lately but we have saved our crop. Without logs the emigration across the Mountains is quite small this fall so that we can't sell anything in that way.

The letter from Hiram and Jane (Glover) Duncan is as follows:

Dear friends,

Perhaps you may wish to hear from us as we wish to hear from you all in Oregon. This leaves us all in Health, able to stir about, except your Mother. She is in a very helpless condition. She was confined to her bead from the middle of January last to near the last of March, when she recovered so as to be able to walk out in the yard at times, and in do[ing] so on the first day of April, suddenly fell, helpless, was carried to her bead, and had not been able to leave it, nor even to sit up in it since. Ever since her fall she has had no use atall of her left leg. The main leader by which it is moved appears to be broken loose, and it is now much perished away, is often very painful to her, and throws her into fevers.

She has to be lifted and turned without scarcely any assistance of her own. Her speech and hearing is latterly much failed. Her appetite is tolerable good, and often seems to rest in sleep tolerable well. Jane has a very hard time of it in waiting on her. Until the first of this month we had Susan Mourning living with us to assist her, her father has taken her away to send her to school, so she now, only occasionally, can have any assistance, and that from our neighbor women, in coming to see her. We have had a Doctor to see her, and you may rest assured that we have shunned no Expense, Services, or attention in order to make her Situation as comfortable as possible. Your Mother sometime ago had me to write to James Glover for the Money he owes her, stating her kneed of it and the propriety of his assisting in taking care of her.

His answer was insulting to me. She then got Azro Holmes to write to him for it, offering (by my own proposal) to knock off all interest on his note, if he would only pay the Principal. His answer to Azro, which I have read, is an abuse on me, and insulting to Jane. And that his Sister Nelly and himself was coming after her in this month to take her Home with them. To think what servants Jane and myself have been to her so many years, with so little assistance, and now to be insulted and abused for merely calling on you all who are equally obligated with us to help in such a matter as that is more than I can well bear. Your Mother requested Azro to write to James Glover that he kneed not come for her, that she was not nor never had been willing to live with his Wife, nor with Thomas Elton, that she had rather if compelled go upon the County, or beg her support among her neighbours. James Glover and Thomas Elton's plea is that we all once agreed and promised to take care of her gratis. I have no recollection of it. He is useless for any of you to try to clear yourselves upon such grounds as that when the treatment she met with among you, was such that she could not long live with any of you. With Some of her children she tried to live with, but on account of Disagreement soon left. With the Same Propriety I could have treated her in like manner (so that she could not have lived with me). And as it is turned out, I am truly sorry that ever I took her back without the rest of you being bound to contribute equally with us, towards her Support. I always was Disposed to go fully my part, and none of you has any just right to require any more of us. It is no light matter to have any one so old and helpless to work. I could bear it better, but am now not able to work much and in poor circumstances. And of course such a task tends to sink us in Poverty. For

Chapter Sixteen: A Post Office and a Diary

This letter asked Matilda and her siblings who moved west to help with the costs of caring for their mother.

WASHINGTON STATE LIBRARY'S COLLECTION OF THE JACKSON, KOONTZ, GLOVER FAMILY PAPERS, 1837-1952.

we do but little else since her confinement than wait on her as prudence requires, without any chance of ever going to Meeting or to visit a neighbor together at all. The treatment towards us from James Glover has hurt our feelings so much that we wish to know how you all feel towards us. I wish to reason with you all friendly and to be Plain with you, but not to hurt your feelings. I will continue for Justice, and the Welfare of my own family. And as I have before said your Mother has not, nor shall not, suffer for anything that is in our power to furnish. And as to what amount we may ever get for it, I know not. You have us in your Power, to give, or withhold. The matter is with you. Do as you Please. Only let us know your determination Soon as convenient. The Church of which your Mother is a Member has (as I understand) considered our condition waiting to hear from you all in Oregon, intending to contribute to her kneed if you will not. Only Deal fair with us and you will ever have our friendship. Best Wishes.

If not, I expect never to write to any of you again. Then fare well, and may the Lord have Mercy upon us all, the time will Soon come when all our Contentions and Trouble here will be done away, and we all return to our common Mother Dust.

Hiram Duncan

Jane Duncan

Your Mother and Jane send their love to you all in Oregon. Your Mother has me to say to you all that she expects it is the last time you will ever hear of her being alive.

N.B. Please read this letter and send it by mail or otherwise soon as convenient to each other to whom it is written.

H. Duncan

Hiram Duncan

No record of Matilda's letters sent in reply could be found. Her mother died in 1856 in Benton County, Missouri, at age eighty-six.

Chapter Seventeen
Indian Wars and Grievous Loss

TENSIONS AMONG THE NATIVE TRIBES and the white settlers who claimed land for themselves increased as more emigrants arrived in Washington Territory in the mid-1850s.

Writer Donna Tisdale mentioned in a September 9, 1941, write-up about the Elkanah Mills family that the Indians referred to Elkanah, with his golden hair and blue eyes, as "the White Spirit," according to his granddaughter, Esther Brown Grant.[1] The entire family learned the Chinook dialect to communicate with the natives, and Elkanah's son William could speak two dialects by the time he was ten. He later helped Indian agent Sidney S. Ford as an interpreter.

When a smallpox epidemic struck, Elkanah's wife, Vianna Lorinda (Wisdom) Mills, placed a pan of bread and milk for the natives on a charred stump a hundred feet from her house but didn't let local tribal members inside her home.

Tensions increased after Governor Isaac Stevens negotiated the Treaty of Medicine Creek in 1854 that took away Nisqually land. Nisqually Chief Leschi, who signed the treaty under protest, opted to fight rather than give away land. Other tribes involved in the Puget Sound War and the Yakama War were the Muckleshoots, Puyallups, Klickitats, and Yakamas.

The governor, who also served as superintendent of Indian Affairs, ordered the Washington Territorial Volunteers to construct blockhouses or small forts to protect settlers and supplies.[2] The Army built several posts too. To the north, Olympia had several blockhouses and forts erected in Thurston County. On Grand Mound Prairie, just north of Centralia, settlers built Fort Henness with two blockhouses attached at opposite corners in a stockade and huts. Thirty families took refuge there. Among them were Mrs. Mary Borst, Joseph's wife, and baby daughter Eva and her mother, Mrs. J.H. Roundtree, and two sisters.

But her husband, Joseph, stayed on his farm on the Chehalis River near the mouth of the Skookumchuck River, where Oregon Volunteers erected a blockhouse to store grain and other supplies for volunteer soldiers fighting near Puyallup and White River. Thirty Army soldiers remained headquartered near the Borst blockhouse for three months, the number later dropping to fifteen. The Borst blockhouse later was moved first to Riverside Park and then to Fort Borst Park in Centralia, where it remains today.

To the south, settlers near Castle Rock built Fort Arkansas, a blockhouse on the lower Cowlitz River. Washington militiamen constructed a blockhouse with a stockade on the Cowlitz River at Cowlitz Landing near Toledo.

Centralia's founder, George Washington, built a small stockade on his farm.

Men were organized into companies, and John R. Jackson was listed as a captain in the *List of the Names of Lewis County Rangers, 1855*. The book lists the names of others in Volunteer Company K: S.S. Saunders, James V. Stark, Louis Sacks, W.B. Busey, J. Barton, E. Mills, Charles Layton, J.L. Mitchel, P.O. Roundtree, Andrew J. Roundtree, Thomas Davis, John Southerland, John McCormick, J.P. Mannen, C.C. Pagett, T.M. Pearson, Henry Coonse, J.B. Roberts, T.J. Carter. According to Charles Layton, the company didn't participate in active service. He also served in the company of Captain Edward Warbass.

On November 13, 1855, Jackson dictated a note to Washington Territory's Acting Governor Charles H. Mason to report on scouting activities around the Highlands.[3]

Governor Mason—Dear Sir: I have deemed it my duty to keep a diligent watch in this portion of the territory. Yesterday a party of scouts in charge of Lieut. Roundtree were out up the Newaukum some five or six miles east of my place and east of the meridian line where they found a considerable Indian trail along which from five to seven horses had traveled that morning in the direction of the Klickitat country or upper Cowlitz and none of our Indians had passed that way. Just before finding said trail Lieut. Roundtree met a Klickitat Indian who said there was no trail in that direction and seemed to be very anxious that the party of scouts should not penetrate the woods any farther in that direction. I have also sent a party up the Cowlitz to Klickitat prairie to bring away two of my command who reside there, also to take observations there. I have also stationed a party on the trail south of the Cowlitz leading from the Klickitat to Lewis River pass, all of which acts I most respectfully submit for your consideration. I shall keep parties out on these trails every day.

Please inform me from time to time of the course you wish me to pursue.

As tensions grew, white settlers were urged to seek safety behind the walls of the forts and blockhouses.

The Mills family was told to move into Fort Henness on Grand Mound Prairie but instead spent the winter with Judge Sidney S. Ford, the Indian agent, three miles northwest of Centralia. Mary Jane Brown, Elkanah Mills' daughter, described it as a scary time for all. She said the government had taken the Indians' guns, but she worried about bows and arrows.[4]

One night, fifteen friendly Indians asked Judge Ford for guns to ward off hostile natives lurking around the camp, Brown recalled.

"At about eleven o'clock that night they [hostile Indians] shot off the guns and all came running to the house and as they came in through the door, one red man said to another, 'We kill Mr. Ford first,' and I know God was with us that night, for I prayed for Him to keep us from their wicked hands," Brown said. "Tom [Ford]'s wife, Maskeefe, understood what he said and called out that they came to kill us all just as Mr. Ford was in the act of handing them some more ammunition. Tom said, 'Father, your life's in danger!' I tell you there was an exciting few minutes in that house.

"Tommy Ford held his two hands up with a revolver in each of them and shouted at them, 'I'll shoot every one of you if you don't get out of here.' Judge Ford was a brave man and he commanded them to leave the house. My father punched a half dozen of them in the stomach and shoved them out the door. My husband was busy, too. They certainly got those Indians well scared out. There wasn't much sleep in the place the remainder of the night."

Men who heard the gunfire warned the settlers at Fort Henness. They raised the alarm with Captain Hennessey, stationed with seventy-five volunteers, and Captain Goff at the Borst blockhouse on the Skookumchuck River with about seventy or eighty volunteers. They arrived at Fords' the next morning anticipating that all had been slaughtered.

"But for Tommy Ford's Indian wife, we would have all been killed," she said.

Schuyler and Eliza Saunders, who homesteaded property in 1851 near the confluence of the Chehalis and Newaukum Rivers, fled during the Indian Wars to the blockhouse at Claquato. When they returned home, they discovered their home, barn, and fences burned and their livestock slaughtered.[5] All their belongings were stolen or destroyed.

But despite the tensions, many of the local Indians liked Schuyler, who preached the gospel and sang hymns while riding on his horse. Some referred to him as "King George's Man."[6]

Simon Plamondon, a well-respected man who had wed two Cowlitz women, was appointed local Indian agent by J. Cain, acting superintendent of Indian Affairs. His goal was "to exercise a general supervision over all the Indians who may come into one camp and surrender their arms. Also to furnish them such provisions as may be necessary." Cain said he would pay for the provisions at current market rates.[7]

During the height of the Indian Wars, Plamondon received a note from J. Cain of Olympia urging him to secure weapons.

"Owing to the recent alarming intelligence of the movements of the hostile Indians, I will direct that the locks be taken off the guns, belonging to Indians, in your possession and that great precaution be taken to have them in a secure place, where there would be no possibility of their falling into the hands of the hostiles in case of any attack."[8]

But Matilda Coonse Jackson refused to leave her home for the safety of the fort at Cowlitz Landing.

That's because her son, Felix "Grundy" Coonse, was suffering from white swelling of the knee. The disease struck the knee joint and caused it to swell and whiten because of the stretching of tight skin. It could cause the cartilage to ulcerate, sometimes requiring amputation. It primarily affected people in middle age, but at times struck children who had passed through puberty, according to *The Complete Herbalist* by Dr. O. Phelps Brown.

Matilda knew her son was too weak to travel, and she would never leave him.

"If the Indians killed him, they will have to kill me," she said, according to her granddaughter, Anna Koontz. "The Jackson family did not leave home for the fort."

Matilda treated him at home. She placed hot cloths dipped in water infused with arnica flowers and lobelia on his knee and added a liniment of hemlock oil, croton oil, camphor, and tincture of iodine. She changed the cloths whenever they cooled. White swelling of the knee can refer to tuberculous arthritis.

Although the disease most often attacked the lungs, it could affect other body parts. Untreated, it could be fatal.

Even treated by a loving mother, Felix Grundy Koontz succumbed to the disease. He died at fourteen on December 7, 1855, and he was buried in the Jackson family cemetery. Another ache pierced Matilda's heart as she buried her son. The headstone reads:

Felix G. Koontz Died Dec. 7, 1855
Age 14 years
Here I Lay My Burden Down,
Change the Cross into the Crown

Friction also occurred among natives, settlers, and the militia in Eastern Washington. Miners who crossed tribal lands to pursue gold strikes near Colville sometimes stole Indian horses or mistreated native women.[9] Some Yakama braves killed miners in retaliation. An Indian subagent at The Dalles was killed in September 1855 while investigating the reports. Then, on October 5, 1855, three hundred Yakama warriors

LEWIS COUNTY HISTORICAL MUSEUM PHOTOS

The headstone of Felix Grundy Koontz, who died at fourteen in 1855. He was buried in the old Jackson Cemetery. Below is a 1900 photo of the Borst blockhouse in Centralia used for grain storage during the Indian wars.

Chapter Seventeen: Indian Wars and Grievous Loss

led by Chief Kamiakin battled Major Granville O. Haller and his eighty-four troops near Toppenish Creek, starting the Yakama War. Both sides suffered casualties. A month later, Major Gabriel J. Rains led seven hundred troops against Kamiakin and his warriors along the Yakima River at Union Gap.

The Indians fled to the Saint Joseph Mission, which the soldiers burned to the ground after finding gunpowder buried in the garden. By 1858, after losing 90 percent of their tribal lands, the Yakama were ordered onto a reservation.

During 1855, Second Lieutenant Philip Henry Sheridan served in Oregon, stationed in U.S. Army barracks on the Columbia River. In August he commanded a survey team determining a railroad route from Fort Redding in California to Portland, and in the spring of 1856, he relieved the Ninth Infantry after its attack by Yakama, Klickitat, and Cascade warriors. He continued to travel throughout Washington Territory and stopped at the Jacksons' overnight. He later served at Fort Yamill in Oregon Territory and left for St. Louis, Missouri, in 1861 to fight in the Civil War.

In October 1855, Captain Charles Eaton led a citizen militia dubbed "Eaton's Rangers" and, during a clash with the Nisqually, two men died—Joseph Miller and Abram Benton Moses. Other skirmishes took place in Tacoma, Seattle, and Walla Walla. On October 28, 1855, a Muckleshoot war party killed eight settlers in what became known as the White River Massacre, after which the militia captured four thousand natives and moved them to Fox Island, where many died. Fearful Americans also raided native villages to disarm the Indians.

At one point, an Indian was chained to the fireplace in the Jackson courthouse. He moaned all through the night and kept Matilda awake.

The Puget Sound War ended after an ambush of 110 Washington Territorial Volunteers March 10, 1856, by 150 natives, including the Nisqually leader, Chief Leschi, who was arrested in November 1856 and tried for the murder of Abram Moses.

The jury couldn't reach a unanimous decision in the first trial, questioning whether someone can be charged with "murder" during warfare. He was tried again in 1857 and convicted.

At his second trial, Leschi spoke through an interpreter.[10] "I do not know anything about your laws. I have supposed that the killing of armed men in wartime was not murder; if it was, the soldiers who killed Indians are guilty of murder too... I went to war because I believed that the Indian had been wronged by the white men, and I did everything in my power to beat the Boston soldiers, but for lack of numbers, supplies, and ammunition, I have failed. I deny that I had any part in the killing... As God sees me, this is the truth."

Three hundred people witnessed the hanging of Leschi February 19, 1858, at Fort Steilacoom, according to historylink.com. The hangman, Charles Grainger, described Leschi as cool and calm with a firm step as he mounted the scaffold. "I felt then I was hanging an innocent man, and I believe it yet," Grainger wrote later. According to Alexandra Harmon, author of *Indians in the Making*, pioneer Ezra Meeker, who voted to acquit Leschi, described him as "a patriotic martyr" to Governor Isaac Stevens' "political ambition and ill-conceived policies." (A Washington State Senate resolution March 4, 2004, recognized the hanging as an injustice and honored Chief Leschi as "a courageous leader.")

Most of the forty-seven blockhouses and forts with names in Washington Territory were abandoned at wars' end in 1856 with the signing of new treaties, which forced the natives to give up large tracts of land.

George Roberts, who served as overseer of the Cowlitz Farms for years, referred to the fight as Governor Stevens' war in Western Washington. While describing him as a "brave energetic man," Roberts said the conflict "should have been easily dealt with by three or four small parties of thirty men each."[11] He said it was unlikely Indians in the eastern part of the territory would come to the aid of those in the west. "Indians are merely grown-up children, they often have the keenest sense as to right and wrong."

In July 1856, Governor Stevens proclaimed that local Indian agents would be paid one thousand dollars a year and each would provide a bond of two thousand dollars "for the faithful disbursement of property and funds placed in his hands."[11] Assistants at the local agencies received sixty dollars a month and other employees fifty dollars a month or less.

Letter from Matilda to John

On April 12, 1855, while her husband was serving in the Washington Territorial Legislature, Matilda wrote him the following letter:[13]

Chapter Seventeen: Indian Wars and Grievous Loss

Dear Husband

I received your note to day by the hand of Mr. Gallagher— Just at twelve o'clock. Poor Dr. Wylie just packed up for San Francisco. They both sat down and eat dinner for they started. I suppose you want to hear about the Grafting. Old Mr. Gates came here last evening on his way to Portland he never received the word you sent. I sent for Joseph and he [showed] him how to graft. He is still grafting but he says he would rather [mall?/make/ haul] rails than graft.

The other boys is knocking along slowly. Bosworth was plowing yesterday. Stafford was digging a little in the Garden. Henry went to the Mill yesterday and [hauled/baled] up 5 bushels of Spring wheat. They are plowing, sowing today. I want to send two pairs of drawers by the mail carrier tomorrow. I want you to write by the next mail and let me know when you expect to get through the Business and when I may look for you home.

Nothing more at present.

I still remain your Effectionate Wife
Matilda N. Jackson

Matilda's Letter from brother John

In early 1855, Matilda received a letter from her brother, John P. Glover, who lived in Clackamas County in Oregon Territory, in which he told about the death of his three-year-old son, William, and the grave illness of his eldest son, Joseph. It was dated January 8, 1855.[14] [Joseph Glover, the son of John P. and Rachel (Gray) Glover, died in September 1856 at the age of twenty-six.]

Dear Brother and Sister,

As Joseph has been confined and not able to write to his Cousin any longer and feeling anxious to hear from you all, I embrace this opportunity of writing you a few lines to let you know how we are. Dear Sister, time has roled along

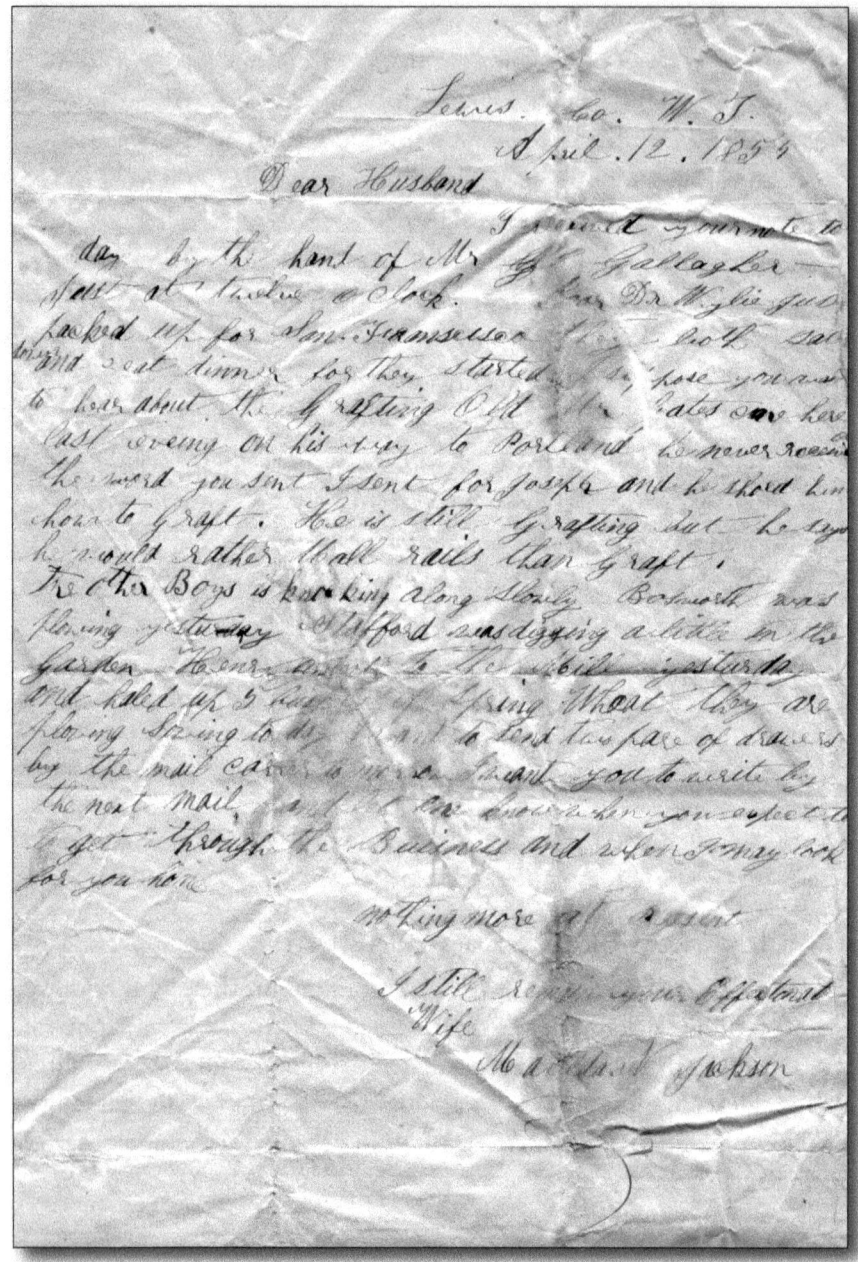

WASHINGTON STATE LIBRARY'S COLLECTION OF THE JACKSON, KOONTZ, GLOVER FAMILY PAPERS, 1837–1952.

This is the only letter preserved in Washington State Library archives written by Matilda (Glover) Koontz Jackson to her husband, John.

Chapter Seventeen: Indian Wars and Grievous Loss

and has brought with it not only the trials and scenes of affliction, but it has been the will of our Heavenly Father for a purpose known to Himself to remove from us by Death our dear little William. He died 1st day of September. The scenes of his sufferings was the most afflicting and heart rending trial J ever have had to pass through, and J can truly say that J rejoiced when it pleased God to take him out of his misery and felt perfectly resined to Heavenly Will and can say with Job the Lord giveth and the Lord taketh away and Blessed be the name of the Lord. He died in convulsion fits, J think his disease was caused by teething, Joseph kept able to walk about through the summer and fall until eight or nine weeks ago, he was taken down violent bad with pain in his breast and side and misery all over him, so that we thought every day would be his last. We set up with him constantly for over one month and we still have to be up with him at times to wait on him through the night. He is able when helped out of bed to sit in an armed rocking chair for 2 or 3 hours every day. His cough is very troublesome but don't complain of much severe pain. He seems to be very much oppressed when sleeping and often wakes up. His appetite is as good as might be expected. He has quit taking the Dr. medicine since he was taken down and is taking Cherry Pectoral. He thinks it has helped him but how long he will be permitted to remain with us is uncertain. He is in the hands of our Heavenly Father who is able to raise him up again if it is his gratious will, and if it is His will to remove him hence, J feel a hope from the evidence he has given us that the Lord has prepared him for that great and awful change.

Rachel is jenerly quite weakly though is mostly able to keep about. J am a good deal troubled with Rheumatism. This winter the rest of our family are all well. J have just recived a letter from Phillip. He said he had been to see William who was very bad off with kidney affection. The rest of them are all well.

> We have a three months school just commenced if your children are not going to school there, J would be very glad if Henry could come over and go to school here. J think you ough both to be willing to spare him that long as it will be for his good. Joseph wishes Mr. Jackson to take care of his property and do the best for him that he can. J shall conclude by saying that we have a great desire to see you once more this side of eternity and hope you will try to come and see us next summer. Be sure and write to us on the receipt of this. Rachel and Joseph joins me in love to you all. Give our respects to Joseph Mannen & wife and tell them we hope they will pardon us for not writing to them before now. Ask them to please write to us and let us know how they are getting along.
> J remain your affectionate Brother
> John P. Glover

Matilda's nephew, her brother Philip's son William Glover, who, with his wife, Jane, traveled the Oregon Trail with the Coonses, also sent a letter in 1855. They were living in Marion County in Oregon Territory.[15]

> Dear Aunt,
> J have delayed writing to you for several reasons. One is J have been expecting you to visit us for a year or more and another is no good opportunity of sending the letter. Howsomever, Mr. Powel call the other day and informed us that he had seen you and your family and that you were all well and doing well wich was gratifying news to us. He said that he would have a chance to send a letter to you and J happily avail myself of the opportunity of writing. Papa and family are all well and well pleased with the Country. Papa has settled on the place that we settle when we first came to the Country. He talks of coming to see you but there is such a difficult way of getting there J do not know whether any of us

Chapter Seventeen: Indian Wars and Grievous Loss

John Glover wrote this letter to his siblings January 8, 1855.

> Clackamas Co. O. T. Jan. 8th 1855
>
> Dear Bro & Sister As Joseph has been confined and not able to write to his Cousin any longer and feeling anxious to hear from you all, I embrace this opportunity of writing you a few lines to let you know how we are. Dear Sister time has rolled along and has brought with it not only the trial & scenes of affliction but it has been the will of our Heavenly Father for a purpose known to Himself to remove from us by death our dear little William he died 1st day of September. The scenes of his sufferings was the most afflicting and heart rending trial I ever have had to pass through, and I can truly say that I rejoiced when it pleased God to take him out of his misery and felt perfectly resigned to our Heavenly Will and can say with Job the Lord giveth and the Lord taketh away and Blessed be the name of the Lord. He died in Convulsion fits, I think his disease was caused by teething. Joseph kept able to walk about through the Summer and fall until 6 or 7 weeks ago he was taken down violent bad with pain in his breast & side and misery all over him so that we thought every day would be his last. We set up with him constantly for over a month and we still have to be up with him at times to wait on him through the night he is able when helped out of bed to sit in an armed rocking chair for 2 or 3 ours every day his cough is very troublesome but dont coplain of much severe pain he seems to be very much oppressed when sleeping and often wakes up his appetite is as good as might be expected he has quit taking the Dr. medicine... be sure and write to us on the receipt of this. Rachel & Joseph joins me in love to you all, Give our respects to Joseph Monnen & wife and tell them we hope they will pardon us for not writing to them before now ask them to please write to us and let us know how they are getting along. I remain your affectionate Brother &c
>
> John R. Glover

WASHINGTON STATE LIBRARY'S COLLECTION OF THE JACKSON, KOONTZ, GLOVER FAMILY PAPERS, 1837-1952.

will ever get there or not but we are all very anxious to come. The children have all grown very much. Brother Philip is larger than William. He is improving a claim eight miles from Papa. He is a promising youth indeed. Samuel and George are nearly grown. Samuel is just as good a boy as ever if not better. George is a steady industrious boy and such a house full of boys can't be [reared] up easy, not even in Oregon. Papa has been very busy improving. He has very comfortable buildings and will do well no dout if he keeps well. Mama is not so fleshy as she was when you saw her but she looks as young and is perter than I ever saw her. John and Maridad and children are well. They have only three. The youngest is a girl. She was born on the road. They call her Sarah Jane. She is a pretty little black eyed girl, I can assure you.

Uncle John Glover has located himself at the foot of the Mountains ware Mr. Foster's. They were all well the last I heard from them. I have not seen any of them since last harvest. Cousin James was up to see us then for the last time but we little thought so then. He was at work at Milwaukie last winter and was taken sick and walked home and died in a few days. He told his father he was willing to die. He was truly an amible young man. His death was regretted by all who knew him and Mary Glover was married last summer to a man by the name of Forrester. They live near her father's and are doing well. Uncle Philip Coons and family reach here last September. They lost there little girl on the road. They have three boys living. He has not taken a claim yet. He rented a farm in three miles of us last fall. He had a very hard spell of fever lately but they are all well at this time. He is not well pleased with the country so he sais.

Friend Turner and family starting here last spring, him and Mary Jane and Elizabeth died on the road. Joseph Gibson was with them and brought Mrs. Turner and her three children to Bardolph Gibson's who came through in forty nine. One of Mrs. Turner's children were sick when she landed there and Mrs. Gibson in her too little boys were taken sick and all three died in a week. So Mrs. Turner lives with her brother. She told me she went to see your Mother the Sunday before she left. She was quite smart and wished her to tell you to write to her without fail as she had a great wish to hear from you before she died. How you are pleased and soon. She had never heard whether you were married or not.

Dr. Wilmot Jessy Leheat and family and a great many more of our acquaintances came through last year. We have heard from Missouri as late as December. Our friends were all well then and a great many talking of coming here this year. There has been a great many marriages there and among them was David Evans to Polly Thornhill. We heard from Thomas Fine in California lately. He was married last spring to a very fine young lady. He has made a fortune there. He intends moving to this country as soon as he can come by land.

We live twelve miles from Papa. Me and Mariah live about the same distance apart as we did in Missouri. She wishes her best love to you and family. I have written all that I think would interest you. I must close by requesting you to write soon as your friends are more than anxious to receive a letter from you. Give my best respects to Uncle Jackson and the children and accept for yourself the best love and well wishes of your niece and nephew.

Jane and William Glover

1856 Military Road

As the Indian Wars wound down, the political battle over construction of the military road ensued. John Jackson wasn't happy when he learned that the surveyors planned to build the road from Monticello, following

William Glover, Matilda's nephew who crossed the trail with her in 1847, remained in close contact with her through the years.

WASHINGTON STATE LIBRARY'S COLLECTION OF THE JACKSON, KOONTZ, GLOVER FAMILY PAPERS, 1837–1952.

Chapter Seventeen: Indian Wars and Grievous Loss

the west side of the Cowlitz River, to St. Urban, Napavine, and Claquato. That meant the new road would completely bypass the Cowlitz Trail, along which the Jacksons had built their Highland home, inn, and eatery. He wrote a letter complaining about the proposed route, and J. Patton Anderson, the first territorial marshal, responded.

Anderson's letter of November 6, 1856, republished in *The Bee-Nugget*, was addressed to Captain John R. Jackson at the Highland Post Office.[16]

> Dear Captain: Your letter of the 21st September reached me yesterday at this place where I have been stopping with my family since the adjournment of congress.
>
> Your letter gives me the first intelligence that I have received in relation to any difficulty about the location of the military road from Vancouver to Steilacoom. I supposed when Gibbs had thoroughly reconnoitered the route, and had recommended the old road as the best and most practicable that there would be no more squabbling about it. It seems to me very plain that it will cost the government a good deal more to make the road by the Boistfort route than on the old one, inasmuch as the latter traverses an open level country nearly the entire distance from the landing to Steilacoom. Even if such was not the case, the report of the officer appointed to make the reconnaissance ought to be satisfactory on the point to the secretary of war, and such will no doubt be the case.
>
> At all events on my return to Washington City I shall lose no time in ascertaining what the war department intends to do about it and shall acquaint Col. Davis of all the particulars of the case. It seems to me very palpable that they make too many crossings of the Chehalis on the Boistfort route to insure anything like certainty of transportation in times of high water. But all of this shall be laid before Col. Davis and the true interest of the territory attended to.

We will leave here in a few days for Washington City. Mrs. Anderson desires to be remembered to Mrs. Jackson and the children. She says tell Andrew that he must be ready to teach her boy (now four months old) how to ride on horseback by the time we come out to Highlands again. He is a large, fine looking sprightly fellow and I hope will continue to enjoy his present good health.

We were much grieved to hear of the death of Judge Monroe. What a blow it will be to his old mother and his three little orphans.

Let me hear from you often.

Your friend and obedient servant,

J. Patton Anderson.

Chapter Eighteen
More Tragedy and Heartache

DURING THE LATE SUMMER OF 1856, Matilda received yet another letter from her nephew, William Glover. The letter was dated July 30, 1856, from Marion County in Oregon Territory.[1]

Dear Aunt

J embrace this opportunity to let you hear from me. J have no excuse to offer for not writing you before excep meanness and neglect. Letter writing has always been an uphill business to me, there fore J have not done much of it. Jett has written you several letters for which she has received no answers my dear Aunt J have been afflicted for the last nine or ten months there fore J have not felt much like doing much of any thing. J was taken down last fall with the inflammation of the kidneys and bladder and from that time to this J have not been able to do any thing except walk and set about the house. J have been under the care of as good a doctor as there is in the Territory during that time and he has not done but very little for me and J think it very doubtful whether J ever will get well and if it is God's will J never should J feel to say he has done all things well. J am made to believe some times that God for Christ sake has forgiven all my sins. My dear aunt let me say to you reflect about these things and endeavor to put your trust in him that above to save your soul. There is no happiness in this world and if you dy out of Christ you must be undone for ever. I professed religion one year ago last May. Joined the regular Baptist Church last June. Was baptized last Sunday and I can say of a truth there is great difference in severing the devel and trying to serve God. Religion should our thoughts engage amids our youthful bloom it will fit us for declining age and for the awful toumb. Father is very feeble this summer. He thinks his time is about at hand. Mother is as well as usual. Maria has five children. Philip has two. Brother Nicholas died last winter. Samuel has been in California four years. We look for him home this fall. George retuned from uncle John Glover's last week. Joseph was some better. We have not heard from Missouri for twelve months or more. Friend Magone is very near dead with the Bronkituz. He was taken sick in New York whilst visiting his people. Thomas Fine and family are well.

Jett joins me in love to you uncle and the children. I heard a few days that Henry was going to school below Oregon City near Mt. Durham. I hope he will come to see us before he returnz home. I want you to be sure to write to me. Direct your letters to Silverton.

No more but ever remain your affectionate nephew.
Wm Glover

Both William and his father, Philip, survived their ailments discussed in this letter. Philip died December 20, 1872, in Marion County, Oregon, at seventy-seven. William died August 23, 1892, in Marion County at the age of seventy.

Henry's Journal

Henry continued writing in his journal during 1855, starting with a Happy New Year's greeting January 1. He, Barton, and Jimmy hauled

Chapter Eighteen: More Tragedy and Heartache

potatoes and firewood on a cold January 2. When it snowed the next day, all hands threshed peas.

"I hauled Mrs. Montgomery to Cowlitz Landing," he wrote January 4.[2]

They threshed and fanned peas, but rested on a rainy and snowy Sabbath. They rested every week on the Sabbath.

Most of the notations simply spoke of their hard work—threshing rye, working at the barn, threshing and cleaning oats. They traveled to Mrs. Small's for oak timber. But then the notations disappeared in the middle of 1855.

Two years later, his little brother John wrote a note in Henry's diary. It said simply, "Goodbye John."

That's about the time when John lost yet another big brother. First he lost his father in 1847. Then Grundy died in 1855.

Henry, a hardworking teenager who rested only on the Sabbath, often retrieved his stepfather's horses from the Cowlitz Landing south of Toledo, where travelers had rented and returned them. On June 1, 1857, when the deep waters of the Cowlitz River flowed swiftly downstream, churning with snowmelt from the mountains, Henry crossed the river and drowned. He was only eighteen.

How did it happen? Did he fall off his horse? Did the horse struggle and plunge under water? Did he find himself caught in an undercurrent and dragged down? After his father's death in the Snake River, did the boys learn to swim? Would swimming skills help him in a fight against the strong current?

Henry was with two other men at the time.

The Pioneer and Democrat, an Olympia newspaper, published a notice of Henry's death and burial June 5, 1857.[3]

By drowning in the Cowlitz River, at the Cowlitz Landing, on Monday, June 1st, Henry M. Coonce, stepson of J.R. Jackson, aged about 18 years.

Oregon papers please copy:

The many virtues, industrious habits, manly deportment, and urbane manners, which were universally conceded as qualities possessed by the deceased, are the best eulogy and epitaph that could be inscribed to perpetuate the memory of the deceased. Alltho' so young, he had won the confidence and esteem of all who knew him:

"None knew him but to love him,
None named him but to praise."

We deeply sympathise with the relatives and friends of the deceased, and more particularly with his mother in their bereavement. To the latter will the blow be most severely felt, first in the loss of her husband, in the Snake River, in 1847, and now in the death of her oldest son. But she should bear with her afflictions, and bow in submission to the will and visitations of an all-wise Providence, for soon we, too, shall be numbered among the dead. Burdens and tribulations are not visited upon us, but with it the strength to support them. In the full hope then of a glorious resurrection, let her, as well as other relatives, find comfort and consolations.

Thus friend after friend departs, and we perform the last sad and solemn rites to the dead, only the more forcibly to admonish us to prepare for that death from which there is no escape, again to mingle with the dust from whence we came, and thence, as we hope, rejoin the kindred and friends who have preceded us in the realms of bliss and a happy eternity.

From: Pioneer and Democrat
Olympia, Washington Territory

After Henry drowned, his two companions knocked on the door of the Jackson home. Matilda answered, with four-year-old Louisa at her heels.

Upon hearing the heartbreaking news that her oldest son had drowned in the Cowlitz River, Matilda bid the men goodbye in a quiet voice. Louisa remembered her mother reached down to hold her hand.

"Come, Lulie, let us walk in the orchard," she said.[4]

They shuffled outside to the orchard, where Matilda gazed in silence at the majestic snow-covered peak serving as backdrop to the apple, cherry, and other fruit trees. She found comfort in her Bible, in the New Testament kept on a stand near the chimney corner, in the silence of the orchard.

Chapter Eighteen: More Tragedy and Heartache

DIED,

By drowning, in the Cowlitz river, at the Cowlitz Landing, on Monday, June 1st, HENRY M. COONCE, stepson of J. R. Jackson, aged about 18 years.

[Oregon papers please copy.]

The many virtues, industrious habits, manly deportment, and urbane manners, which were universally conceded as qualities possessed by the deceased, are the best eulogy and epitaph that could be inscribed to perpetuate the memory of the deceased. Altho' so young, he had won the confidence and esteem of all who knew him:

"None knew him but to love him,
None named him but to praise."

We deeply sympathise with the relatives and friends of the deceased, and more particularly with his mother, in their bereavement. To the latter will the blow be most severely felt, it being the second death in her family by a like fatality—first in the loss of her husband, in Snake river, in 1847, and now in the death of her oldest son. But she should bear with her afflictions, and bow in submission to the will and visitations of an all-wise Providence, for soon we, too, shall be numbered among the dead. Burdens and tribulations are not visited upon us, but with it the strength to support them. In the full hope then of a glorious resurrection, let her, as well as other relatives, find comfort and consolation.

Thus friend after friend departs, and we perform the last sad and solemn rites to the dead, only the more forcibly to admonish us to prepare for that death from which there is no escape, again to mingle with the dust from whence we came, and thence, as we hope, rejoin the kindred and friends who have preceded us in the realms of bliss and a happy eternity.

THE PIONEER AND DEMOCRAT, JUNE 5, 1857

The story about Henry Koontz's drowning in June 1857.

LEWIS COUNTY HISTORICAL MUSEUM

The headstone for Henry M. Koontz at the old Jackson Cemetery.

Louisa remembered the day because she never before had seen her mother cry.

Henry's death proved a hard blow for Matilda, according to her granddaughter, Anna Koontz. She stayed busy to keep her mind off the pain, spun and carded wool, knit socks, sewed, and cooked.

The crown of Henry's headstone was inscribed with the following words:

Henry M. Koontz
Died June 1, 1857
Age 18 Yr. 10 Mo.
Where Immortal Spirits Reign
There We Shall Meet Again

Chapter Nineteen

End of a Deadly Decade

AFTER THE PUGET SOUND AND YAKAMA INDIAN WARS ended, the Pacific Northwest settled into a peaceful coexistence between white settlers and natives in the late 1850s.

Oregon gained statehood February 14, 1859, the thirty-third state admitted to the Union of the United States. Its motto was "Alis Volat Propiis," translated as "She Flies with Her Own Wings." A prelude to the coming American Civil War occurred when abolitionist John Brown and a group of twenty men raided the arsenal at Harpers Ferry, West Virginia, October 16, 1859.

Matilda kept in touch with the man who saw her family safely across the Oregon Trail after the death of her husband, Nicholas. On July 4, 1850, Captain Magone had married Miss Mary Ann Tomlinson, a woman he met on the plains. She died nine years later. Magone fought in the Cayuse War that began after the massacre of Doctor Marcus and Narcissa Whitman and ended in 1855. He earned a promotion to major, and later traveled to California to work in the gold mines. He signed an Oath of Allegiance July 24, 1863, pledging his loyalty to the Union, which he fought for in the Civil War. Major Magone, who was awarded a certificate for his service June 29, 1867, earned a reputation for honesty: "If the Major said he did it, then he did it."[2]

Magone is said to have discovered a picturesque lake in Grant County in Eastern Oregon in 1880 and built a cabin there. Magone Lake is named in his honor. So is Magone Park in West Linn, Oregon.

In 1893, after construction of the railroad, Magone retraced his westward journey east from Canyon City, Oregon, to Chicago for the World's Fair. He returned to his native state of New York, where he died February 15, 1902, in Ogdensburg.

As for Matilda, she continued to offer gracious hospitality to all travelers, cooked, cleaned, gardened, sewed, and raised her younger children.

But she closed the decade of the 1850s with a heavier heart than ever. By then the mother of eight children had buried two sons and a daughter as well as her first husband.

Chapter Twenty

Life and a Girl's Diary

THE JACKSON FAMILY HIRED WORKERS to help in the fields, and several lived with them. During the 1860 census, the immediate family consisted of John, who was sixty; fifty-year-old Matilda; twenty-year-old Barton; fifteen-year-old John; ten-year-old Mary; nine-year-old Andrew; and Louisa, seven. But they also had others living in the household listed as laborers: John Brown, a twenty-three-year-old from Germany; and thirty-year-old Lewis Lerby, a laborer from the West Indies, and his eight-year-old son, Lewis Lerby Jr.[1]

Jackson was listed as a farmer with real estate valued at twelve thousand dollars and a personal estate worth ten thousand. The value of his estate in today's dollars would be about $621,262.

The family owned quite a bit of livestock, which Jackson recorded June 13, 1860.[2] He listed some of the cattle by name: Bald, Black Butte, Speck, Black Cutman cow, Lady Pink, Lucy, Old Seesaw, Gypsy, Flower, Nancy, Cherry, Spot, and Bows. The livestock included twenty-two cows, fifteen calves, twenty-two yearlings, and twenty-three two-year-olds, including Dandy Cow and Tinny. He had three oxen, three four-year-olds, four three-year-olds, and two bulls. He listed a yearling filly, two mares, four colts, four draft horses, a stud horse, and a mare with foal, plus five ewes and eight lambs, probably at the house. He also listed upward of a hundred head of sheep and forty head of hogs. His equipment included four sets of harnesses, three wagons, two reapers, a threshing machine, plows, harrows, and two fanning mills.

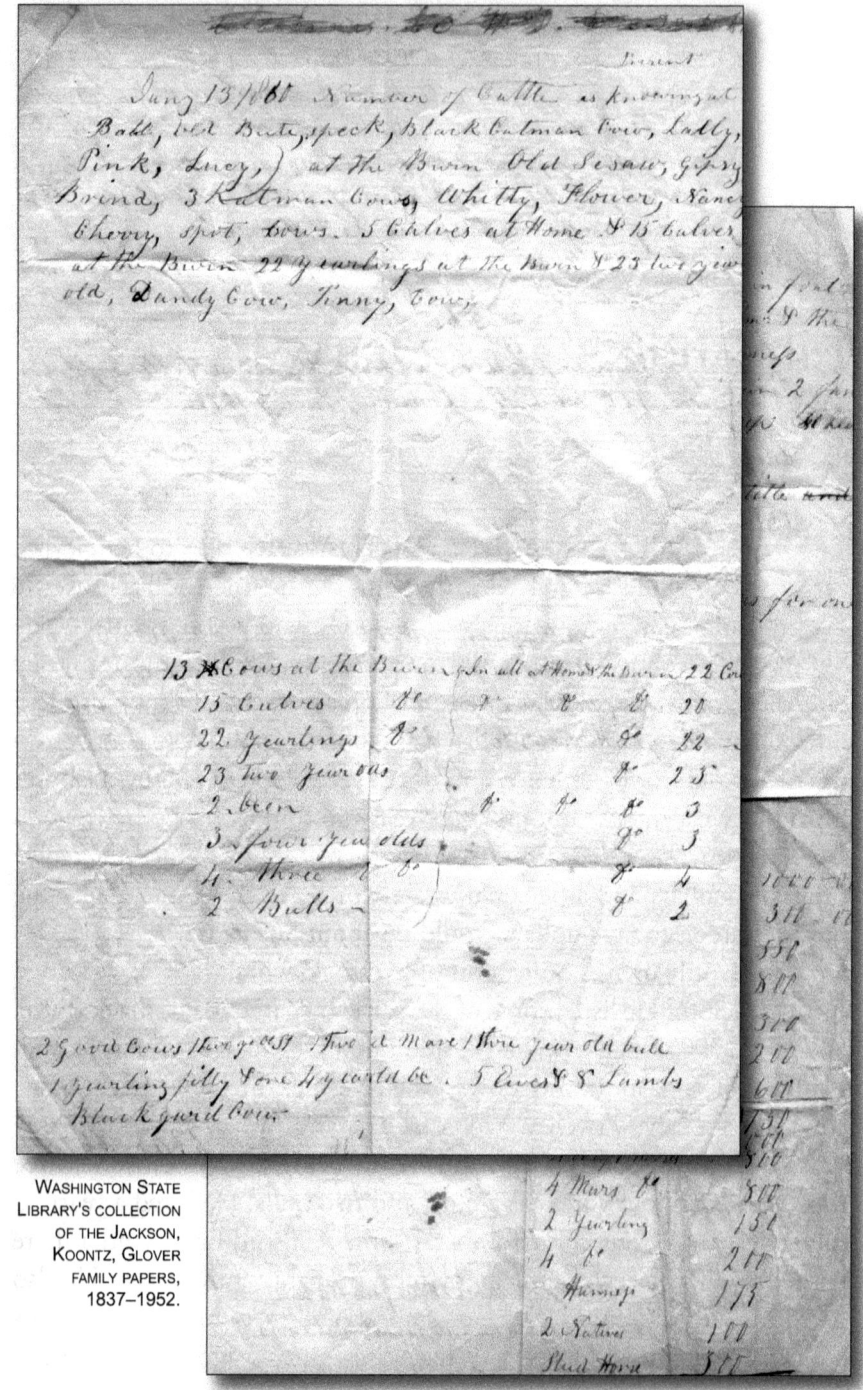

WASHINGTON STATE
LIBRARY'S COLLECTION
OF THE JACKSON,
KOONTZ, GLOVER
FAMILY PAPERS,
1837–1952.

An inventory of the cattle at the Jacksons' Highland Farms in 1860.

Chapter Twenty: Life and a Girl's Diary

WASHINGTON STATE LIBRARY'S COLLECTION OF THE JACKSON, KOONTZ, GLOVER FAMILY PAPERS, 1837–1952.

The United States Internal Revenue license granted in 1864 gives John R. Jackson the authority to operate a hotel at Highland in Lewis County.

Despite the decision to construct the Military Road to the west, the Jackson home continued to provide lodging most nights for travelers who passed by en route to Puget Sound during the 1860s.

In fact, John Jackson paid $3.22 to tax collector H.A. Goldsborough for a license to run a hotel at Highland in Washington Territory from September 1, 1863, to May 1, 1865. Philip D. Moore, an Internal Revenue Service collector in Olympia, granted a license to Jackson on July 1, 1864, to carry on the business of Hotel Keeper with rentals earning less than two hundred dollars a year. The new license expired May 1, 1865. Jackson paid a tax of $8.33 under "an act to provide internal revenue to support the government and to pay interest on the public debt."

One of the Jacksons' visitors, a man they knew well as the homesteader of Saundersville, which later became Chehalis, fell ill while traveling south on business. Schuyler S. Saunders died February 4, 1861,

LEWIS COUNTY HISTORICAL MUSEUM

After his death at Highland Farms, Schuyler Saunders was buried at the Jackson cemetery north of where the cabin is today.

at the Jackson farm. He was forty-seven.³ They buried him in the Jackson cemetery, which was north of the Highlands in a grove of trees near what later became North Prairie Road. Vandals later destroyed the headstones. He left his wife, Eliza, a widow with five children. She owned 320 acres of their homestead, ran the post office, and reluctantly sold parts of her land to pioneers. She also built a hotel, opera house, and Catholic Church in Chehalis.

The Jacksons' welcoming kindness backfired in 1861, after Matilda and John hosted a family with a sick child. They helped tend to the child, who recovered from diphtheria, a serious bacterial infection that attacks the mucous membranes of the nose and throat.

But within a few days, it became clear that the disease had spread inside the Jackson home when their ten-year-old son, Andrew, fell ill with a sore throat.⁴ Fever, swollen glands, and weakness followed, but the thick gray material blocked his airway.

Matilda tended her youngest boy as he gasped for breath. But all attempts to save him failed. He breathed his last February 27, 1861. The tall gray headstone marking the grave of ten-year-old Andrew M. Jackson at Fern Hill Cemetery in Chehalis contains this sentiment: "Safe and sheltered from sorrow."⁵

Grief engulfed Matilda. What wrenching heartache she must have felt as the dirt covered the grave of her third son, her fourth child to die. Matilda, who had just turned fifty-one, was left with only two of her sons with Nicholas—Barton and John—and the two daughters fathered by Jackson, Mary and Louisa.

Chapter Twenty: Life and a Girl's Diary

AUTHOR PHOTO

The headstone of Andrew Jackson, the ten-year-old son of John and Matilda Jackson, who died of diphtheria in 1861. He is buried at Fern Hill Cemetery south of Chehalis.

But she carried on. They all did. What choice did they have? It's likely she relied on her Christianity to help her through the pain. In testament to Matilda's faith, books tucked into the shelves at the Highlands included a Saunders School Reader, published in 1862; a Watson School Reader published in 1868; a McGuffey Fourth Reader from 1853; an 1824 Bible; an 1853 Bible; hymns from 1856; a Polyglott Bible from 1833; *The Rose and the Ring* by William Makepeace Thackery, published in 1855; and an 1843 Common Prayer Book.[1]

The winter of 1861 proved a cold one with snow two to three feet deep. The ground remained frozen until late February. The stage company that carried mail and passengers from Olympia to Pumphrey's Landing on the Cowlitz River and then by canoe to Monticello used four-horse bobsleds, according to J.B. Cutting, whose family settled in Napavine. The fare was fifteen dollars.[6] Many people who lacked feed for their animals lost their stock that winter, he said.

In May 1861, John received a bill from L.L. Dubeau & Co. for nine dollars that listed purchases since the first of the year.[7] It included a hat for Barton for two dollars, a ball of cotton for Andy at thirteen cents, rice and dried apples for A.B. Delling at seventy-five cents, another ball of goods for thirteen cents, an almanac for twenty-five cents, another two dollar hat for Barton, seven yards of bleached cotton at $1.75, three-quarters of a dozen screws for sixty-three cents, a dozen screws for twelve cents, two candles for a dollar, and other items.

The Jacksons also sold food from their farm to Dubeau to peddle in his store on Cowlitz Prairie.

Dubeau, a Canadian, moved to Cowlitz Prairie in the 1850s and operated Chappellier & Daulne's mercantile business, which he later purchased. He served as county commissioner, postmaster, stage agent, justice of the peace, and sheriff. In 1863, he married Isabel Cottonier, one of Simon Plamondon's descendants, and they had fifteen children.[8]

A stickler for paperwork, Jackson had requested information about his property. At the end of 1861, he received a letter from the Surveyor General's Office in Olympia, Washington Territory, dated December 18, 1861.[9]

> Dear Sir,
> In accordance with your request, I herewith send you a plat of your donation claim. I have calculated the

Chapter Twenty: Life and a Girl's Diary

acre of each fractional track and marked them with red ink. I have also given the distance of all the intersections … and mark it in every respect correct, which I suppose is what you wanted. Please acknowledge its receipt by return mail.

I have not yet received that piece of Bacon.

My kind regards to Mrs. Jackson and family

Respectfully

E. Giddings C.C.

In addition to their hotel, the Jacksons continued to operate the Highland Post Office from their home. In a letter dated December 10, 1862, the third assistant postmaster general stated: "Sir: You are required within two days after the close of each quarter to forward your Quarterly Account to this Department; or, if there be no mail from your office within that time, then by the next mail. The quarters end on the 31st March, 30th June, 30th September, and 31st December."[10]

The letter continued with directions on how to keep the accounts of Mail Sent and Mail Received up-to-date so it was ready to forward within a few hours.

In January 1862, under an act passed by the Legislative Assembly of the Territory of Washington, the Lewis County seat officially shifted to Claquato, three miles west of Saundersville, which later became Chehalis. The act outlined that the

LEWIS COUNTY HISTORICAL MUSEUM

In 1862 the Lewis County seat was officially moved to the courthouse in Claquato, above, built by Lewis H. Davis.

county seat would be located on the land claim of Lewis H. Davis, who donated land and materials to build a two-story courthouse large enough for court sessions with separate offices for the sheriff and county auditor. Deadline for completing the building was January 1, 1865. The county seat remained there until an act of the Legislature passed November 11, 1873, shifted it the following summer to Chehalis, through which the Northern Pacific Railroad passed.

While no longer hosting the Lewis County court, John Jackson continued as postmaster. A pay stub from February 25, 1863, shows that Postmaster John R. Jackson provided Sheriff Javan Hall with thirteen dollars for taxes.[12]

Other correspondence saved for more than a century includes a note from W.W. Miller to his friend Jackson dated September 10, 1863.[13]

> Dear Esquire,
> I left my cane in your waggon this morning, and you have probably taken it home. Will you please send it to me by the first waggon coming this way. Mason gave to me and I therefore prize it very highly.
> Don't forget to send it.

In January 1864, Mary, who was away at school in Olympia, wrote a newsy letter to her younger sister, Louisa.[14]

> Dear Sister Lou—
> This pleasant Sabbath morning in Mrs. Giddings dinning room, sitting in Mr. [Edward] Giddings' big arm chair by the stove with pen and paper in my lap, not a very pleasant way to write. I spose you'll think the folks have all gone to Church except myself and thought I would not go this morning as Mr. Whitworth is absent and Mr. Elder preaches he preached on last Sunday and we had such a poor sermon. I do hope that Mr. Whitworth will be back by next Sunday. I think he is such a good man, an English man of course. Last evening we saw a

Chapter Twenty: Life and a Girl's Diary

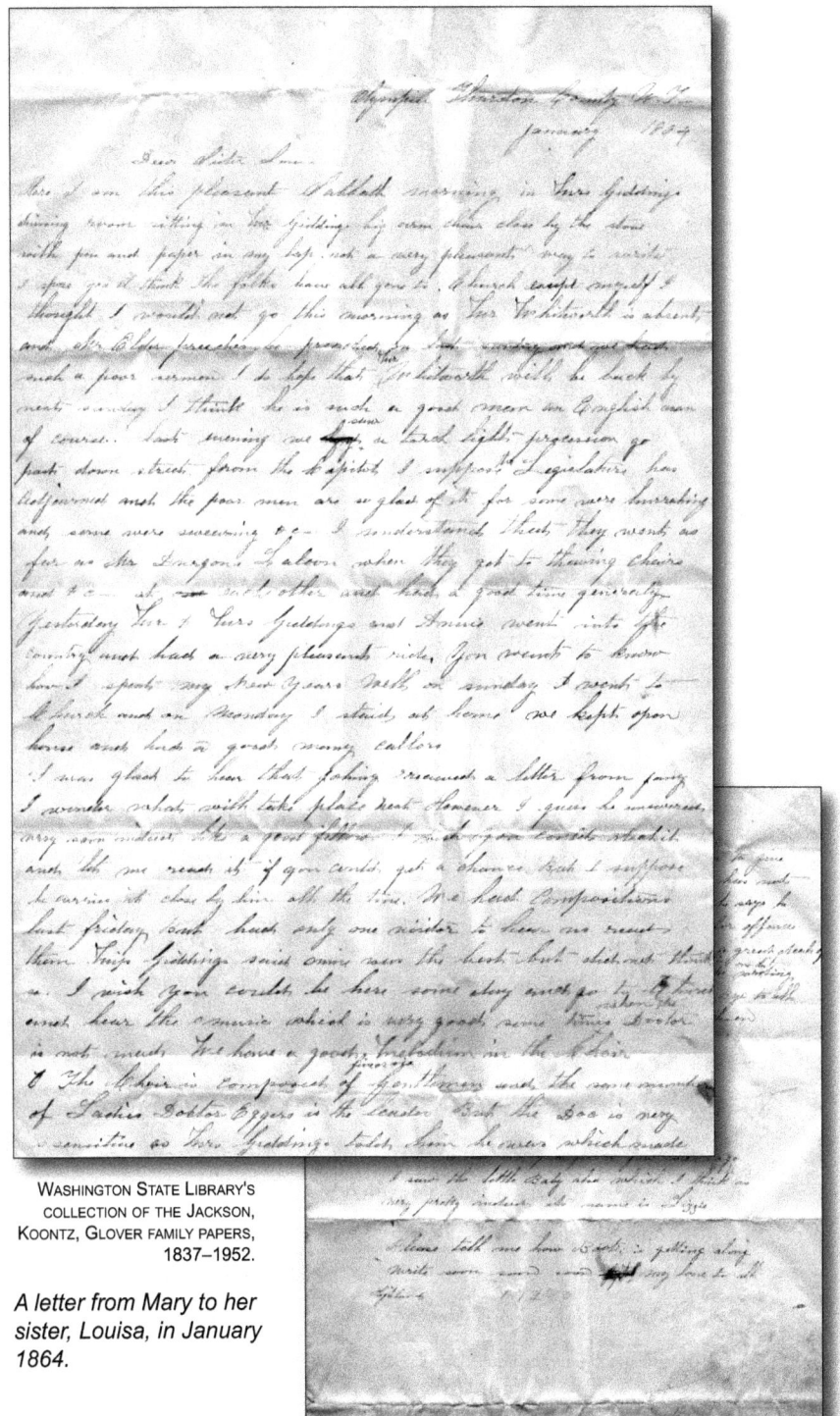

WASHINGTON STATE LIBRARY'S COLLECTION OF THE JACKSON, KOONTZ, GLOVER FAMILY PAPERS, 1837–1952.

A letter from Mary to her sister, Louisa, in January 1864.

torch light procession go past—down street—from the Capitol. I suppose the Legislature has adjourned and the poor men are so glad of it for some were hurrahing and some were swearing and as I understand that they went as far as Mr. Durgons Saloon when they got to throwing chairs and [to cuss] at each other and had a good time generally yesterday. Mr. and Mrs. Giddings and Annie went into the country and had a very pleasant ride. You wanted to know how I spent my New Years. Well on Sunday I went to Church and on Monday I staid at home. We kept open house and had a good many callers.

I was glad to hear that [brother] Johnny received a letter from [Jamy].

I wonder what will take place next. However I guess he answered very soon indeed like a good fellow. I wish you could steal it and let me read it. If you could get a chance. But I suppose he carries it close by him all the time. We had compositions last Friday. But had only one visitor to hear us read them. Mrs. Giddings said mine was the best, but did not think so. I wish you could be here some day [and] go to church and hear the music, which is very good some times when the Doctor is not much. We have a good Melodium in the choir and the choir is composed of fine old gentlemen and the same number of Ladies. Doctor Eggers is the leader. But the Doc is very sensitive as Mrs. Giddings told him he was which made him very angry and he will not come to give Annie or I our music lessons any more and has not for four or five weeks past. I am sorry but he says he won't come until Mrs. Giddings asks his pardon for offences poor man! Mrs. Giddings says he thinks a great deal of me but I don't believe he does. I am sure I don't like him one bit. Must stop writing and go and [light] a fire in the parlor. So good Bye to all

Ever ever your Affectionate Sister Mary Jackson

Chapter Twenty: Life and a Girl's Diary

> P.S. I saw Mr. Gangloff a few days ago. He inquires about you all. I went to see Mrs. Grainger a few weeks ago. I saw the little Baby also which I think is very pretty indeed. Its name is Lizzie.
>
> Please tell me how Bootie is getting along.
>
> Write soon soon soon. My love to all

Mary's friend Ann Judson mailed a letter filled with news and gossip March 18 from Beaver in Washington Territory, although the year is missing.[15] Some of the writing is hard to decipher and the letter refers to mutual friends.

In 1864, one of the visitors to the Jackson house was William West, who became known as the father of Chehalis. He arrived at Monticello near present-day Longview and traveled north. During his stop for dinner at the Jacksons, he and John enjoyed visiting about Scotland, a country both knew well.[16] West was born in England, not far from where Jackson had lived. Scotsmen who pioneered in Lewis County were the Urquharts and MacDonalds.

PHOTO FROM *THE CHEHALIS BEE-NUGGET*

William West, known as the father of Chehalis, visited the Jacksons when he arrived in Lewis County in the 1860s.

French Canadians also populated the region, many of whom started as employees of the Hudson's Bay Company. Other French-Canadians moved south as the Oregon Trail opened the land to settlement. Among the French Canadians were the Chappelliers, Pintos, Henriots, Sareaults, Connaires, Bouchards, and L.L. Dubeau. American settlers included the Howes, Spencers, Russells, and Halls.

A telegraph line between Portland and Olympia was completed the afternoon of September 4, 1864, with the first telegraphic notice sent the following day from Washington Territorial Governor William Pickering to President Abraham Lincoln.[17] The following day, September 6, Lincoln acknowledged "your patriotic dispatch of yesterday" and noted it would be published.

A change came to the Highland in late 1864, when Jackson received a letter dated December 5 telling him to merge his home post office with the Cowlitz Post Office, which was nearby at the Cowlitz Landing. He had operated the Highland Post Office for a decade.

On December 9, 1864, President Abraham Lincoln signed a land patent giving Jackson public lands he purchased for himself and his heirs. Little did they know the tall, lanky man who served as the nation's sixteenth president would be assassinated only five months later on April 14, 1865.

While the Civil War divided the northern and southern states in the east, pioneers in the West remained relatively untouched by the War Between the States. The states of Oregon and California sided with the Union, and regular Army troops traveled east to join the fight. But the people who lived in the Northwest paid close attention to the happenings across the country.

When she was almost twelve, Louisa Matilda Jackson noted in her calico-covered diary the assassination of President Abraham Lincoln.

"We hear the report of Lincoln's death," she wrote April 18.[18] "He was shot, died last Saturday night at eight, and Mr. Seward is not expected to live." Seward, who served as Lincoln's Secretary of State, was wounded in an attack at his home, but he survived.

John Jackson had encouraged his children to keep diaries. In letters he had urged Matilda to remind Grundy to keep his journal, and his youngest daughter also faithfully filled in her diary throughout 1865. The handwritten diary has been preserved in the Jackson-Koontz-Glover Collection at the Washington State Library in Tumwater. In May 2004, Serene A. Johnson and Karen L. Johnson transcribed the diary, complete with its phonetic spellings and lack of punctuation, and provided annotations about pioneers mentioned within its pages.

"Every other page has an embossed crest in the upper left corner, evidence of stationery of good quality," the Johnsons wrote.[19] "The calico fabric, though somewhat faded and stained, still retains its squiggles on a dark blue background."

In her diary, Louisa mentions the weather each day—snowy, rainy, showery, fair, storming, cloudy, foggy, cold, windy, or pleasant. She primarily describes the work done outside by her half-brothers Barton and John, as well as day laborers she referred to as Mr. Orton (perhaps Nathan Orton who later settled on Delameter Creek in Cowlitz County), Mr. Ledo (perhaps Louis LaDue, who lived east of the Jacksons), Mr. Moses, Mr. Clair, Mr. Miller, and Tom, a Cowlitz Indian. The diary provides a glimpse into the hardworking lifestyles of early pioneers.

They built sheds, hauled rails, fixed fences, and thrashed wheat, oats, and peas. They boiled mash for pig slop, shoed horses, hooped barrels, sorted apples, pulled and hauled turnips, and dug potatoes. They cut oak for spokes and timber for wagon wheel rims and cut, split, and hauled cedar. They shaved boards for timber, cut and hauled firewood, and sharpened plows. They built doors, stairs, gates, small troughs, a wheelbarrow, a bedstead, and a doubletree wagon axle. They fixed buggy beds. They sealed the front porch, repaired the telegraph line, and cleaned the barn. They washed, greased, mended, and fixed harnesses. They killed hogs and cut them up, chopped and stuffed sausage, and hung up meat. They hauled manure, drove cattle, and rounded up lost lambs and stray heifers. They plowed and harrowed fields, planted peas and sowed seeds, and sacked potatoes. They trimmed fruit trees in the orchard, staked the grapevine, and hauled loads of ash.

They planted and covered pea seeds, grubbed out stumps, sheared sheep, cut brush and logs, sowed white turnips among the corn, built one shed, tore down another, and replaced a roof on yet another, worked in the milk room, fixed the roads, hauled shavings from the woodshed, crafted a breadboard, built wagon racks, mowed the yard and field, hunted horses and stray cattle, repaired machinery, raked hay, washed and painted the buggy, cut and bound wheat, shocked oats, and thrashed peas.

Reading the diary, it's understandable why Matilda's brother a decade earlier had complained that John Jackson worked his stepsons too hard.

They rested only on the Sabbath each week, although occasionally some of them would visit neighbors.

Occasionally Louisa would note that one of her brothers had "done one thing & nother" or they or the hired man were "musing away at something," which could mean tinkering on some project or even daydreaming.

The diary also shows that John Jackson relied on his stepsons and hired help to run the farm while he kept the books for the farm and the hotel. Louisa told an interviewer in 1922 that she accompanied her father outdoors more often after the death of her brother, Andrew. She joined him as he herded horses and cattle. Later he rode in a two-horse buggy because of his rheumatism.

Louisa seldom mentions her mother, perhaps thinking the daily household chores of a woman baking bread, churning butter, washing clothes, cooking, sewing, cleaning, and caring for the family not as noteworthy. Years later, during a newspaper interview, she described her mother as "a wonderful worker."[20] Sometimes a hired man helped with the cooking, including one named Gus Gangloff, and according to Edward Yates, who worked on the farm in the early 1850s, John helped out around the house. But everyday tasks required much effort in the 1860s when water had to be drawn from a well, clothes and dishes washed by hand, and floors scrubbed on hands and knees.

On January 5, Louisa wrote that she and Ma washed, while Barton headed to Claquato for Mr. Lewis H. Davis's mill but his wagon broke down, so Mr. Orton and "Johny" helped with repairs all day. Again on January 21, while John and Bart fanned oats, she mentions that "Ma and I scrubed today."

Beyond that, her only references to Matilda were July 8, when she noted that Mr. Orton "went away," Barton and John "cut a road to the creek," and "Pa & Ma & Mrs. Jackson went to Mr. Robertses."

On September 16, she said her parents started to Mr. Manning's, and that Mr. and Mrs. Decker came and three men stayed all night. The following day John and Matilda returned home, the same day that Andrew and Ellen Urquhart visited. They were children of James and Ellen Urquhart, Scottish immigrants, whose other children included Margaret, John, James, William, Alee, Robb, Noble, and David.

The following month, on October 11, she noted that "Pa & Ma started to Claquato," and they returned the next night, October 12, when Mr. Yantis stayed overnight.

Chapter Twenty: Life and a Girl's Diary

WASHINGTON STATE LIBRARY'S COLLECTION OF THE JACKSON, KOONTZ, GLOVER FAMILY PAPERS, 1837–1952.

Louisa (Jackson) Ware, left, with her niece, Anna Koontz, in the 1920s.

That's it for references to Matilda, the gracious hostess who kept the Jackson home running, greeted and fed visitors, changed bedsheets, sewed clothes, carded wool, and cared for her family.

But Louisa did mention, often by name, the frequent visitors who stayed the night at their place.

A stage run by Englishman Charles Grainger of Olympia, who executed Chief Leschi and described him as an innocent man, often stopped at the Jacksons with passengers on the way from the capitol city to Monticello on the Columbia River near present-day Longview.

Louisa also mentioned when people stopped for dinner.

On February 5, John stayed home and answered a letter from someone named Jane, while Louisa's brothers searched for lost lambs and stray cattle. Louisa occasionally wrote about the birth of new lambs and the death of others. Her brothers killed four hogs one day, she wrote.

On January 12, she noted visits by Thomas Pearson, a New York wagonmaker referred to as a "squatter" on Cowlitz Farm property by former Hudson's Bay Company manager George Roberts, and his family. The grownups traveled to the Skookumchuck for a benefit ball to raise money for wounded Union soldiers.[21] The relief effort raised one hundred and sixty-five dollars for the soldiers' care. Their daughter Mary remained at the Jacksons with Louisa.

Louisa received a letter from her sister Mary February 1 and responded right away. She noted trips to Cowlitz Landing by her father, her brothers, and even herself when she joined her pa. Men visited the Jacksons to purchase beef cattle and sheep, bushels of oats and wheat and potatoes, and pounds of bacon and lard. They hauled large quantities of food to the Cowlitz Landing where it could be sold. People also stopped to purchase coal.

The hired man fell sick in mid-February and didn't work for several days. When he felt better, he worked upstairs indoors. Bart, who had driven colts home from Newaukum February 11, thrashed while John crafted a wooden maul and later a butter knife handle. Louisa noted on a showery February 13 that "the horse doctor passed."[22]

Mary returned home from Olympia February 24, fetched by John in the buggy. He and Barton drove cattle later. Barton and John were joined by hired hands at times, including Louis Ledo (LaDue) and Mr. Orton.

Chapter Twenty: Life and a Girl's Diary

Louisa mentioned March 10 that John Rubin of Castle Rock told her father he'd pay only fifty cents per bushel of oats. Seven days later, she wrote that Mr. Ledo, most likely Louis LaDue, purchased a bushel of wheat, two dollars' worth of flour, and fifty cents worth of pork. Mr. Ensine's man bought three pounds of bacon and thirty-three pounds of butter August 9, and another three pounds of butter August 15.

Jackson visited Cowlitz Landing March 25, perhaps to elect delegates to the Democratic Territorial Convention in Olympia in April, the Johnsons wrote.

Louisa spoke about accompanying her father to Newaukum on a wet April 3 to get colts. Her father, Barton, and John butchered a beef.

On April 4, Jackson attended a meeting at the home of Judge O.B. McFadden in Saundersville, which is a home that still stands in modern-day Chehalis, to discuss construction of a plank road from Skookumchuck near present-day Centralia through soggy Saunders Bottom to the Cowlitz Landing at today's Toledo. *The Washington Democrat* in Olympia January 7, 1865, reported on incorporation of a company to build the road from planks, stone, gravel, or some other material. The report said no one disputed the need for it. Among the company's commissioners were Jackson, McFadden, Marcel Bernier, Marcell Chappellier (who owned a store and sawmill on Cowlitz Prairie), A.B. Dillenbaugh, Sidney S. Ford Sr., Wesley B. Gosnell, John McIlroy, Henry Miles, James T. Phillips, Henry Winsor, and Timothy R. Winston.

In April, Louisa reported the sighting of what she called "a panther," but it was likely a cougar or mountain lion. However, the men didn't kill it.

She also worked alongside her brothers at times. On May 9, Louisa wrote, "Barton and I planting peas. John and Mary planting corn and beans." She wrote that one man stopped at their place overnight.

Only once is a birthday party mentioned, not on May 11 when Louisa turned twelve but rather October 3, when Marcel and Cecelia Bernier gave a party to honor daughter Frances, who was thirteen or fourteen.

On May 21, Louisa wrote that Mr. Urquhart, Mr. Bernier, and Mr. Hennessey stopped by to discuss a school at Newaukum. She, John, and Mary attended the school at the George Roberts home, taught by law student Daniel Dodge. Later, Patrick Hennessey, a fifty-four-year-old Irishman, taught in the second school on the prairie, Louisa said

Dr. John R. Jackson P.M. "Highland" Washington Ty, in a/c with the U.S. Cr.

To Balance due on a/c Sents	8 68	June 30 56	By Balance on a/c Sents		96
" Quarterly Returns from		2 qr 57	" Amt. paid Henry Gray		2 50
Jan 1 to Mar 31 56	.. 12	Apl 27 58	" "	Do	2 87
Apl 1 " June 30	" See [illegible]	2 qr "	" "	Do	1.25
July 1 " Sept 30	" due no Stps	4 " "	" "	H Wilson	75
Oct 1 " Dec 31	" 6 57	2 " 59	" "	Do	55
Jan 1 " Mar 31 57	2 25	4 " "	" "	Do	50
Apl 1 " June 30	" due no Stps	1 " 61	" "	Do	37
July 1 " Sept 30	" " "	2 " "	" "	Do	25
Oct 1 " Dec 31	" 1 54	4 " 62	" "	Do	75
Jan 1 " Mar 31 58 due		2 " "	" "	Do	50
Apl 1 " June 30	" due no Stps	" " "	" "	Do	25
July 1 " Sept 30	" "	Apl 8 63	" "	F Chable	75
Oct 1 " Dec 31	" "	July 13 "	" "	Do	25
Jan 1 " Mar 31 59	"	June 2 64	" "	Do	25
Apl 1 " June 30	" " no Stps	Oct 20 "	" "	Do	50
July 1 " Sept 30	" " "	Feb 2. 65	" "	Do	25
Apl 1 " June 30	" "				
July 1 " Sept 30	" "				
Oct 1 " Dec 31	" "				
Jan 1 " Mar 31 62	"				
Apl 1 " June 30	" " no Stps				
July 1 " Sept 30	" "				
Oct 1 " Dec 31	" "				
Jan 1 " Mar 31 63	"				
Apl 1 " June 30	" " no Stps				
July 1 " Sept 30	" "				
Oct 1 " Dec 31	" "				
Jan 1 " Mar 31 64	"				
Apl 1 " June 30	" " no Stps				
July 1 " Sept 30	" "				
Oct 1 " Dec 5	" " no Stps				
May 15 65 " Stamps Sent 2 qr 65	9 00				
	$28 10				$28 10
To Balance	$14 60				

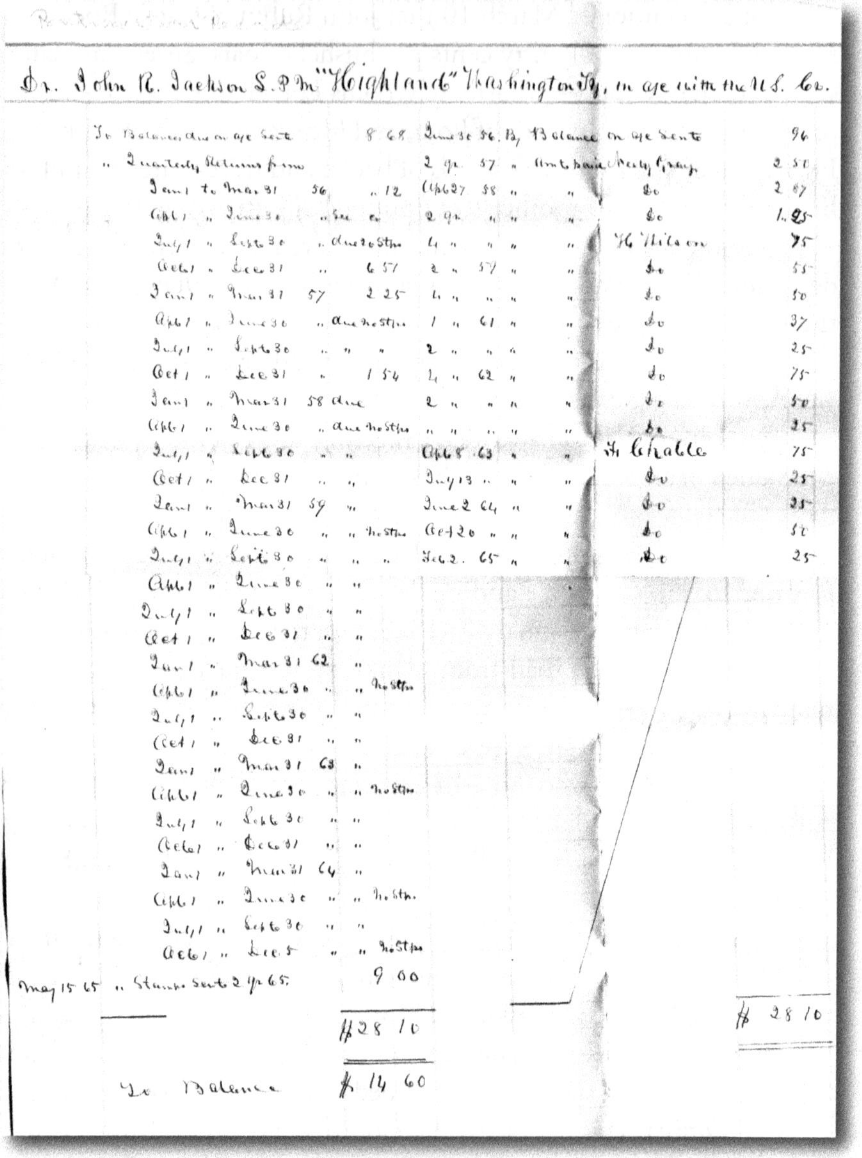

WASHINGTON STATE LIBRARY'S COLLECTION OF THE JACKSON, KOONTZ, GLOVER FAMILY PAPERS, 1837–1952.

John R. Jackson kept meticulous records as Highland postmaster, as seen above in 1865.

during a 1922 interview.²³ She and John began attending the school May 29, and Mary joined them the next day and on a few other occasions. But for the most part, only John and Louisa attended school until the term ended July 30, which is when they retrieved their books from the schoolhouse.

Barton and his stepfather left for Olympia May 25, hauling thirteen bushels of wheat and ninety-four fleeces of wool. They returned three days later on the Sabbath.

Jackson, Barton, and John, accompanied by Mr. Orton, traveled to the Cowlitz Landing June 5 to elect local officials—county commissioner, sheriff, auditor, surveyor, and coroner.

Later in the month, Jackson took Mary with him to Olympia in the buggy, leaving June 19 and returning four days later. A peddler passed by the next day.

Mr. Tucker and his family spent the pleasant Sabbath of June 25 overnight at the Jacksons. Another Sabbath they hosted the Tuckers, the Laytons, the MacDonalds, the Lanes, and the Hennesseys.

On June 26, Mr. Orton took the loft out of the kitchen and sealed it, and later in the month he fixed the pantry.

Louisa noted the holidays—Independence Day, Christmas, the New Year—and special events like a wedding and the end of the school term. On the Fourth of July, Louisa mentioned that they raised the flag to honor the nation's independence.

Soldiers from Fort Steilacoom camped at the Jacksons July 6, the same day Louisa wrote that one of the lambs broke its leg. On July 8, Barton and John cut a road to the creek while Louisa's parents visited the George Roberts family. On July 10, Barton and John hauled 37½ bushels of wheat to Olympia. They returned three days later. Mr. Bernier bought 25½ pounds of bacon July 21 but still needed to pay for it. John H. Foster bought sixteen pounds of salt from them August 21. Mr. Foster bought four pounds of butter September 2.

Even in the 1860s, competition for labor proved fierce. On July 25, Louisa wrote that Barton and Mr. Green raked and hauled hay while John and Mr. Jones mowed, but a man named Peter Smith passed by and mentioned to the workhands they could earn higher wages at another farm. Both Green and Jones left the following day, leaving Barton to rake and John to mow.

On July 28, James Urquhart stopped by with tickets, or invitations, to his daughter Margaret's wedding to John Alexander, who had settled in Washington Territory in 1858. Barton, John, Mary, and Louisa attended the wedding of John and Margaret (Urquhart) Alexander, a ceremony performed on a pleasant August 1 by J.D. Clinger, justice of the peace. "We had a very nice time and good dinner," Louisa wrote.[24]

On August 6, Mary and John bought eighty-three pounds of beef from Marcel Bernier. The following day, Barton propped up apple trees while John mended harnesses. Afterward, they went to some sort of a performance at the Cowlitz.

As the harvest ended, the men had bound and shocked eight acres of wheat and twenty-two acres of oats. They paid a Mr. Clair twenty dollars for his work August 27. He went home but returned to continue assisting on the farm. Clair also helped fan up wheat, while Mr. Miller picked up a cradle at Marcel Bernier's and John installed window glass. Clair made stirrups and left September 4. They paid Miller nine dollars.

On August 22, John Jackson, accompanied by Simon Plamondon and Henry Miles, left for Victoria in British Columbia to testify at the Hearings of the British and American Joint Commission, which was seeking to determine compensation for the Hudson's Bay Company for its property losses after the U.S.-Canadian boundaries were settled in 1846. The three old-time settlers, as well as Michael T. Simmons, founder of Tumwater, were asked to estimate the value of the Hudson's Bay Company's land that became the property of the United States. They returned to Lewis County September 3. But George Roberts, who had managed the company's Cowlitz Farm, didn't return home until September 24.

Louisa also shared sad news, but in a matter-of-fact manner.

"We heard that Mr. MacDonald's youngest girl died this morning," Louisa wrote September 10. Karen and Serene Johnson, in annotations to their transcription of Louisa's diary, noted that Martha Harriet MacDonald, the daughter of John M. and Mary J. MacDonald, was two years and twenty-five days old when she died.[25]

In mid-September, Barton and John built a cider mill and made cider. John made ten gallons of cider September 21 for Mr. Dubeau. The following day, John Jackson took pears, apples, and cider to the Cowlitz Landing.

Chapter Twenty: Life and a Girl's Diary

About that time, John and Matilda visited Mr. Manning and returned the following day.

They finished harvesting for the season September 19 and spent the rest of the day binding and hauling oats. The Jacksons hired two of Marcel Bernier's boys, Peter and Frank, to work on the farm hauling in and setting out oats. They left to spend the Sabbath October 1 at home but returned the next day. Louisa also helped with the harvest hauling in wagons of oats. They finished the harvest October 2.

After shoeing a horse October 5, Barton and John hauled thirty-eight bushels of wheat and three dozen chickens to Olympia. They "got home all safe" October 8.

Barton hauled manure and his brother John gathered apples and pressed cider. John and four Indians dug potatoes October 16 and 17. Barton and John gathered apples, plowed, and ground apples for cider. Sometimes they worked on the road that passed by their homestead.

On October 11, John and Matilda left for Claquato, returning the following day, and on October 22, Mr. James, Johny, Mary, and Louisa visited Mr. Roberts. On November 3, John Jackson, Barton, and John attended a school meeting at Marcel Bernier's.

On November 1, Barton sowed and plowed while John harrowed. Barton cut cabbages while John and Louisa made apple butter.

Some days the men butchered beef and often sold it to neighbors such as Mr. Gosnell and Marcel Bernier, who received eighty-seven pounds in mid-November. John stayed overnight at the Berniers, and the next day, Barton arrived for a sheep.

He and John hauled out straw. Barton thrashed and John separated the colts November 22, and the next day he got the hogs up. On November 27, Barton threshed and John boiled cider.

December 1 brought snow showers. "Pa and John went to mill," Louisa wrote. "George Roberts come and got two sheep."

Barton and John fanned twenty-two bushels of wheat, which John and his stepfather hauled to the mill a few days later. Then they hauled another seventeen bushels of wheat to the mill the next day.

John, Barton and three Indians finished digging potatoes December 9. Three days later, John boiled hog food, and the next day he fixed a shed while Barton and Tom fanned wheat. The two brothers thrashed and fanned oats for a few days. On a cloudy December 17, they put up eight beef and thrashed. As the weather grew worse, Louisa wrote December 20 "they are not doing much." But with snow two inches deep, Barton and Tom thrashed and John fixed a shed and boiled food.

"I wish all a merry Crismas & a happy New year," Louisa wrote December 25.

Two days later, snow about six inches deep didn't prevent Barton from thrashing oats, John from boiling food, and Louisa and her father from traveling to the Cowlitz.

They killed two hogs December 29, thrashed and boiled food, and the next day, fanned a hundred bushels of oats.

On December 31, a snowy Sabbath, Barton went to the Cowlitz. Louisa closed her 1865 diary with these lines:[26]

> The year is past and gone
> How quickly it has fled
> And never to return
> And no one knows
> How soon we'll be numbered
> With the dead
>
> When this you see remember me
> Louisa M Jackson

By 1865, John Jackson had acquired 2,200 acres of land. He bred and trained horses. He had served as a territorial legislator and operated a freight line between Tumwater and the Cowlitz River.

During one winter in the mid-1860s, Barton Coonse recalled that Indian squaws who lived near Ethel trudged through deep snow to the Jacksons' home begging for provisions. He gave them all the oats they could carry.

The winter of 1867 saw the Cowlitz River overflow its banks and wash away buildings at Cowlitz Landing, but by then much of the commercial activity had moved north a mile toward what later became Toledo. However, in the 1860s and 1870s, the community was simply referred to as Cowlitz.

Paperwork for a legal transaction, preserved at the Washington State Library, shows that on December 29, 1866, John Jackson paid $750 to Horace H. Pinto for land in the Joseph St. Germain claim.[27]

Witnesses were George B. Roberts and C.C. Pagett, and L.L. Dubeau notarized it. A warranty deed from Pinto to Jackson was received January 30, 1867, by the deputy auditor, J.D. Clinger.

Barton "Coontz" received official notice May 23, 1867, that he had been appointed supervisor of Road District No. 4 for the year.[28] He was twenty-seven when he signed a paper solemnly swearing to the county auditor that he would support the United States constitution and laws of the territory and faithfully discharge his duties. He earned payment of four dollars for his services, according to a receipt.

His paperwork lists the names of local property owners, the value of their property, and the amount of road tax. John R. Jackson owned the highest valued property, followed by Marcel Bernier, Edward Yates, Mrs. Mary Moore, A.B. Dillenbaugh, Erastus Garrison, and Julien Bernier (Marcel's father). Other owners without a property value listed were brothers Barton and John L. Koontz, brothers Isadore and Peter Bernier, Richard Wood, John Brushas, and Baryeal Bersia.

A Wedding

In 1865, Michael T. Simmons moved his family south from Tumwater, formerly known as New Market, to Lewis County, where he settled near Drew's Prairie. His daughter, Charlotte, married Matilda's son, John Koontz, November 13, 1867. At the time, John was twenty-three and Charlotte seventeen.

The Simmons family had a rich history in Washington Territory. On January 20, 1835, Simmons, who was born August 5, 1814, married Elizabeth Kindred, who was born February 15, 1820. They traveled across the Oregon Trail in 1844 and settled at New Market in 1845. Their children included George W., David K., Enos F.M.D., Macdonald, Christopher, Benjamin, Charlotte E., Douglas Woodbury, Mary, Catherine, Charles Mason, and Michael T.

Like Louisa, John Koontz kept a journal in 1868, beginning on a snowy March 14. He said he had struck out to do something for himself and his wife. He worked for Mr. Gosnell and Father Richard, hauling lumber and rails, plowing with mules, and fixing fences. His mother visited March 22. He hauled manure, sorted apples, planted potatoes, and hoed the garden.

"Charlotte and I went up to C.C. Pagett's shopping and in the afternoon went fishing," John wrote March 29.²⁹ "Caught one trout. I did it."

On March 30, he wrote that they moved up to Mrs. Simmons' place to take a claim. In April he fixed up an office, cut and hauled wood, planted peas, and hoed a garden. He went to the Cowlitz Landing for grain and "up home to see the folks."

It's doubtful his hard work outside afforded him much time to write in the journal but he did for a month or so.

It was Charlotte who changed the spelling of her surname to make it consistent. It had been spelled Coonse, Coonce, Coontz, and Koontz. In 1876, she opted to spell the name "Koontz," which is how it has remained for future generations. Just north of the Jackson place is an east-west road by that name. The nearly four-mile road crosses Interstate 5 so the words "Koontz Road" are prominently displayed on the overpass.

Cowlitz Steam Navigation Company

The year 1867 is when John R. Jackson joined with M. Chappellier and John T. Kerins as trustees in the new Cowlitz Steam Navigation Company.

Paperwork indicates they worked with the Willamette Iron Works Company in Portland, builders of steam engines, boilers, saw and grist mills, and mining machinery, for iron shutter work and blacksmithing.³⁰

A document dated October 11, 1867, at Cowlitz Landing certifies that John Jackson was entitled to five shares in the capital stock of the company. Another stock certificate dated July 20, 1867, lists a hundred shares at one hundred dollars each for $10,000.

William S. Ogden, whom Jackson had met in Portland, sent a packet of papers to Matilda and a letter to her husband dated September 13, 1867.

> Dr Sir—
> It affords me a great deal of pleasure to open a correspondence with you. I send package of papers— not for you to read but for Mrs. Jackson and you may

be sure that I intend to keep sending papers to Mrs. Jackson and not to you—

If the direction I give the papers is not correct please inform me of it.

As you are a steamboat man, I want to tell you one thing in this letter, which besides what I told you in Portland is well worth bearing in mind. "Keep your business to yourself." Some of the owners of your Cowlitz boat don't do this.

I am as ever
Your friend
Wm S. Ogden

No explanation is offered as to why the papers would be sent to Matilda rather than to John Jackson.

M. Chappellier sent John R. Jackson a Western Union Telegraph June 3, 1868, which noted that neither Pinto nor Hall was home, but he would see Gosnell the following day to discuss investing together in the steamboat business.[31]

Jackson was in Portland in July when a letter from Dean Blanchard to "Friend Hall" dated July 11, 1868, from Rainier, Oregon, spoke of the impending sale of the steamboat *Rainier*, which was built by John Holland in 1867 in Rainier, according to Nathan Stueve, who wrote "Steamboats on the Cowlitz."[32]

"I can put 600 to 1,000 dollars towards buying her if you can raise the balance to buy her, in that is I mean yourself, Mr. Jackson, Gosnell, Pinto and others on the Prairie," he wrote. "We ought to have about $3,000 to be sure of getting her though I believe she will go for about $2,000. Please let me hear from you."

Jackson invested $2,500 in the Cowlitz Steam Navigation Company and paid $109.85 in county taxes in 1870.

In October 1868, the *Rainier* was launched into service between Monticello and Cowlitz Landing, a ten-hour trip upriver that took half as long going downstream. However, within months of its beginning operation, federal Customs officials seized the 110-ton ship after learning that she transported passengers without a license, according to

Washington State Library's collection of the Jackson, Koontz, Glover family papers, 1837–1952.

Jackson's Cowlitz Steam Navigation Co. stock certificate, above, and a receipt from Willamette Iron Works Company for steam engines below.

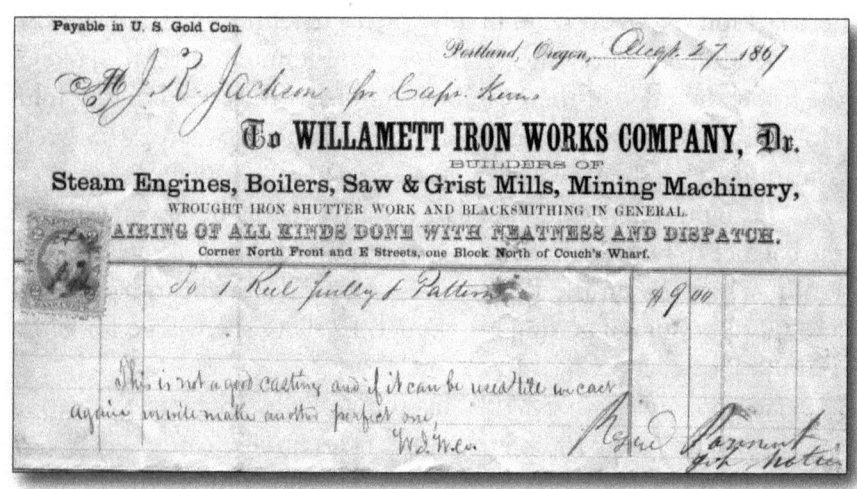

Chapter Twenty: Life and a Girl's Diary

Stueve. The government sold the steamer to three river captains, who rebuilt and renamed the steamer *Carrie*, operating it on a new route between Portland and Monticello (present-day Longview).

So ended Jackson's involvement in steamboat transportation. Eventually, the Portland-based Oregon Steam Navigation Company bought out steamboat competitors and became what Stueve referred to as a "benevolent monopoly."

At the end of 1868, L.L. Dubeau closed out his general store accounts and sent a notice to Jackson saying that he owed a small balance of $6.94. He provided an itemized list to Jackson showing things he had purchased, including sugar, slippers, booties, buttons, pants, tobacco, and coal oil.

A year later, Dubeau sent a new notice to Jackson asking for payment and listing what had been purchased from M. Chappellier & Co., dealers in dry goods, groceries, liquors, and general merchandise.[33]

"I am need of money in the later part of this month," he wrote. "Permit me to call your attendance."

On February 18, 1869, Jackson paid W. Walmito thirty-four dollars, clearing his account. The paperwork doesn't say what the purchase was.

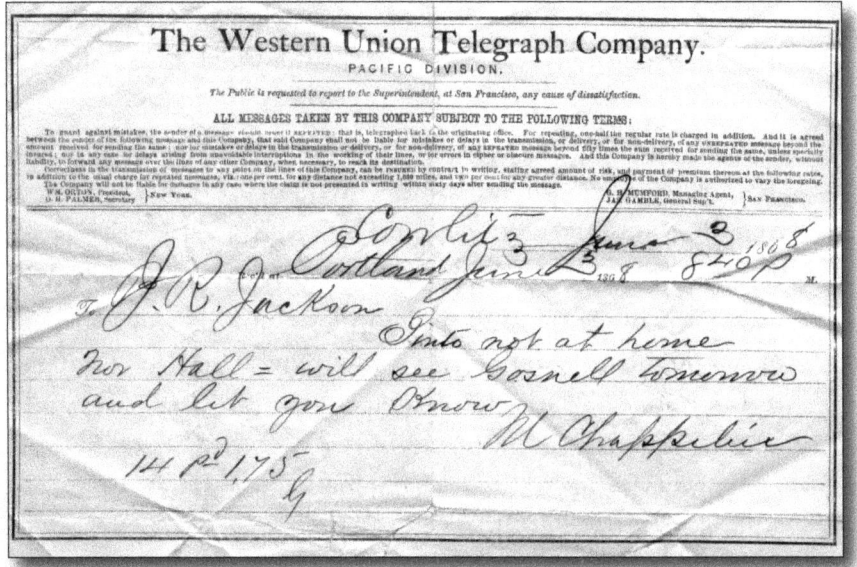

WASHINGTON STATE LIBRARY'S COLLECTION OF THE JACKSON, KOONTZ, GLOVER FAMILY PAPERS, 1837–1952.

The Western Union telegram from M. Chappellier to John R. Jackson.

On March 1, 1869, Jackson sent a note to J.H. Myres asking that Hiram Smith be paid fifty dollars in gold coin on a gray mare.

Barton Coonce

Barton worked hard on the farm and spent most of his life at Highland, but he did some extended traveling in the spring of 1869. On May 7, 1869, Barton Coonce, who was in Portland, sent a letter to his mother and stepfather.[34]

> Respected parents,
>
> After leaving home I stoped at Johns the first evening. The next day I went as far as Mr. Jacksons [no relation] where I left the horse and took the steamer for Portland where I remained almost one day and from here I took the steamer and went to Oregon City in the evening. From here I went to Mr. Carsons where I remained one day from here I went to G Trullinger where I stopped one week from here I went to Uncle John's where I remained about three weeks and from there I came here where I will take the steamer this evening and go by Victoria on the sound.
>
> All of the Folks are well over here and I hope this will find you all the same. I was at T. Forrester's also they have 10 children, 6 boys and 4 girls
>
> Trullinger has put up another saw mill in which he has a circular saw and plaining machine. He got one of his thumbs almost cut off a few weeks before I got to his house. It has healed up but it pains him very much. John as we understood is married.
>
> There is no news here of any importance. The mills belonging to the railroad company are now closed and they are not doing much except hauling some timbers on the track. Have paid for the Oregon

Herald one year. Nothing more at present
   Yours with respect
   Barton Coonce

A Sketch of Matilda Koontz Jackson by Nettie Beireis, her Granddaughter

Most of the women pioneers had been reared in farmhouses and were courageous, adventurous, thrifty, and used to hard work. Most were religious and patriotic. Many had large families. Women were ranked according to their skills as a housewife, and among those early pioneer women, Matilda Jackson stands out.

At the request of Noah B. Coffman and Charles Miles, authors of the Claquato Landmarks column published regularly in *The Chehalis Advocate*, Nettie (Koontz) Beireis of Chehalis wrote a sketch about her grandmother's home life, based on recollections, research, and remembrances of family and friends. She was one of the four daughters of John and Charlotte Koontz.

"What this faithful, retiring, courageous and devoted wife and mother accomplished in her daily household duties staggers comprehension," Coffman and Miles noted in the introduction to the sketch, which was published in 1939.[35]

"Matilda Ann Nettle Glover Jackson was a dignified, serene gentlewoman, erect of form even to her last days, having lived nearly a century. In winter months she was clad in plainly fashioned dress of 'waterproof,' a durable, dark wool material much used by the early settlers. In summer, black cotton cloth replaced the heavier material. A small shoulder cape made of material like the dress completed the costume.

"Mrs. Jackson never wore a coat—for outdoor wear she used a long cape made of waterproof fabric.

"Housekeeping in her new home at Highlands was begun May 1848 in a one-room log cabin housing herself, husband, and four young sons by a former marriage. It was in this crowded cabin, over the fireplace (small Franklin stove) that she prepared the meals eaten by judge, jury and prisoners during the first court session.

"Very soon after this session of court, the family moved into the new log courthouse building (standing now). This was truly a happy day for

> Portland May the 7 - 1869
>
> Respects folks After leaving home I stoped at Johns the first evening the next day I went as far as Mr Jacksons where I left the horse and took the Steamer for Portland where I remained almost one day and from here I took the Steamer and went to Oregon City in the evening from here I went to Mr Casons where I remained one day from here I went to S Trullingers where I stopped one week from here I went to Uncle Johns where I remained about three weeks and from there I came here where I will take the steamer this Sevening and go by Victoria on the Sound All of the folks are well over here and I hope this will find you all the same I was at J Forreaters also they have 10 children 6 Boys and 4 girls S Trullinger has put up another Saw mill in which he has a circular saw and planing machine he got one of his thumbs almost cut off a few weeks before I got to his house it has healed up but it pains him very much John as we understood is martied there is no news here of any importance the Mills belonging to the railroad company are now closed and they are not doing much except hauling some timbers on the track I have paid for the Oregon herald for one year nothing more at present
>
> Yours with respect
> Barton Coonc

The May 7, 1869, letter from Barton to his parents.

Washington State Library's collection of the Jackson, Koontz, Glover Family Papers, 1837-1952.

Mrs. Jackson. Besides the combined living room and kitchen, there were two small bedrooms downstairs and more room for six beds upstairs.

"Within a few years extensive additions were made to the courthouse building. When completed, it was one of the most spacious, comfortable, even luxurious homes in the county at that time. These rooms were really four separate low buildings, one built against another, all rooms on the ground floor, except the upper floor in the courthouse building.

"With the addition of the new buildings, the court room was only used upon rare occasions and finally only as a passage to the front door, two small bedrooms and the stairway.

"In this old home the three Jackson children were born, Mary (Mrs. S.A. Phillips), Louisa (Mrs. J.G. Ware), and Andrew, who died when a small boy. (Seven children to care for.)

"No domestic help being available (she would not have Indians in the house because they were dirty and had fleas), the amount of work turned off by Mrs. Jackson seems now impossible (incredible). The house was maintained in an orderly, dignified manner.

"In addition to the routine household tasks, there fell upon her the burden of seasonal work all of which were vital to the family's comfort and well being.

"In the springtime after the garden ground was prepared, she planted the vegetable seeds, carefully saved from the previous autumn's harvest.

"At regular intervals throughout the year, soap must be made in the big iron kettle set up in the back yard. Odds and ends of all kinds of grease were saved for this purpose and combined with the hardwood ash lye from the big ash leach set up in the corner of the woodshed.

"The leach made of hand-split cedar boards five feet in length formed a hopper, wide at the tops, narrowing sharply to a peak at the bottom where a bundle of clean straw was placed to act as a strainer. The choicest hardwood ashes from the fireplace were used to fill the hopper. When filled, a depression made in the ashes, several pails of water were poured in and, in due time, a strong lye seeped through the straw into the container placed beneath. Frequent stirring with a long wooden paddle and close watch must be maintained since to be boiled down and stirred just enough was the secret of good soap. When done the thick mass was poured into shallow containers and, when cool, cut in squares convenient to use.

"As the season advanced into warm summer with its generous offering of foods, saving some of this abundance for the long winter was imperative. Wild blackberries, plums, apples, green beans, and pumpkin were dried and stored in white muslin bags on the 'buttery' shelves against winter needs.

"Advantage was taken of the warm sunny weather to wash fleeces of wool to be put away in readiness for winter use. The sharp ends of the picket fence surrounding the yard offered choice places upon which to drape the wool for drying.

"During the late spring and summer, many pounds of butter were made, molded into two-pound rolls in wooden molds and packed in barrels of brine. This butter was made in a barrel-like wooden churn, larger at the bottom than top, bound by stout metal hoops and operated with a dasher.

"Numbered among the routine tasks throughout the entire year was roasting coffee. At this time only the green coffee berries were available, which were bought in fifty-pound bags, equal parts Mocha, and were the popular blends. Until stoves could be bought, Mrs. Jackson did this work at the open fireplace. Great care must be exercised that the berries did not become overdone, thereby imparting a bitter flavor. Just the right amount of coffee for the meal would be ground at one time in the coffee mill, securely fastened to the kitchen wall.

"Candle-making throughout the entire year was a necessity. Into tin molds of twelve-candle capacity was threaded the wick, double twisted, making a loop at one end into which was run a slender round stick—the wick then pulled taut through the tapering end of the mold end tied into a knot to prevent the melted tallow from seeping out. The melted mutton tallow poured into the molds soon hardened, the knots clipped off and the candles easily removed by pulling on the stick threaded through the loops of wick, six on each stick.

"With other work not too pressing, a number of candles would be made in one day. This was the only means of light at night. Even the lanterns used by the menfolk were lighted by tallow candles.

"Cold weather heralded hog butchering time. The only market for hogs in those days was in the sale of bacon and lard.

"Mrs. Jackson's husband in his younger days, being a butcher by trade, was well trained in curing meats. A dozen or more hogs would be butchered at a time, at different periods through the cold weather. The weather being clear and cold, the long row of dressed hogs would be left hanging out in the open overnight.

"There was, of course, the round of sausage making, head cheese, souse, and lard rendered in the big iron kettle in the back yard.

"There were no periods of idleness. As the years advanced, there was the ever-increasing numbers of travelers seeking food and shelter.

"Upon one occasion, a traveler was so gravely ill he died in a few days after his arrival. A coffin was made from cedar and he given a burial in the graveyard on the east side of the farm. (Long silk box, relatives notified.)

"Among the many travelers, two soldiers of fortune in different years were found who were willing to remain through the winter months and teach the children the three R's.

"Mrs. Jackson's early years of work and privation was largely compensated for by the comforts and even luxuries of her (later) home.

"The addition first built to and joining the court building was a spacious living room made of boards and lighted by three windows. At one end was a grand old fireplace with a high black mantel and facings. On this mantel would always be found an old-fashioned vase filled with candle lighters. Matches were the rarest luxury and only to be used in an emergency. These lighters were a tightly rolled strip of paper, sharply crimped at the end to hold the twist.

"A pair of long-handled tongs companioned a poker, possibly made in Mr. Jackson's own blacksmith shop, a shovel, and a turkey wing to brush up the hearth made up the fireplace set.

"During the making of quilts and comforters, the quilting frames were suspended from four stout hooks in the ceiling near the center of the living room. After the quilting was finished for the day, the frames were elevated above the range of the family heads.

"The walls were covered with paper, having a white ground on which were rows of stiff medallion-like figures.

"The baseboard and chair rail with the other woodwork were painted a light grey. At the end of the room opposite the fireplace was a bulky combination of bookcase in the upper part with glass doors and

AUTHOR PHOTOS

The Jackson cabin at Highland Farm was located on the main route from the Cowlitz River near present-day Toledo north to Puget Sound, so visitors often stopped overnight. The farm expanded to include several barns, an office, and other outbuildings. Below are trees along the old Cowlitz Trail leading to the courthouse.

a cabinet in the lower part. Also in this room was a dulcimer with its two padded hammers.

"In the winter months, the spinning wheel found a place in the back of the room to be handy for its share of the work. A what-not, bearing the usual burden of miscellaneous objects collected down through the years, occupied one corner of the room. A round center stand was always in the middle of the room.

"A carpet, somewhat like the ingrain type, covered the floor from wall to wall. This was later replaced with a homemade rag carpet.

"At right angles to the fireplace was a long homemade lounge with hand-hewn, carved maple arms at each end, worn smooth and showing the grain handsomely from the polish of years of use.

"On the walls were pictures of noted Americans and a fine old weight clock held ceaseless vigil over both tragic and happy events that took place in the room.

"Opening off this room near the fireplace was a large, well-lighted white-washed kitchen. On one side of it was a long, sturdy dining table covered with a durable, dark oilcloth with a white and gold pattern. Next to the wall and running the full length of her table was a high-backed, wooden bench. There was a large cupboard for food in one corner. Across one end were a work table and a long wooden sink fitted at one end with a cleverly contrived wooden cross bar to serve as a drain board.

"The back of the living room fireplace jutted out into the kitchen, a mass of bricks put together in a rather irregular fashion creating shelves and crannies, all used for some purpose. Sometimes cobs of corn being cured for seed would be seen in one or more of the apertures. Pegs were driven between the bricks in places on which to hang various cooking utensils.

"The only other room opening off the kitchen was the 'entry.' Besides other uses, this entry served as a passageway from the kitchen to the 'buttery,' woodshed, and backyard. At the side of this entry was a long, wooden sink furnished with tin basins, homemade soap, a roller towel, and a comb case beneath a small looking glass. Distinguished guests, family, and hired hands all tidied themselves here. This arrangement was luxurious as compared with some others of the times. The real purpose of this entry was to provide a home for the well with its genuine oaken buckets, a combination of large, wooden wheel and well sweep. The bucket was lowered by real labor as the operator pulled down on the rope hand over hand. The weight of the end of the well sweep drew up the filled bucket. The big wheel worked on a wooden shaft and, if not kept greased, creaked and groaned in protest.

"The 'buttery' opened off this entry. It had rows of shelves around the wall and work tables near the center. It was on these tables that much of the culinary mixing was done. Here were stored the precious food supplies, bags of flour, wooden barrels of brown sugar, the sauerkraut, corned beef, and butter barrels.

"The meals prepared by Mrs. Jackson were very plain and substantial with both meat and potatoes a part of all three meals. Mutton was the meat most often used. Unlike many pioneer families, dependence for meat was not placed upon wild game. The favored ways of cooking the mutton were roasting and broiling. Mr. Jackson was especially fond of a dish he called broiled bones. Also, he liked mutton soup and wheat hominy. To make hominy, the whole grain was 'lyed off' with lye from the ash leach, a very delicious dish much used during the winter months.

"Desserts were not the rule. The one most often made before stoves came to the home was a boiled English pudding. The raw mixture was tied in a muslin cloth and boiled in an iron kettle. With the acquisition of a stove and ovens, pie (and cake) became popular with the family.

"Salt-rising bread was made for years, there being no yeast available such as that used in these modern times. The batter for this was mixed in a small iron kettle set in a larger one containing warm water and placed on the hearth in the early morning. This would be carefully tended all day by testing the temperature of the water in the outer kettle by hand and stirring the batter frequently. When this became a light, fluffy leaven, it was ready to make into loaves and, when baked, made a fine-grained pleasingly flavored bread.

"There were at first long periods of time with no newspapers or word from the outside world. During these days Mr. Jackson would sit beside the fireplace the greater part of the night, discussing affairs of the day with any traveler who came along. Not until the military road was established and regular stage lines ran from California was there a regular mail. At one time a post office was kept in the home.

"With the gray days of winter and long evenings, the living room became Mrs. Jackson's workshop. Here sitting beside the blazing hearth,

Chapter Twenty: Life and a Girl's Diary

AUTHOR PHOTOS

Some of the utensils used for cooking by Matilda Jackson at her home on Highland Farm. These utensils remain in the cabin today.

working with the wool, preparing it for either spinning into yarns or carding into bats for comforters and quilts, she worked surrounded by her family. Sometimes hymns would be sung and psalms read. Mrs. Jackson was deeply religious, always feeling the nearness of God. In working with the wool, if for spinning into yarn, she would place a shallow vessel of lard on the hearth to melt and lightly apply by dipping the palm of her hand into the melted fat and working it into the wool.

"No dyes were used to color the yarn. The black sheep of the flock furnished the most valued fleece of all. By mixing this with the white wool, while carding rolls to spin, various shades of gray could be made. (She knitted socks, stockings, and mittens for the family. You know all of the clothes for the children and for herself had to be made in the home and without a sewing machine.)

"With a goodly supply of rolls on hand, the spinning wheel could be brought near the fireplace. An inner corn husk, saved for just this purpose, would be quickly dipped in hot water and tightly wound on the steel spindle. Deftly attaching the end of the roll to the spindle, the wheel was given a whirl and to the accompaniment of the resounding zoom, she paced slowly backward, drawing firmly on the roll. At just the right moment, the wheel was stayed by her hand, a quick reverse motion given the wheel end still holding the thread taut, a fine flawless wool strand would reel up on the husk-covered spindle. The next roll would be welded with skillful fingers to the bit of unspun wool left or the reeled strand and the wheel would be off again. In her lifetime she must have walked an endless number of miles in this work.

"This yarn was used for making socks, stockings, mittens, tippets, and other articles used by the family. Thus Mrs. Jackson during any leisure time through the day and the long evening would sit knitting with a watchful eye upon an iron kettle of wheat hominy simmering over the coals or a tray of apples baking before the fire. While thus engaged, she frequently would reach for her nearby prayer book to read the Word that stilled the hidden pain in her heart.

"The even tenor of her busy life was marred by grim tragedy. Answering the summons to her door one day, she was told her firstborn, Henry, a fine manly lad of nineteen [eighteen] years, had that day gone to his death in the swollen Cowlitz river. She lost [Grundy] a younger fifteen-year-old son after years of cruel suffering, due to a severe knee injury. There were only simple home remedies to ease the pain. It was during the last days of this lad, when the settlers were moving into the blockhouses to seek safety from threatened Indian attacks, that Mrs. Jackson stoutly refused to move the sick lad, saying if it must be, the Indians will take us here. The lad is too ill to be moved from the home.

"Some years later, a party of travelers with a sick child sought the hospitality of the Jackson home. The child's illness proved to be the dreaded diphtheria. While the stranger child was successfully nursed through the illness, Mrs. Jackson's ten-year-old Andrew (named for President Andrew Jackson), her last-born, lost a gallant fight against the disease.

"In 1883, the Jackson family, consisting now of herself, her son Barton Koontz, and daughter Louisa Jackson moved into their new house, located nearby and just beyond the site of the cabin that she came to as the bride of John R. Jackson. Here she lived until February 14, 1901, when she passed away peacefully at the age of ninety.

"The last years of her life were years of invalidism caused from a hip injury, the result of a fall. Through it all she was still serene and uncomplaining. A fine example to all who were fortunate enough to know her.

"Comfort for Mrs. Jackson in her bereavements was found in reading the Bible. Her New Testament had its place on a stand near the chimney corner, at hand for daily reading. In the presence of overpowering grief or sorrow, she would possess herself in silence and composure and steal out into the quiet of the orchard."

Nettie's sister, Anna Koontz, remembered her grandmother as deeply religious. She lived her faith without preaching. She based her character on her faith.

"Once she said to me, 'You must forgive if you want to be forgiven,'" she recalled in an article published by Dan Bush in *The Chehalis Bee-Nugget*. "The brevity of that statement, spoken in her firm convincing voice, made it effective. She was a person of few words, but rather a meditative spirit who valued silence. Her speech was never flippant, nor was she given to idle chatter."

As her eyesight failed, Anna Koontz said she read to her from her New Testament, which sat on a stand beside her chair. When she read

The old Jackson homestead in May 1869. John R. Jackson is riding on the horse with stepchildren of Mary (Jackson) Phillips. Mary later married Charles C. Gregg, and

Chapter Twenty: Life and a Girl's Diary

LEWIS COUNTY HISTORICAL MUSEUM

Eddie Phillips on the hitching rail and Mary "Mollie" Phillips on the block. They were their children included historian and author Dr. Kate Gregg.

a psalm and skipped the word "Selah" because she didn't know how to pronounce, her grandmother inserted the word. She knew her Bible. Then she read a chapter from the gospels. Matilda often quoted the words silently ahead of her granddaughter.

"I felt a reader was not needed," she said. "She had a generous store of Scripture in her memory for her contemplation and comfort."

In addition to opening her home to Eddie and Mary Phillips after their mother died, Matilda nurtured Nellie Boone, who lived with the Jacksons while attending school taught by Louisa Jackson, who received a teaching permit from Henry Stearns Sr. after attending the Claquato Academy for a year or longer and Seattle Preparatory School.

Years later, when Nellie Boone Simonton visited Chehalis from her home in California, she told Anna Koontz, "I can't tell you how much it meant to me in character development to have lived with Grandma Jackson when I did."

Anna remembered her grandmother's gentleness.

"She never scolded, nagged, shook or spanked us, with one exception," she recalled.

Mattie, the oldest of John and Charlotte's daughters, went missing one day, and Matilda heard a "queer sound" coming from a big kitchen cupboard that extended from the floor to the ceiling.

"She opened one of the lower doors—and there sat Mattie eating a piece of blackberry pie," Anna recalled. "She was pulled out gently and given one spank. That did something for Mattie. A few years later, Mattie one day dramatically raised one hand to her head and declared, 'All I am that is worthwhile I owe to Grandmother Jackson.' I recall how I stared at her in amazement at this fervent pronouncement."

One time Matilda missed her new flannel nightgown and discovered it in the hired girl's room.

"Let her have it if she needs it that much," she said.

Matilda's plain clothes were cut from the same pattern but she dressed her daughters like ladies.

"She started to tell me one day about a low-necked dress she had when a young girl," Anna recalled. "Suddenly she stopped and exclaimed, 'Oh, how foolish!' Vanity was not one of her faults, nor was malicious gossip. Those who knew her said they never heard her speak an unkind word about anyone."

Chapter Twenty-One

Death of a Gentleman Farmer

DURING THE LAST THREE YEARS of his life, John R. Jackson continued to oversee operations at his Highland Farm and track expenditures and income. He saw his eldest daughter married to his good friend before suddenly falling ill.

In the August 15, 1870 census, Jackson was listed as a seventy-year-old farmer with real estate valued at $20,000 and a personal estate of $3,000. Matilda, sixty, was "keeping house," while Barton N. Coonse, thirty, worked as a farm laborer. Louisa was seventeen at the time, but the census also listed a child at the home, eight-year-old Mary Phillips, who attended school.[1]

Mary was the daughter of Sylvanus "Vean" A. Phillips, a native of Niagara County, New York, who was born in 1830 and sailed from New York City to San Francisco in 1852 via Panama. A year later, he traveled north to Washington Territory where a brother lived on Chambers Prairie near Olympia. He settled on a ranch near Chehalis. In 1856, he lived on Jackson Prairie for a few months. He served during the Indian Wars as a corporal in Company C, the first regiment of Washington volunteers, under Charles Bishop, a first lieutenant and good friend. He married Sarah Jane Moore in 1857. They had four children, but two died in childhood. Sarah Jane died in April 1867.[2]

Three years later, left a widower with a son, Edward B., and daughter Mary Adelia, Sylvanus courted Mary Louisa Jackson, the eldest daughter of John and Matilda Jackson. She was eighteen years younger than him. They married May 3, 1870. J.D. Clinger performed the ceremony and certified the license dated April 30, 1870. The wedding took place May 3 at the Jackson home. Witnesses were Peter Smith and Barton Koontz. Clinger as justice of the peace signed the marriage license May 10, 1870, when he filed the notice with the county.

"This is to certify that the undersigned, a Justice of the Peace by authority of license, having date of April 30, 1870, and issued by the Auditor of Lewis County, did on the third day of May A.D. 1870 at the house of John R. Jackson in the county and territory aforesaid joined in lawful wedlock Sylvanus Phillips of the county of Lewis and territory of Washington and Mary Jackson of the county and territory aforesaid with their mutual assent in the presence of Peter Smith and Barton Koons witnesses."[3] [The spelling of the surname remained inconsistent until John's wife, Charlotte, established it as Koontz.]

Sylvanus and Mary Phillips had no biological children of their own. Sylvanus's son, Edward, died October 21, 1888, apparently never having married, and their daughter, Mary Phillips, married Charles Gregg. They had at least eight children, including their eldest, Kate Gregg, an academic, historian, and author. Sylvanus served one term as Lewis County commissioner.

On May 10, 1870, John Jackson swore an oath of office as road supervisor. Other road supervisors at the time were John Alexander, Ammund Ammuns, F. Chable, Charles Clark, J.H. Goff, Richard Griffith, John Koontz (Jackson's stepson), T.B. Mitchell, Salim Plant, Levi Prince, Joseph Pyett, John Rayton, James Tullis, James Urquhart, and William West.[4]

Jackson kept a diary throughout 1870 in a black leather-covered book published in San Francisco. The book included hack fares in San Francisco ($1.50 per person), distances from San Francisco, tide tables, astronomical calculations, populations in 1867 (New York was the largest in the United States with 200,000 people and Liverpool in England had 450,000), an almanac, and a monthly calendar. He and others jotted numbers that he added and subtracted in the front and back covers.[5]

The journal records the rhythms and flavor of Jackson's final years of life. Like his daughter, Jackson listed the weather each day: at times warm and pleasant, fine, rainy, tremendous storm, cold, snow, very warm, colder, windy but fair, and raining. He spoke about the farming

Chapter Twenty-One: Death of a Gentleman Farmer

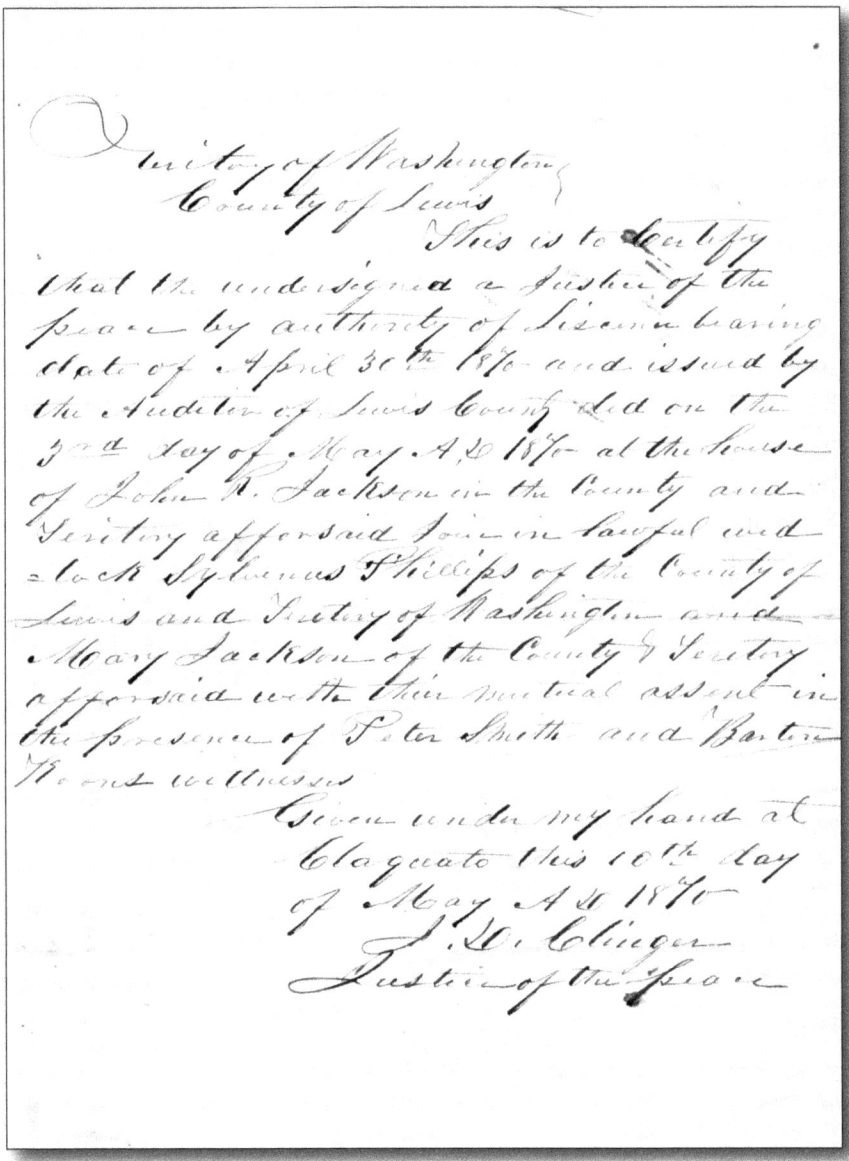

WASHINGTON STATE LIBRARY'S COLLECTION OF THE JACKSON, KOONTZ, GLOVER FAMILY PAPERS, 1837–1952.

The April 30, 1870, marriage certificate for Mary Jackson and Sylvanus Phillips, a widower with two children.

activities each day, with notations about the travelers who enjoyed a meal or overnight stay at Highland.

In the early part of the year, the work—much of it done by Barton—included cleaning a well, laying up fence, harvesting, feeding two yoke of oxen belonging to someone named Mick, and plowing. He noted someone named Henry went to the Cowlitz with fourteen sacks to purchase twenty-five bushels of wheat seed from A.J. Simmons. Plowing continued into March and April. Although he employed hired hands, John Jackson also performed some of the farm chores. For example, he spent March 29 counting sheep—110—and lambs, seventy-eight. Henry had to serve in District Court but returned a few days later. They hauled manure and plowed after dinner. On April 3 they traveled to Cowlitz to buy eighteen bushels of seed at ninety cents per bushel from A.J. Simmons. In April they plowed the field behind the orchard, turned up manure in the barnyard, and sold forty pounds of bacon to A.J. Simmons.

Visitors included David Chambers in April. Mr. Brower returned from Portland, and Mr. Ensign stopped by on his way to Portland. On April 11, Barton went home with S. Phillips. He returned two days later.

"All hands sowing and harrowing in wheat," Jackson wrote April 14. "Mike came after his oxen and wagon."

The next day, three travelers with two horses stayed the night. Later two wagons with families bound for Oregon stopped.

The weather was "fine" on "Easter Sunday," April 17. The next day, they sowed nearly twenty bushels of peas, which they harrowed in the next day.

"Mr. Bower came, got sixteen bushels of oats and one thousand pounds of hay," he wrote. Queen mare had a filly colt.

On April 20, Jackson wrote, "Mrs. & I self went to the Cowlitz. One team finished harrowing in pease. Mr. Myres put the new papers on the dining room."

The spring continued with harrowing and sowing of oats. On April 22, he and Barton marked the lambs' withers. They had fifty-four lambs and forty-seven ewes. Barton sowed oats after dinner. Mr. James Urquhart stopped by.

Barton finished sowing oats and started plowing and harrowing the garden. He planted potatoes and peas. Two young lambs were born. Louisa accompanied Jackson to the Cowlitz. Barton plowed in front of

Chapter Twenty-One: Death of a Gentleman Farmer

John R. Jackson kept a diary in the last years of his life.

Washington State Library's collection of the Jackson, Koontz, Glover family papers, 1837–1952.

the shop until a big thunderstorm struck April 29. He finished the plowing and sowing the next day, and another lamb arrived.

On Tuesday, May 3, Jackson jotted a rather unemotional note. "Mary married to S. Phillips by Esqr. Clinger. Webfoot had a mare cold. Henry went to Nowaucum with Linch's potatoes. One ham eighteen pounds."

S. Phillips and Mary left for home May 5, and Barton tilled the garden. Jackson harnessed the horses and rode in the pleasant afternoon of May 6. Barton plowed for potatoes, and the W.B. Gosnell family stayed on their way to Olympia. The weather May 9 was hot and fine, eighty-five in the shade.

Barton visited the McDonalds with Mrs. Lane and Henry left for Portland. Barton planted potatoes, and Jackson rolled oats. Charles Eaton stayed the night.

On May 15, Matilda and Barton visited Mr. Mitchell's and A.I. Miller spent the night. Barton hauled manure onto the potato patch in heavy rain May 18. Barton and John Wright, a hired hand, hauled firewood while Jackson and Louisa went to the Cowlitz.

Visitors who stayed the night included Mr. Bernier and Kitson, and Gabriel Jones another night, while S. Phillips and Mary visited the evening of May 21.

On Monday, May 23, Territorial Governor Edward Selig Salomon visited the Jacksons. He had been appointed to the position March 4, 1870, and served until April 1872.

On May 28, a cold and showery day, Jackson attended the county convention at Claquato. At the farm, they sacked 368 pounds of wool. The next day, Barton visited S. Phillips and Jackson went to the Cowlitz Landing in the evening for the mail. James Urquhart called to visit.

On May 31, Jackson took his 360 pounds of wool to the Cowlitz Landing and sold it to H.H. Pinto at twenty cents per pound. Barton returned home that evening.

On June 1, James Holmes came to work for Jackson. They plowed and hoed potatoes, and A.J. Simmons stayed the night. Two day later, the Honorable O.B. McFadden, a judge, and his party traveled to the Cowlitz and returned, stopping at the Jacksons for the night. Mr. Pemberton also stayed with his four horses.

On a "very pleasant" Sunday, June 5, Barton visited his brother John and his family at Cowlitz Landing.

Chapter Twenty-One: Death of a Gentleman Farmer

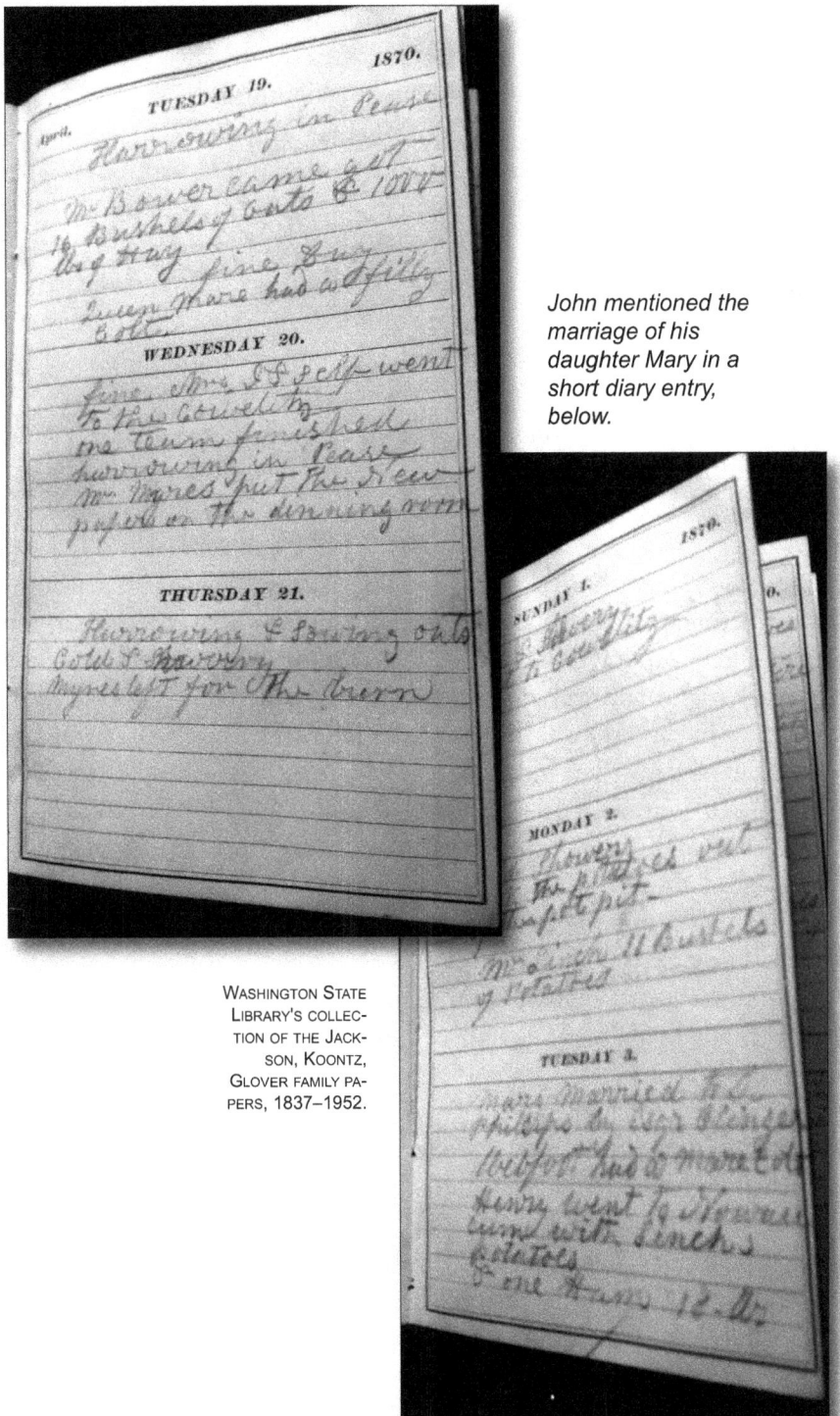

John mentioned the marriage of his daughter Mary in a short diary entry, below.

WASHINGTON STATE LIBRARY'S COLLECTION OF THE JACKSON, KOONTZ, GLOVER FAMILY PAPERS, 1837–1952.

"The great election" took place Monday, June 6, and Mary stayed the night at her folks' home. Mr. Winsor returned with Jackson after the election. The visitors all left the following morning.

Visitors stopped even at midnight. Dubeau called the governor to Claquato to qualify as sheriff. On June 11, Jackson visited the Cowlitz Landing for the election returns. Sunday, June 12, was "very pleasant and a very quiet day." Jackson liked to stay abreast of world, national, and regional news. In fact, he lined the walls of his home with newspapers.

In mid-June, Yates, Garrison and other men worked on the road in hard rain. Jackson stayed the night June 16 with S. Phillips and his daughter, Mary.

On June 17, Jackson said he helped herd cattle toward Yakima and then returned home. Yates and Garrison continued working on the road.

Matilda's son John and his family visited the Jacksons Sunday, June 19. A heavy shower and thunderstorm of hail fell the next day as Jackson traveled to Newaukum.

Barton and "Indian Tom" pulled out and hauled puncheon for the road. They laid down the crossway. S. Phillips and his family returned from Portland and stayed with the Jacksons all day. It rained hard in the morning and they didn't work. The following day, a rainy Saturday, the Phillips family left for home.

Work continued on the road.

On June 29, Jackson visited Cowlitz Landing in the morning and, after dinner, he and Louisa left for Olympia. They stayed the night at Mary and S. Phillips's home. Tom and Barton worked on the road. The next day, Jackson and Louisa arrived at Olympia at seven or eight in the evening and stopped at the Pacific Hotel. The following morning, July 1, they visited Mr. Rowland's home, where Louisa stayed the night.

"Went over to Mr. Rowland's and found Louisa in very good spirits," Jackson wrote July 2. "She walked over to town with me and hitched up the buggy and took her and her trunk back to Mr. Rowland's."

On Sunday, July 3, Jackson returned home, stopping for dinner at Mary and Sylvanus Phillips's place and arriving home to find John and his family visiting. On the Fourth of July, both Mary and John with their families joined their folks for the Independence Day celebration.

Temperatures approached a hundred, and the Phillips family left for home in the evening.

Work slowed down in the hot stifling weather. A slight breeze from the north made it more pleasant and temperatures dropped to ninety-four by July 7.

Temperatures remained hot as they finished haying. Barton left July 28 to help S. Phillips haul in hay. Tom ground oats in front of the Jackson home the next day and then bound and shocked what they had cut before visiting S. Phillips in the buggy. The Phillips family arrived at the Jacksons' on the Sabbath, but Barton stayed a day or two longer to help with the haying.

A hot Monday, August 1, found John Jackson "all alone and nothing doing." He was alone the next day too. But on August 3, he helped Tom cut a few rounds. Barton returned home that evening, and the next day they cut the rest of the oats and bound them up. They commenced cutting wheat August 5, but the sickle broke and needed to be mended at Cowlitz Landing the next day before they could resume work.

Jackson visited Cowlitz Landing on August 7 and, when he returned, Barton left for Newaukum on what proved to be a fruitless search for a binder. He and Tom bound the wheat and later in the week Barton and his stepfather hauled new oats to Skookumchuck near present-day Centralia. Barton and Tom finished cutting the fall wheat August 10, but then needed to bind and haul it.

On Friday, August 12, Sylvanus and Mary Phillips visited in the evening and spent the night. The next morning, Jackson and Barton hauled three loads of wheat in the morning and hauled oats in the afternoon. They cut oats behind the orchard and hauled them to the front of the house.

"S. Phillips sent Ed [his son] up at noon with a nice piece of fresh beef," Jackson wrote August 16. "We had some for dinner."

By mid-August, they finished cutting oats and started harvesting the spring wheat, which they finished August 19. The following day it started to rain and poured steady all day. Light clouds and showers followed the next day.

"S. Phillips and family came up to see me," Jackson wrote Sunday, August 21. "Staid till after dinner. Louisa came home."

Rain continued in the night with heavy showers the next day and evening thunderstorms. When the weather cleared August 23, the "boys" shocked the oats while Jackson went to Cowlitz Landing. They bound up the spring wheat the next few days, and Jackson said he helped with the shocking.

Rain arrived again, and Jackson left for the mills in Olympia August 28, stopping for the night at the home of his daughter, Mary, and Sylvanus Phillips. He arrived in Tumwater at seven the next day and left twenty bushels of wheat before going on to Olympia. He visited "Swantown," which is in East Olympia today, and saw John Roland. He picked up medicine for Louisa and left town at noon. He returned to the Phillips home and spent the night before leaving in the morning for home.

"Boys got done harvesting this evn," he wrote August 31. "All in good order."

Early September brought cleaning of the barn, threshing of wheat, cleaning twenty-five bushels, and sowing a patch of turnips. Jackson paid Peter Smith for his help on the farm and he left. Barton planted while Jackson traveled to Olympia, stopping at the Phillips home.

He was alone September 6 and 7, when he traveled to Newaukum to meet with Marcel Bernier and Mrs. Valaro and see if Mr. Inatir was coming. The following day, he met Barton returning from Olympia.

"Gave him my pony to go and get some help to thrash and I brought the wagon home," Jackson wrote September 8. "The machine came this evn."

Threshing of fall wheat commenced with help from William McFadden and two Irishmen from Newaukum, Jackson Layton and G. Layton. They reaped 220 bushels. The next day, they thrashed 163 bushes of oats.

"The family all here and Mrs. Gosnell and baby," Jackson wrote Sunday, September 11.

The next day, they threshed 166 bushels of spring wheat with help from the two Irishmen, finishing by two in the afternoon. Barton cut and hauled firewood later in the week.

Jackson noted that a Mr. Calhound had his outbuildings burned and saved the house with great trouble. Sunday visitors included Mr. and Mrs. Mannen and John Koontz. The next day, Jackson visited Sylvanus Phillips in the buggy and Barton shoed horses to go to the

Chapter Twenty-One: Death of a Gentleman Farmer

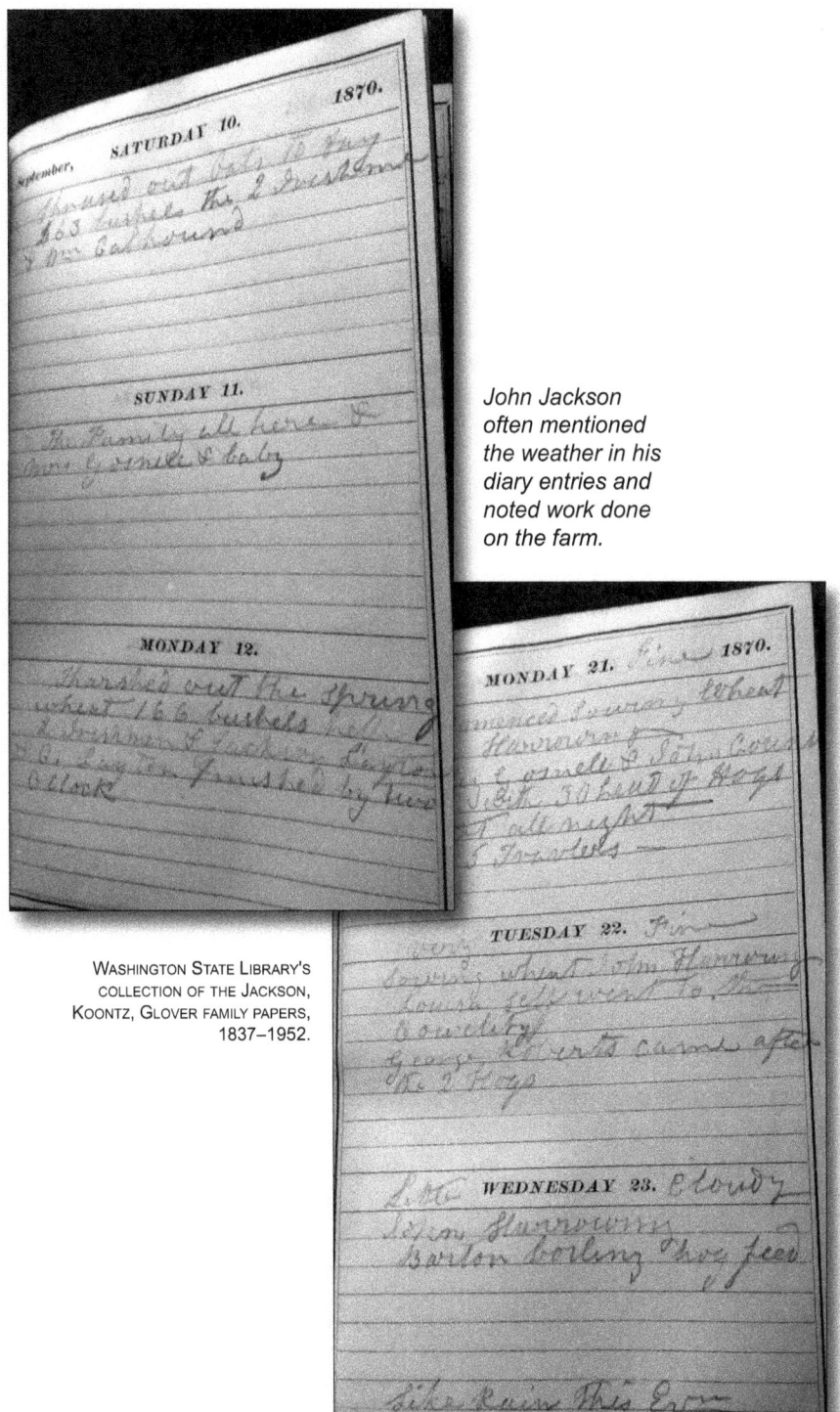

John Jackson often mentioned the weather in his diary entries and noted work done on the farm.

WASHINGTON STATE LIBRARY'S COLLECTION OF THE JACKSON, KOONTZ, GLOVER FAMILY PAPERS, 1837–1952.

John Jackson kept track of some expenditures in his diary.

mill. When Jackson returned with Sylvanus in the buggy, Barton left for the mill in the evening. A Mr. Kelly from British Columbia visited September 20, and Jackson accompanied him to Cowlitz Landing the next day. Mrs. Case stayed at the Jackson home that evening. After Barton returned from the mill September 23, he loaded up and left for Sylvanus Phillips' home in the evening.

Peter Smith fixed up the wagon and took a load of wheat to Sylvanus Phillips' place September 24, returning the next day with Sylvanus for another load of wheat.

"I got one of the sorrel's colts," Jackson wrote September 25. "Mrs. McDonald and family and Mr. and Mrs. Winsor and family paid a visit."

The next week, Peter Smith hauled another load of wheat each day. Mrs. C. Bishop and two children along with Mr. Jimmy Welsh stayed

Chapter Twenty-One: Death of a Gentleman Farmer

at the Jacksons' October 1 before leaving for Sylvanus Phillips' home the next morning.

"I went to Claquato and paid the tax," Jackson wrote October 3.

The following day, Kelly C. Garrison called on the way to Klickitat Prairie, near present-day Mossyrock. John Chambers spent the night.

Sylvanus Phillips and his family visited October 6 and spent the night. They returned home the following evening. Peter Smith went to Cowlitz for grain. Kelly and G. Garrison stayed the night with some cattle October 7, leaving in the morning. Jackson sold Kelly his bull.

The fall brought the time for chopping and hauling firewood and picking apples.

Visitors included John Browning and James Phillips and his son, M. Mitchell and his wife, Mr. Manning and Emmy, and Sam Coulter, who purchased 122 head of sheep from the Jacksons. Jackson let R. Garrison have his mare, Veto, to work. They fixed Louisa's bedroom and Jackson hired two men to dig potatoes. They were paid a dollar a day each.

On Sunday, October 23, Jackson wrote, "Found three sheep killed by panthers." The culprits were most likely cougars.

Later in the month, Jackson visited George Roberts to obtain two rams. Sylvanus and Mary Phillips stayed the evening of October 29. The following day, the Phillips family visited Cowlitz Landing to see John Koontz and his family and spent the night.

Peter Smith and Edding took the mares, colts, and wagons home. On October 31, Jackson left for Olympia in a wagon with twenty bushels of wheat and peas for the nineteen hogs he was taking to Sam Bowlt. He was accompanied by Indians. They stayed the night at Sylvanus Phillips' home. Jackson headed to Tumwater and then Olympia. He stayed at the Hummons' home, leaving after dinner. He returned to Tumwater and loaded grist from the mill and started home. Tom, an Indian, drove the wagon and Jackson rode the mare. They stayed the night at the Phillips' place and returned home by eleven o'clock November 4 after traveling through stormy weather all morning.

Jackson said Matilda's nephew Sam Glover, Philip's son, came that day. They traveled to G. Manning's, spent the night at William Pumphrey's, and arrived at Monticello in cold and stormy weather at half past ten November 5. They boarded the stage and arrived in

Portland by five o'clock that night. They stayed at the Russ house and paid twenty-five cents per meal. They met several old acquaintances and crossed the river to East Portland November 6. Jackson completed his work in the city and prepared to return home November 8. He left at six o'clock in the morning and arrived at Monticello by one in the afternoon. He reached Pumphrey's home by ten that night. The next day, he reached the Mannings' home by six o'clock for breakfast and arrived home by noon.

"A man came and fixed the clock and went to work on the pumps," Jackson wrote November 12. He worked all the next day on the pump and fixed it.

Barton plowed in mid-November and Jackson hired a young man named Tom Tyling to help so they'd have two teams plowing. Jackson left November 19 for Cowlitz Landing for wheat seed. Louisa left the next day to visit her sister, Mary Phillips, and Mrs. Mitchell stopped for dinner.

Workers began sowing wheat and harrowing. Wesley Gosnell and John Count stopped for the night with thirty head of hogs. Five travelers also stayed the night.

Jackson and Louisa visited Cowlitz Landing November 22 and George Roberts stopped at the Jacksons' for two hogs. Barton boiled hog feed and later hauled manure.

Jackson left November 24 for Olympia and traveled in the rain. The weather was showery while he was in town and he stayed November 27 at Sylvanus and Mary Phillips' home. He arrived home by eleven o'clock the next morning. That evening Colonel Ross and his wife joined them for dinner. Other visitors late in November included Mr. War and six hands, who spent the night and ate supper and breakfast, and a Northern Pacific Railroad surveying party camped nearby. On December 7, Jackson wrote that Vice President Richard D. Rice of the Northern Pacific Railroad and his party of six passed through on the way to Olympia. Rice was vice president for the Pacific coast. They returned from the Puget Sound December 13.

On August 22, 1870, paperwork filed at the Lewis County courthouse in Claquato showed that Jackson had paid in full all that was owed for purchasing one hundred and twenty acres of public lands. A U.S. land patent was deposited in the General Land Office of the

Chapter Twenty-One: Death of a Gentleman Farmer

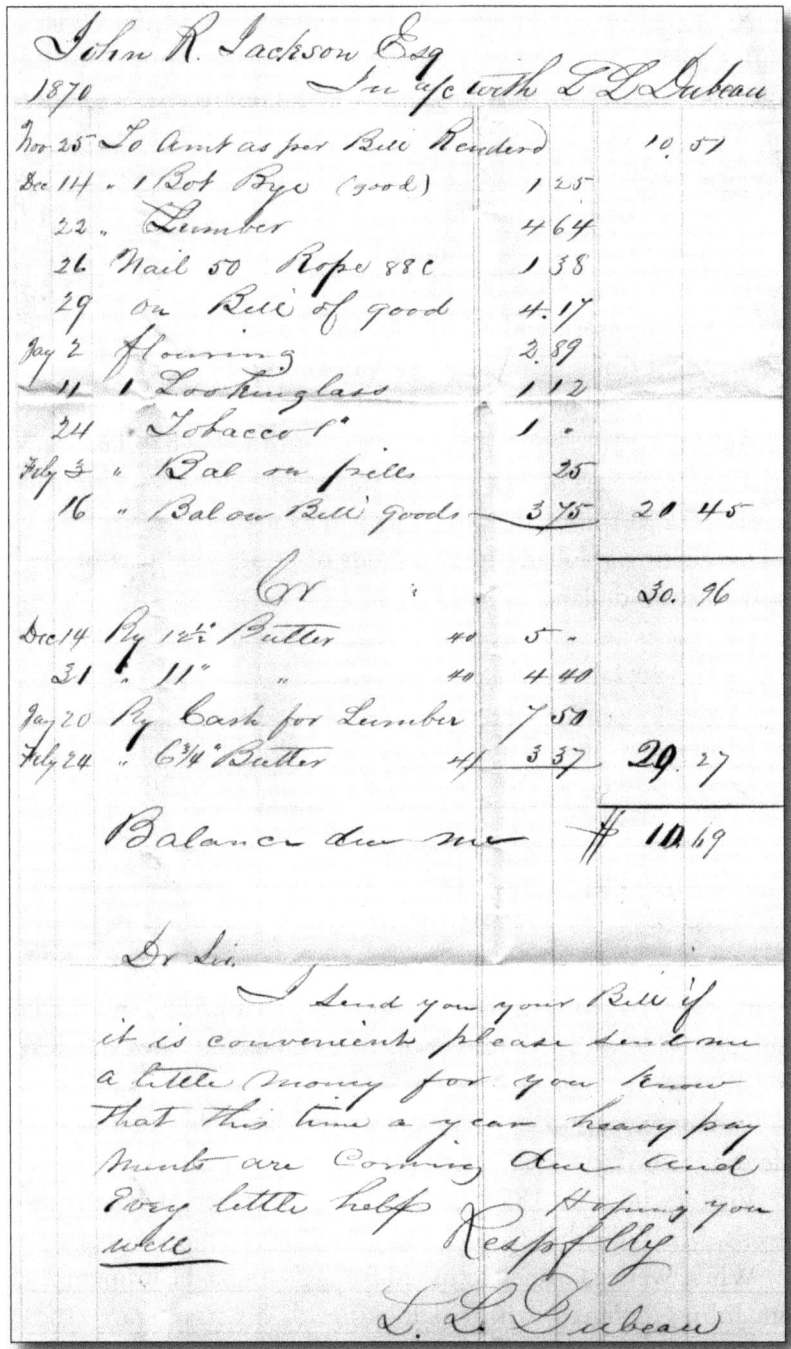

WASHINGTON STATE LIBRARY'S COLLECTION OF THE JACKSON, KOONTZ, GLOVER FAMILY PAPERS, 1837–1952.

Above is one of the many invoices sent by L.L. Dubeau to John R. Jackson.

United States and a Certificate of the Register of the Land Office filed at Olympia, Washington Territory. The paperwork was signed September 9, 1870, in Washington City by President U.S. Grant.[6]

With property comes taxes. On January 21, 1871, L.L. Dubeau, as sheriff and tax collector, issued a receipt to John R. Jackson stating that he had received $109.85 for his county, territorial, and school taxes for 1870.[7] A later notice from A.L. Davis outlined how much John R. Jackson owed. The total due was $126.85—$67.12 for Lewis County, $33.56 for Washington Territory, and $26.17 for the school. Although noting that Jackson wasn't delinquent in his taxes, Davis said he needed to settle the amount or it would be turned over to the sheriff with a 10 percent fee.

An 1870 bill from L.L. Dubeau outlined what Jackson had purchased and paid for with goods traded to Dubeau, with a balance due of $10.19. Among the purchases was a looking glass for $1.12 and tobacco costing a dollar. Thirty pounds of butter paid part of the bill, nearly thirteen dollars.[8]

> Dear Sir,
> I send you your Bill if it is convenient please send me a little money for you know that this time a year heavy payments are coming due and every little help
> Hoping you well
> Respfully
> L.L. Dubeau

The year 1871 progressed much as the previous year, with plenty of work every day to keep the farm operating. Barton and the hired help labored outside while Matilda cooked, cleaned, and cared for travelers who stopped overnight.

"A very pleasant day," Jackson wrote March 9.[9] "Louisa and self rode round the farm."

Visitors in early 1871 included a Mr. Traver of Portland, Mr. Stevens, Mr. Tullis the assessor, and John Bower, among others.

When Wesley Gosnell returned from Olympia, he brought a letter from John Chapman, who was looking for his stray mare. The rain poured and gorged the rivers and creeks. When M. Barton returned from Olympia, he said the Chehalis and Newaukum rivers had flooded their banks.

Chapter Twenty-One: Death of a Gentleman Farmer

"Louisa and self rode round the farm to hunt the old Bernier cow," Jackson wrote March 12, 1871. The next day, Barton searched for the missing cow but couldn't find her.

On a showery and cold March 15, Marcel Bernier arrived to take back John Chapman's mare, while Jackson and Louisa rode to Cowlitz. Weather continued to worsen with winds gusting to the north, snow and sleet with a bit of sunshine. Barton found Bernier's cow and calf March 17.

Ben Mitchell arrived March 20 for some seed oats, while Jackson visited Sylvanus and Mary Phillips. He said she'd been sick, but she was a bit better. He spent the night.

"This morning S. Phillips harnessed up his team to his new gang plow," Jackson wrote March 21. "The ground was very wet but it appears to work first rate. P. Smith came home with me. Cold showery this morning."

Although it didn't rain during that day, at nine o'clock March 22, it stormed and continued all night. The rainy weather continued with winds blowing hard from the south. The first lamb of the season arrived March 26.

The next day dawned clear and fine. Barton left for S. Phillips' to borrow his gang plow. Five lambs arrived alive but one was born dead. The next day, Barton returned with the plow and three more lambs were born. Peter Smith arrived at noon March 29 to help with the plowing. They started the gang plow in the evening. Six more lambs were born.

While Peter Smith wielded the gang plow, Barton fixed the harness for the two-horse plow. Two more lambs were born on a warm March 30, while ten arrived the next day. Barton plowed during the day. Six travelers stayed the night.

April dawned with showers in the morning.

"The boys cleaning up oats," Jackson wrote April 1. "John Coonse came back from his homestead on the Skookum chuck this morning. Sick with a bad cold. Raining most of the day. No plowing done."

The next day, Jackson wrote, James Urquhart stopped by in his capacity as treasurer of the school district. He "stated the amount of money on hand and wanted to have a teacher employed," Jackson wrote. Two more lambs arrived.

One of the early French Canadian settlers in the area died June 8. A notice in the June 17, 1871, *Washington Standard* told of Julien Bernier's passing.[10]

Julien Bernier—

D. at Newaukum Prairie June 8th 1871, Mr. Julien Bernier, a native of Quebeck, Canada, aged 87 years.

Mr. Bernier was one of the Canadian voyageurs who accompanied John G. McTavish in the service of the Northwest Company to Astoria, in 1813. After several years of active life on the upper and lower Columbia, Mr. Bernier retired to a farm on the Red River of the North, but was in 1841 induced by Sir George Simpson to cross the plains and settle on Puget Sound.

In a *Seattle Times* column December 20, 1948, columnist C.T. Conover wrote that Julien's son, Marcel, was the first white child born in what later became Washington Territory. He was born near Spokane Falls November 10, 1819.

A January 14, 1872, receipt from L.L. Dubeau, sheriff of Lewis County in Washington Territory, showed that Jackson paid $172.77 for his share of the county, territory, and school taxes for the year 1871.[11]

Cowlitz January 14th 1872

Received of J.R. Jackson one hundred & seventy two 77/100 dollars for his County Territory and School tax for the year A.D. 1871.

L.L. Dubeau
Sheriff of Lewis Co. W.T.
Lewis County W.T.

A December 9, 1872, receipt shows that John Koontz received $10.90 for his work on the public highway in 1872.[12]

Dec. 9th A.D. 1872

I hereby certify that John Koontz has performed labor on the public highway, in road Dist. No. 10 Lewis

County, W.T., to the amount of ten dollars and ninety cents in full of his roads tax for the year 1872.

Wm. Champs
Supervisor

The year 1872 opened with eighteen inches of new snow on the ground.

"Commenced to thaw and made the roads awful," Jackson wrote January 1.[13] "I went to the Cowlitz."

According to Jackson's diary, wintry weather continued with strong winds from the south and fast snow mixed with a little rain pouring from the skies. They put up six hams weighing one hundred forty-four pounds and other meat, which they probably needed to feed the houseguests as their place was full.

The snow melted by January 3, when George Roberts took fourteen sacks of potatoes to the Cowlitz Landing.

Sylvanus and Mary Phillips arrived in the evening of January 4 and brought Louisa home with them. The next day, the Phillips family returned home as did George Roberts. A man named Nelson from Oregon stayed with eight horses, and the next day Mr. Thons stopped by for potatoes.

Jackson loaned "Indian Tom" two dollars January 7 and Barton shot two deer that evening. Two days later, John McDonald's boys arrived and killed a beef.

"The weather turned cold and disagreeable with showers all day," Jackson wrote.

On Saturday, January 13, George Roberts and Mr. Stevens enjoyed a "good dinner" with the Jacksons to celebrate John's birthday. He was seventy-two.

Two days later, Jackson experienced a frustrating and eventful day.

"Started with the six steers, six head that I sold to Mr. Rogers, to be delivered of the halfway house," he wrote January 15. "Got into the woods between this and Newucum (Newaukum) and lost every one of them and could not get them out of the wood again. The dog treed a panther and G. Roberts came home, got his gun, and shot it. I'm packing the panther out of the woods. The dog treed a she bear with two cubs. G.B. shot the bear and nocking two cubs in head."

Early the next morning, Barton, George Roberts, Tom, and Jackson left to hunt the cattle.

"Barton found them about 12 p.m. but could not get them out of the woods," Jackson wrote. The next day, he wrote to John Rogers to say that he could not start the cattle as they'd gotten lost in the woods.

The cost of some items in mid-January 1872 included flour, four dollars; salt, one dollar; candles, twenty-five cents; crackers, fifty-five cents; white corn meal, two dollars; cheese, twenty-five cents; coffee, eighty-five cents; and eggs, sixty cents.

Sylvanus Phillips stopped January 20 on his way to Cowlitz, and the next day Jackson and Louisa visited Mr. Mitchell. James Urquhart stopped and spent the day.

In late January, on frosty clear days, Barton hauled manure. He attempted to plow the afternoon of January 25 after the ground froze hard, but it proved too hard to plow, so instead Barton hauled rails.

As temperatures rose and the rain returned, the ground softened. A light frost dried it up enough for Barton to plow in the afternoon. A man named Alec arrived to help plow and sow wheat.

"Finished pulling turnips and ploughing and sowing this forenoon," Jackson wrote January 31. "Alec commenced plowing in the timothy lot by the house. Mr. Wiley came this afternoon after the cattle I sold to Mr. Rogers. Barton went to hunt them in the woods but did not find them."

While Alec plowed, Barton looked for the cattle the following day but still couldn't find them. Again, he tried the next day and brought the cattle out in the evening. "We put them in the lot by the barn," Jackson wrote February 2.

"We got two out of the woods and got them started," Jackson wrote February 3. "Alec and self went as far as the Nowuckum (Newaukum) and Barton went on as far as S. Phillips with Wiley. Alec and I brought three bulls home."

They herded the cattle into the shed, tied them together in pairs, and started them through the fields when they broke for the timber. Two escaped into the timber and they had to cut them apart. One bull, as soon as loosed from the rope, raged toward Alec, caught him on his horns and carried him ten or fifteen feet. He survived and soon was cutting firewood on the farm. Barton returned from the Phillips' home

Chapter Twenty-One: Death of a Gentleman Farmer

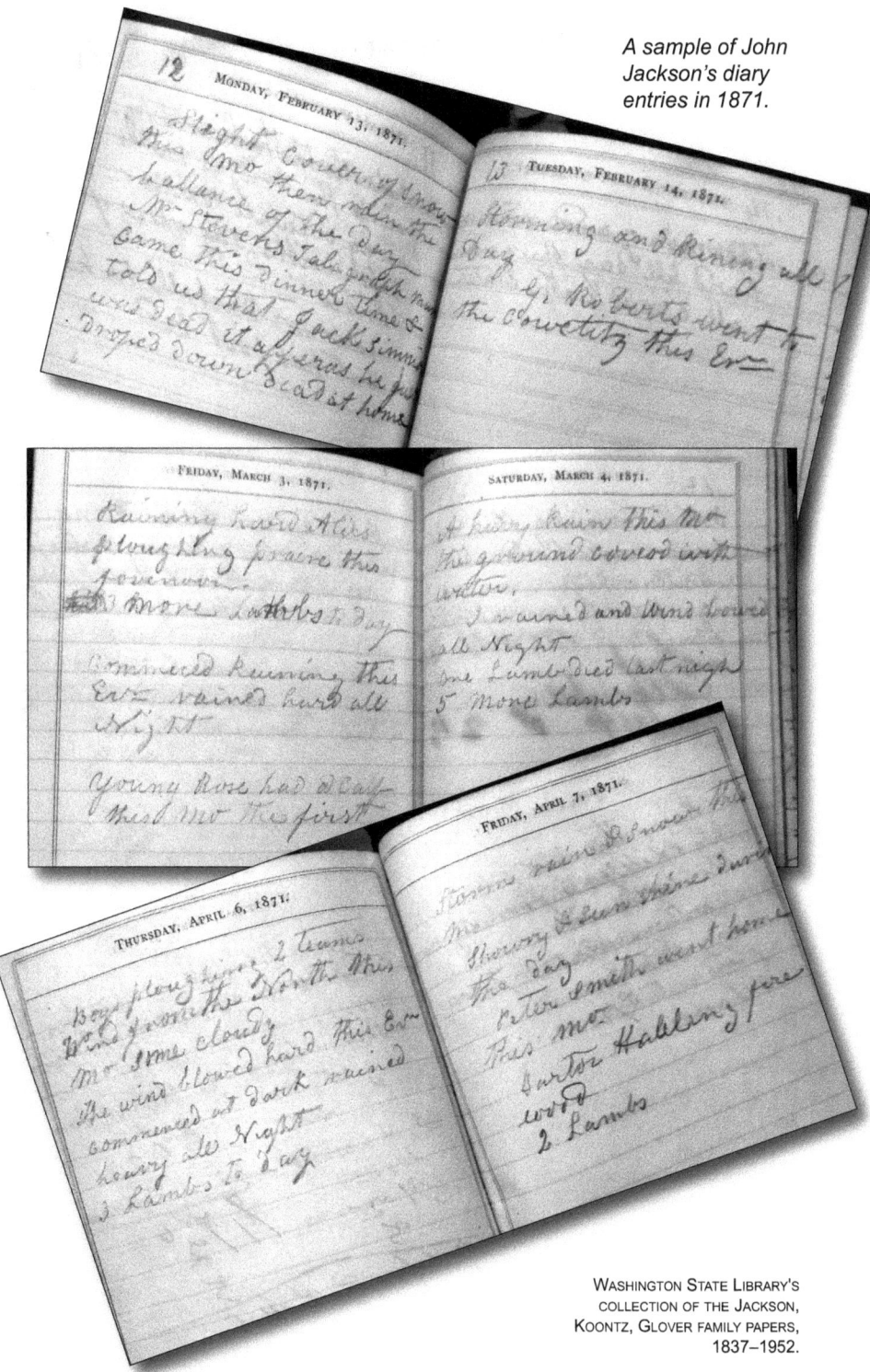

A sample of John Jackson's diary entries in 1871.

WASHINGTON STATE LIBRARY'S
COLLECTION OF THE JACKSON,
KOONTZ, GLOVER FAMILY PAPERS,
1837–1952.

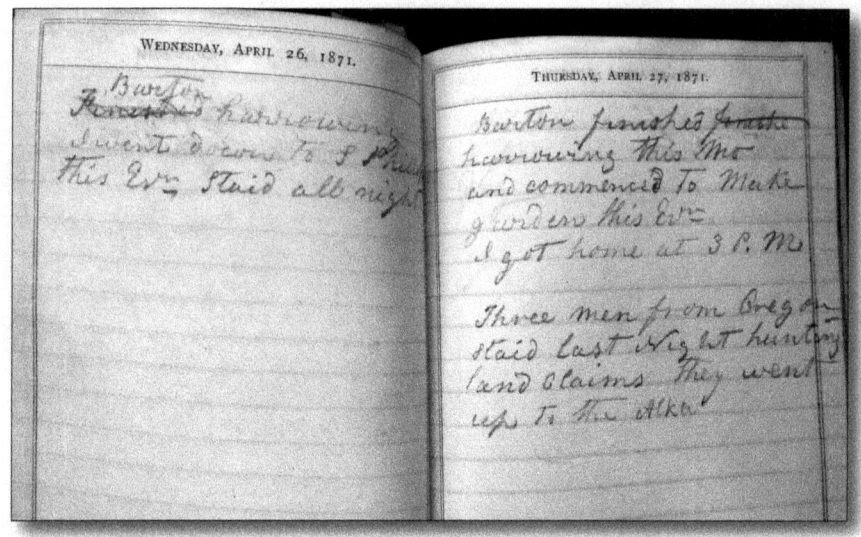

WASHINGTON STATE LIBRARY'S COLLECTION OF THE JACKSON, KOONTZ, GLOVER FAMILY PAPERS, 1837–1952.

John Jackson's precise penmanship grew a bit quavery as he aged.

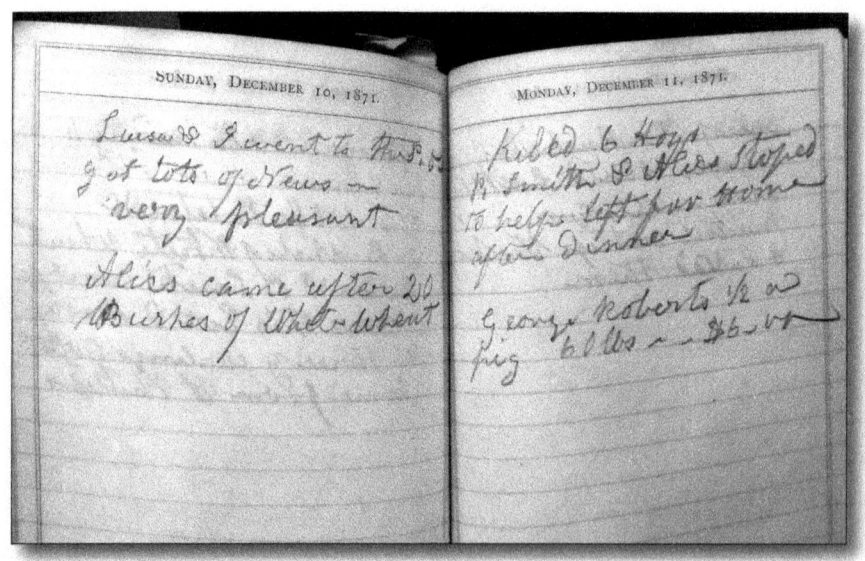

Chapter Twenty-One: Death of a Gentleman Farmer

the evening of February 5. He and Alec hunted and chopped firewood, plowed, and sorted potatoes.

Jackson wrote a letter February 7 while Barton went hunting. They cleaned the barn and cooked hog feed the next day.

A thunderstorm with lightning, wind, and rain drenched the region February 9. Two days later, Jackson left for the Cowlitz but found the bridges washed away so he had to turn back. He saw Mr. Mitchell, who had cut his foot badly.

Snow covered the ground lightly the next morning. Mr. Stevens, the telegraph man, stopped for dinner and told them that Jack Simmons had died. "It appears he just dropped down dead at home," Jackson wrote February 12. George Roberts went to the Cowlitz the next evening. A storm continued to rage, soaking the ground. On February 17, Jackson wrote that one of the ewes, pregnant with two lambs, died in the morning.

Sylvanus and Mary arrived with their family the evening of February 24. Sylvanus went to Cowlitz the next day. The Phillips family left for home February 26 and the boys returned to plowing the wheat field. Four more lambs were born that day, and three the next. On February 28, Alec went with Mr. Twiss, who bought six bushels of potatoes and fifty pounds of bacon and other groceries. Barton plowed and six more lambs were born.

Two teams plowed until eleven February 29, but the rain poured so they had to quit. Six more lambs arrived. Plowing continued the next morning and three more lambs were born. It rained hard all night. Young Rose had a calf in the morning.

Water covered the ground and the wind howled all night. Five more lambs were born, but one died. River levels rose as the rain continued. George Roberts came for his plow March 3. Two more lambs arrived.

"Rain—rain—rain," Jackson wrote March 4. "The sun made its appearance at noon, the first time for several days. One lamb died last night. One more lamb."

The plowing continued as did the birth of lambs.

Jackson noted that he bought soap, stamps, and tobacco for $1.25. He and Barton marked twenty-one pigs and sowed cabbage seed in boxes.

Mr. Mitchell arrived March 8 for applesauce. Jackson counted the lambs that evening and they numbered forty-eight. Only two had died.

Alec continued plowing. Jackson went to the Cowlitz. A Mr. Nelson from Victoria stayed the night of March 9 with eight horses.

Mr. Wiley arrived from Olympia March 10 wanting sheep. By March 12, Jackson counted sixty lambs total. The Chapmans and others stayed the night of March 15 and 16. George Roberts arrived and stopped before leaving for court in Olympia the next morning.

"Jimmy Urquhart and Ellen came and spent the day with us," Jackson wrote March 17. "Very pleasant day. The Rose's heffer (heifer) fell in the well at the barn. We got her out."

Alec and Barton plowed, harrowed, and sowed oats until March 22.

"The little humming bird came to see us to day, the first time this spring," Jackson wrote March 22. "Is twelve days earlier than last spring."

John Robinson Jackson's diary ended, but he might have seen the hummingbird arrive once more before he died in the spring of 1873. He had settled on untamed land in the Pacific Northwest in 1844 and carved out a large ranch and farm from the land, with help from his wife and stepsons. He kept track of purchases and sales, perhaps fancying himself as an English squire, but he failed to write a will. So when he died May 23, 1873, at the age of seventy-three years, four months, and ten days, Matilda was forced to sell the livestock to pay off debts. She retained the land, which her children inherited when she died in 1901.

Edward Yates recalled Jackson's death during an interview with editor Judd C. Bush published in *The Chehalis Bee-Nugget* March 17, 1922.

"I do not know how old he was when he died but he was getting along in years," Yates said. "I attended his funeral. He was buried on Jackson prairie in the little cemetery where his son, Andrew, at the time of his death about twelve years old, and a number of others had been laid away. I understand the Jacksons were removed to the Urquhart cemetery."

John R. Jackson was buried in the family plot beside his son, Andrew, but after Matilda died in 1901, both bodies were exhumed and moved to Fern Hill Cemetery (formerly Urquhart Cemetery), where she was buried.

On May 30, 1873, *The Morning Oregonian* published a notice about Jackson's death.[15]

John R. Jackson, for thirty years a resident of Washington Territory, died at his home at Highland, Lewis county, on the 23rd last, at the age of 73 years.

Chapter Twenty-One: Death of a Gentleman Farmer

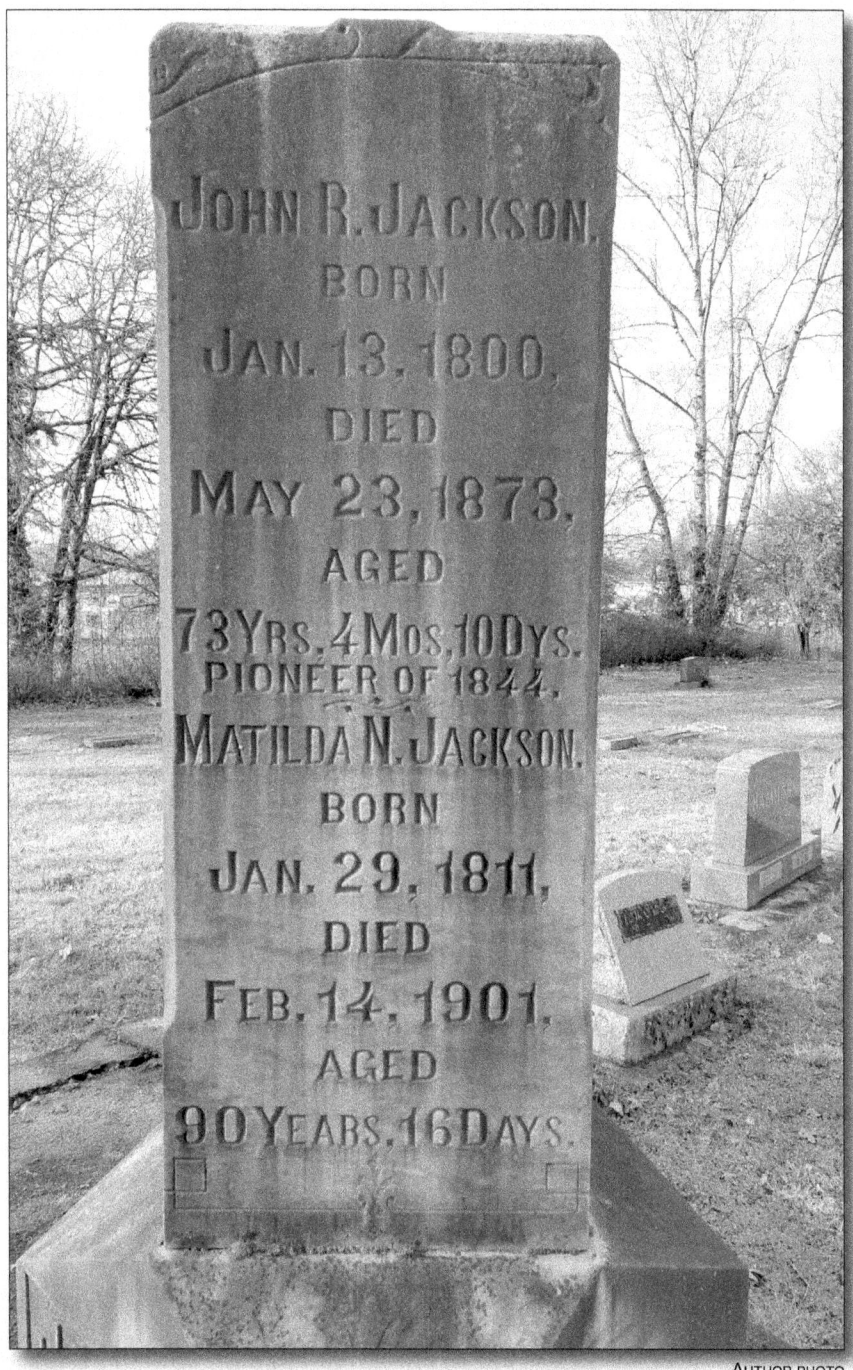

John R. Jackson was initially buried at the Jackson cemetery but later moved to Fern Hill Cemetery, where he rests beside his wife, Matilda.

The Washington Standard published a bit more June 7, 1873, but reported his age erroneously.[16]

DEATH OF A PIONEER.—*John R. Jackson, Esq., one of the oldest and most respected citizens of Lewis county, died at his home on the Cowlitz, on the 25th ult. [ultimo, meaning "last month."] Deceased was 72 years of age, nearly half of which have been passed in this Territory. All the older settlers remember the many manly virtues of the deceased and will drop a tear to his memory.*

Sylvanus A. Phillips served as executor of Jackson's estate. He published an administrator's notice in several issues of *The Washington Standard* during the summer of 1873.

The undersigned having been appointed by the Probate Court of Lewis county, W.T., Administrator of the estate of John R. Jackson, deceased, hereby gives notice to all persons indebted to said estate to pay the same to him and that all claims against said estate must be filed within one year from date properly sworn to or they will be forever barred.

S.A. Phillips, adm'r estate John R. Jackson, deceased

June 28, 1873

The obituaries, while fine notices, failed to mention Jackson's contributions to the region. He had served as Lewis County's acting sheriff under the Oregon provisional government from 1845 to 1847, probate judge and court clerk from 1847 to 1849, acting U.S. District Court clerk from 1854 to 1856, justice of the peace and representative to the territorial legislature. He and his wife offered friendly welcomes to countless pioneers who passed through on their way to settle Puget Sound.

As Matilda dealt with the loss of her husband, she likely leaned heavily on her son, Barton. Her brother, John Glover, had died December 20, 1872, in Marion County, Oregon.

At the same time, another Lewis County family struggled to survive after a horrendous fire burned the home and store operated near Cowlitz Landing by Louis L. Dubeau in March 1874.[17] Olympia's *Pacific Tribune* reported on the loss April 1, 1874:[18] "Dubeau and a young man named

Chapter Twenty-One: Death of a Gentleman Farmer

DEATH OF A PIONEER.—John R. Jackson, Esq., one of the oldest and most respected citizens of Lewis county, died at his home on the Cowlitz, on the 25th ult. Deceased was 72 years of age, nearly half of which have been passed in this Territory. All the older settlers remember the many manly virtues of the deceased and will drop a tear to his memory.

THE WASHINGTON STANDARD, JUNE 7, 1873.

Newspapers reported the death of John R. Jackson but said he was seventy-two when he was actually seventy-three when he died.

THE MORNING OREGONIAN, MAY 30, 1873.

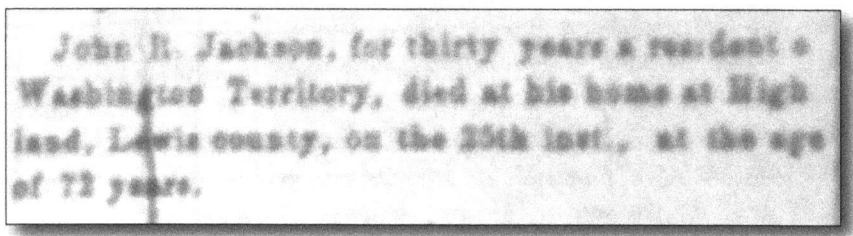

John R. Jackson, for thirty years a resident of Washington Territory, died at his home at Highland, Lewis county, on the 25th inst., at the age of 72 years.

St. Peters had two hundred and fifty dollars in greenbacks burned, the former one hundred and the latter the remainder. The entire loss is estimated at $3,000." The family survived, and by the time Dubeau died a decade later, in 1885, his estate was valued at almost five thousand dollars.

An 1874 tax receipt from Thomas Waterbury, Lewis County treasurer, shows that "Widow Jackson" paid $27.36 in county, territorial, and school taxes for the year 1874.[19]

Barton continued to live with his mother, Matilda, on the Jackson homestead. He wrote to his sisters, and they in turn corresponded with him.[20]

> Seattle, W.T.
>
> Feb. 28, 1875
>
> Dear Brother
>
> I received your kind letter on 15 and were very glad to hear from you all once more. Mary wrote me a nice interesting letter which I fully appreciated as it was the first news I have had from home since I left— I called on Mrs. Maynard a few days ago She has changed very much in the past few years, looks quite old—and her hair is almost white. She says she does not receive any letters from Mrs. Simmons family and thinks very unkind of them not to write—I think our school is excellent—it opened every morning with singing and prayer. This term will close with an exhibition about— the 15 of April as Mrs. Whitson has 14 weeks in a term.
>
> Last Friday evening we all had our pictures taken that an artist photographed the school in a group standing and looks a view of the University building. I expect we all looked sweet—as we were in such graceful positions. Mr. Whit had a dificult time to keep the little folks quite enough to have their picture taken. I hope you attended Mrs Kiltze party and enjoyed yourself nicely. How is Mrs. Mitchell health? Is it improving as she has gone east?
>
> And how Johnnie Grange progressing tell him I want him to write and give me all the news he can think

Chapter Twenty-One: Death of a Gentleman Farmer

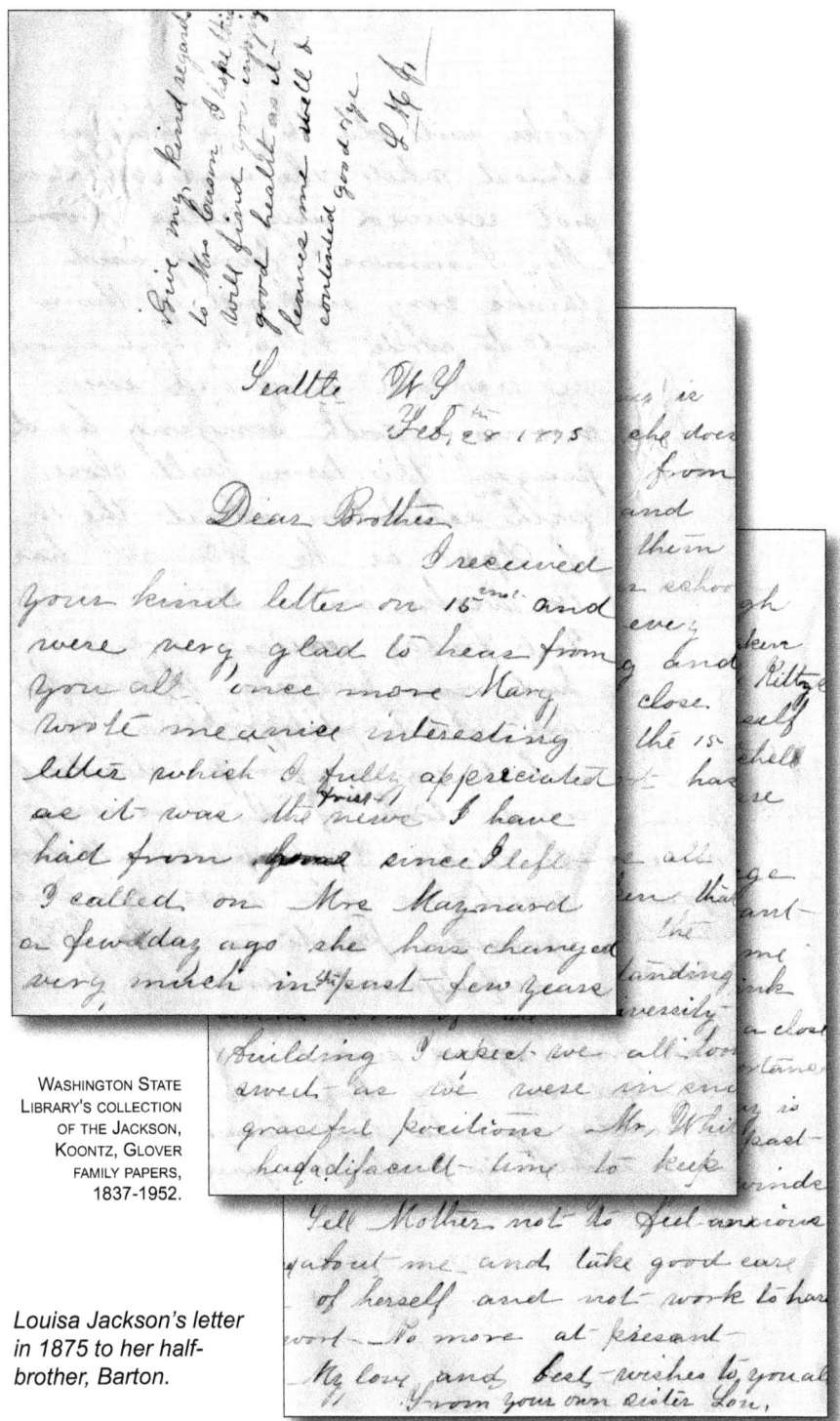

WASHINGTON STATE LIBRARY'S COLLECTION OF THE JACKSON, KOONTZ, GLOVER FAMILY PAPERS, 1837-1952.

Louisa Jackson's letter in 1875 to her half-brother, Barton.

of. I'll bring my letter to a close as have nothing of importance to add. The weather to day is quite pleasant—during the past week we had very high winds. Tell Mother not to feel anxious about me and take good care of herself and not work to hard—No more at present—
    My love and best wishes to you all
    From your little sister Lou
To Mr. Barton Koontz
Write soon soon

On May 5, 1875, Matilda deeded 161.48 acres of her husband's donation land claim to her youngest son, John N. Koontz "in consideration of the love and affection which she ... bears ... and also for the better maintenance, support and protection and livelihood." Conditions of the transaction called for Matilda to "occupy, unmolested, the premises in which she now resides, to wit, the dwelling house on the said John R. Jackson's Donation Claim, and the free use of such other buildings in said Donation Claim as she said party of the first part may need for housing stock and produce—and provide her the said party of the first part with all necessary food, clothing, medical and other necessary allowance for her maintenance and support during the period of her natural life."

If they failed to fulfill the requirements stated in the document, the transaction would become null and void. The paperwork was recorded June 12, 1875, and attested to by Charles P. Twiss, justice of the peace.

Barton kept a record of firsts for Lewis County jotted on a paper under the heading "Old Dates." It noted the first flour mill powered by a water wheel was built by Simon Plamondon at Drew's Prairie in 1847, the first brick made at Plamondon's place on Cowlitz Prairie in 1848, and the first flag, school, and stove at the Jacksons' in 1853.[22]

"They carried the mail by pony express, on an Indian trail, the Columbia to Steilacoom, the first post office in the old courthouse, called the Highlands Post Office, from the early 1850s to 1863-64," he wrote. "Next post office was at Cowlitz Prairie."

Chapter Twenty-One: Death of a Gentleman Farmer

After the death of her husband, Matilda deeded property to her youngest son, John Koontz, in 1875.

WASHINGTON
STATE LIBRARY'S
COLLECTION OF THE
JACKSON, KOONTZ,
GLOVER FAMILY
PAPERS,
1837–1952.

WASHINGTON TERRITORY'S GRAND LADY

Twenty-six years after losing her first husband, Matilda (Glover) Koontz Jackson was once again a widow. The probate records at right list S.A. Phillips, John's son-in-law, as executor of his estate, with John Koontz and Matilda Jackson also listed. Below is a tax receipt showing the amount paid by Widow Jackson on December 12, 1874.

LEWIS COUNTY PROBATE RECORD

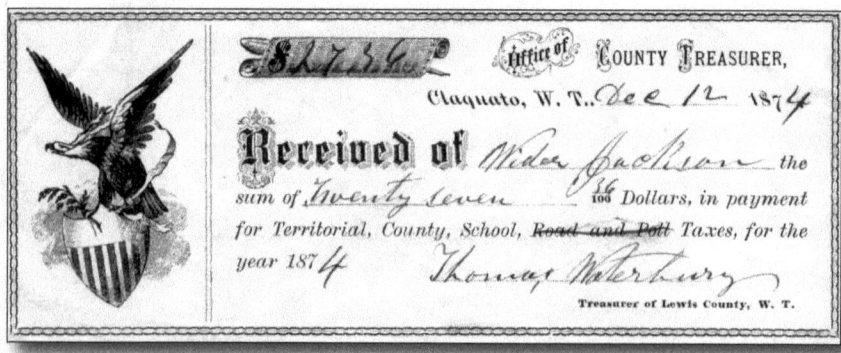

WASHINGTON STATE LIBRARY'S COLLECTION OF THE JACKSON, KOONTZ, GLOVER FAMILY PAPERS, 1837–1952.

Chapter Twenty-Two

A Widow Living with Her Son

MATILDA KOONTZ JACKSON lost her first husband in 1847, when she was thirty-four. She lost her second husband, John R. Jackson, in 1873, when she was sixty-two. She had given birth to eight children and buried four of them.

Barton remained with his mother throughout her life. He never married until after she died. Matilda's eldest daughter, Mary, became the wife of Sylvanus A. Phillips, who had two children from his first marriage. Matilda was grandmother to them and their children.

John married Charlotte Simmons and they had four children—Matilda, who married John U. Smith; Anna, who worked as Chehalis city librarian; Nettie, who married George Beireis; and Jessie, who lived in Seattle.

John worked on the highways in Lewis County, and a July 25, 1880, receipt showed he earned $13.88 for seven days' work.[1]

In 1885, John Koontz drove a herd of hogs through Chehalis on his way to the city of Olympia, according to a piece by Carl P. Staeger in *The Chehalis Advocate* November 9, 1950.[2]

The 1880 census described the Widow Jackson as simply someone who "keeps house." But in the nineteenth century, keeping house entailed a lot of work, especially when she ran a hotel and restaurant too.

On May 30, 1883, John D. Dement of Portland sent Matilda a letter asking her to sign and return paperwork granting power of attorney to Sylvanus Phillips.[3]

Matilda relied on her son-in-law to help her navigate the legalities after the death of her husband.

WASHINGTON STATE LIBRARY'S COLLECTION OF THE JACKSON, KOONTZ, GLOVER FAMILY PAPERS, 1837-1952.

> Portland Oregon
> May 30th 1883.
>
> Mrs M Jackson
> Napavine
> W.T.
>
> Dear Madam
>
> I have been for some time anxiously expecting the return of the powers of attorney sent you for Mr Phillips execution, but as you know have been disappointed to the present time.
>
> Mr Phillips would have but very little trouble in having the administration opened for the purpose of endorsing the draft or signing the power of attorney sent you. In representing the matter to the probate judge, he could not, nor do I believe he would hesitate for a moment in granting the request; the cost would be but trifling.
>
> Business calls me away from the State, and I shall probably be absent for two or more months. I will leave the draft in the hands of Mess" Mitchell and Dement attorneys at Law in this City, who will on receipt of the powers of attorney properly executed remit to you without delay Ninety dollars ($90.00)
>
> Hoping Mr P. will attend to this matter at as early a day as possible I remain
>
> Yours Very respectfully
> John D Dement
>
> P.S. Don't forget to send with power of atty a certified Copy of Mr P's appointment.
> D

Chapter Twenty-Two: A Widow Living with Her Son

I have been for some time anxiously expecting the return of the power of attorney sent you for Mr. Phillips execution, but as you know have been disappointed to the present time.

Mr. Phillips would have but very little trouble in having the administration opened for the purpose of endorsing the draft, or signing the powers of attorney sent you.

On representing the matter to the probate judge, he could not, nor do I believe he would, hesitate for a moment in granting the request. The cost would be but trifling.

Business calls me away from the state, and I shall probably be absent for two or three months. I will leave the draft in the hands of Miss Mitchell and Dement attorneys at law in this city, who will on receipt of the powers of attorneys properly executed remit you without delay Ninety dollars; /$90.00)

Hoping Mr. P will attend to this matter at as early a day as possible. I remain

Yours very respectfully
John D. Dement

P.S. Don't forget to send with power of atty a certified copy of Mr. P's reappointment.
D

A post office was established at Toledo November 30, 1880, and Horace Pinto's general store was home to the Cowlitz post office beginning February 3, 1881, and operated by Abel P. Henriot April 10, 1882.[4]

In 1882, Matilda, Barton, and Louisa moved from the cozy log house into a new wooden frame building erected by Barton. That's where Matilda lived the rest of her days.

Toward the end of the decade, Matilda saw her youngest child married. Louisa Matilda Jackson married Josiah Greenbury Ware July 4, 1888, at the Chehalis Hotel. He had farmed in Illinois. They had no children.

Matilda lived long enough to see Washington become not only a territory in 1853 but a state in 1889, when Washington was admitted as the forty-second state to the United States of America November 11. Congress had passed an act in February 1889 enabling Washington, North Dakota, South Dakota, and Montana territories to apply for statehood. To achieve statehood, the territory needed to adopt a constitution. Normally, her husband would have been in the thick of drafting that constitution, as he had been in the territorial days. But not now.

Seventy-five men served as delegates to a Constitutional Convention at the Territorial Capitol Building in Olympia between July 4 and August 24, 1889, and on October 1, 1889, citizens approved the Washington State Constitution by a vote of 40,152 to 11,879, according to Historylink.org. President Benjamin Harrison signed the bill that admitted Washington to the United States November 11, 1889.[5]

A decade earlier, fifteen men had gathered in Walla Walla during the summer of 1878 to draft a state constitution, but it was never approved by Congress. That document was used as a basis for creating the Washington State Constitution in 1889.

Chapter Twenty-Three

Preserving Pioneer History

BY THE 1890s, people living in Washington State realized the importance of preserving the history of the people who settled the region. The Washington State Historical Society was founded in 1891. One of the early members, Colonel Charles W. Hobart, interviewed Matilda Jackson, "one of the oldest female pioneers," in 1894.[1] Hobart, who served as the historical society's secretary at the time, was accompanied by former Senator J.H. Long, who met him at Chehalis. Long, who traveled from Iowa in 1864, settled the following year in Lewis County, where a quarter of a century later he owned a farm of several hundred acres in Chehalis. He had worked for Lewis Davis in Claquato.

Upon his return, Hobart shared what he learned during the interview with Matilda, who had never ridden a train. He spoke about the trip with a reporter for the *Tacoma Daily Ledger*.

"On reaching Chehalis and thus meeting Senator Long with horse and buggy, we proceeded last Friday to the home of Mrs. Matilda Jackson, on Jackson's prairie, about ten miles southeast of Chehalis," Hobart said. *"Mrs. Jackson is the widow of John R. Jackson, who crossed the plains in 1844, and in 1845 took a donation claim on this prairie which is on the divide between the Columbia and Chehalis rivers. He soon built a cabin and improved and fenced a few acres.*

"Mrs. Jackson is a native of Maryland, born January 29, 1810 [sic, should be 1811], and fairly educated. At the age of 26 she first married Nicholas Koontz in Missouri. In 1847 Mr. Koontz with his wife and four boys crossed the plains for the Willamette Valley, Oregon, and when they, with others of their company, reached the Snake river in what is now Idaho, Mr. Koontz was drowned therein in his effort to rescue an ox while crossing. Here Mrs. Koontz, with her four young boys, was left alone. She proceeded to Fort Walla Walla, where Dr. Whitman was then located, to whose company of pioneers he preached a sermon during their visit.

"The captain of their company across the plains kindly assisted Mrs. Koontz to Oregon City, the destination of her husband. Here she remained until May, 1848, where she had formed the acquaintance of John R. Jackson, a bachelor, who like others had to come from their claims to Oregon City for supplies, and in that month she married Mr. Jackson, and he took her and her four boys, Henry, Barton, Grundy, and John N. Koontz, to his home on Jackson Prairie. Subsequently Henry and Grundy died leaving Barton and John N., who reside on the prairie. Barton, a bachelor, remains with and takes care of his mother, who is now 84 years old. John, on another part of the prairie allotted to him, is a well-to-do farmer and his hospitality Senator Long and myself shared the following night.

"The following day we visited Mrs. Jackson and heard her story of pioneer days which we noted down. Mr. Jackson was an Englishman by birth, and knew the Hudson's Bay Company people. We often heard the name of Edward Huggins, the treasurer of the State Historical society, mentioned by these very early pioneers in this section.

"Jackson's Prairie is on the road from Fort Vancouver to Fort Steilacoom, along which soldiers used to pass and often stop for supplies. Mrs. Jackson remembers with pride that Gen. U.S. Grant had stopped at their house; that Generals McClellan and Sheridan had also been there. She gave us some incidents of Indian experiences, mentioning the fact that after the Indians learned that Mr. Jackson was an Englishman and not one of the hated 'Bostons,' they were not molested and often fed the Indians. In early times they were obliged to employ Indians to help in their harvesting—there

Chapter Twenty-Three: Preserving Pioneer History

Handwritten receipt:

Barton Koontz 1882
Bought of Woods & Cuples

Jun 9	1018	White Lead	8	81 44
	50 Gal	Boiled Linseed Oil	70	35 00
	20 "	Turpentine	92½	18 50
	½ "	Prussian Blue		25
	½ "	Chrome Yellow		25
	1 "	Light Oak Graining		25
	1 "	Dark "		25
	1 "	Walnut		25
	5 "	Whiting		25
	5 "	Venn Red		30
	5 "	Yellow Ocher		30
	1½ "	Vermillion		40
	2 "	Vandyke Brown		35
	2 Bot	Shelack Varnish		1 75
	¼ "	Rose Lake		25
	½ Gal	Copal Varnish		1 25
	½ "	Coach "		1 50
	1	Flat point Brush		1 25
	8 "	Putty		50
				$144.29

WASHINGTON STATE LIBRARY'S COLLECTION OF THE JACKSON, KOONTZ, GLOVER FAMILY PAPERS, 1837–1952.

Above is a detailed receipt of purchases by Barton Koontz, while below is a road supervisor's certificate showing John Coonse continued work maintaining local roads. Note again the inconsistent spelling of the Koontz surname.

Road Supervisor's Certificate.

I hereby certify that John Coonse has performed 7 day's labor on the highways in Lewis Coun'y, Washington Territory, under my direction, to the amount of 13.88 cents dollars, in payment of his road tax for the year 1880.

Henry Lucas, Supervisor,

Road District No. 30

Dated at Highland this 25 day of July 25 A.D. 1880

being no other help—and they always paid them in blankets or their equivalents. Blankets were their basis of values, and if they took shirts or other goods a blanket was the basis of their value. The natives then knew nothing about money or its value.

"After Washington territory was set off from Oregon in 1853, Mr. Jackson was asked by the judge if he could prepare a building in the new territory. In a week he and the boys cut the logs and other necessary material and erected a structure 16 by 26 feet ready for the court. Holes were cut for windows and doors, but no floor. A fire was made in the middle of the structure on the ground, the smoke ascending through an opening in the roof. Here the first and some subsequent terms of court in Washington territory were held. After this, Mr. Jackson lived in the building, with some additions, until his death in May, 1873, in his 73rd year of age. Photographic views of this historic building are to be taken for use. He was prominent in early-day public affairs, having been assessor, sheriff, representative in first territorial legislature, etc. Mr. Jackson is reputed by some to be the first pioneer settler north of the Columbia, and by others Col. Michael T. Simmons is awarded this honor, he having also crossed the plains in 1844 and located at and around Tumwater Falls. He was also a conspicuous person in pioneer days and a strong friend of George Bush, of Bush's Prairie, Thurston County.

"Mrs. Jackson has lived at her present home on Jackson's Prairie for 46 years and never rode on a railroad, never saw a railroad or train of cars but once and those a few years ago at Napavine, some six miles from her home."

The two men gathered photos of the Jacksons, Michael T. Simmons and his daughter Charlotte Koontz, John's wife, and other historic figures. They obtained a lock and key from one of Peter Bernier's sons. It fastened the door of his early house five or six miles from the Jacksons' home, a home purchased from the Hudson's Bay Company large enough for a penitentiary, according to Hobart. They took home a six-tube lead candle mold that John R. Jackson bought from the Hudson's Bay Company but that his wife found too heavy. He later bought a twelve-tube tin mold for her.

They also visited Bernier's home and Claquato, where Lewis A. Davis had taken a donation land claim and erected a building as a courthouse. His son, Henry C. Davis, owned the property in 1894.

"Mingling as I did among the people in various localities while on the trip, I could not close my ears to political gossip. From the general expression I heard there appeared to be no doubt among the Republicans but that they will carry the county by an increased Republican majority," Hobart said. *"But that is not yet 'historical.'"*

When she was eighty, Matilda left the house to gather fallen apples from the ground, but she fell on the frosty back steps and shattered her hip. Afterward, she was confined to her bed or a chair, unable to move easily.

Granddaughters who visited Matilda Jackson sometimes reported home to their mother, saying, "Grandma Jackson was sad today," and their mother would reply, "I suppose she has been remembering some of the sorry things that have happened to her," according to a newspaper column by Betsy Hemenway and Karin Soderland.

In June 1899, *The Winlock Pilot* published a story about Jackson Prairie and Matilda, describing her as "one of the most interesting personages in the state of Washington among the pioneers."[2] It recapped her early history, John R. Jackson's trip across the Oregon Trail in 1844, her first husband's tragic death in the Snake River in 1847, their stay at Fort Walla Walla where Doctor Marcus Whitman preached to them, and her life in Oregon City. The story described how she married John R. Jackson in 1848 and brought her family north to his place on the prairie that bears his name, Jackson Prairie.

"Two of the sons have since died, but two others, John and Barton, are still living on the prairie, and are respected citizens of the county," the article states.

The Oregonian correspondent who wrote the article, which was also published in *The Seattle Post-Intelligencer* May 24, 1899, described Matilda, at eighty-eight, as still an interesting person.

"Her mind is bright, and her memory is still good," the article states.[3] "She has lived on the prairie for about fifty-two years, and her life has been one of the most regular habits."

The article speaks of the construction of the Jackson Courthouse but says it was built in 1853 rather than 1850. After its use as a courthouse, the article states that Jackson used the building until his death in 1873.

By 1899, the building was still standing but overgrown with ivy and myrtle. The author described it as "an interesting relic of Washington's early history, and within sight of the comfortable home of her son, Barton Koontz, with whom Mrs. Jackson is spending in peace and quietude her declining years."

LEWIS COUNTY HISTORICAL MUSUEM P21504

Sometimes Matilda's grandchildren described her as "sad" in later years.

Chapter Twenty-Four

Legacy of a Great Lady

O N VALENTINE'S DAY OF THE NEW CENTURY, February 14, 1901, Matilda Koontz Jackson died at home, just sixteen days after her ninetieth birthday.
The Chehalis Examiner published news of her death February 22, 1901.[1]

Mrs. Matilda Jackson was born in Maryland January 29, 1811. She spent her youth in that state. Later she went to Missouri, where at the age of 26, she married Nicholas Koontz. This was in 1837. In 1847, they, with four children, all boys, started for Oregon. The journey was an arduous one, being made in wagons, the only available means of crossing the plains in those days. In Idaho, while attempting to rescue an ox in the Snake River, Mr. Koontz was drowned.

The widow with her boys accompanied their fellow immigrants as far as Fort Walla Walla. During their stay there they met Dr. Whitman, who preached to them. When Mr. and Mrs. Koontz left their home in Missouri, their destination was the Willamette Valley, and after a short sojourn at Fort Walla Walla, Mrs. Koontz continued her journey and finally settled at what is now Oregon City. In 1844 Mr. John R. Jackson crossed the plains and took up a donation claim on the prairie which later assumed his name. In those days there was no Portland and the nearest place at which Mr. Jackson and his fellow settlers could obtain supplies was Oregon City. There he met Mrs.

Koontz, whom in 1848 he married. After the ceremony Mr. and Mrs. Jackson and the four boys returned to the homestead in Lewis County, where they continued to live until Mr. Jackson's death occurred in 1873, and where his widow lived up to the time of her death last week. Two of the boys who crossed the plains are dead, but the other two, John and Barton, are still alive, the former a resident of Chehalis, and the latter still a resident on the old prairie homestead.

Mrs. Jackson's mind and memory were clear until the end. Strange to say she never rode on a railroad train and only saw a train of cars once, a few years ago when she visited Napavine only six miles distant from her home.

The Jackson home was on the old military road from Fort Vancouver to Fort Steilacoom, and she remembered perfectly well General U.S. Grant stopping at her home while engaged in his military duties in the Northwest. She also met in the same way Generals Sheridan and McClellan. [The three men were not generals at the time.]

On the old homestead was built the first courthouse in Lewis County, and it stands today as a monument to the enterprise of Mr. Jackson and his stepsons. In 1850, the judge asked Mr. Jackson to prepare a place in which to hold the first court. Mr. Jackson and his boys cut the logs and built a house 16 by 26. There were only holes for windows and there was no floor save one of earth. In this building court was held for several years. Subsequently it was occupied by Mr. Jackson and it was there that he died in 1873 in his 73rd year.

Of late years, Mrs. Jackson lived with her son, Barton. It is to be hoped that the old courthouse will be preserved in memory of the old pioneer days.

Mrs. Jackson also left two daughters, Mrs. Phillips and Mrs. Ware.

Many other newspapers carried the story of her death, including *The Chehalis Bee-Nugget* March 1, 1901, with much of the information repeated.

Mrs. Matilda Jackson, better known as "Grandma Jackson," died at her home on Jackson Prairie, twelve miles southeast of

Chapter Twenty-Four: Legacy of a Great Lady

THE MORNING OREGONIAN, MARCH 11, 1901

One of the many tributes to Matilda Jackson upon her death.

Chehalis, Thursday night of last week. The funeral occurred Saturday morning and the remains were interred in the Urquhart cemetery near Chehalis.

Mrs. Jackson was the widow of John R. Jackson, who crossed the plains in 1844, and in 1845 took a donation land claim on this prairie, which is on the divide between the Cowlitz and Chehalis river valleys. Mrs. Jackson is a native of Maryland and was born in 1811....

During the later years of her life, Mrs. Jackson lived in a comfortable, modern house, but the remains of the first court house in the territory still stand on the prairie, grown over with briars, a curiosity to those who know its history. Mrs. Jackson was a woman of fair education, but the habit of staying at home became firmly fixed and it is related that she never rode on a railroad train and never but once saw a train of cars although a railway is only six miles distance from the prairie.

She leaves two sons who are living, Barton Koontz and John Koontz. Mrs. Jackson leaves two daughters, Mrs. Louisa Ware and Mrs. S.A. Phillips.

The Morning Oregonian published a photo of Matilda Jackson and another of her home March 11, 1901, under the headline "The Late Mrs. Matilda Jackson, Washington Pioneer of 1847."[2] It repeated the information in The Chehalis Bee-Nugget obituary but described the location of Jackson Prairie, twelve miles southeast of Chehalis, Washington.

THE CHEHALIS BEE-NUGGET, MARCH 1, 1901

Another obituary described her life and her death under the headline, "Death of Lewis County's Oldest Pioneer" and noted that she died at midnight at the home of her son, Barton Koontz. The funeral took place at the Jackson home with the Reverend L.S. Mochel of Toledo officiating. She was laid to rest at the Urquhart Cemetery, today known as Fern Hill Cemetery. The remains of her husband, John R. Jackson, were also moved to that cemetery. It noted she was survived by two sons, John and Barton Koontz, and two daughters, Mrs. S.A. (Mary) Phillips and Mrs. J.G. (Louisa) Ware. It noted that two of her sons, Henry and Grundy, died some years ago, but it failed to mention Andrew.

The loss of Grandma Jackson was compounded later in the year when her youngest surviving son, John Nicholas Koontz, died December 21. He was buried in Chehalis.

An obituary was published in *The Chehalis Bee-Nugget* December 27, 1901.[3]

Another Pioneer Has Passed Away.

John N. Koontz, a well known pioneer citizen of Lewis county, died at his home in this city Saturday, December 21, 1901, of heart failure brought on by an attack of pneumonia, aged 57 years.

He left a wife and four daughters, Misses Anna, Nettie and Jessie and Mrs. J.U. Smith, now a resident of the Hawaiian Islands; also a brother, Barton Koontz, and two half-sisters, Mrs. S.A. Phillips and Mrs. Joseph Ware, all of this county, together with a large circle of friends, to mourn his loss.

The deceased was one of Lewis county's most highly respected citizens and the history of his life forms an important part of the early history of what is now the State of Washington.

Funeral services were conducted at the family home in McFadden Addition by Rev. Monfort of the Chehalis Presbyterian church. The services at the grave were conducted by Chehalis Lodge No. 28, A.F. and M., of which order Mr. Koontz was an honored member.

Messrs. John T. Newland, John Goff, W.M. Urquhart, Francis Donahoe, T.B. Mitchell and William West, all old pioneers, acted as pall-bearers.

The deceased, with his parents and three brothers crossed the plains in '47, bound for Oregon City. Mr. Koontz's father was acci-

PEOPLE'S ADVOCATE.

Chehalis, Washington, Friday, December 27, 1901.

Another Pioneer Has Passed Away.

John N. Koontz, a well known pioneer citizen of Lewis county, died at his home in this city Saturday, December 21, 1901, of heart failure brought on by an attack of pneumonia, aged 57 years.

He left a wife and four daughters, Misses Anna, Nettie and Jessie and Mrs. J. U. Smith, now a resident of the Hawaiian Islands; also a brother, Barton Koontz, and two half-sisters, Mrs. S. A. Phillips and Mrs Joseph Ware, all of this county, together with a large circle of friends, to mourn his loss.

The deceased was one of Lewis county's most highly respected citizens and the history of his life forms an important part of the early history of what is now the State of Washington.

Funeral services were conducted at the family home in McFadden Addition by Rev. Monfort of the Chehalis Presbyterian church. The services at the grave were conducted by Chehalis Lodge, No. 28, A. F. and A. M., of which order Mr. Koontz was an honored member.

Messrs. John T. Newland, John Goff, W. M. Urquhart, Francis Donahoe, T. B. Mitchell and William West, all old pioneers, acted as pall-bearers.

The deceased, with his parents and three brothers crossed the plains in '47, bound for Oregon City. Mr. Koontz's father was accidentally drowned in the Snake River while the immigrating party was in camp on the bank of that stream. Mrs. Koontz came on to Oregon City where the following year she married John R. Jackson who had already taken up a donation land claim in this county, and made her subsequent home on Jackson's Prairie where the deceased grew to manhood. On November 13, 1867 he was united in marriage to Miss Charlotte Simmons, who survives him. She is a daughter of Col. M T Simmons, a pioneer of '44.

The Jackson home was on the road from Ft. Vancouver to Ft. Steilacoom and the family entertained Generals Grant, Sheridan, McClellan and other notable men. Mr. Jackson and the boys, at the direction of the territorial judges, built the first court house in the territory, which was located on their farm where it still stands, an interesting relic of pioneer days. Mr. Jackson, who

had been elected to various offices of honor and trust, died in 1873. Mrs. Jackson enjoyed reasonably good health almost up to the hour of her death which did not occur till in Feburary of this year, she having attained a full "four score and ten."

THE PEOPLE'S ADVOCATE, DECEMBER 27, 1901

Matilda's youngest surviving son, John, died the same year she passed away. Below is a photo of Matilda Jackson in her later years.

C2016.0.185 WASHINGTON STATE HISTORICAL SOCIETY, TACOMA, WASHINGTON

dentally drowned in the Snake River while the immigrating party was in camp on the bank of that stream. Mrs. Koontz came on to Oregon City where the following year she married John R. Jackson who had already taken up a donation land claim in this county, and made her subsequent home on Jackson's Prairie where the deceased grew to manhood. On November 13, 1867 he was united in marriage to Miss Charlotte Simmons, who survives him. She is a daughter of Col. M.T. Simmons, a pioneer of '44.

Six years later, Mary (Jackson) Phillips lost her husband, Sylvanus. *The Lewis County Advocate* reported his death July 19, 1907, under the headline, "Another Old Pioneer Gone."[4]

S.A. Phillips, for Many Years an Honorable Citizen, Passes Away

S.A. Phillips, one of Lewis County's most respected and honored citizens, and an old pioneer of this section, died of Bright's disease, July 14, 1907, at his home in Chehalis.

Mr. Phillips was born in Niagara County, N.Y., Nov. 1, 1830, and was in his seventy-seventh year at the time of his death. He left New York when 22 years of age and first settled in Michigan, but a short time later he left that state and came West to Washington and has been a citizen of this state and of Lewis County for the past 50 years.

In 1859 he first settled on his old home place near Chehalis, and has lived there continuously up to the time of his death. Mr. Phillips was married twice, his wife who survives him, formerly being Miss Mary Jackson, of the well known Jackson family on Jackson Prairie, whom he married in 1870. He had four children by his first marriage, all of whom, with the exception of Mrs. Mary Gregg of Clarkston, Wash., are dead.

The deceased was one of Lewis County's best citizens, was public spirited and always ready with his wise counsel to help the needy and deserving. Mr. Phillips was an Indian war veteran, having served his country faithfully through all the trying years of the life of the early pioneers.

He served Lewis County as county commissioner for one term, and has held several positions of trust and prominence. He was an excellent neighbor, a true friend, and no one ever went away from Uncle Vean, as he was commonly called, with an empty hand. He was honest, fearless and capable, and no one will be missed more than Uncle Vean Phillips.

The funeral was one of the most largely attended ever held in Chehalis, the services being conducted by Rev. Dickson of the Episcopal church.

The following year, Barton Koontz likely surprised many people when the lifelong bachelor married Jane E. Riches. Barton was sixty-eight at the time; Jane was sixty-five. They were married September 24, 1908, in Chehalis. The October 2, 1908, *Chehalis Bee-Nugget* reported on the nuptials.[5]

Barton Koontz and Mrs. Jane E. Riches of near Chehalis were united in marriage in this city September 24, Justice W. A. Westover officiating.

But their marriage lasted only three years as Jane died July 6, 1911, in Chehalis.

It's likely that Louisa comforted her sister and brother upon the deaths of their spouses, and they probably did the same for Louisa after her husband wound up in prison in 1909.

Louisa's husband, Joe Ware, and a neighbor fought over stolen rope and a hammer. The dispute escalated to violence when Joe shot and killed the man. He was charged with first-degree murder but

THE PEOPLE'S ADVOCATE, JULY 19, 1907

convicted of manslaughter and sentenced to serve time in the Walla Walla penitentiary.

On May 28, 1909, *The Washington Standard* ran a story about the shooting.[6]

KILLS FRIEND ON TRIVIAL CAUSE.—Joe Ware, a pioneer farmer living on Jackson prairie, 12 miles southeast of Chehalis, shot and instantly killed his neighbor, J.M. Corp, during a dispute over a picket rope, Tuesday, which Ware accused the ten-year-old son of Corp of stealing. Corp leaves a large family.

The Evening Statesman in Walla Walla ran a short piece about the shooting May 31, 1909.[7]

Pictures of Murder Scene

CENTRALIA, Wash., May 30—J.R. Buxton, prosecuting attorney of Lewis county, yesterday had pictures taken of the scene of the murder of James M. Corp by Joseph Ware, to be used in evidence at the trial of Ware. Ware shot and instantly killed Corp Tuesday night because a son of Corp, while playing, found a piece of rope in a road and carried it away. The rope belonged to Ware. Corp leaves a widow and 12 children. Ware is a wealthy farmer and formerly respected.

Mary (Jackson) Phillips died early February 25, 1914. *The Chehalis Bee-Nugget* published the following notice.[8]

Mrs. S.A. Phillips died at her home two miles east of Chehalis early Wednesday morning, aged 65 years. Mrs. Phillips was well known by the people of Lewis County who have lived here many years. She was born July 9, 1849, on Jackson Prairie and was a daughter of J.R. Jackson, one of the earliest settlers in this county. She was married May 3, 1870, to S.A. Phillips and has lived since then in the home in which she died. She is survived by one sister, Mrs. J.G. Ware, and a brother, Barton Koontz, both of Jackson Prairie. The funeral will be held this Friday afternoon from the residence at 1 o'clock.

The Lewis County Advocate ran a story the same day under the headlines, "Mary E. Phillips, Native Daughter of County, Passes On" and "Born on Jackson Prairie 65 Years Ago, Died Wednesday Morning at Home on Phillips Farm Near This City," "Was Daughter of First Lewis County Sheriff," and "Home of Early Childhood Was Old Jackson Prairie Court House—Had Never Lived Outside Lewis County—The Funeral Will Be Held This Afternoon at 1:00 O'Clock."[9]

Mrs. Mary E. Phillips, one of the first white children born in Lewis County or in the state of Washington, passed away at her home on the Phillips farm, two miles south of this city Wednesday morning at one o'clock. Death came after a slow decline which began about a year ago, and was due to paralysis.

Mary E. Phillips was the daughter of John R. Jackson, first sheriff of Lewis County and one of the first settlers in this section of the state. She was born on Jackson Prairie, which was named for her father, July 9th, 1849, and would have been 65 years of age at her next birthday. Her early youth was spent at the home of her father, known as the old Jackson Prairie court house because of its use for the purpose of holding court during the early years of Mary's life.

On May 3, 1870, Mary E. Jackson and S.A. (Vean) Phillips were married and they made their home on the Phillips farm near Chehalis. The husband died about six years ago and after his death Mrs. Phillips continued to make her home there until her death. All her life, then, has been spent in Lewis County with the exception of a short time when she attended school in Seattle. Her residence has never been elsewhere. She was well known in every part of the county and had a great many friends in this city. A sister, Mrs. J.G. Ware, and a half-brother, Barton Koontz, both of whom are residents of Jackson Prairie, survive her.

The funeral service will be held from the home this afternoon at one o'clock, E.D. Fissel in charge. Rev. A.H. Chittenden will conduct the services. Interment will be in the Phillips cemetery.

With the loss of her mother, brother, and sister, Louisa (Jackson) Ware may have felt some urgency to honor her mother before it was too late.

Chapter Twenty-Four: Legacy of a Great Lady

The family's homestead had passed into other hands after the death of Matilda Jackson. In 1915, Augustine Donahoe and his wife, who owned the property on which the deteriorating Jackson Courthouse stood, donated the building and a 100- by 200-foot tract of land to the Washington State Historical Society.

At that time, members of the St. Helens Club of Chehalis decided to renovate the dilapidated historic landmark. Among the club's members was Matilda's granddaughter, Chehalis librarian Anna Koontz, and Ethel M. Bush, whose husband published many historic articles in *The Chehalis Bee-Nugget*. The club members solicited donations from Chehalis businessmen to pay for completely restoring the log cabin built of stripped fir logs with a loft overhead accessed for years by cleats nailed to the side of the wall and a hole in the top floor. They preserved as much of the original wood as possible, such as the steep staircase that eventually replaced the cleats. Afterward, the courthouse and surrounding 1.4 acres became

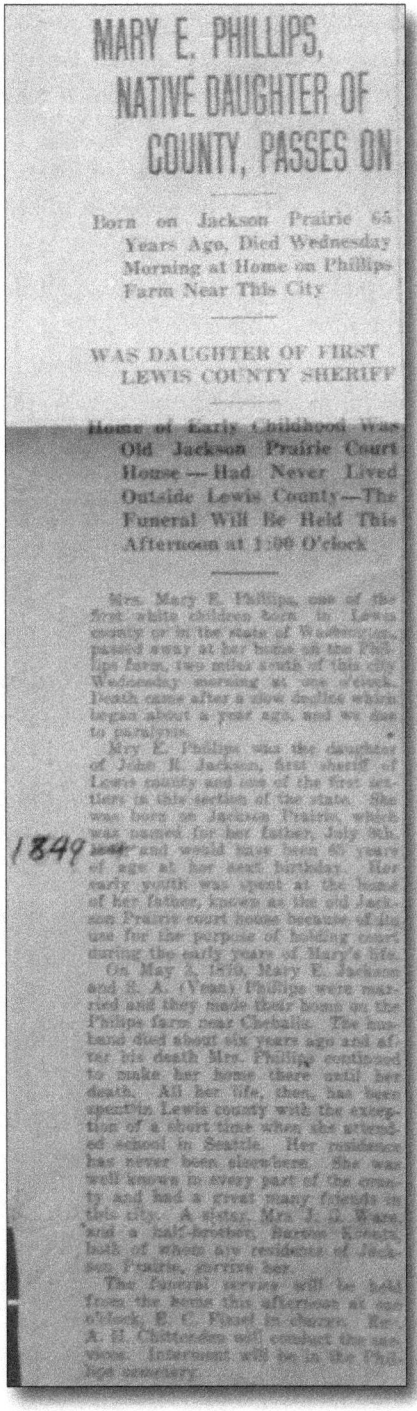

Lewis County Advocate, February 25, 1914

Washington's second state park. (The first state park was created in October 1915 after Pacific Realty Company, representing the Larrabee estate of Bellingham, donated twenty acres south of Bellingham for park purposes.)

The following year, in 1916, Louisa set aside five acres to the north of the courthouse as a park in honor of her mother.

The Chehalis Bee-Nugget published a story about the park dedication September 1, 1916, with the headline "In Honor of Mrs. Jackson" and the subheadline stating "Mrs. Louisa Ware to Dedicate Park on Jackson Prairie." Another subheadline states: "Five Acre Tract Will Be Set Aside to Public in Honor of Mrs. Ware's Mother, Matilda N. Jackson, Famed Early Pioneer."[10]

Readers of the Bee-Nugget will remember with much interest the fact that recently A. Donahoe donated to the state the site of the old courthouse on Jackson Prairie, and that following the tendering of the deed, the St. Helens Club and state historical society of the state got busy and had the old courthouse restored. Another historical spot in Lewis County has been deeded to the public.

Mrs. Louisa Ware, daughter of Mrs. Matilda N. Jackson, has donated a five-acre tract about the middle of the Jackson prairie, on the right hand side of the road, going south, and on the Pacific highway. This tract is to be improved and made a comfort station and park for the benefit of the public. It is located in a beautiful spot on the prairie, easily accessible, and will prove a great convenience to the traveling public. It is planned to park the spot, and in every way possible improve it. A big fireplace will be built, good, cool water piped to it, etc. Governor Lister will be asked to dedicate the new park a little later.

Mrs. Ware will donate the tract with the understanding that it will be dedicated to the memory of her mother, Mrs. Matilda N. Jackson.

The Bee-Nugget story recapped her early life, her historic trek westward in 1847, the drowning of her first husband in the Snake River, and her marriage to John R. Jackson in May 1848.

Chapter Twenty-Four: Legacy of a Great Lady

Mrs. Jackson died in 1900. The Jackson home, at the site of the old courthouse mentioned above, was the favorite stopping place for travelers for years, and was known all over the west for the fine hospitality given. The Jacksons bore an excellent reputation, Mrs. Jackson in particular being highly spoken of for her many admirable qualities.

Nicholas Koontz, Mrs. Jackson's first husband, and who was drowned in the Snake River, was the grandfather of Misses Anna Koontz, Nettie Koontz and Jessie Koontz of Chehalis and Mrs. John U. Smith.

Lewis County people, and the public in general, will be pleased to learn of the new park, which will be a boon to travelers, and serve to help preserve the memory and the history of one of the famous characters of the west in the very early days.

Louisa Ware did something quite smart when she deeded those five acres along the Pacific Highway (Old Highway 99, now known as Jackson Highway) north of Mary's Corner at the U.S. Highway 12 intersection. She insisted in the deed that it perpetually serve as a waystation for travelers, which has prevented the state from selling the land during tight financial times. The park, nestled among tall Douglas fir trees about a half mile north of the

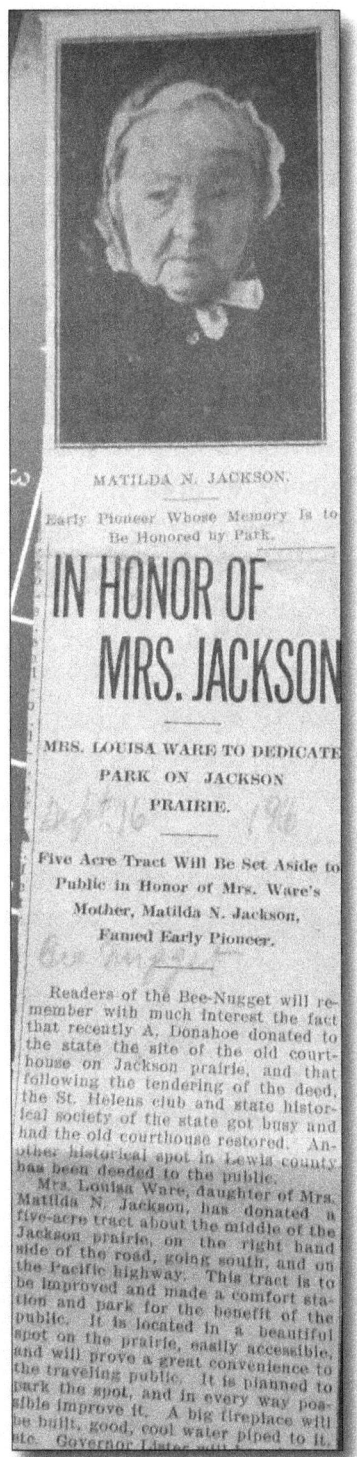

Jackson Courthouse, features picnic tables and a shelter. A brass plaque on a stone marker, placed at the entrance to the park by the Daughters and Sons of the American Revolution in 1916, commemorates its location along the Oregon Trail with the date 1844. Marking the Oregon Trail was the brainchild of Ezra Meeker, who first crossed the trail in 1852 with his wife, Eliza Jane, and their newborn son, Marion. After living in Portland, he moved north to Puyallup, Washington, in 1862 and established a hops farm. When he was seventy-six, Meeker set out January 29, 1906, to cross the country in an ox-drawn prairie schooner and raise awareness of the need to mark the historic trail that brought so many pioneers west.

Eight months after the park dedication, Louisa's last surviving sibling passed away. *The Chehalis Bee-Nugget* published his obituary May 25, 1917, under the headline "B. Koontz, Pioneer, Passes" and "Came to Lewis County 69 Years Ago, Settling on Jackson Prairie."[11]

The death of Barton Koontz, 12 miles southeast of Chehalis, at the home of his sister, Mrs. L.M. Ware, on Jackson Prairie, Saturday, May 19, recalls the early history of that section of Lewis County which has a noteworthy significance.

Mr. Koontz' parents left his birthplace in Missouri in 1847, where he was born in 1840, and started for Oregon. The father died on the journey, and after reaching Oregon, a short time before coming to Lewis county, his mother married J.R. Jackson. They settled on the homestead on Jackson prairie 69 years ago. Here was located the old Jackson prairie court house where Generals Grant and Sherman and other prominent men in the early Northwest history [stopped by]. The old log court house began to decay and about two years ago the St. Helens club of Ladies of Chehalis interested the state Historical Society in the little house and it has now been restored. The Jackson homestead has been the home of the family ever since it was first settled, though Mrs. Jackson died some years ago. The first territorial court held in the state of Washington was held in the little one-room log hut. A. Donahoe, who owned the site on which the old court house stands, donated the site to the state. It is alongside the Pacific highway. Recently Mrs. Ware donated another five-acre tract near the old court house

Chapter Twenty-Four: Legacy of a Great Lady

to the state, which was accepted and will be made into a park by the state for automobile and other travelers on the highway.

Mr. Koontz funeral will be held at Sticklin's chapel in Chehalis tomorrow afternoon at 2 o'clock, interment being in Fern Hill cemetery.

Deceased is survived by his sister, Mrs. L.M. Ware of Jackson prairie, and four nieces, Mrs. John U. Smith of Newberg, Ore., and Misses Anna Nettie and Jessie Koontz, all of Chehalis.

Anna Koontz also belonged to the Washington State Historical Society, which helped provide money for further restoration of the courthouse. William P. Bonney, secretary of the state organization, told *The Chehalis Bee-Nugget* March 10, 1922, that work would commence in the summer to restore the cobblestone wall and archway and lay cement in front of the building.[12]

A dedication ceremony of the renovated Jackson Courthouse on October 21, 1922, drew about 150 people to the prairie, where they

---

B. KOONTZ, PIONEER, PASSES

Came to Lewis County 69 Years Ago, Settling on Jackson Prairie.

The death of Barton Koontz, 12 miles southeast of Chehalis, at the home of his sister, Mrs. L. M. Ware, on Jackson prairie, Saturday, May 19, recalls the early history of that section of Lewis county which has a noteworthy significance. Mr. Koontz' parents left his birthplace in Missouri in 1847, where he was born in 1840, and started for Oregon. The father was drowned in the Snake river on the journey and after reaching Oregon, a short time before coming to Lewis county, his mother married J. R. Jackson. They settled on the homestead on Jackson prairie, 69 years ago. Here was located the old Jackson prairie courthouse, where Generals Grant and Sherman and other prominent men in the early northwest history held court. The old log courthouse began to decay and about two years ago the St. Helens club of ladies of Chehalis interested the State Historical Society in the little house and it has been preserved. The Jackson homestead has been the home of the family ever since it was first settled, though Mrs. Jackson died some years ago. The first territorial court held in the state of Washington was held in the little one-room log hut. A. Donahoe, who owned the site on which the old courthouse stands, donated the site to the state. It is alongside the Pacific highway. Recently Mrs. Ware donated another five-acre tract near the old courthouse to the state, which was accepted and will be made into a pary by the state for automobile and other travelers on the highway.

Mr. Koontz' funeral was held from Sticklin's chapel Monday, May 21, interment being in Fern Hill cemetery under direction of L. J. Sticklin & Son.

Deceased is survived by his sister, Mrs. L. M. Ware of Jackson prairie, and four nieces, Mrs. John U. Smith of Newberg, Ore., and Misses Anna, Nettie and Jessie Koontz, all of Chehalis.

THE CHEHALIS BEE-NUGGET, MAY 25, 1917

listened to speakers under a beautiful autumn sun on a Saturday afternoon.¹³ The event, organized by the St. Helens Club and the Washington State Historical Society, opened with a patriotic song performed by Zella McMicken followed by an invocation delivered by the Reverend F.C. Stannard.

Senator W.S. Davis of Tacoma addressed the gathering, followed by Anna Koontz, who delivered a heartfelt tribute to her Grandma Jackson, recounting Matilda's rich life and hard work on the Jackson homestead, which served as an inn, grocery store, post office, and wedding chapel. She told Professor Edmond S. Meany of the University of Washington about her grandmother.

"Mrs. Jackson, as I knew her, was one of the finest, truest, and noblest women I have known," she said of her grandmother.

Ethel M. Bush, St. Helens Club president, reviewed the work that the club members did to renovate the old homestead.

Meany, a historian, spoke with eloquence about the personal lives of John and Matilda Jackson and other stalwart Washington pioneers.

W.P. Bonney delivered the main address.

"Mr. Chairman, Ladies and Gentlemen: The Washington State Historical Society has to do with the past, the present, the future; we are here today especially to do honor to pioneers who erected a home on this spot, a home that became a haven of rest for travelers as they plodded their weary way from the Columbia River to Puget Sound. John R. Jackson was born in the parish of Staindrop county of Durham, England, on the 13th day of January [1800]. He came to the United States in 1833, landing in New York September 27 of that year. Looking for frontier life he proceeded to Illinois, then to Missouri, finally on across the continental divide to Oregon in 1844. In those days the Willamette Valley was considered the Mecca of immigrants over the Oregon trail; however, the elevation of the valley, the proximity of rivers, showing flood conditions deterred Mr. Jackson from attempting permanent settlement; he started north to find land more to his liking and arrived on this prairie late in the fall of 1844; the spot met with his approval and he named it 'Highland.' In 1845 he erected a cabin, had it far enough along to entertain the Simmons party (the first American settlers on Puget Sound) as they passed here in October of that year. The house that was built in 1845 was not nearly so pretentious as the one which stands here now; this building was erected by Mr. Jackson, assisted by

Chapter Twenty-Four: Legacy of a Great Lady

NATIONAL REGISTER OF HISTORIC PLACES APPLICATION PHOTOS

In the decades after Matilda Jackson's death, the old courthouse cabin began to fall down. The St. Helens Club, led by Matilda's granddaughter, Anna Koontz, sought donations to pay for repairing the historic building. It was then given to the Washington State Historical Society in 1922.

Leander Wallace in the winter of [Anna Koontz corrected the date to 1850], and is far more commodious than the first cabin; it was planned with the idea of a home for a family, for during one of Mr. Jackson's trips to Oregon City he had met the widow Matilda N. Koontz.

"Just a few days ago while looking through our files of old newspapers, I came across the notice of a wedding, printed in the *Oregon Spectator* of May 4, 1848. It reads: 'Hymenial: Married, on the 4th inst., by Rev. H. John, J.R. Jackson, Esq., of Lewis County, to Mrs. Matilda N. Coonse of this city.' Before leaving his highland home on this auspicious trip to Oregon City, Mr. Jackson arranged with his man, Leander Wallace, to meet him and his family at Cowlitz Landing, with horses.

"The family came down the Willamette River, across the Columbia, up the Cowlitz in a chinook canoe, to the landing, then by horseback the intervening ten miles to Highland, where they arrived the evening of May 7, having been three days making the trip from Oregon City. Mr. Jackson was a good provider, a sociable host; Mrs. Jackson a competent housekeeper and a sympathetic woman. Highland, or Jackson's, as it was better known, soon gained a reputation for hospitality.

"Governor Stevens brought his family over this road from Cowlitz Landing to Olympia late in the fall of 1854. To give an intimate description of conditions at Jackson's at that time, I quote from Mrs. Stevens' diary: She writes: 'After another long day's tiresome travel, we stopped at a log house for the night; upon entering from the porch, we found a big room with a wood fire filling up one side, blazing and crackling; low chairs in front; in the center of the room was a table with a clean cloth on it, and a repast of well cooked food, relishing and abundant was placed upon it, to which we did ample justice.

"'Our host was an Englishman, a farmer, who was getting on well, a genial hospitable man; his wife was a superior woman; she was a fine looking woman and a thorough housekeeper. At night she took us across the yard into another log house and where we found a bright fire burning on the hearth, and nice, clean beds; I felt like staying in this comfortable shelter, hearing the rain patter on the roof until the rainy season was over, at least.'"

"I have frequently heard commendations similar to this from other pioneers of the early fifties; last week I talked with a lady who crossed

Chapter Twenty-Four: Legacy of a Great Lady

The program for the dedication of the stone wall and memorial tablets in 1922.

the plains in 1851 and she still retains pleasant memories of the night at Jacksons'; she is here on the platform today, Mrs. A.E. Bigelow of Olympia. Another lady from Seattle, who we expected here today, has told me recently of her stay here in 1853; she also remembers the entertainment at Jackson's at different times when she made the stage trip from Olympia to Monticello. Speaking of that stage trip reminds us of the perquisites enjoyed by mail passengers; the fare from Olympia to Monticello was $10. Some stretches of the road were extremely muddy; to lighten the burden for the horses, men were permitted to walk along these places and carry a fence rail on their shoulder so as to pry the wagon loose when stalled.

"Not only private affairs concerned the Jackson home; among records of court being held in Lewis County we find that in Sidney S. Ford's home court was held in October 1847, and several subsequent terms being held in the same place; Mr. Jackson's name is mentioned as being present in official capacity. In October of 1849, there was a session of federal court at Fort Steilacoom, and December 5, 1850, court was

> Exercises *to be held on the* Grounds *in*
> Front *of the* "Old Jackson Home"
> **Saturday October 21st, 1922**
> at 1:30 o'clock P. M.
>
> MUSIC
>
> Invocation .... Rev. F. C. Stannard
> Statement .... Senator W. S. Davis, Chairman
> Address .... Miss Anna C. Koontz
>   Grandma Jackson
> Address .... Mrs. D. W. Bush
>   Restoration of Old Cabin
> Address .... W. P. Bonney, Secretary
>   Washington State Historical Society
>
> Music
>
> UNVEILING THE TABLETS
>
> Statement by .... The Chairman
>
> *Responsive Reading*
>
> *Chairman* — In the name of God the Father of all; the builder of the universe.
> *People* — We gather here today.
> *Chairman* — For the honor of our commonwealth and benefit of the traveler.
> *People* — With ready minds and willing feet we come.
> *Chairman* — To honor the past.
> *People* — We have set these stones.
> *Chairman* — To enlighten the people of today and future generations.
> *People* — We unveil these tablets.
>
> Mrs. Louisa Ware, Miss Nettie Koontz, lift flags from tablets
> Reading the inscription on tablets.

WASHINGTON STATE LIBRARY'S COLLECTION OF THE JACKSON, KOONTZ, GLOVER FAMILY PAPERS, 1837–1952.

held here at the Jackson home. In addition to being a genial host, John R. Jackson was a man of affairs in a business way and politically. In 1847 he was sheriff of Lewis County; the boundaries of the county at that time were the Columbia River on the south to the British possessions on the north; from the Pacific Ocean on the west to the summit of the Rocky Mountains on the east, practically the entire territory that afterwards became the commonwealth of Washington. A vast domain for one man to keep in order. In our records we find no complaint that it was not kept in order, but we do find that in open court, held in the home of Sidney S. Ford, October 4, 1847, that the report of Sheriff John R. Jackson was accepted and approved.

"It was said by one of Sheriff Jackson's admirers that 'he could see farther with one eye than most men could with two.'

"In connection with the federal court held at Fort Steilacoom, copy of record at Olympia reads: 'At a district court of the United States for the County of Lewis in the Territory of Oregon, begun and held at Steilacoom in said county, on Monday, the 1st day of October, in the year of our Lord, one thousand eight hundred and forty-nine, before the Hon. William P. Bryant, sole judge of said court; the said court being opened in due form, by proclamation made by Joseph Meek, esquire, marshal of the said territory of Oregon.' The record shows that John R. Jackson, a 'good and lawful man,' was foreman of the grand jury and that the grand jury did on the second day of October, return in open court an indictment against six Indians for the murder of Leander G. Wallace. Further, the records show that the petty jury found four of the Indians not guilty and two of them, Kussass and Quallahworst, guilty of murder as charged. On the morning of the third of October, 1849, those two men were executed in the presence of Patkanim and several other members of the Snoqualmie tribe. This speedy and sure justice influenced the warriors of this tribe to respect the white man's law and they were allies of the whites in the war which came a few years later.

"Time does not permit that I should enumerate all of the tasks that Mr. Jackson performed as a public benefactor, but I will add that he was a member of the Cowlitz convention of August 29, 1851; a member of the Monticello convention of November 25, 1852; a member of the first territorial legislature, 1854; a captain of a volunteer company during the Indian war of 1855–56.

"When I first saw the Jackson home it was lined on the inside with newspapers that had been printed in the early sixties; I spent some time in reading various items; I recall that near the southeast corner of the room was a small item in a paper issued in July, 1864. It was a proclamation by Abraham Lincoln, then president of the United States; it recited that Congress had set aside a certain room to be known as 'statuary hall,' and invited the individual states to place in that hall statues of either bronze or marble representing men of the state who were considered worthy of such distinction; not more than two such statues were allowed from each state. I might say in passing that the state of Washington has never yet acted on that invitation; many of the other states have; personally, I should like to see the statues of Isaac I. Stevens, our first territorial governor, and Elisha P. Ferry, our first state governor, placed in statuary hall."

The dedication featured a responsive reading as two memorial tablets were unveiled.

Chairman—In the name of God the Father of all; the builder of the universe

People—We gather here today.

Chairman—For the honor of our commonwealth and benefit of the traveler.

People—With ready minds and willing feet we come.

Chairman—To honor the past.

People—We have set these stones.

Chairman—To enlighten the people of today and future generations.

People—We unveil these tablets.

One of two stone tablets explaining the significance of the courthouse was by the flag Matilda and others sewed in 1853 from wool bunting brought north from San Francisco. At the dedication, the two flags were removed by the Jacksons' daughter, Louisa Ware, and granddaughter Nettie Koontz. Over the gate in a cobblestone wall were the words "1847 Jackson House" and "1850 Courthouse." One of the tablet inscriptions reads: "Highland. John R. Jackson selected this spot for a home in 1844. It became famous as a stopping place for pioneer travelers over the Oregon trail. Governor Stevens and family spent a night here in 1854 on way to Olympia." The other tablet inscription states: "Court House. In addition to being the Jackson home, this was used as a courthouse as early as 1850. House and lot donated to the Washington State Historical Society by Augustine Donahoe and wife 1915."

Also attending the dedication were Charlotte (Simmons) Koontz, the widow of John Koontz, and Nettie Koontz, their daughter and Anna's sister.

The ceremony ended with everyone singing "Hail, Columbia," a popular song written in 1798 by Judge Joseph Hopkinson and sung to the tune of "The President's March," which was composed by Philip Phile for George Washington's inauguration.

Hail! Columbia, happy land! Hail! Ye heroes, heaven-born band, who fought and bled in freedom's cause, who fought and bled in freedom's cause, and when the storm of war is gone, enjoyed the

peace your valor won; Let Independence be your boast, ever mindful what it cost, ever grateful for the prize, let its altar reach the skies.
CHORUS:
Firm united, let us be, rallying round our liberty, as a band of brothers joined, peace and safety we shall find.

The Sunday Oregonian also reported on the dedication of the restored courthouse.

Since that initial renovation, the Jackson Courthouse has been revamped several times. The Washington State Parks Commission set aside $3,500 in the mid-1930s to rebuild and fix up the Jackson home with help from the Civilian Conservation Corps. *The Tacoma News Tribune* published a story about a National Parks Service restoration effort February 26, 1936, and recapped the significance of the historic Jackson Prairie courthouse, the finest cabin in the county for many years with its long spacious veranda.

"The cabin became famous as a stopping place and was the community center for miles around," the article noted.[14] "Young folks came there to get married. The pioneers came to hold celebrations, swap articles, and repair farm implements and wagons."

Anna Koontz tried to retrieve as many of the family's memorabilia as possible, including a candlestick sold by her uncle Barton.[15]

> H.J. Miller Lumber Company
> Seattle Wash.
> April 22, 1936
> My dear Anna Koontz:
> Pardon me for being remiss in answering your letter of March 29th.
> No, I am not mistaken in what I paid Barton Koontz for the candle stick, and as I negotiated with him alone, your Aunt may not have known of that particular transaction. I really would like you to have it for the old Court House, but don't like to lose the amount of difference between my purchase price and your offer. Did you speak to Mrs. Coleman regarding it? I am sure she would remember it, as she was with me that day.

Somewhere in my file I have considerable data compiled a long time ago on the Glover and one other family, of Maryland. The latter name I do not remember, but it was one of your own line connected with the Glover family. At the time of my copying this material I was sure it was your own, though I do not remember the details now, not having seen the material lately. It is somewhere in my files, probably not filed correctly. If you would send me Mrs. Root's Portland address I might submit same to her when I find the material.

You really should be a member of the D.A.R. inasmuch as your early ancestors in the State of Washington hold so much historical interest.

With all good wishes, I am,
Cordially yours,
Mabel J. Miller

Among the relics from the home of John and Matilda Jackson, given to the Washington State Historical Society by Anna C. Koontz July 10, 1947, were the following books: large Bible, inscribed "Mrs. Matilda Jackson's Book"; small Bible, inscribed "Mrs. Matilda Jackson's Book"; prayer book given to Mrs. Jackson by her friend Louise E. Kiser; a book of psalms and hymns of Dr. Watts, given to her by her brother John R. Glover; Common Prayer of the Protestant Episcopal Church; and a hymnal used for many years in the Jackson home. When she inscribed the books, she spelled her grandmother's first name as "Mathilda."

The Chehalis Bee-Nugget reported that the "Last of Historic Jackson Family Passes" January 18, 1938. "Death Takes Last Member of Pioneers," the subheadline states, and "Mrs. Louisa M. Ware, 84, Died Sunday Morning in Chehalis," "Born on Prairie," "Jackson Home on Prairie One of Most Famous in State History." Louisa Matilda (Jackson) Ware died January 16, 1838.[16] The article erroneously listed her father's middle name as Roberson instead of Robinson.

Mrs. Louisa M. Ware, 84, the last member of the historic Jackson family of pioneer fame, passed away early Sunday morning at the home of a niece, Mrs. Nettie Beireis, in Chehalis.

Chapter Twenty-Four: Legacy of a Great Lady

Louisa Jackson was born in the old family home on Jackson prairie May 11, 1853, and lived near there practically all of her life.

She was married on July 4, 1888, to Josiah G. Ware, who survives her. She had no children but is survived by four nieces, Mrs. John U. Smith, Miss Anna Koontz, city librarian, and Mrs. George Beireis, all of Chehalis, and Miss Jessie Koontz of Seattle. She had been ill at her home for some time before being brought to the home of her niece some weeks ago.

While not calling herself a pioneer, she was a daughter of early settlers of western Washington and a brief review of the lives of her parents is of historic interest.

In his articles on "living pioneers of Washington," Edmund S. Meany, professor of history at the University of Washington, said: "In March 1845 John R. Jackson started for Puget Sound from the Columbia river. He turned back from Simon Plomondon's place near the Newaukum river and in early July he started again with a number of companions. The latter turned back at the Chehalis river and Mr. Jackson staked a claim on what has since been known as Jackson prairie. Jackson was born in Durham, parish of Steindrop, January 13, 1800. He landed in New York September 27, 1823, and went directly to Illinois. He was naturalized as an American citizen in 1835. He came to Oregon in 1844.

He named his home on the prairie "Highland Farm." He was acting sheriff of Lewis county, which then comprised most of the territory north of the Columbia river, under the provisional government. He also served as probate judge, clerk of the courts, justice of the peace and was a member of the territorial legislature.

Mrs. Ware's mother was Mrs. Matilda Nettle Glover Koontz, a native of Maryland, who crossed the plains in 1847 with her first husband, Nicholas Koontz, who was drowned while fording the Snake river. Mrs. Koontz continued with her four little boys with the immigrant train. Near Walla Walla in October 1947, she heard Marcus Whitman preach a sermon just a month before his death in the Indian massacre at his mission. She continued on to Oregon City where she became the wife of John Roberson Jackson, and proceeded with him to Highland Farm, where she died in 1901 at the age of 90.

THE CHEHALIS BEE-NUGGET

CHEHALIS, LEWIS COUNTY, WASHINGTON, TUESDAY, JANUARY 18, 1938

RUSH KIDNAPER-MURDERER

Last Of Historic Jackson Family Passes

DEATH TAKES LAST MEMBER OF PIONEERS

Mrs. Louisa M. Ware, 84, Died Sunday Morning In Chehalis

BORN ON PRAIRIE

Jackson Home on Prairie One of Most Famous in State History

Mrs. Louisa M. Ware, 84, the last member of the historic Jackson family of pioneer fame, passed away early Sunday morning at the home of a niece, Mrs. Nettie Beireis, in Chehalis.

Louis Jackson was born in the old family home on Jackson prairie May 11, 1853, and lived near there practically all of her life. She was married on July 4, 1888 to Josiah G. Ware, who survives her. She had no children but is survived by four nieces, Mrs. John W. Smith, Miss Anna Koontz, city librarian, and Mrs. George Beireis, all of Chehalis, and Miss Jessie Koontz of Seattle. She had been ill at her home for some time before being brought to the home of her niece some weeks ago.

While not calling herself a pioneer, she was a daughter of early

(Please Turn to Page Three)

DEATH TAKES LAST MEMBER OF PIONEERS

(Continued from Page One)

settlers of western Washington and a brief review of the lives of her parents is of historic interest.

In his articles on "living pioneers of Washington," Edmund S. Meany, professor of history at the University of Washington said: "In March, 1845 John R. Jackson started for Puget Sound from the Columbia river. He turned back from Simon Plomondon's place near the Nawaukum river and in early July he started again with a number of companions. The latter turned back at the Chehalis river and Mr. Jackson staked a claim on what has since been known as Jackson prairie. Jackson was born in Durham, parish of Steindrop, January 13, 1800. He landed in New York September 27, 1823, and went directly to Illinois. He was naturalized as an American citizen in 1835. He came to Oregon in 1844.

He named his home on the prairie "Highland Farm." He was acting sheriff of Lewis county, which then comprised most of the territory north of the Columbia river, under the provisional government. He also served as probate judge, clerk of the courts, justice of the peace and was a member of the territorial legislature.

Mrs. Ware's mother was Mrs. Matilda Nettle Glover Koontz, a native of Maryland, who crossed the plains in 1847 with her first husband, Nicholas Koontz, who was drowned while fording the Snake river. Mrs. Koontz continued with her four little boys with the immigrant train. Near Walla Walla in October, 1847, she heard Marcus Whitman preach a sermon just a month before his death in the Indian massacre at his mission. She continued on to Oregon City where she became the wife of John Roberson Jackson, and proceeded with him to Highland Farm where she died in 1901 at the age of 90.

Jackson home was one of most famous of territorial In the fall of 1851 a new home was built, 16 by floor dimensions. Before [family] moved into it as sessions the federal court was held. Hundreds of pioneers traveling to or from Oregon stopped at the Jackson home and partook of the Jackson hospitality. There, a small girl Louisa saw U. S. George B. McClellan and J. Sheridan, while junior in the Northwest, traveled between Forts Vancouver and [home], who stayed overnight [at] home.

[Wash]ington Territory was created a short time before Louisa [was born]. Her father decided that [they] should have an American flag [over the] house and sent to San [Francis]co for materials and his [folk]s made the flag. It was [un]furled there on July 4 of [that ye]ar. It is believed to be the [first] American flag made in the [area], now forming the state of [Washin]gton and was in the possession of Mrs. Ware up to the [time of] her death.

[The] old Jackson cabin stands by [the side] of the Pacific highway. It [was] restored by the St. [Helens] club of Chehalis. This [small] tract of land 100 by 200 [feet wa]s deeded to the Washington [Sta]te Historical society and is [now the] property of the state. Mrs. [Ware la]ter deeded to the state five [acres o]n the old homestead on the [road a]nd asked that it be known [as Mati]lda Jackson park, in honor [of her] mother.

[Fune]ral services were held Tuesday [at] the John W. Boone mortuary. [The] Rev. Herbert E. Gordon [offic]iating. Interment was in the family plot in the Fernhill cemetery.

Pallbearers will be C. R. Mitchell, John W. Alexander, Henry Lucas and John Young, all of Chehalis, and A. D. Boone and George J. Galvin, both of Centralia.

THE CHEHALIS BEE-NUGGET,
JANUARY 18, 1938

Chapter Twenty-Four: Legacy of a Great Lady

The Jackson home was one of the most famous of territorial days. In the fall of 1851, a new log cabin home was built, 16 by 26 in floor dimensions. Before the family moved into it a session of the federal court was held in it. Hundreds of pioneers traveling to or from Oregon stopped at the home and partook of the famed Jackson hospitality. There, as a small girl, Louisa saw U.S. Grant, George B. McClellan and Philip H. Sheridan, while junior officers in the Northwest, traveling between Forts Vancouver and Steilacoom, who stayed overnight at the home.

Washington Territory was created by an act of Congress March 2, 1853, a short time before Louisa was born. Her father decided that he should have an American flag for his house and sent to San Francisco for materials and his home folks made the flag. It was the first unfurled there on July 4 of that year. It is believed to be the first American flag made in the area now forming the state of Washington and was in the possession of Mrs. Ware up to the time of her death.

The old Jackson cabin stands by the side of the Pacific highway. In 1915, it was restored by the St. Helens club of Chehalis. This, with a tract of land 100 by 200 feet, was deeded to the Washington State Historical Society and is now the property of the state. Mrs. Ware later deeded to the state five acres on the old homestead on the prairie and asked that it be known as the Matilda Jackson park, in honor of her mother.

Funeral services were held Tuesday at the John W. Boone mortuary, the Rev. Herbert E. Gordon of the Presbyterian church officiating. Interment was in the family plot at Fernhill cemetery.

Pallbearers will be C.R. Mitchell, John W. Alexander, Henry Lucas and John Young, all of Chehalis, and A.D. Boone and George J. Galvin, both of Centralia.

Two of Matilda's granddaughters, Chehalis librarian Anna Koontz and Dr. Kate L. Gregg, the daughter of Mary Phillips and a professor emeritus of English at Lindenwood College in St. Charles, Missouri, were honored in May 1947 by the Daughters of the Pioneers of Washington at their annual convention.

Gregg, the first woman to earn a doctorate degree from the University of Washington, wrote two books published by Oklahoma

University Press—*Westward with Dragoons* and *The Road to Sante Fe*—as well as many historical articles on Missouri and Washington history. She addressed the convention, speaking about "A Pioneer—Defined in Action."

Koontz, the granddaughter of two pioneer families—Michael T. Simmons and Matilda Koontz Jackson—served as president of the local chapter of the Daughters of Washington Pioneers and on the state association's board. Her involvement included participation in the St. Helens Club, the Women's Association of the Westminster Presbyterian Church, and other women's groups.

On December 12, 1950, a newspaper reported that the courthouse on Jackson Prairie would be restored after visits by the Historical Sites Advisory Board and members of the State Parks and Recreation Commission, legislative delegates including Senator Virgil R. Lee, and Chehalis Women's club members. The amount set aside for the work was $2,500. The group also decided to seek more antiques and curios of historical value for the cabin.

Later, in 1953, William K. Glenn, superintendent of Matilda Jackson State Park, said Anna Koontz was helping him to recreate the original floor plan of the building in preparation for spending another $1,500 restoring the courthouse. He said only the parlor remains intact. Workers planned to replace rotted logs, clean the interior, landscape the grounds, and set up a display of pioneer relics. Flossie Lucas, the wife of Henry Lucas, served as curator of the courthouse during the centennial week.

In the 1960s, a *Daily Chronicle* article by reporter George Blomdahl noted that an average of four hundred people a week stop by Jackson Courthouse, and more than a thousand signed a visitors' book in 1963.

On January 11, 1974, the John R. Jackson House was listed on the National Register of Historic Places.

The Washington State Parks and Recreation Commission maintained the building through the decades and invested money in its upkeep. A major renovation took place in 1995, complete with a rededication ceremony after work was completed. Workers identified and replaced deteriorating logs and repaired the foundation, fireplace, and chimney. The rededication featured a welcome and closing by J.A. Vander Stoep, presentation of colors by the Civil Air Patrol, and comments from Lewis County Commissioner Carl Hemenway, St. Helens Club member Jane Minear, Washington State Supreme Court Justice Gerry L. Alexander, and Cleve Pinnix, director of the Washington State Parks and Recreation Commission.

In 2016, the Jackson Courthouse was relisted on the Washington Heritage Register. A search of the National Register of Historic Places still shows the 1974 listing of the John R. Jackson House.

A major restoration of the old courthouse took place in the summer and fall of 2017. The state invested $216,000 to redo the cabin's front porch, repair water damage, restore the roof, and replace soft, rotten logs. Workers also added wheelchair-accessible pathways and three new interpretive panels. They retained as much of the original structure and construction as possible to retain the courthouse's listing as a state landmark on historic registries.

The Washington State Parks and Recreation Department hosted a rededication ceremony the afternoon of October 6, 2017. As a special treat, inside the courthouse, the Washington State Historical Society displayed the flag stitched together by Matilda and her neighbors, flown July 4, 1853, to mark the creation of Washington territory in March. Jackson sent to San Francisco for the wool bunting, and the women stitched until they ran out of cloth. Hence, the flag bears 13 stars and eight stripes.

During his presentation, former Washington Secretary of State Ralph Munro described the St. Helens Club's 1915 restoration of the courthouse as "the oldest historic preservation effort in Washington."

A bookmark commemorating the event, organized by area manager Pam Wilkins of the Washington State Parks and Recreation Department, describes the courthouse as "a rustic cabin reconstructed through the efforts of local women."

"This building really tells us a story, and that's why it's so important," Munro said.[17] "So much of our state's history lies in this yard and this building. If we don't understand our past, then we have no idea of how to conquer the future."

He focused his remarks on Matilda Koontz Jackson, giving a brief recap of a remarkable life. He told how she left Missouri with her husband, Nicholas, and their four boys, filled with high hopes as they traveled the prairies, avoided cholera in the Platte River Valley and crossed the Rocky Mountains. On September 7, 1847, only five hundred miles from Oregon City, Nicholas drowned crossing the Snake River. The next day, Matilda miscarried the daughter she was carrying. Later, someone even stole her oxen and wagon.

Matilda and her sons, he told the crowd, finally arrived at Oregon City on the Willamette River, the territory's first capital and a commercial hub for early settlers. In January 1848, she met John R. Jackson, a British native and naturalized American who had crossed the Oregon Trail four years earlier. He had visited Oregon City for supplies and returned home to Jackson Prairie in May with a wife and four sons. They traveled by flatboat, or barge, down the Willamette and Columbia rivers to the mouth of the Cowlitz, where Indians in canoes paddled them upstream to Cowlitz Landing at present-day Toledo.

"That same lady gave us every reason in the world to preserve and to protect this home," Munro said. "But it wasn't just for that.... In so many ways, she was the first lady of the territory."

Visitors saw the Jackson home as a bright beacon of hospitality, and Matilda served as gracious hostess to all, including Governor Isaac Stevens and his wife and Ulysses S. Grant, George McClellan, and Philip Sheridan who later became generals. She helped her husband in his roles as postmaster, judge, sheriff, and tax collector.

"Everybody talks about him, but I have to look at it through her eyes, and what a pioneer for our state that she was and the job that she did," Munro said.

He's right. Most of the history preserved in legal paperwork and court proceedings recount the life of John R. Jackson, but Matilda shines as pioneer woman who worked hard, cared for her family, friends, and strangers, and persevered when she endured heartache and loss. Her story exemplifies the journey of many early pioneer women. And her legacy is preserved forever at the Jackson Courthouse and the Matilda Jackson State Park in Lewis County, Washington.

> The Jackson House State Park Heritage Site is at 4277 Jackson Highway on Jackson Prairie. The website is at https://parks.state.wa.us/1060/Jackson-House. A Facebook page is dedicated to the Matilda Jackson State Park at https://www.facebook.com/pages/Matilda-Jackson-State-Park/105927436130135.

Chapter Twenty-Four: Legacy of a Great Lady

AUTHOR PHOTOS

A ceremony marked the Washington State Parks and Recreation Department's rededication of the Jackson Courthouse in October 2017. Area manager Pam Wilkins speaks to the audience in front of the courthouse, above. Below, former Secretary of State Ralph Munro cuts the ribbon to the renovated courthouse held by local Boy Scouts.

AUTHOR PHOTOS

The five-acre Matilda Jackson State Park, nestled in a forest of tall trees just north of the historic Jackson Courthouse, provides a peaceful place to picnic and rest. Matilda's daughter Louisa Ware donated the property to honor her mother, whose hospitality to weary travelers earned her a reputation for graciousness throughout the region and even the nation.

Endnotes

All references to today's dollar values come from the government CPI calculator or from West-egg, https://westegg.com/inflation/infl.cgi.

PROLOGUE
[1] Koontz, Anna. "Grandma Jackson Remembered," typewritten recollections. Washington State Library. 1953
[2] Ancestry.com, 1810 Census, nine slaves, https://search.ancestry.com/cgi-bin/sse.dll?indiv=1&dbid=7613&h=83861&tid=&pid=&usePUB=true&_phsrc=EZw1388&_phstart=successSource
[3] Lord Baltimore settling Maryland https://www.history.com/this-day-in-history/the-settlement-of-maryland
[4] Koontz, Anna. "Grandma Jackson Remembered," typewritten recollections. Washington State Library. 1953.
[5] Letter from Mabel Glover Roots, October 11, 1955, and Ancestry.com military records showing applications for pensions by both James and Philip Glover.
[6] Hannon, Trudy R. *John R. Jackson: Washington's First American Pioneer*. Advocate Printing. 1998.

CHAPTER ONE: THE COONTZ FAMILY
[1] Hahn, Dennis J. "Kountz Fort and The Boone's Lick Road," posted May 26, 2002. Regarding DAR marker for Kountz Fort in danger of being destroyed. dhahn@alvey.com
[2] Miles, Shute & Kons website on Nicholas Coonce/Kountz, 1759-1820. http://www.miles-shute-kouns-families.com/getperson.php?personID=I115&tree=Kouns-GalliaCo.O
[3] Bryan, William Smith. *A History of the Pioneer Families of Missouri: With Numerous Sketches, Anecdotes, Adventures, Etc., Relating to Early Days in Missouri. Also the Lives of Daniel Boone and the Celebrated Indian Chief Black Hawk with Numerous Biographies and Histories of Primitive Institutions.* 1876. Bryan Brand & Company. 528 pages.
[4] "Welcome to St. Charles County, Missouri: Forts." http://genealogytrails.com/mo/stcharles/hist_forts.htm
[5] St. Charles County Place Names. The State Historical Society of Missouri. https://shsmo.org/manuscripts/ramsay/ramsay_saint_charles
[6] Zimmerman, Jim. "Re: John, Jacob & Nicholas Coonce, St. Chas. MO." https://www.genealogy.com/forum/surnames/topics/coonce/36/
[7] Boone's Lick Road—Kountz Fort (1800). http://www.waymarking.com/waymarks/WM5T8B
[8] Gregg, Kate L. "The Boonslick Road in St. Charles County." From Missouri Historical Review, Volume 27 Issue 4, July 1933, pp. 307–314. http://statehistoricalsocietyofmissouri.org/cdm/compoundobject/collection/mhr/id/13394/rec/1
[9] *Old Franklin Intelligencer*, April 23, 1819, edition.
[10] Hahn, Dennis J. "Kountz Fort and The Boone's Lick Road," posted May 26, 2002. Regarding DAR marker for Kountz Fort in danger of being destroyed. dhahn@alvey.com

CHAPTER TWO: THE GLOVERS IN MISSOURI
[1] Missouri Compromise https://www.history.com/topics/missouri-compromise and https://www.history.com/topics/abolotionist-movement/missouri-compromise
[2] Missouri Compromise, https://en.wikipedia.org/wiki/Missouri_Compromise
[3] Handwritten notes from Anna Koontz. Washington State Library.
[4] "Marriage in the Colonies," https://classroom.synonym.com/age-marriage-us-1800s-23174.html

CHAPTER THREE: NICHOLAS AND MATILDA COONSE
[1] Panic of 1837. Ohio History Central. http://www.ohiohistorycentral.org/w/Panic_of_1837 and Panic of 1837 http://lehrmaninstitute.org/history/Andrew-Jackson-1837.html
[2] Receipt in the Jackson, Koontz, Glover family papers. Washington State Library.

³ *The Boon's Lick Times* of Fayette, Missouri, June 22, 1844. Page 2. https://www.newspapers.com/image/49666604. Downloaded May 15, 2018.
⁴ Daly, Walter J., M.D., "The Black Cholera Comes to the Central Valley of America in the 19ᵗʰ Century—1832, 1849, and Later," Transactions of the American Clinical and Climatological Association, The National Center for Biotechnology Information, https://www.ncbi.nlm.nih.gov/pmc/articles/PMC2394684/
⁵ Manifest Destiny. https://www.history.com/topics/westward-expansion/manifest-destiny
⁶ Manifest Destiny. http://www.ushistory.org/us/29b.asp
⁷ Francis Parkham and the Oregon Trail. https://www.univie.ac.at/Anglistik/easyrider/data/parkoret.htm
⁸ Hastings, Lansford Warren. *The Emigrants' guide to Oregon and California : containing scenes and incidents of a party of Oregon emigrants, a description of Oregon, scenes and incidents of a party of California emigrants, and a description of California : with a description of the different routes to those countries : and all necessary information relative to the equipment, supplies, and the method of traveling.* 1845. Cincinnati: G. Conclin. https://archive.org/details/emigrantsguideto04hast
⁹ Root, Mabel Clarissa Glover. *Family history of the Oregon pioneer families of Philip Glover and John H. Palmer.* Portland, Ore.: M.G. Root. 1966. Archived at the Oregon Historical Society's Research Library.

CHAPTER FOUR: WESTWARD BOUND
¹ Beireis, Nettie B. "A Sketch of Mrs. Matilda N. Jackson's Life: An Old Pioneer of Lewis County." Typed copy of handwritten and nearly illegible information at the Washington State Historical Society. 1939. Jackson, Koontz, Glover family papers. Washington State Library. Published by N.B. Coffman and Charles Miles in "Claquato Landmarks." *The Chehalis Bee-Nugget.* 1939.
² Letter from Captain Joseph Magone to Matilda (Coonse) Jackson January 20, 1848 from the Dallas Mission. Archived in the Jackson, Koontz, Glover family papers. Washington State Library.
³ Lyman, H.S. "Reminiscences of James Jory," *The Quarterly of the Oregon Historical Society,* Vol. 3, No. 3 (Sep., 1902), pp. 271–286 Published by: Oregon Historical Society. Stable URL: http://www.jstor.org/stable/20609535. Accessed: 21/10/2014 14:30.
⁴ End of the Oregon Trail Interpretive and Visitor Information Center. Oregon City, Oregon.
⁵ Hannon, Trudy R. *John R. Jackson: Washington's First American Pioneer.* Advocate Printing. 1998. pp. 13–14.
⁶ Coonse, Nicholas. One-page diary from May 1947. Archived in the Jackson, Koontz, Glover family papers. Washington State Library.
⁷ Gibson, James, 1834–1920. Typeset recollections of overland travel from Bates County, Missouri, to Linnton, Oregon, between May 15, 1847, and November 1847. Dictated to Minnie M. Richards. 1914. Seven pages. Archived in the Oregon Historical Society's Research Library.
⁸ Coonse, Nicholas. One-page diary from May 1947. Archived in the Jackson, Koontz, Glover family papers. Washington State Library.
⁹ Flora, Stephenie, and Nancy Prevost, compilers. "Emigrants to Oregon in 1847." Listing for Surnames A–L, M–Z. Oregonpioneers.com. http://www.oregonpioneers.com/1847
¹⁰ "Apples to Oregon: The Journey of Henderson Luelling." North Carolina Department of Natural and Cultural Resources. https://www.ncdcr.gov/blog/2015/12/28/apples-to-oregon-the-journey-of-henderson-luelling
¹¹ Blanchet, Rt. Rev. Augustine Magloire Alexander. Edward J. Kowrach; Jean Baptiste Abraham Bouilett. *Journal of a Catholic Bishop on the Oregon Trail: The Overland Crossing of the Rt. Rev. A.M.A. Blanchet, Bishop of Walla Walla, from Montreal to Oregon Territory,* March 23, 1847 to January 23, 1851. Ye Galleon Press, Fairfield, Wash. 1978.
¹² Blanchet, Rt. Rev. Augustine Magloire Alexander. Edward J. Kowrach; Jean Baptiste Abraham Bouilett. *Journal of a Catholic Bishop on the Oregon Trail: The Overland Crossing of the Rt. Rev. A.M.A. Blanchet, Bishop of Walla Walla, from Montreal to Oregon Territory,* March 23, 1847 to January 23, 1851. Ye Galleon Press, Fairfield, Wash. 1978.

Endnotes

[13] Lyman, H.S. "Reminiscences of James Jory," *The Quarterly of the Oregon Historical Society*, *Vol. 3, No. 3* (Sep., 1902), pp. 271–286 Published by: Oregon Historical Society. Stable URL: http://www.jstor.org/stable/20609535. Accessed: 21/10/2014 14:30

[14] Blanchet, Rt. Rev. Augustine Magloire Alexander. Edward J. Kowrach; Jean Baptiste Abraham Bouilett. *Journal of a Catholic Bishop on the Oregon Trail: The Overland Crossing of the Rt. Rev. A.M.A. Blanchet, Bishop of Walla Walla, from Montreal to Oregon Territory*, March 23, 1847 to January 23, 1851. Ye Galleon Press, Fairfield, Wash. 1978.

[15] Milne, Mrs. Frances W. 1847 Oregon Trail Emigrant Families. 1990. Updated October 9, 2014. Warren Forsythe. https://wc.rootsweb.com/cgi-bin/igm.cgi?op=GET&db=oregon1847&id=I2528

CHAPTER FIVE: JUNE AND THE PLATTE RIVER

[1] Blanchet, Rt. Rev. Augustine Magloire Alexander. Edward J. Kowrach; Jean Baptiste Abraham Bouilett. *Journal of a Catholic Bishop on the Oregon Trail: The Overland Crossing of the Rt. Rev. A.M.A. Blanchet, Bishop of Walla Walla, from Montreal to Oregon Territory*, March 23, 1847 to January 23, 1851. Ye Galleon Press, Fairfield, Wash. 1978.

[2] Blanchet, Rt. Rev. Augustine Magloire Alexander. Edward J. Kowrach; Jean Baptiste Abraham Bouilett. *Journal of a Catholic Bishop on the Oregon Trail: The Overland Crossing of the Rt. Rev. A.M.A. Blanchet, Bishop of Walla Walla, from Montreal to Oregon Territory*, March 23, 1847 to January 23, 1851. Ye Galleon Press, Fairfield, Wash. 1978.

[3] Hockett, William A. "Experiences of W.A. Hockett on the Oregon Trail 1847." Typed by the William Albert Hockett, in 1914. Archived at the University of Oregon Libraries, Special Collections and University Archives, Eugene, Oregon.

[4] Lyman, H.S. "Reminiscences of James Jory," *The Quarterly of the Oregon Historical Society*, Vol. 3, No. 3 (Sep., 1902), pp. 271–286 Published by: Oregon Historical Society. Stable URL: http://www.jstor.org/stable/20609535. Accessed: 21/10/2014 14:30.

[5] Lyman, H.S. "Reminiscences of James Jory," *The Quarterly of the Oregon Historical Society*, Vol. 3, No. 3 (Sep., 1902), pp. 271–286 Published by: Oregon Historical Society. Stable URL: http://www.jstor.org/stable/20609535. Accessed: 21/10/2014 14:30.

[6] Blanchet, Rt. Rev. Augustine Magloire Alexander. Edward J. Kowrach; Jean Baptiste Abraham Bouilett. *Journal of a Catholic Bishop on the Oregon Trail: The Overland Crossing of the Rt. Rev. A.M.A. Blanchet, Bishop of Walla Walla, from Montreal to Oregon Territory*, March 23, 1847 to January 23, 1851. Ye Galleon Press, Fairfield, Wash. 1978.

[7] "Fort Laramie." Wyoming State Historic Preservation Office. https://www.wyohistory.org/encyclopedia/fort-laramie

[8] Hieb, David L. "Fort Laramie National Monument, Wyoming." National Park Service Historical Handbook Series No. 20. September 18, 2018.

[9] Lyman, H.S. "Reminiscences of James Jory," *The Quarterly of the Oregon Historical Society*, Vol. 3, No. 3 (Sep., 1902), pp. 271–286 Published by: Oregon Historical Society. Stable URL: http://www.jstor.org/stable/20609535. Accessed: 21/10/2014 14:30.

[10] Geer, Elizabeth Dixon Smith. "Diary of Mrs. Elizabeth Dixon Smith Geer. Transactions of the Thirty-Fifth Annual Reunion of the Oregon Pioneer Association. Portland, Oregon. June 14, 1906.

[11] Gibson, James, 1834–1920. Typeset recollections of overland travel from Bates County, Missouri, to Linnton, Oregon, between May 15, 1847, and November 1847. Dictated to Minnie M. Richards. 1914. Seven pages. Archived in the Oregon Historical Society's Research Library.

CHAPTER SIX: OREGON TRAIL LANDMARKS IN JULY

[1] Geer, Elizabeth Dixon Smith. "Diary of Mrs. Elizabeth Dixon Smith Geer. Transactions of the Thirty-Fifth Annual Reunion of the Oregon Pioneer Association. Portland, Oregon. June 14, 1906.

[2] Blanchet, Rt. Rev. Augustine Magloire Alexander. Edward J. Kowrach; Jean Baptiste Abraham Bouilett. *Journal of a Catholic Bishop on the Oregon Trail: The Overland Crossing of the Rt. Rev. A.M.A. Blanchet, Bishop of Walla Walla, from Montreal to Oregon Territory*, March 23, 1847 to January 23, 1851. Ye Galleon Press, Fairfield, Wash. 1978.

³ Blanchet, Rt. Rev. Augustine Magloire Alexander. Edward J. Kowrach; Jean Baptiste Abraham Bouilett. *Journal of a Catholic Bishop on the Oregon Trail: The Overland Crossing of the Rt. Rev. A.M.A. Blanchet, Bishop of Walla Walla, from Montreal to Oregon Territory*, March 23, 1847 to January 23, 1851. Ye Galleon Press, Fairfield, Wash. 1978.

⁴ Gibson, James, 1834–1920. Typeset recollections of overland travel from Bates County, Missouri, to Linnton, Oregon, between May 15, 1847, and November 1847. Dictated to Minnie M. Richards. 1914. Seven pages. Archived in the Oregon Historical Society's Research Library.

⁵ Blanchet, Rt. Rev. Augustine Magloire Alexander. Edward J. Kowrach; Jean Baptiste Abraham Bouilett. *Journal of a Catholic Bishop on the Oregon Trail: The Overland Crossing of the Rt. Rev. A.M.A. Blanchet, Bishop of Walla Walla, from Montreal to Oregon Territory*, March 23, 1847 to January 23, 1851. Ye Galleon Press, Fairfield, Wash. 1978.

⁶ Geer, Elizabeth Dixon Smith. "Diary of Mrs. Elizabeth Dixon Smith Geer. Transactions of the Thirty-Fifth Annual Reunion of the Oregon Pioneer Association. Portland, Oregon. June 14, 1906.

⁷ Blanchet, Rt. Rev. Augustine Magloire Alexander. Edward J. Kowrach; Jean Baptiste Abraham Bouilett. *Journal of a Catholic Bishop on the Oregon Trail: The Overland Crossing of the Rt. Rev. A.M.A. Blanchet, Bishop of Walla Walla, from Montreal to Oregon Territory*, March 23, 1847 to January 23, 1851. Ye Galleon Press, Fairfield, Wash. 1978.

⁸ Lyman, H.S. "Reminiscences of James Jory," *The Quarterly of the Oregon Historical Society, Vol. 3, No. 3* (Sep., 1902), pp. 271–286 Published by: Oregon Historical Society. Stable URL: http://www.jstor.org/stable/20609535. Accessed: 21/10/2014 14:30.

⁹ Blanchet, Rt. Rev. Augustine Magloire Alexander. Edward J. Kowrach; Jean Baptiste Abraham Bouilett. *Journal of a Catholic Bishop on the Oregon Trail: The Overland Crossing of the Rt. Rev. A.M.A. Blanchet, Bishop of Walla Walla, from Montreal to Oregon Territory*, March 23, 1847 to January 23, 1851. Ye Galleon Press, Fairfield, Wash. 1978.

¹⁰ Geer, Hon. Ralph C. "Occasional Address for the Year 1847." Transactions of the Seventh Annual Re-Union of the Oregon Pioneer Association. E.M. Waite Steam Printer and Bookbinder. Salem, Oregon. 1879.

¹¹ Blanchet, Rt. Rev. Augustine Magloire Alexander. Edward J. Kowrach; Jean Baptiste Abraham Bouilett. *Journal of a Catholic Bishop on the Oregon Trail: The Overland Crossing of the Rt. Rev. A.M.A. Blanchet, Bishop of Walla Walla, from Montreal to Oregon Territory*, March 23, 1847 to January 23, 1851. Ye Galleon Press, Fairfield, Wash. 1978.

¹² Bagley, Will. "Fort Bridger." WyoHistory.org, a Project of the Wyoming State Historical Society. https://www.wyohistory.org/encyclopedia/fort-bridger

¹³ "Pathways of the Pioneers. Soda Springs." Idaho Public Television. http://idahoptv.org/outdoors/shows/pathwaysofpioneers/sodasprings.cfm

CHAPTER SEVEN: REACHING THE ROCKY MOUNTAINS

¹ Tompkins, Professor Jim. "Mileposts along the Oregon Trail." http://www.oregonpioneers.com/Milepost4.htm

² National Historic Trails Auto Tour Route Interpretive Guide. "Along the Snake River Plain Through Idaho." National Trails System. National Park Service. U.S. Department of the Interior. October 2008.

³ "The Oregon Trail: Soda Springs." HistoryGlobe.com. http://www.historyglobe.com/ot/sodasprings.htm

⁴ Pathways of Pioneers. "Soda Springs." http://idahoptv.org/outdoors/shows/pathwaysofpioneers/oldfortboise.cfm

⁵ National Historic Trails Auto Tour Route Interpretive Guide. "Along the Snake River Plain Through Idaho." National Trails System. National Park Service. U.S. Department of the Interior. October 2008.

⁶ The Oregon Trail: Fort Hall. http://oregontrail101.com/fthall.html

⁷ Lyman, H.S. "Reminiscences of James Jory," *The Quarterly of the Oregon Historical Society, Vol. 3, No. 3* (Sep., 1902), pp. 271–286 Published by: Oregon Historical Society. Stable URL: http://www.jstor.org/stable/20609535. Accessed: 21/10/2014 14:30

Endnotes

[8] Lyman, H.S. "Reminiscences of James Jory," *The Quarterly of the Oregon Historical Society*, Vol. 3, No. 3 (Sep., 1902), pp. 271–286 Published by: Oregon Historical Society. Stable URL: http://www.jstor.org/stable/20609535. Accessed: 21/10/2014 14:30

CHAPTER EIGHT: TRAGEDY ON THE SNAKE RIVER

[1] National Park Service: Three Island Crossing. https://www.nps.gov/oreg/planyourvisit/site9.htm

[2] Lyman, H.S. "Reminiscences of James Jory," *The Quarterly of the Oregon Historical Society*, Vol. 3, No. 3 (Sep., 1902), pp. 271–286 Published by: Oregon Historical Society. Stable URL: http://www.jstor.org/stable/20609535. Accessed: 21/10/2014 14:30

[3] Lyman, H.S. "Reminiscences of James Jory," *The Quarterly of the Oregon Historical Society*, Vol. 3, No. 3 (Sep., 1902), pp. 271–286 Published by: Oregon Historical Society. Stable URL: http://www.jstor.org/stable/20609535. Accessed: 21/10/2014 14:30

[4] Lyman, H.S. "Reminiscences of James Jory," *The Quarterly of the Oregon Historical Society*, Vol. 3, No. 3 (Sep., 1902), pp. 271–286 Published by: Oregon Historical Society. Stable URL: http://www.jstor.org/stable/20609535. Accessed: 21/10/2014 14:30

[5] Coffman, Noah B. "Old Lewis County, Oregon Territory, an address delivered before the Southwest Washington Pioneers." Rochester, Thurston County, Washington. August 12, 1926.

[6] Coffman, Noah B. "Old Lewis County, Oregon Territory, an address delivered before the Southwest Washington Pioneers." Rochester, Thurston County, Washington. August 12, 1926.

[7] Geer, Elizabeth Dixon Smith. "Diary of Mrs. Elizabeth Dixon Smith Geer. Transactions of the Thirty-Fifth Annual Reunion of the Oregon Pioneer Association. Portland, Oregon. June 14, 1906.

[8] Geer, Elizabeth Dixon Smith. "Diary of Mrs. Elizabeth Dixon Smith Geer. Transactions of the Thirty-Fifth Annual Reunion of the Oregon Pioneer Association. Portland, Oregon. June 14, 1906.

[9] Pathways of Pioneers. "Old Fort Boise." http://idahoptv.org/outdoors/shows/pathwaysofpioneers/oldfortboise.cfm

[10] Flora, Stephenie, compiler. "Nathan Scofield Kimball." OregonPioneers.com. http://www.oregonpioneers.com/NathanKimball.htm

[11] Lyman, H.S. "Reminiscences of James Jory," *The Quarterly of the Oregon Historical Society*, Vol. 3, No. 3 (Sep., 1902), pp. 271–286 Published by: Oregon Historical Society. Stable URL: http://www.jstor.org/stable/20609535. Accessed: 21/10/2014 14:30

[12] Lyman, H.S. "Reminiscences of James Jory," *The Quarterly of the Oregon Historical Society*, Vol. 3, No. 3 (Sep., 1902), pp. 271–286 Published by: Oregon Historical Society. Stable URL: http://www.jstor.org/stable/20609535. Accessed: 21/10/2014 14:30

[13] Lyman, H.S. "Reminiscences of James Jory," *The Quarterly of the Oregon Historical Society*, Vol. 3, No. 3 (Sep., 1902), pp. 271–286 Published by: Oregon Historical Society. Stable URL: http://www.jstor.org/stable/20609535. Accessed: 21/10/2014 14:30

[14] Ware, Louisa Jackson. Handwritten note describing her mother hearing Marcus Whitman preach. Washington State Library.

[15] Young, John Quincy Adams. "Recollections." Typescript. Oregon Historical Society, Portland.

[16] Coonc, Elizabeth Ann Fenn. "Reminiscences of a Pioneer Woman." The Washington Historical Quarterly. Volume VIII. The Washington University State Historical Society. University Station. Seattle, Washington. 1917.

[17] Fort Walla Walla Museum. Walla Walla, Washington. https://www.fwwm.org/

[18] Barber, Katrine. "Celilo Falls." The Oregon Encyclopedia. https://oregonencyclopedia.org/articles/celilo_falls/#.XDEgs1xKiUk

[19] Lyman, H.S. "Reminiscences of James Jory," *The Quarterly of the Oregon Historical Society*, Vol. 3, No. 3 (Sep., 1902), pp. 271–286 Published by: Oregon Historical Society. Stable URL: http://www.jstor.org/stable/20609535. Accessed: 21/10/2014 14:30

[20] Coffman, Noah B. "Old Lewis County, Oregon Territory, an address delivered before the Southwest Washington Pioneers." Rochester, Thurston County, Washington. August 12, 1926.

[21] Boyd, Robert. "Wascopam Mission." The Oregon Encyclopedia. https://oregonencyclopedia.org/articles/wascopam_mission/#.XDEhVVxKiUk

CHAPTER NINE: WHITMAN MISSION TO OREGON CITY

[1] Beireis, Nettie B. "A Sketch of Mrs. Matilda N. Jackson's Life: An Old Pioneer of Lewis County." Typed copy of handwritten and nearly illegible information at the Washington State Historical Society. 1939. Jackson, Koontz, Glover family papers. Washington State Library. Published by N.B. Coffman and Charles Miles in "Claquato Landmarks." *The Chehalis Bee-Nugget.* 1939.

[2] Webber, Bert and Margie. *Oregon City (By Way of the Barlow Road) At the End of the National Historic Oregon Trail.* Webb Research Group. Publishers of Books about the Oregon Country. Medford, Oregon. 1993.

[3] Letter from Captain Joseph Magone to Matilda (Coonse) Jackson January 20, 1848 from the Dallas Mission. Archived in the Jackson, Koontz, Glover family papers. Washington State Library.

[4] Addis, Cameron. "Whitman Massacre." The Oregon Encyclopedia. https://oregon encyclopedia.org/articles/whitman_massacre/#.XDEkkFxKiUk

[5] Tate, Cassandra. "Cayuse attack mission, in what becomes known as the Whitman Massacre, on November 29, 1847." HistoryLink.org Essay 5192. http://www.historylink.org/File/5192 Posted September 24, 2014.

[6] Tate, Cassandra. "Trial of five Cayuse accused of Whitman murder begins on May 21, 1850." HistoryLink.org Essay 9401. http://historylink.org/File/9401 Posted April 16, 2010.

[7] Letter from Captain Joseph Magone to Matilda (Coonse) Jackson January 20, 1848 from the Dallas Mission. Archived in the Jackson, Koontz, Glover family papers. Washington State Library.

[8] Letter from Captain Joseph Magone to Matilda (Coonse) Jackson January 20, 1848 from the Dallas Mission. Archived in the Jackson, Koontz, Glover family papers. Washington State Library.

[9] Milne, Frances. Joseph Magone. https://wc.rootsweb.com/cgi-bin/igm.cgi?op=GET&db=oregon1847&id=I6372

[10] Glover, Matthew. Letter to his sister, Matilda (Glover) Coonse, Oregon Territory, from Montgomery County, Missouri, dated April 2, 1848.

[11] Glover, William. Letter to his aunt, Matilda (Glover) Coonse, April 1848.

CHAPTER TEN: JOHN ROBINSON JACKSON

[1] Hannon, Trudy R. *John R. Jackson: Washington's First American Pioneer.* Advocate Printing. 1998.

[2] Smith, Frederic A., Dutchess County clerk. Letter from the Office of the County Clerk of Dutchess County, Poughkeepsie, New York, March 28, 1952, to Walter Twiss, and note from Twiss to Anna Koontz, Matilda's granddaughter.

[3] Paperwork from John R. Jackson dated May 28, 1836. Archived in the Jackson, Koontz, Glover family papers. Washington State Library.

[4] Jackson, John R. November 1835 paperwork. Archived in the Jackson, Koontz, Glover family papers. Washington State Library.

[5] Jackson, John R. October 1837 and January 1840 paperwork. Archived in the Jackson, Koontz, Glover family papers. Washington State Library.

[6] Jackson, John R. September 1838 and January 1845 paperwork. Archived in the Jackson, Koontz, Glover family papers. Washington State Library.

[7] Jackson, John R. October 1838 paperwork. Archived in the Jackson, Koontz, Glover family papers. Washington State Library.

[8] Jackson, John R. September 1839 paperwork. Archived in the Jackson, Koontz, Glover family papers. Washington State Library.

[9] Jackson, John R. March 1840 paperwork. Archived in the Jackson, Koontz, Glover family papers. Washington State Library.

[10] Jackson, John R. March and July 1839 paperwork. Archived in the Jackson, Koontz, Glover family papers. Washington State Library.

[11] Jackson, John R. September 1839 and April 1840 paperwork. Archived in the Jackson, Koontz, Glover family papers. Washington State Library.

Endnotes

[12] Jackson, John R. 1843 paperwork. Archived in the Jackson, Koontz, Glover family papers. Washington State Library.

[13] Jackson, John R. May 1844 paperwork. Archived in the Jackson, Koontz, Glover family papers. Washington State Library.

[14] Flora, Stephenie. "Emigrants to Oregon in 1844." OregonPioneers.com. http://www.oregonpioneers.com/1844.htm

[15] Camp, Charles L., editor. "James Clyman, American Frontiersman, 1792–1881. The adventures of a trapper and covered wagon emigrant as told in his own reminiscences and diaries." California Historical Society, Special Publication No. 3. http://www.archive.org/details/jamesclymanameri01cali

[16] Jones, Pat. *The Chronicle*. "Billy Packwood—part legend, part mountain man." November 4, 2006.

[17] Camp, Charles L., editor. "James Clyman, American Frontiersman, 1792–1881. The adventures of a trapper and covered wagon emigrant as told in his own reminiscences and diaries." California Historical Society, Special Publication No. 3. http://www.archive.org/details/jamesclymanameri01cali

[18] Camp, Charles L., editor. "James Clyman, American Frontiersman, 1792–1881. The adventures of a trapper and covered wagon emigrant as told in his own reminiscences and diaries." California Historical Society, Special Publication No. 3. http://www.archive.org/details/jamesclymanameri01cali

[19] Blomdahl, George H. "John R. Jackson was versatile man." *The Daily Chronicle* Bicentennial Edition. June 28, 1976.

[20] Quick, Cindy, and Julie McDonald Zander, eds. *The Toledo Community Story, 1800–2008*. Chapters of Life. Originally published in 1953. Updated in 1976 and 2008.

[21] Gibson, James R. *Farming the Frontier: The Agricultural Opening of the Oregon Country 1786–1846*. University of Washington Press. Seattle and London. 1985.

[22] Blomdahl, George H. "John R. Jackson was versatile man." *The Daily Chronicle* Bicentennial Edition. June 28, 1976.

[23] Atwood, A. The Conquerors: Historical Sketches of the American Settlement of the Oregon Country. Published with the Indorsement of the Officers of the Washington State Historical Society. Tacoma, Washington. Jennings and Graham. 1907.

[24] Meany, Edmond S., professor of History, University of Washington "Living Pioneers of Washington: Louisa M. Ware." *The Seattle Post-Intelligencer*. April 22, 1920.

[25] Simmons, Christopher Columbus. Ancestors and descendants of Christopher Columbus Simmons and Asenath Ann Kennedy Simmons, Washington State pioneers, [198-] / compiled by their granddaughter, Margaret Moore Keck. Washington State Library Northwest Genealogy.

[26] Plamondon, George F. "First settlers from Cowlitz Prairie to Tumwater." Cowlitz County Historical Society. November 1959.

[27] Rector, Elaine. "Looking Back In Order to Move Forward An Often Untold History Affecting Oregon's Past, Present and Future Timeline of Oregon and U.S. Racial, Immigration and Education History." Timeline of Oregon's Racial and Education History—The City of Portland. https://www.portlandoregon.gov/bps/article/412697 May 16, 2010.

[28] *Centralia's First Century 1845–1955*. Citizens of Centralia. H.J. Quality Printing. 1955.

[29] Plamondon, George F. "First settlers from Cowlitz Prairie to Tumwater." Cowlitz County Historical Society. November 1959.

[30] Cascades Volcano Observatory, USGS. "Henry Warre, September 1845 eruption of Mount St. Helens." https://volcanoes.usgs.gov/observatories/cvo/Historical/volcanoes_henry_warre_1845.shtml

[31] Jackson, John R. Paperwork from fall 1845. Archived in the Jackson, Koontz, Glover family papers. Washington State Library.

[32] Crowell, Sandra. *The Land Called Lewis*, Panesko Publishing. 2007.

[33] Zander, Julie McDonald. *Images of America: Chehalis*. Arcadia Publishing. September 5, 2011.

[34] Jackson, John R. Paperwork from 1846. Archived in the Jackson, Koontz, Glover family papers. Washington State Library.

[35] Cascades Volcano Observatory, USGS. "Paul Kane, 1847 Eruptions of Mount St. Helens." https://volcanoes.usgs.gov/observatories/cvo/Historical/volcanoes_henry_warre_1845.shtml
[36] Koontz, Barton. Handwritten notes recording old dates and firsts in Lewis County. Dictated in the year before his death in 1917.
[37] *The Oregon Spectator*, Oregon City, Oregon. July 8, 1847.
[38] Bush, J.C. "The Records Are Ancient: Summaries of County Commissioners' Meetings Held in 1854; Little to Show the History of Lewis County from 1845 to 1859—Grown People of Those Days Are Gone." *The Chehalis Bee-Nugget*, Feb. 4, 1921.
[39] Lewis County, Oregon Territory, records of first meetings. https://web.archive.org/web/20110523015333/http://users.bentonrea.com/~tinear/lewis-ot.htm
[40] Secretary of State. Washington State Digital Archives. Title Info: 1847, Lewis County Heads of Family Census, Lewis County Territorial Auditor. https://www.digitalarchives.wa.gov/Collections/TitleInfo/405

CHAPTER ELEVEN: QUICK COURTSHIP AND A WEDDING
[1] Bonney, William P. "The Murder of Leander Wallace," History of Pierce County, Washington. Chicago: Pioneer Historical Publishing Company, 1927. pp. 54–61.
[2] *The Oregon Spectator*, May 4, 1848.
[3] *The Oregon Spectator*, May 18, 1848.
[4] Beireis, Nettie B. "A Sketch of Mrs. Matilda N. Jackson's Life: An Old Pioneer of Lewis County." Typed copy of handwritten and nearly illegible information at the Washington State Historical Society. 1939. Jackson, Koontz, Glover family papers. Washington State Library. Published by N.B. Coffman and Charles Miles in "Claquato Landmarks." *The Chehalis Bee-Nugget*. 1939.
[5] Hannon, Trudy R. *John R. Jackson: Washington's First American Pioneer*. Advocate Printing. 1998.
[6] Glover, Matthew. Letter to his sister, Matilda (Glover) Coonse, Oregon Territory, from Montgomery County, Missouri, dated April 2, 1848.
[7] McDonald, Julie. "Highlighting Lewis County: First U.S. Flag in Lewis County Flew July 4, 1853." *The Chronicle*. July 3, 2018.
[8] Bush, J.C. "The Records Are Ancient: Summaries of County Commissioners' Meetings Held in 1854; Little to Show the History of Lewis County from 1845 to 1859—Grown People of Those Days Are Gone." *The Chehalis Bee-Nugget*, Feb. 4, 1921.
[9] Glover, Matilda Nettle, Montgomery County, Missouri, letter to daughter Matilda Coonse Jackson dated April 1, 1849. Archived in the Jackson, Koontz, Glover family papers. Washington State Library.
[10] Bonney, William P. "The Murder of Leander Wallace," History of Pierce County, Washington. Chicago: Pioneer Historical Publishing Company, 1927. pp. 54–61.

CHAPTER TWELVE: BUILDING A COURTHOUSE
[1] Jackson, John R. Receipt from 1850. Archived in the Jackson, Koontz, Glover family papers. Washington State Library.
[2] Hannon, Trudy R. *John R. Jackson: Washington's First American Pioneer*. Advocate Printing. 1998.
[3] "Historic Jackson Prairie: Lewis County Home, in which Grant, Sheridan and McClellan were Entertained." *The Weekly Oregonian*. June 2, 1899.
[4] Hannon, Trudy R. *John R. Jackson: Washington's First American Pioneer*. Advocate Printing. 1998.
[5] Quick, Cindy, and Julie McDonald Zander, eds. *The Toledo Community Story, 1800–2008*. Chapters of Life. Originally published in 1953. Updated in 1976 and 2008.
[6] Hannon, Trudy R. *John R. Jackson: Washington's First American Pioneer*. Advocate Printing. 1998.
[7] McDonald, Lucile. "Historic Jackson Courthouse at Chehalis 100 Years Old This Fall." *The Seattle Times*. 1950.
[8] McDonald, Lucile. "First Courthouse in State," *The Seattle Sunday Times Magazine. The Seattle Times*, March 10, 1946.
[9] Koontz, Anna. Information from Oregon State Library, Salem, Oregon, with quotations are from Judge Strong's records, as found in an article by his grandson, Robert Strong.

Endnotes

[10] Bush, J.C. "Early History Two Pioneers." Reproduced recollections of Huggins, Edward, overseer at the Hudson's Bay Co.'s Puget Sound Agricultural Co. *The Oregonian* 1900 and *The Chehalis Bee-Nugget* September 28, 1900.
[11] "The Donation Land Claim Act of 1850 Law and Legal Definition.: USlegal.com. https://definitions.uslegal.com/t/the-donation-land-claim-act-of-1850/
[12] Scott, Leslie M. "Oregon's Provisional Government, 1843–49." Oregon Historical Quarterly. Vol. 30, No. 3. September 1929.
[13] Zander, Julie McDonald. *Images of America: Chehalis*. Arcadia Publishing. September 5, 2011.
[14] Donation Land Claim Holdings at the Washington State Library. www.sos.wa.gov/library/landrecords.aspx
[15] McDonald, Julie. "Highlighting Lewis County: Is Blueberry Cheesecake in Toledo's Future?" *The Chronicle*. August 7, 2018.
[16] Roberts, George B. "Letters to Mrs. F.F. Victor, 1878–83." Oregon Historical Quarterly. Vol. 63, No. 2/3. June to September 1962, pp. 175-236. https://www.jstor.org/stable/20612688
[17] Roberts, George B. "Letters to Mrs. F.F. Victor, 1878–83." Oregon Historical Quarterly. Vol. 63, No. 2/3. June to September 1962, pp. 175-236. https://www.jstor.org/stable/20612688
[18] Roberts, George B. "Letters to Mrs. F.F. Victor, 1878–83." Oregon Historical Quarterly. Vol. 63, No. 2/3. June to September 1962, pp. 175-236. https://www.jstor.org/stable/20612688
[19] Shine, Gregory P. "Hudson's Bay Company." The Oregon Encyclopedia. https://oregonencyclopedia.org/articles/hudson_s_bay_company/#.XDFtnlxKiUk
[20] Gray, Mary A. "Settlement of the Claims in Washington of the Hudson's Bay Company and the Puget's Sound Agricultural Company." Washington Historical Quarterly 21, No. 2 (1930), pp. 95–102.

CHAPTER THIRTEEN: TRYING TO CREATE A TERRITORY

[1] Receipt from Simon Plamondon, the treasurer, accepted by John R. Jackson, Clerk of Probate, January 10, 1851. Archived in the Jackson, Koontz, Glover family papers. Washington State Library.
[2] Jones, Pat. "Plenty still to learn from pioneer woman," *The Chronicle*, June 10, 2006.
[3] Grant, Esther (Brown), Seaside, Oregon. *The Centralia Daily Chronicle*, July 21, 1938, and *The Chehalis Advocate*, 1939.
[4] Jackson, John R. Papers dated April 12, 1851. Archived in the Jackson, Koontz, Glover family papers. Washington State Library.
[5] Undated note to Matilda Jackson. Archived in the Jackson, Koontz, Glover family papers. Washington State Library.
[6] Bush, Judd C. "County Dads Busy in 1851. Met at Jackson's—Effort to Move the Seat of Government to Olympia Olympia-Cowlitz Landing Road, From Monticello, Cathlamet-Boistfort Road and Others Under Consideration." *The Chehalis Bee-Nugget*, April 1, 1921.
[7] Meany, Edmond S. "The Cowlitz Convention: Inception of Washington Territory," The Washington Historical Quarterly. Vol. XIII, No. 1. January 1922, pp. 3–19 Published by: University of Washington Stable URL: http://www.jstor.org/stable/40473582
[8] *The Oregonian*, September 20, 1851, and *The Oregon Spectator* September 23, 1851.
[9] Bush, Judd C. "County Seat Trouble In '51. Commissioners Move From Jackson's To Courthouse on Ford's Prairie. Effort Made to Compel Clerk of District Court, County Clerk, Probate Court and Commissioners to Make New Headquarters." *The Chehalis Bee Nugget*, April 8, 1921.
[10] McDonald, Lucile. "Courthouse Battle Led to Forming County," *The Seattle Sunday Times Magazine, The Seattle Times*. January 6, 1952.
[11] McDonald, Lucile. "Courthouse Battle Led to Forming County," *The Seattle Sunday Times Magazine, The Seattle Times*. January 6, 1952.
[12] Bush, Judd C. "County Seat Trouble In '51. Commissioners Move From Jackson's To Courthouse on Ford's Prairie. Effort Made to Compel Clerk of District Court, County Clerk, Probate Court and Commissioners to Make New Headquarters." *The Chehalis Bee Nugget*, April 8, 1921.
[13] Dougherty, Phil. "Thurston County—Thumbnail History." HistoryLink.org Essay 7979. http://www.historylink.org/File/7979 Posted November 15, 2006.

[14] Glover, Matilda Nettle. Letter to her daughter, Matilda Jackson, November 17, 1851. Archived in the Jackson, Koontz, Glover family papers. Washington State Library.

CHAPTER FOURTEEN: LIFE AT HIGHLAND FARM
[1] Hannon, Trudy R. *John R. Jackson: Washington's First American Pioneer*. Advocate Printing. 1998.
[2] Jackson, John R. Records kept listing expenses. December 1851 and throughout 1852. Archived in the Jackson, Koontz, Glover family papers. Washington State Library.
[3] Meany, Edmond S., professor of History, University of Washington "Living Pioneers of Washington: Louisa M. Ware." *The Seattle Post-Intelligencer*. April 22, 1920.
[4] Bush, J.C. "Jackson Twice Naturalized? Evidence Shows He Was Admitted to Citizenship in 1835 and Again in 1850." *The Chehalis Bee-Nugget*. March 31, 1922.
[5] Bonney, William P., secretary. Washington State Historical Society. Letter to the editor dated March 17, 1922. Published in *The Chehalis Bee-Nugget*. Chehalis, Washington. March 31, 1922.
[6] Tisdale, Donna. "Chapter XV: The Elkanah Mills Family." First marriage at courthouse. *The Daily Chronicle*, Centralia, Washington. Sept. 8, 1941.
[7] Bush, Judd C. "Washington A Territory: The First Legislature Met at Olympia Early in 1854; Doings of the Commissioners in 1852 and 1853—Met at Various Places—Seven School Districts Established—Road Work." *The Chehalis Bee-Nugget*. Chehalis, Washington. April 15, 1921.
[8] "Territorial Timeline: Settlers met at Monticello to sign a petition asking Congress to create a separate territory north of the Columbia River." Legacy Washington, Washington Secretary of State. https://www.sos.wa.gov/legacy/timeline/detail.aspx?id=214
[9] "Lewis County's First Elected Sheriff John R. Jackson," *The Chronicle*. Centralia, Washington. July 19, 2013.
[10] Meany, Edmond S. "The Cowlitz Convention: Inception of Washington Territory." *The Washington Historical Quarterly*, Vol. 13, No. 1 (Jan., 1922), pp. 3–19 Published by: University of Washington Stable URL: http://www.jstor.org/stable/40473582. Accessed: 24-05-2018 16:39.

CHAPTER FIFTEEN: FLYING THE FIRST FLAG
[1] Koontz, Barton. Handwritten notes recording old dates and firsts in Lewis County. Dictated in the year before his death in 1917.
[2] Bush, Judd C. "John R. Jackson Came in 1845: First from the United States to Settle Permanently in County. Mrs. Weir, Jackson's Daughter, and Mr. Yates, Who Knew Him in 1853, Talk for the Bee-Nugget Readers." *The Chehalis Bee-Nugget*. March 17, 1922.
[3] "Flag, 92 Years, To Be Shown." *The Chehalis Bee-Nugget*. August 23, 1945.
[4] Koontz, Barton. Handwritten dates.
[5] Winkler, Pat. "Famed Jackson Flag Presented to State Museum: Patriotism Woven Deep in Fabric of Century-Old 4th of July Flag." *The Tacoma News Tribune*. July 4, 1958.
[6] "The Cowlitz Celebration," *The Columbian*, Olympia, Puget Sound, Washington Territory. July 16, 1853.
[7] Hannon, Trudy R. *John R. Jackson: Washington's First American Pioneer*. Advocate Printing. 1998.
[8] Hutchins, C.C. "Here First Court Sat in State: In Lewis County History Sits by Pacific Highway." *The Seattle Post-Intelligencer*. Seattle, Washington. June 12, 1921 or 1927.
[9] "Jacksons left lasting imprint on Lewis County." April 24, 1989.
[10] Winkler, Pat. "Famed Jackson Flag Presented to State Museum: Patriotism Woven Deep in Fabric of Century-Old 4th of July Flag." *The Tacoma News Tribune*. July 4, 1958.
[11] Bush, Judd C. "John R. Jackson Came in 1845: First from the United States to Settle Permanently in County. Mrs. Weir, Jackson's Daughter, and Mr. Yates, Who Knew Him in 1853, Talk for the Bee-Nugget Readers." *The Chehalis Bee-Nugget*. March 17, 1922.
[12] Bush, Judd C. "John R. Jackson Came in 1845: First from the United States to Settle Permanently in County. Mrs. Weir, Jackson's Daughter, and Mr. Yates, Who Knew Him in 1853, Talk for the Bee-Nugget Readers." *The Chehalis Bee-Nugget*. March 17, 1922.
[13] Jackson, John R. Accounting book November 1853 to July 1855. Archived in the Jackson, Koontz, Glover family papers. Washington State Library.
[14] Bush, Judd C. "Washington A Territory: The First Legislature Met at Olympia Early in 1854;

Doings of the Commissioners in 1852 and 1853—Met at Various Places—Seven School Districts Established—Road Work." *The Chehalis Bee-Nugget*. Chehalis, Washington. April 15, 1921.

CHAPTER SIXTEEN: A POST OFFICE AND A DIARY

[1] McDonald, Lucile. "Diary of a Pioneer Boy." *The Seattle Times*, Sunday, July 11, 1954.

[2] Coonse, Henry, and Andrew Levitt Diary, December 1851 to January 1855. (Henry Coonse papers. Accession 4709-001.) Diaries of Andrew Levitt and Henry Coonse. University of Washington Libraries, Pacific Northwest Historical Documents Digital Collections. PNW00121. https://digitalcollections.lib.washington.edu/digital/collection/pioneerlife/search/searchterm/4709001/field/source/mode/all/conn/and/cosuppress/ pp. 1–50. 1851–1855.

[3] Ramsey, Guy Reed. *Postmarked Washington: Lewis and Cowlitz Counties*. The Lewis County Historical Society. 1978.

[4] Bush, Judd C. "Little Details of Life on Jackson Prairie in the Early Days: Jackson Had a Military Company in '55—The Road Change—Prices in Early Days—Recollections of Barton Koontz." *The Chehalis Bee-Nugget*, Chehalis, Washington. March 24, 1922.

[5] Coffman, N.B., and Charles Miles. "Claquato Landmarks: Grandma Jackson." *The Chehalis Bee-Nugget*. October 3, 1939.

[6] Stevens, Hazard. "Canoeing Up the Cowlitz," *The Life of Isaac Ingalls Stevens, Volume 1*. Boston and New York: Houghton, Mifflin and Company. 1901.

[7] Jackson, John R. Letter to his wife, Matilda Jackson, dated March 1, 1854. Jackson, Koontz, Glover family papers. Washington State Library.

[8] Jackson, John R. Letter to his wife, Matilda Jackson, dated March 2, 1854. Jackson, Koontz, Glover family papers. Washington State Library.

[9] Jackson, John R. Letter to his wife, Matilda Jackson, dated April 25, 1854. Jackson, Koontz, Glover family papers. Washington State Library.

[10] Duncan, Jane and Hiram, from Lincoln County, Missouri. Letter to Jane's brother Philip Glover, forwarded to his brother, John Glover, who forwarded it to their sister, Matilda (Glover) Jackson. Dated May 15, 1854, and sent to Matilda Jackson September 8, 1854. Part of the Jackson, Koontz, Glover family papers. Washington State Library.

CHAPTER SEVENTEEN: INDIAN WARS AND GRIEVOUS LOSS

[1] Tisdale, Donna. "Chapter XV: The Elkanah Mills Family." First marriage at courthouse. *The Daily Chronicle*, Centralia, Washington. Sept. 8, 1941.

[2] Denfeld, Duane Colt, Ph.D. "Forts of Washington Territory, Indian War Era, 1855–1856." HistoryLink.org. http://www.historylink.org/File/10087. Posted April 9, 2012.

[3] Bush, Judd C. "Little Details of Life on Jackson Prairie in the Early Days: Jackson Had a Military Company in '55—The Road Change—Prices in Early Days—Recollections of Barton Koontz." *The Chehalis Bee-Nugget*, Chehalis, Washington. March 24, 1922

[4] Tisdale, Donna. "Chapter XV: The Elkanah Mills Family." First marriage at courthouse. *The Daily Chronicle*, Centralia, Washington. Sept. 8, 1941.

[5] Zander, Julie McDonald. *Chapters of Life in 1915 Chehalis. The Chehalis Bee-Nugget Historical Souvenir Edition, May 14, 1915. Illustrated and Republished*. Chapters of Life. 2011.

[6] Zander, Julie McDonald. *Images of America: Chehalis*. Arcadia Publishing. September 5, 2011.

[7] Cain, J. Note to Simon Plamondon. Undated. Archived with the Jackson, Koontz, Glover family papers. Washington State Library.

[8] Cain, J. Note to Simon Plamondon. Undated. Archived with the Jackson, Koontz, Glover family papers. Washington State Library.

[9] Becker, Paula. "Yakama Indian War begins on October 5, 1855." HistoryLink.org Essay 5311. http://www.historylink.org/File/5311 Posted February 26, 2003.

[10] Denfeld, Duane Colt, Ph.D. "Nisqually Chief Leschi is hanged on February 19, 1858." HistoryLink.org. http://www.historylink.org/File/5145 Posted Jan. 29, 2003.

[11] Roberts, George B. "Letters to Mrs. F.F. Victor, 1878–83." Oregon Historical Quarterly. Vol. 63, No. 2/3. June to September 1962, pp. 187. https://www.jstor.org/stable/20612688

[12] Stevens, Governor Isaac, and Superintendent of Indian Affairs. Circular from Olympia dated

July 1856. Archived with the Jackson, Koontz, Glover family papers. Washington State Library.
[13] Jackson, Matilda (Glover) Koontz. Letter to her husband, John R. Jackson, dated April 12, 1855. Archived with the Jackson, Koontz, Glover family papers. Washington State Library.
[14] Glover, John P., Clackamas County, Oregon Territory. Letter to his sister, Matilda Jackson, dated January 8, 1855. Archived with the Jackson, Koontz, Glover family papers. Washington State Library.
[15] Glover, William and Jane. Marion County, Oregon Territory. Letter to his aunt, Matilda (Glover) Koontz Jackson in 1855. Archived in the Jackson, Koontz, Glover family papers. Washington State Library.
[16] Bush, Judd C. "Little Details of Life on Jackson Prairie in the Early Days: Jackson Had a Military Company in '55—The Road Change—Prices in Early Days—Recollections of Barton Koontz." *The Chehalis Bee-Nugget,* March 24, 1922.

CHAPTER EIGHTEEN: MORE TRAGEDY AND HEARTACHE
[1] Glover, William. Marion County, Oregon Territory. Letter to his aunt, Matilda (Glover) Koontz Jackson dated July 30, 1856. Archived in the Jackson, Koontz, Glover family papers. Washington State Library.
[2] Coonse, Henry, and Andrew Levitt Diary, December 1851 to January 1855. (Henry Coonse papers. Accession 4709-001.) Diaries of Andrew Levitt and Henry Coonse. University of Washington Libraries, Pacific Northwest Historical Documents Digital Collections. PNW00121. https://digitalcollections.lib.washington.edu/digital/collection/pioneerlife/search/searchterm/4709001/field/source/mode/all/conn/and/cosuppress/
[3] *The Pioneer and Democrat,* June 5, 1857.
[4] Soderland, Karin, guest columnist for Mrs. Betsy Hemenway. "Between Us Neighbors." *The Daily Chronicle.* April 4, 1959.

CHAPTER NINETEEN: END OF A DEADLY DECADE
[1] Slip of paper listing books in the cabin. Dated April 9, 1959, in the Jackson file at the Lewis County Historical Museum.
[2] Magone, Joseph. https://www.geni.com/people/Joseph-Magone/3189294

CHAPTER TWENTY: LIFE AND A GIRL'S DIARY
[1] Ancestry.com 1860 census records.
[2] Jackson, John R. Account book listing land and property. June 13, 1860. Archived in the Jackson, Koontz, Glover family papers. Washington State Library.
[3] Zander, Julie McDonald. *Chapters of Life in 1915 Chehalis. The Chehalis Bee-Nugget Historical Souvenir Edition, May 14, 1915. Illustrated and Republished.* Chapters of Life. 2011.
[4] Koontz, Anna. "Grandma Jackson Remembered," typewritten recollections. Washington State Library. 1953.
[5] Jackson, Andrew M. Headstone photograph. Fern Hill Cemetery.
[6] Cutting, J.B. First-person account. "When I started for Napawyna (now Napavine)." London, England, 1851. Published in the 1890s.
[7] L.L. Dubeau & Co. invoice for John R. Jackson dated May 1861. Archived in the Jackson, Koontz, Glover family papers. Washington State Library.
[8] Hannon, Trudy R. *John R. Jackson: Washington's First American Pioneer.* Advocate Printing. 1998.
[9] Giddings, E. Surveyor General's Office, Olympia, Washington. Letter to John R. Jackson dated December 18, 1861. Archived in the Jackson, Koontz, Glover family papers. Washington State Library.
[10] Third assistant postmaster. Letter to John R. Jackson, postmaster, Highland, dated December 10, 1862. Archived in the Jackson, Koontz, Glover family papers. Washington State Library.
[11] Cutting, J.B. First-person account. "When I started for Napawyna (now Napavine)." London, England, 1851. Published in the 1890s.
[12] Jackson, John R. Postmaster. Pay stub for Sheriff Javan Hall dated February 25, 1863. Archived in the Jackson, Koontz, Glover family papers. Washington State Library.

Endnotes

[13] Miller, W.W. Letter to his friend John R. Jackson dated September 10, 1863. Archived in the Jackson, Koontz, Glover family papers. Washington State Library.

[14] Jackson, Mary. Letter to sister Louisa in January 1864. Archived in the Jackson, Koontz, Glover family papers. Washington State Library.

[15] Judson, Ann. Letter to friend Mary Jackson dated March 18 with the year missing. Archived in the Jackson, Koontz, Glover family papers. Washington State Library.

[16] Zander, Julie McDonald. *Chapters of Life in 1915 Chehalis. The Chehalis Bee-Nugget Historical Souvenir Edition, May 14, 1915. Illustrated and Republished.* Chapters of Life. 2011.

[17] Johnson, Karen L. and Serene A. "Louisa Jackson's Diary of 1865." Transcribed. Lewis County Historical Museum. May 2004.

[18] Ware, Louisa Jackson, 1853–1938. Diary/daily journal 1865. MS 0078, Box 1, Folder 7—Part of the Jackson, Koontz, Glover family papers. Washington State Library.

[19] Johnson, Karen L. and Serene A. "Louisa Jackson's Diary of 1865." Transcribed. Lewis County Historical Museum. May 2004.

[20] Ware, Louisa Jackson, 1853–1938. Diary/daily journal 1865. MS 0078, Box 1, Folder 7—Part of the Jackson, Koontz, Glover family papers. Washington State Library.

[21] *The Pacific Tribune.* January 21, 1865.

[22] Ware, Louisa Jackson, 1853–1938. Diary/daily journal 1865. MS 0078, Box 1, Folder 7—Part of the Jackson, Koontz, Glover family papers. Washington State Library.

[23] Bush, Judd C. "John R. Jackson Came in 1845: First from the United States to Settle Permanently in County. Mrs. Weir, Jackson's Daughter, and Mr. Yates, Who Knew Him in 1853, Talk for the Bee-Nugget Readers." *The Chehalis Bee-Nugget.* March 17, 1922.

[24] Ware, Louisa Jackson, 1853–1938. Diary/daily journal 1865. MS 0078, Box 1, Folder 7—Part of the Jackson, Koontz, Glover family papers. Washington State Library.

[25] Johnson, Karen L. and Serene A. "Louisa Jackson's Diary of 1865." Transcribed. Lewis County Historical Museum. May 2004.

[26] Ware, Louisa Jackson, 1853–1938. Diary/daily journal 1865. MS 0078, Box 1, Folder 7—Part of the Jackson, Koontz, Glover family papers. Washington State Library.

[27] Receipt from John R. Jackson to Horace H. Pinto dated December 29, 1866. Jackson, Koontz, Glover family papers. Washington State Library.

[28] "Notice to Barton "Coontz" of appointment as Road District No. 4 supervisor, dated May 23, 1867. Archived in the Jackson, Koontz, Glover family papers. Washington State Library.

[29] Jackson, John R. Journal kept in 1868. Archived in the Jackson, Koontz, Glover family papers. Washington State Library.

[30] Stock certificate dated October 11, 1867, for shares in Cowlitz Steam Navigation Company. Another stock certificate dated July 20, 1867, lists a hundred shares at one hundred dollars each for $10,000. Archived in the Jackson, Koontz, Glover family papers. Washington State Library.

[31] Chappellier, M. Western Union Telegraph to John R. Jackson dated June 3, 1868. Archived in the Jackson, Koontz, Glover family papers. Washington State Library.

[32] Stueve, Nathan. "Steamboats on the Cowlitz." Cowlitz Historical Quarterly. January 8, 2010. Jim LeMonds. http://writeteknorthwest.com/archives/14831/steamboats-on-the-cowlitz.

[33] Receipts and accounts. 1868 and 1869. Archived in the Jackson, Koontz, Glover family papers. Washington State Library.

[34] Coonce, Barton. Letter from Portland to his mother, Matilda (Glover) Jackson, and stepfather, John R. Jackson, dated May 7, 1869. Archived in the Jackson, Koontz, Glover family papers. Washington State Library.

[35] Beireis, Nettie B. "A Sketch of Mrs. Matilda N. Jackson's Life: An Old Pioneer of Lewis County." Typed copy of handwritten and nearly illegible information at the Washington State Historical Society. 1939. Jackson, Koontz, Glover family papers. Washington State Library. Published by N.B. Coffman and Charles Miles in "Claquato Landmarks." *The Chehalis Bee-Nugget.* 1939.

CHAPTER TWENTY-ONE: DEATH OF A GENTLEMAN FARMER
[1] Ancestry.com 1870 census.
[2] Obituary for Sylvanus A. Phillips. *The Centralia Chronicle*, July 25, 1907. Page One.
[3] Marriage certificate signed by J.D. Clinger uniting Sylvanus Phillips with Mary Jackson May 3, 1870. Archived in the Jackson, Koontz, Glover family papers. Washington State Library.
[4] Bush, J.C. "The Records Are Ancient: Summaries of County Commissioners' Meetings Held in 1854; Little to Show the History of Lewis County from 1845 to 1859—Grown People of Those Days Are Gone." *The Chehalis Bee-Nugget*, Feb. 4, 1921.
[5] Jackson, John R. Diary for 1870 to 1873 in black leather-covered book. Archived in the Jackson, Koontz, Glover family papers. Washington State Library.
[6] Land patent dated September 9, 1870. Archived in the Jackson, Koontz, Glover family papers. Washington State Library.
[7] Receipt from L.L. Dubeau to John R. Jackson dated January 21, 1871. Archived in the Jackson, Koontz, Glover family papers. Washington State Library.
[8] Invoice from L.L. Dubeau to John R. Jackson. 1870. Archived in the Jackson, Koontz, Glover family papers. Washington State Library.
[9] Jackson, John R. Diary for 1870 to 1873 in black leather-covered book. Archived in the Jackson, Koontz, Glover family papers. Washington State Library.
[10] Obituary for Julien Bernier. *The Washington Standard*, Olympia, Washington. June 17, 1871.
[11] Receipt from L.L. Dubeau to John R. Jackson dated January 14, 1872. Archived in the Jackson, Koontz, Glover family papers. Washington State Library.
[12] Receipt for John Koontz dated December 9, 1872. Archived in the Jackson, Koontz, Glover family papers. Washington State Library.
[13] Jackson, John R. Diary for 1870 to 1873 in black leather-covered book. Archived in the Jackson, Koontz, Glover family papers. Washington State Library.
[14] Bush, Judd C. "John R. Jackson Came in 1845: First from the United States to Settle Permanently in County. Mrs. Weir, Jackson's Daughter, and Mr. Yates, Who Knew Him in 1853, Talk for the Bee-Nugget Readers." *The Chehalis Bee-Nugget*. March 17, 1922.
[15] *The Morning Oregonian*, May 30, 1873.
[16] *The Washington Standard*, June 7, 1873.
[17] Hannon, Trudy R. *John R. Jackson: Washington's First American Pioneer*. Advocate Printing. 1998.
[18] *The Pacific Tribune*, Olympia, Washington. April 1, 1874.
[19] Tax receipt for Widow Matilda Jackson. 1874. Archived in the Jackson, Koontz, Glover family papers. Washington State Library.
[20] Ware, Louisa (Jackson). Letter from Seattle, Washington Territory, to brother Barton Koontz dated February 28, 1875. Archived in the Jackson, Koontz, Glover family papers. Washington State Library.
[21] Deed from Matilda Jackson to her son, John N. Koontz. Recorded June 12, 1875. Archived in the Jackson, Koontz, Glover family papers. Washington State Library.
[22] Koontz, Barton. Handwritten notes recording old dates and firsts in Lewis County. Dictated in the year before his death in 1917. Washington State Library.

CHAPTER TWENTY-TWO: A WIDOW LIVING WITH HER SON
[1] Receipt for John Koontz's work on highways dated July 25, 1880. Archived in the Jackson, Koontz, Glover family papers. Washington State Library.
[2] Staeger, Carl P. "Sixty-five years ago in 1885." *The Chehalis Advocate*. November 9, 1950.
[3] Dement, John D., Portland. Letter to Matilda Jackson dated May 30, 1883. Archived in the Jackson, Koontz, Glover family papers. Washington State Library.
[4] Ramsey, Guy Reed. *Postmarked Washington: Lewis and Cowlitz Counties*. The Lewis County Historical Society. 1978.
[5] Lange, Greg. "Washington is admitted as the 42nd state to the United States of America on November 11, 1889." HistoryLink.org Essay 5210. http://www.historylink.org/File/5210 Posted February 15, 2003.

Endnotes

CHAPTER TWENTY-THREE: PRESERVING PIONEER HISTORY
[1] Hobart, Colonel Charles W. *Tacoma Daily Ledger*. 1894. Newspaper article archived in the Jackson, Koontz, Glover family papers. Washington State Library.
[2] "Historic Jackson Prairie: Home in which Grant, Sheridan and McClellan stopped." *Winlock Pilot*, Winlock, Lewis County, Washington. June 2, 1899, V. 13, No. 47.
[3] *The Seattle Post-Intelligencer*, Seattle, Washington. May 24, 1899.

CHAPTER TWENTY-FOUR: LEGACY OF A GREAT LADY
[1] "Mrs. Jackson Passes Away At the Age of Ninety Years: A Resident of Lewis County for Over Fifty Years—She Entertained Grant, Sheridan and McClellan," *The Chehalis Examiner*, Chehalis, Washington. February 22, 1901.
[2] "The Late Mrs. Matilda Jackson, Washington Pioneer of 1847," *The Morning Oregonian*, Portland, Oregon. March 11, 1901.
[3] "Another Pioneer Has Passed Away," *The Chehalis Bee-Nugget*, Chehalis, Washington December 27, 1901.
[4] "Another Old Pioneer Gone," *The Lewis County Advocate*, Chehalis, Washington. July 19, 1907.
[5] Marriage announcement Barton Koontz. *The Chehalis Bee-Nugget*, Chehalis, Washington. October 2, 1908.
[6] *The Washington Standard*, Olympia, Washington. May 28, 1909.
[7] *The Evening Statesman*, Walla Walla, Washington. May 31, 1909.
[8] Obituary for Mary (Jackson) Phillips. *The Chehalis Bee-Nugget*, Chehalis, Washington. February 25, 1914.
[9] "Mary E. Phillips, Native Daughter of County, Passes On: Born on Jackson Prairie 65 Years Ago, Died Wednesday Morning at Home on Phillips Farm Near This City" and "Home of Early Childhood Was Old Jackson Prairie Court House—Had Never Lived Outside Lewis County—The Funeral Will Be Held This Afternoon at 1:00 O'Clock." *The Lewis County Advocate*, Chehalis, Washington. February 25, 1914.
[10] "In Honor of Mrs. Jackson: Mrs. Louisa Ware to Dedicate Park on Jackson Prairie." Another subheadline states: "Five Acre Tract Will Be Set Aside to Public in Honor of Mrs. Ware's Mother, Matilda N. Jackson, Famed Early Pioneer." *The Chehalis Bee-Nugget*, Chehalis, Washington. September 1, 1916.
[11] B. Koontz, Pioneer, Passes" and "Came to Lewis County 69 Years Ago, Settling on Jackson Prairie." *The Chehalis Bee-Nugget*, Chehalis, Washington. May 25, 1917.
[12] "Improvement at Jackson." *The Chehalis Bee-Nugget*, March 10, 1922.
[13] "Territorial Court House Is Dedicated: Ceremony Held Last Saturday Afternoon Fittingly Commemorates Work of Lewis County Pioneers," *The Lewis County Advocate*, Chehalis, Washington. October 27, 1922.
[14] *The Tacoma News Tribune*, Tacoma, Washington. February 26, 1936.
[15] Miller, Mabel J. Letter to Anna Koontz dated April 22, 1936. Archived in the Jackson, Koontz, Glover family papers. Washington State Library.
[16] "Last of Historic Jackson Family Passes." Louisa (Jackson) Ware obituary. *The Chehalis Bee-Nugget*, January 18, 1938.
[17] McDonald, Julie. "Highlighting Lewis County: History Now Preserved for Future Generations at Jackson Courthouse," *The Chronicle*, Centralia, Washington. October 10, 2017.

Bibliography

"100th Birthday of Court Due: Observance Set in Lewis County." *The Oregonian*, Nov. 12, 1950.

"100-year-old Cabin Sheltered Famous Men," August 9, 1945.

"A Neighbor is 100 Years Old." The Oregonian. December 1945.

"A Review of Three Pioneer Lives of the Southwest." *The Chehalis Bee-Nugget*, August 21, 1931.

"Another Old Pioneer Gone," *The Lewis County Advocate*, Chehalis, Washington. July 19, 1907.

"Another Pioneer Has Passed Away," *The Chehalis Bee-Nugget*, Chehalis, Washington December 27, 1901.

"Another Pioneer Has Passed Away." Obituary for John Koontz. *The Chehalis Bee-Nugget*, December 27, 1901.

"Apples to Oregon: The Journey of Henderson Luelling." North Carolina Department of Natural and Cultural Resources. https://www.ncdcr.gov/blog/2015/12/28/apples-to-oregon-the-journey-of-henderson-luelling

"B. Koontz, Pioneer, Passes: Came to Lewis County 69 Years Ago, Settling on Jackson Prairie." *The Chehalis Bee-Nugget*. May 25, 1917.

"Board met at the house of John R. Jackson." *The Chehalis Bee-Nugget*, April 16, 1921.

"Boone's Lick Road Opened New Westward Progress," *St. Charles Journal*, Monday, August 9, 1971.

"County Notes 100th Anniversary of Court at Historic Jackson Courthouse." *The Chehalis Advocate*. November 9, 1950.

"Exercises Dedicating the Stone Wall and Memorial Tablets at Jackson Prairie." Program from event, Sunday, Oct. 21, 1922, at 1:30 p.m.

"Fifty Years Ago: Semi-Centennial Washington a Territory; Observe Day at Olympia; Anniversary Is Made an Occasion for Speeches; Many Pioneers are Present." *The Morning Oregonian*. Portland, Ore. March 3, 1903.

"First Emigrants on the Oregon Trail: Beginning the great migration to Oregon." Oregon-California Trails Association. http://www.octa-trails.org/articles/first-emigrants-on-the-oregon-trail.

"Flag, 92 Years, To Be Shown." *The Chehalis Bee-Nugget*. August 23, 1945.

"Fort Laramie." Wyoming State Historic Preservation Office.

"Frequently Asked Questions About the Oregon Trail." Bureau of Land Management. https://www.blm.gov/sites/blm.gov/files/learn_interp_nhotic_faq.pdf.

"Future Bright For Courthouse. Historic Jackson Prairie: Home in which Grant, Sheridan and McClellan stopped." *Winlock Pilot*, Winlock, Lewis County, Washington. June 2, 1899, V. 13, No. 47.

"Historic Jackson Prairie: Lewis County Home, in which Grant, Sheridan and McClellan were Entertained." *The Weekly Oregonian*. June 2, 1899.

"Improvement at Jackson." *The Chehalis Bee-Nugget*, March 10, 1922.

"In Honor of Mrs. Jackson: Early Pioneer Whose Memory Is to Be Honored by Park: Mrs. Louisa Ware to Dedicate Park on Jackson Prairie." *The Chehalis Bee-Nugget*. September 16, 1916.

"In Honor of Mrs. Jackson: Mrs. Louisa Ware to Dedicate Park on Jackson Prairie." Another subheadline states: "Five Acre Tract Will Be Set Aside to Public in Honor of Mrs. Ware's Mother, Matilda N. Jackson, Famed Early Pioneer." *The Chehalis Bee-Nugget*, Chehalis, Washington. September 1, 1916.

"In Honor of Mrs. Jackson: Mrs. Louisa Ware to Dedicate Park on Jackson Prairie." *The Chehalis Bee-Nugget*. September 16, 1916.

"Initial Homestead at Napavine Taken in 1872 by John Cutting," *The Daily Chronicle*, Centralia, Washington. June 6, 1953.

"Jackson Courthouse: Historic Site Draws Tourists." *The Daily Chronicle*, January 11, 1964.

"Jackson House Rededication Ceremony." *The Chronicle*. June 29, 1995.

"Jacksons left lasting imprint on Lewis County." April 24, 1989.

"John R. Jackson, who lived to be 90 years." Caption for headstone. Centennial Edition, *The Daily Chronicle*, June 7, 1953.

"Last of Historic Jackson Family Passes." Louisa (Jackson) Ware obituary. *The Chehalis Bee-Nugget*, January 18, 1938.

"Lewis County's First Elected Sheriff John R. Jackson," *The Chronicle*. Centralia, Washington. July 19, 2013.

"Marriage in the Colonies," https://classroom.synonym.com/age-marriage-us-1800s-23174.html

"Mary E. Phillips, Native Daughter of County, Passes On." *The Lewis County Advocate*. February 27, 1914.

"Mary E. Phillips, Native Daughter of County, Passes On: Born on Jackson Prairie 65 Years Ago, Died Wednesday Morning at Home on Phillips Farm Near This City" and "Home of Early Childhood Was Old Jackson Prairie Court House—Had Never Lived Outside Lewis County—The Funeral Will Be Held This Afternoon at 1:00 O'Clock." *The Lewis County Advocate*, Chehalis, Washington. February 25, 1914.

"Matilda Nettle Glover Jackson" by Nettie (Koontz) Beireis. 1939.

"Mrs. Jackson Passes Away At the Age of Ninety Years: A Resident of Lewis County for Over Fifty Years—She Entertained Grant, Sheridan and McClellan," *The Chehalis Examiner*, Chehalis, Washington. February 22, 1901.

"Mrs. Jackson Passes Away At the Age of Ninety Years; A Resident of Lewis County for Over Fifty Years—She Entertained Grant, Sheridan and McClellan."

"Pathways of the Pioneers. Soda Springs." Idaho Public Television. http://idahoptv.org/outdoors/shows/pathwaysofpioneers/sodasprings.cfm

"Pioneer Reminiscences As Told By Mrs. Geo. Beireis—Chehalis (Formerly Miss Nettie Koontz)." Lewis County. Pp. 33–34. Told by the Pioneers. Reminiscences of Pioneer Life in Washington. Vol. 2. 1938. Washington Pioneer Project. Printed under W.P.A. Sponsored Federal Project No. 5841. Directed by Secretary of State Ernest N. Hutchinson.

"Pioneer Settler of Chehalis Dies." Barton Koontz obituary. *The Chehalis Bee-Nugget*. May 21, 1917.

"Pioneers' Daughters to Honor Two Chehalins." *The Chehalis Advocate*. May 8, 1947.

"Restoring First Courthouse: Historical Building at Jackson Prairie, South of Chehalis, Will Be Preserved." *The Tacoma News Tribune*, February 26, 1936.

"S.A. Phillips dies: Another Old Pioneer Gone." *The Lewis County Advocate*, July 19, 1907.

"Statehood Day Celebration | Missouri State Parks," https://mostateparks.com/event/61143/statehood-day-celebration

"Territorial Court House Is Dedicated: Ceremony Held Last Saturday Afternoon Fittingly Commemorates Work of Lewis County Pioneers," *The Lewis County Advocate*, Chehalis, Washington. October 27, 1922.

"Territorial Timeline: Settlers met at Monticello to sign a petition asking Congress to create a separate territory north of the Columbia River." Legacy Washington, Washington Secretary of State. https://www.sos.wa.gov/legacy/timeline/detail.aspx?id=214

"The Cowlitz Celebration," *The Columbian*, Olympia, Puget Sound, Washington Territory. July 16, 1853.

"The Donation Land Claim Act of 1850 Law and Legal Definition.: USlegal.com. https://definitions.uslegal.com/t/the-donation-land-claim-act-of-1850/

"The Late Mrs. Matilda Jackson, Washington Pioneer of 1847," *The Morning Oregonian*, Portland, Oregon. March 11, 1901.

"The Oregon Trail: Soda Springs." HistoryGlobe.com. http://www.historyglobe.com/ot/sodasprings.htm

"Welcome to St. Charles County, Missouri: Forts." http://genealogytrails.com/mo/stcharles/hist_forts.htm

100-year-old Cabin Sheltered Famous Men: A Historic "Court House." *The Sunday Oregonian*, December 12, 1950.

Addis, Cameron. "Whitman Massacre." The Oregon Encyclopedia.

An Act to Re-Locate the County Seat of Lewis County." *The Pacific Tribune*. January 21, 1865.

Ancestry.com 1860 census records.

Ancestry.com 1870 census.

Ancestry.com listing for John Philpott Glover, 1769–1843.

Ancestry.com, 1810 Census, nine slaves, https://search.ancestry.com/cgi-bin/sse.dll?indiv=1&dbid=7613&h=83861&tid=&pid=&usePUB=true&_phsrc=EZw1388&_phstart=successSource

Ancestry.com. Andrew M. Jackson headstone. https://search.ancestry.com/cgi-bin/sse.dll?indiv=1&dbid=60525&h=83971509&tid=&pid=&usePUB=true#?_phcmd=u('https://www.ancestry.com/search/?name%3DAndrew_Jackson%26event%3D_lewis-washington-

Bibliography

usa_1748%26birth%3D1851%26successSource%3DSearch','successSource')
Ancestry.com. Listing for Barton Koontz.

Atwood, A. *The Conquerors: Historical Sketches of the American Settlement of the Oregon Country.* Published with the Indorsement of the Officers of the Washington State Historical Society. Tacoma, Washington. Jennings and Graham. 1907.

"B. Koontz, Pioneer, Passes" and "Came to Lewis County 69 Years Ago, Settling on Jackson Prairie." *The Chehalis Bee-Nugget*, Chehalis, Washington. May 25, 1917.

Bagley, Will. "Fort Bridger." WyoHistory.org, a Project of the Wyoming State Historical Society. https://www.wyohistory.org/encyclopedia/fort-bridger

Banel, Feliks. "Cowlitz convention responsible for splitting Washington from Oregon." http://mynorthwest.com/728893/cowlitz-splits-washington-oregon/ August 23, 2017.

Barber, Katrine. "Celilo Falls." The Oregon Encyclopedia. https://oregonencyclopedia.org/articles/celilo_falls/#.XDEgs1xKiUk

Becker, Paula. "Yakama Indian War begins on October 5, 1855." HistoryLink.org Essay 5311. http://www.historylink.org/File/5311 Posted February 26, 2003.

Beireis, Nettie B. "A Sketch of Mrs. Matilda N. Jackson's Life: An Old Pioneer of Lewis County." Typed copy of handwritten and nearly illegible information at the Washington State Historical Society. 1939. Jackson, Koontz, Glover family papers. Washington State Library.

Blanchet, Rt. Rev. Augustine Magloire Alexander. Edward J. Kowrach; Jean Baptiste Abraham Bouilett. *Journal of a Catholic Bishop on the Oregon Trail: The Overland Crossing of the Rt. Rev. A.M.A. Blanchet, Bishop of Walla Walla, from Montreal to Oregon Territory, March 23, 1847 to January 23, 1851.* Ye Galleon Press, Fairfield, Wash. 1978.

Blomdahl, George H. "John R. Jackson was versatile man." *The Daily Chronicle* Bicentennial Edition. June 28, 1976.

Blomdahl, George H. "Old Jackson Courthouse Visited By Thousands of U.S. Travelers: Courthouse Attracts Tourists." *The Daily Chronicle.* July 13, 1957.

Bonney, William P. "The Murder of Leander Wallace," *History of Pierce County, Washington.* Chicago: Pioneer Historical Publishing Company, 1927. pp. 54–61.

Bonney, William P., secretary. Washington State Historical Society. Letter to the editor dated March 17, 1922. Published in *The Chehalis Bee-Nugget*. Chehalis, Washington. March 31, 1922.

Boone's Lick Road—Kountz Fort (1800). http://www.waymarking.com/waymarks/WM5T8B

The Boon's Lick Times of Fayette, Missouri, June 22, 1844. Page 2. https://www.newspapers.com/image/49666604. Downloaded May 15, 2018.

Boyd, Robert. "Wascopam Mission." The Oregon Encyclopedia. https://oregonencyclopedia.org/articles/wascopam_mission/#.XDEhVVxKiUk

Brown, Dr. O. Phelps. The Complete Herbalist: The People Their Own Physicians by the Use of Nature's Remedies. White Swelling (Hydrarthrus). Republished by Kessinger Publishing LLC. March 5, 2004.

Brown, Mrs. Esther Grant. "Pioneer recalls courthouse: Pioneer Visitor From Seaside, Oregon; Mrs. Esther Grant Brown's Parents Married There in 1851; Recalls Early Days, Jackson Courthouse. *The Chehalis Advocate.* November 2, 1939.

Bryan, William Smith. *A History of the Pioneer Families of Missouri: With Numerous Sketches, Anecdotes, Adventures, Etc., Relating to Early Days in Missouri. Also the Lives of Daniel Boone and the Celebrated Indian Chief Black Hawk with Numerous Biographies and Histories of Primitive Institutions.* 1876. Bryan Brand & Company. 528 pages.

Bush, J.C. "Early History Two Pioneers." Reproduced recollections of Huggins, Edward, overseer at the Hudson's Bay Co.'s Puget Sound Agricultural Co. *The Oregonian* 1900 and *The Chehalis Bee-Nugget* September 28, 1900.

Bush, J.C. "Jackson Twice Naturalized? Evidence Shows He Was Admitted to Citizenship in 1835 and Again in 1850." *The Chehalis Bee-Nugget.* March 31, 1922.

Bush, J.C. "The Records Are Ancient: Summaries of County Commissioners' Meetings Held in 1854; Little to Show the History of Lewis County from 1845 to 1859—Grown People of Those Days Are Gone." *The Chehalis Bee-Nugget*, February 4, 1921.

Bush, Judd C. "County Dads Busy in 1851. Met at Jackson's—Effort to Move the Seat of Government to Olympia Olympia-Cowlitz Landing Road, From Monticello, Cathlamet-Boistfort Road and Others Under Consideration." *The Chehalis Bee-Nugget*, April 1, 1921.

Bush, Judd C. "County Seat Trouble In '51. Commissioners Move From Jackson's To Courthouse on Ford's Prairie. Effort Made to Compel Clerk of District Court, County Clerk, Probate Court and Commissioners to Make New Headquarters." *The Chehalis Bee-Nugget*, April 8, 1921.

Bush, Judd C. "John R. Jackson Came in 1845: First from the United States to Settle Permanently in County. Mrs. Weir, Jackson's Daughter, and Mr. Yates, Who Knew Him in 1853, Talk for the Bee-Nugget Readers." *The Chehalis Bee-Nugget*. March 17, 1922.

Bush, Judd C. "Little Details of Life on Jackson Prairie in the Early Days: Jackson Had a Military Company in '55—The Road Change—Prices in Early Days—Recollections of Barton Koontz." *The Chehalis Bee-Nugget*, Chehalis, Washington. March 24, 1922

Bush, Judd C. "The First Legislature Met at Olympia Early in 1854; Doings of the Commissioners in 1852 and 1853—Met at Various Places—Seven School Districts Established—Road Work. *The Chehalis Bee-Nugget*. April 15, 1921.

Cain, J. Note to Simon Plamondon. Undated. Archived with the Jackson, Koontz, Glover family papers. Washington State Library.

Camp, Charles L., editor. "James Clyman, American Frontiersman, 1792–1881. The adventures of a trapper and covered wagon emigrant as told in his own reminiscences and diaries." *California Historical Society, Special Publication No. 3*. http://www.archive.org/details/jamesclymanameri01cali

Cascades Volcano Observatory, USGS. "Henry Warre, September 1845 eruption of Mount St. Helens." https://volcanoes.usgs.gov/observatories/cvo/Historical/volcanoes_henry_warre_1845.shtml

Cascades Volcano Observatory, USGS. "Paul Kane, 1847 Eruptions of Mount St. Helens." https://volcanoes.usgs.gov/observatories/cvo/Historical/volcanoes_henry_warre_1845.shtml.

Centralia's First Century 1845–1955. Citizens of Centralia. H.J. Quality Printing. 1955.

Chapman, John P. *The Oregonian Statesman*, a Democratic newspaper, 1852.

Chappellier, M. Western Union Telegraph to John R. Jackson dated June 3, 1868. Archived in the Jackson, Koontz, Glover family papers. Washington State Library.

The Chehalis Examiner, February 22, 1901.

Coffman, N.B., and Charles Miles "Claquato Landmarks: John R. Jackson diary." *The Chehalis Bee-Nugget*, October 3, 1939.

Coffman, N.B., and Charles Miles. "Claquato Landmarks: Domestic Life of Earliest Washington Settlers." *The Chehalis Bee-Nugget*. September 5, 1939.

Coffman, N.B., and Charles Miles. "Claquato Landmarks: Grandma Jackson." *The Chehalis Bee-Nugget*. October 3, 1939.

Coffman, N.B., and Charles Miles. "Claquato Landmarks: John R. Jackson." *The Chehalis Bee-Nugget*. August 15, 1939.

Coffman, N.B., and Charles Miles. "Claquato Landmarks: Lewis County Gets Going." *The Chehalis Bee-Nugget*. June 27, 1939.

Coffman, N.B., and Charles Miles. "Claquato Landmarks: Twenty-Nine Years Struggle to Pass Donation Land Claim Act." *The Chehalis Bee-Nugget*, October 24, 1939.

Coffman, Noah B. "Old Lewis County, Oregon Territory, an address delivered before the Southwest Washington Pioneers." Rochester, Thurston County, Washington. August 12, 1926.

Conover, C.T. "First White Child in Washington Territory." *The Seattle Times*, December 20, 1948.

Coonc, Elizabeth Ann Fenn. "Reminiscences of a Pioneer Woman." *The Washington Historical Quarterly. Volume VIII*. The Washington University State Historical Society. University Station. Seattle, Washington. 1917.

Coonce, Barton. Letter from Portland to his mother, Matilda (Glover) Jackson, and stepfather, John R. Jackson, dated May 7, 1869. Archived in the Jackson, Koontz, Glover family papers. Washington State Library.

Coonse, Henry, and Andrew Levitt Diary, December 1851 to January 1855. (Henry Coonse papers. Accession 4709-001.) Diaries of Andrew Levitt and Henry Coonse. University of Washington Libraries, Pacific Northwest Historical Documents Digital Collections. PNW00121. https://digitalcollections.lib.washington.edu/digital/collection/pioneerlife/search

Bibliography

/searchterm/4709-001/field/source/mode/all/conn/and/cosuppress/ pp. 1–50. 1851–1855.

Coonse, Nicholas. One-page diary from May 1947. Archived in the Jackson, Koontz, Glover family papers. Washington State Library.

Corp, Mrs. T. "The People's Column: Jackson Courthouse." *The Daily Chronicle.* April 13, 1937.

Crowell, Sandra. *The Land Called Lewis*, Panesko Publishing. 2007.

Cutting, J.B. First-person account. "When I started for Napawyna (now Napavine)." London, England, 1851. Published in the 1890s.

Daly, Walter J., M.D., "The Black Cholera Comes to the Central Valley of America in the 19th Century—1832, 1849, and Later," Transactions of the American Clinical and Climatological Association, The National Center for Biotechnology Information, https://www.ncbi.nlm.nih.gov/pmc/articles/PMC2394684/

Davidsen, Junel. Article about Louisa M. Ware, appeared in *The Seattle Post-Intelligencer* April 22, 1920. http://jtenlen.drizzlehosting.com/wacowlitz/monticello.html

Deed from Matilda Jackson to her son, John N. Koontz. Recorded June 12, 1875. Archived in the Jackson, Koontz, Glover family papers. Washington State Library.

Dement, John D., Portland. Letter to Matilda Jackson dated May 30, 1883. Archived in the Jackson, Koontz, Glover family papers. Washington State Library.

Denfeld, Duane Colt, Ph.D. "Forts of Washington Territory, Indian War Era, 1855–1856." HistoryLink.org. http://www.historylink.org/File/10087. Posted April 9, 2012.

Denfeld, Duane Colt, Ph.D. "Nisqually Chief Leschi is hanged on February 19, 1858." HistoryLink.org. http://www.historylink.org/File/5145 Posted Jan. 29, 2003.

Dickason, Glen. "The Time Machine: Dec. 5, 1864: John Jackson told to move post office." *The Daily Chronicle.*

Donation Land Claim Holdings at the Washington State Library. www.sos.wa.gov/library/landrecords.aspx

Dougherty, Phil. "Thurston County—Thumbnail History." HistoryLink.org Essay 7979. http://www.historylink.org/File/7979 Posted November 15, 2006.

Dressler, Mrs. Mabel C. of Centralia, Washington.

Dubeau, L.L. Invoice for John R. Jackson. 1870. Archived in the Jackson, Koontz, Glover family papers. Washington State Library.

Duncan, Jane and Hiram, from Lincoln County, Missouri. Letter to Jane's brother Philip Glover, forwarded to his brother, John Glover, who forwarded it to their sister, Matilda (Glover) Jackson. Dated May 15, 1854, and sent to Matilda Jackson September 8, 1854. Part of the Jackson, Koontz, Glover family papers. Washington State Library.

Elwang, W.W. *A History of the Pioneer Families of Missouri.* Lucas Brothers, Columbia, Missouri. 1935.

End of the Oregon Trail Interpretive and Visitor Information Center. Oregon City, Oregon. https://www.oregontrailcenter.org/HistoricalTrails/LocalTrailLandmarks.htm.

The Evening Statesman, Walla Walla, Washington. May 31, 1909.

Flora, Stephenie, and Nancy Prevost, compilers. "Emigrants to Oregon in 1847." Listing for Surnames A-L, M-Z. Oregonpioneers.com. http://www.oregonpioneers.com/1847

Flora, Stephenie, compiler. "Nathan Scofield Kimball." OregonPioneers.com. http://www.oregonpioneers.com/NathanKimball.htm

Flora, Stephenie. "Emigrants to Oregon in 1844." OregonPioneers.com. http://www.oregonpioneers.com/1844.htm

"Fort Coontz." http://www.fortwiki.com/Fort_Coontz

Fort Laramie National Historic Site. https://www.wyohistory.org/encyclopedia/fort-laramie

Fort Walla Walla Museum. Walla Walla, Washington. https://www.fwwm.org/

Francis Parkham and the Oregon Trail. https://www.univie.ac.at/Anglistik/easyrider/data/parkoret.htm

Geer, Elizabeth Dixon Smith. "Diary of Mrs. Elizabeth Dixon Smith Geer. *Transactions of the Thirty-Fifth Annual Reunion of the Oregon Pioneer Association.* Portland, Oregon. June 14, 1906.

Geer, Hon. Ralph C. "Occasional Address for the Year 1847." *Transactions of the Seventh Annual Re-Union of the Oregon Pioneer Association.* E.M. Waite Steam Printer and Bookbinder. Salem, Oregon. 1879.

Gibson, James, 1834–1920. Typeset recollections of overland travel from Bates County, Missouri, to

Linnton, Oregon, between May 15, 1847, and November 1847. Dictated to Minnie M. Richards. 1914. Seven pages. Archived in the Oregon Historical Society's Research Library.

Giddings, E. Surveyor General's Office, Olympia, Washington. Letter to John R. Jackson dated December 18, 1861. Archived in the Jackson, Koontz, Glover family papers. Washington State Library.

Glover, John P., Clackamas County, Oregon Territory. Letter to his sister, Matilda Jackson, dated January 8, 1855. Archived with the Jackson, Koontz, Glover family papers. Washington State Library.

Glover, Matilda Nettle, Montgomery County, Missouri, letter to daughter Matilda Coonse Jackson dated April 1, 1849. Archived in the Jackson, Koontz, Glover family papers. Washington State Library.

Glover, Matilda Nettle. Letter to her daughter, Matilda Jackson, November 17, 1851. Archived in the Jackson, Koontz, Glover family papers. Washington State Library.

Glover, Matthew. Letter to his sister, Matilda (Glover) Coonse, Oregon Territory, from Montgomery County, Missouri, dated April 2, 1848.

Glover, Mrs. Matilda, of Lincoln County, Missouri. Letter to daughter Matilda Jackson (Mrs. John R. Jackson.) Folded and fastened by stamp of red sealing wax. Washington State Library.

Glover, William and Jane. Marion County, Oregon Territory. Letter to his aunt, Matilda (Glover) Koontz Jackson in 1855. Archived in the Jackson, Koontz, Glover family papers. Washington State Library.

Glover, William. Marion County, Oregon Territory. Letter to his aunt, Matilda (Glover) Koontz Jackson dated July 30, 1856. Archived in the Jackson, Koontz, Glover family papers. Washington State Library.

Grant, Esther (Brown), Seaside, Oregon. *The Centralia Daily Chronicle*, July 21, 1938.

Gregg, Kate L. "The Boonslick Road in St. Charles County." From *Missouri Historical Review, Volume 27 Issue 4*, July 1933, pp. 307–314.

Hahn, Dennis J. "Kountz Fort and The Boone's Lick Road," posted May 26, 2002. Regarding DAR marker for Kountz Fort in danger of being destroyed. dhahn@alvey.com.

Handwritten notes from Anna Koontz. Jackson papers at Washington State Library.

Hannon, Trudy R. *John R. Jackson: Washington's First American Pioneer*. Advocate Printing. 1998.

Hastings, Lansford Warren. *The Emigrants' guide to Oregon and California : containing scenes and incidents of a party of Oregon emigrants, a description of Oregon, scenes and incidents of a party of California emigrants, and a description of California : with a description of the different routes to those countries : and all necessary information relative to the equipment, supplies, and the method of traveling*. 1845. Cincinnati: G. Conclin. https://archive.org/details/emigrantsguideto04hast

Hieb, David L. "Fort Laramie National Monument, Wyoming." National Park Service Historical Handbook Series No. 20. September 18, 2018.

Hobart, Colonel Charles W. *Tacoma Daily Ledger*. 1894. Newspaper article archived in the Jackson, Koontz, Glover family papers. Washington State Library.

Hockett, William A. "Experiences of W.A. Hockett on the Oregon Trail 1847." Typed by the William Albert Hockett, in 1914. Archived at the University of Oregon Libraries, Special Collections and University Archives, Eugene, Oregon.

Huggins, Edward. Former overseer of the Hudson's Bay Co.'s Puget Sound Agricultural Company at Nisqually. First-person account of his travels south to the Cowlitz Farm near present-day Toledo in the early 1850s, originally published in *The Oregonian* in 1900 and republished in *The Chehalis Bee-Nugget*.

Hutchins, C.C. "Here First Court Sat in State: In Lewis County History Sits by Pacific Highway." *The Seattle Post-Intelligencer*. Seattle, Washington. June 12, 1921 or 1927.

Jackson, Andrew M. Headstone photograph. Fern Hill Cemetery.

Jackson, John R. 1843 paperwork. Archived in the Jackson, Koontz, Glover family papers. Washington State Library.

Jackson, John R. Account book listing land and property. June 13, 1860. Archived in the Jackson, Koontz, Glover family papers. Washington State Library.

Jackson, John R. Accounting book November 1853 to July 1855. Archived in the Jackson, Koontz, Glover family papers. Washington State Library.

Jackson, John R. Diary for 1870 to 1873 in black leather-covered book. Archived in the Jackson, Koontz, Glover family papers. Washington State Library.

Jackson, John R. Journal kept in 1868. Archived in the Jackson, Koontz, Glover family papers. Washington State Library.

Jackson, John R. Letter to his wife, Matilda Jackson, dated April 25, 1854. Jackson, Koontz, Glover

Bibliography

family papers. Washington State Library.

Jackson, John R. Letter to his wife, Matilda. March 1, 1854. Part of the Jackson, Koontz, Glover family papers. Washington State Library.

Jackson, John R. Letter to his wife, Matilda. March 2, 1854. Part of the Jackson, Koontz, Glover family papers. Washington State Library.

Jackson, John R. March 1840 paperwork. Archived in the Jackson, Koontz, Glover family papers. Washington State Library.

Jackson, John R. March and July 1839 paperwork. Archived in the Jackson, Koontz, Glover family papers. Washington State Library.

Jackson, John R. May 1844 paperwork. Archived in the Jackson, Koontz, Glover family papers. Washington State Library.

Jackson, John R. November 1835 paperwork. Archived in the Jackson, Koontz, Glover family papers. Washington State Library.

Jackson, John R. Paperwork dated May 28, 1836. Archived in the Jackson, Koontz, Glover family papers. Washington State Library.

Jackson, John R. October 1837 and January 1840 paperwork. Archived in the Jackson, Koontz, Glover family papers. Washington State Library.

Jackson, John R. October 1838 paperwork. Archived in the Jackson, Koontz, Glover family papers. Washington State Library.

Jackson, John R. Papers dated April 12, 1851. Archived in the Jackson, Koontz, Glover family papers. Washington State Library.

Jackson, John R. Paperwork from 1846. Archived in the Jackson, Koontz, Glover family papers. Washington State Library.

Jackson, John R. Paperwork from fall 1845. Archived in the Jackson, Koontz, Glover family papers. Washington State Library.

Jackson, John R. Postmaster. Pay stub for Sheriff Javan Hall dated February 25, 1863. Archived in the Jackson, Koontz, Glover family papers. Washington State Library.

Jackson, John R. Receipt from 1850. Archived in the Jackson, Koontz, Glover family papers. Washington State Library.

Jackson, John R. Records kept listing expenses. December 1851 and throughout 1852. Archived in the Jackson, Koontz, Glover family papers. Washington State Library.

Jackson, John R. September 1838 and January 1845 paperwork. Archived in the Jackson, Koontz, Glover family papers. Washington State Library.

Jackson, John R. September 1839 and April 1840 paperwork. Archived in the Jackson, Koontz, Glover family papers. Washington State Library.

Jackson, John R. September 1839 paperwork. Archived in the Jackson, Koontz, Glover family papers. Washington State Library.

Jackson, Mary. Letter to sister Louisa in January 1864. Archived in the Jackson, Koontz, Glover family papers. Washington State Library.

Jackson, Matilda (Glover) Koontz. Letter to her husband, John R. Jackson, dated April 12, 1855. Archived with the Jackson, Koontz, Glover family papers. Washington State Library.

Johnson, Karen L. and Serene A. "Louisa Jackson's Diary of 1865." Transcribed. Lewis County Historical Museum. May 2004.

Jones, Pat. "Plenty still to learn from pioneer woman," *The Chronicle*, June 10, 2006.

Judson, A.B., M.D. "A Contribution to the Treatment of White Swelling of the Knee." Read before the American Orthopedic Association, St. Louis, Mo., September 1893. Published November 18, 1893. JAMA Network.

Judson, Ann. Letter to friend Mary Jackson dated March 18 with the year missing. Archived in the Jackson, Koontz, Glover family papers. Washington State Library.

Koontz, Anna. "Grandma Jackson Remembered," typewritten recollections. Lewis County Historical Museum? 1953

Koontz, Anna. Handwritten notes. November 12, 1850, regarding Judge Strong's first regular court session in Washington. Washington State Library.

Koontz, Anna. Information from Oregon State Library, Salem, Oregon, with quotations from Judge

Strong's records, as found in an article by his grandson, Robert Strong.

Koontz, Barton. Handwritten notes recording old dates and firsts in Lewis County. Dictated in the year before his death in 1917. Lewis County Historical Museum.

Koontz, Nettie. Matilda's granddaughter, John's daughter Nettie Koontz, wrote about her grandmother in 1939.

L.L. Dubeau & Co. invoice for John R. Jackson dated May 1861. Archived in the Jackson, Koontz, Glover family papers. Washington State Library.

Land patent dated September 9, 1870. Archived in the Jackson, Koontz, Glover family papers. Washington State Library.

Lange, Greg. "Washington is admitted as the 42nd state to the United States of America on November 11, 1889." HistoryLink.org Essay 5210. http://www.historylink.org/File/5210 Posted February 15, 2003.

Letter from Captain Joseph Magone to Matilda (Coonse) Jackson January 20, 1848, from the Dallas Mission. Archived in the Jackson, Koontz, Glover family papers. Washington State Library.

Lewis County, Oregon Territory, records of first meetings. https://web.archive.org/web/20110523015333/http://users.bentonrea.com/~tinear/lewis-ot.htm

Lord Baltimore settling Maryland https://www.history.com/this-day-in-history/the-settlement-of-maryland

Lyman, H.S. "Reminiscences of James Jory," *The Quarterly of the Oregon Historical Society*, Vol. 3, No. 3 (Sep., 1902), pp. 271–286 Published by: Oregon Historical Society. Stable URL: http://www.jstor.org/stable/20609535. Accessed: 21/10/2014 14:30

Magone, Joseph. https://www.geni.com/people/Joseph-Magone/3189294

Manifest Destiny. https://www.history.com/topics/westward-expansion/manifest-destiny

Marriage announcement Barton Koontz. *The Chehalis Bee-Nugget*, Chehalis, Washington. October 2, 1908.

Marriage certificate signed by J.D. Clinger uniting Sylvanus Phillips with Mary Jackson May 3, 1870. Archived in the Jackson, Koontz, Glover family papers. Washington State Library.

Mayo Clinic staff. "Diphtheria." https://www.mayoclinic.org/diseasesconditions/diphtheria/symptoms-causes/syc-20351897.

McDonald, Julie. "Highlighting Lewis County: First U.S. Flag in Lewis County Flew July 4, 1853." *The Chronicle*, Centralia, Washington. July 3, 2018.

McDonald, Julie. "Highlighting Lewis County: History Now Preserved for Future Generations at Jackson Courthouse," *The Chronicle*, Centralia, Washington. October 10, 2017.

McDonald, Julie. "Highlighting Lewis County: Is Blueberry Cheesecake in Toledo's Future?" *The Chronicle*, Centralia, Washington. August 7, 2018.

McDonald, Lucile. "First Courthouse in State," *The Seattle Sunday Times Magazine*, March 10, 1946.

McDonald, Lucile. "Courthouse Battle Led to Forming County," *The Seattle Sunday Times Magazine*. January 6, 1952.

McDonald, Lucile. "Diary of a Pioneer Boy." *The Seattle Times*, Sunday, July 11, 1954.

McDonald, Lucile. "Historic Jackson Courthouse at Chehalis 100 Years Old This Fall." *The Seattle Times*. 1950.

Meany, Edmond S. "The Cowlitz Convention: Inception of Washington Territory." *The Washington Historical Quarterly*, Vol. 13, No. 1 (Jan., 1922), pp. 3–19 Published by: University of Washington Stable URL: http://www.jstor.org/stable/40473582. Accessed: 24-05-2018 16:39.

Meany, Edmond S., professor of History, University of Washington "Living Pioneers of Washington: Louisa M. Ware." *The Seattle Post-Intelligencer*. April 22, 1920.

Miles, Shute & Kons website on Nicholas Coonce/Koontz, 1759-1820. http://www.miles-shute-kouns-families.com/getperson.php?personID=I115&tree=Kouns-GalliaCo.

Miller, Mabel J. Letter to Anna Koontz dated April 22, 1936. Archived in the Jackson, Koontz, Glover family papers. Washington State Library.

Miller, W.W. Letter to his friend John R. Jackson dated September 10, 1863. Archived in the Jackson, Koontz, Glover family papers. Washington State Library.

Milne, Frances. Joseph Magone. https://wc.rootsweb.com/cgibin/igm.cgi?op=GET&db=oregon1847&id=I6372

Milne, Mrs. Frances W. "1847 Oregon Trail Emigrant Families." 1990. Updated October 9, 2014.

Bibliography

Warren Forsythe. https://wc.rootsweb.com/cgibin/igm.cgi?op=GET&db=oregon1847&id=I2528

Missouri Compromise https://www.history.com/topics/missouri-compromise and https://www.history.com/topics/abolotionist-movement/missouri-compromise

Missouri Compromise, https://en.wikipedia.org/wiki/Missouri_Compromise

The Morning Oregonian, May 30, 1873.

Napavine. http://en.wikipedia.org/wiki/Napavine%2C_Washington

National Historic Trails Auto Tour Route Interpretive Guide. "Along the Snake River Plain Through Idaho." National Trails System. National Park Service. U.S. Department of the Interior. October 2008.

National Park Service: Three Island Crossing. https://www.nps.gov/oreg/planyourvisit/site9.htm

Nguyen, Khoa. "Charcoal Making in the Nineteenth Century." https://charcoalkiln.wordpress.com/2012/11/18/charcoal-making-nineteenth-century/ Posted November 18, 2012.

Notice to Barton "Coontz" of appointment as Road District No. 4 supervisor, dated May 23, 1867. Archived in the Jackson, Koontz, Glover family papers. Washington State Library.

Obituary for Julien Bernier. *The Washington Standard*, Olympia, Washington. June 17, 1871,

Obituary for Mary (Jackson) Phillips. *The Chehalis Bee-Nugget*, Chehalis, Washington. February 25, 1914.

Obituary for Mary (Jackson) Phillips. *The Chehalis Bee-Nugget*. February 27, 1914.

Obituary for Sylvanus A. Phillips. *The Centralia Chronicle*, July 25, 1907. Page One.

Obituary of Matilda Jackson. *The Chehalis Bee-Nugget*. March 1, 1901.

Old Franklin Intelligencer, April 23, 1819, edition.

Oldham, Kit. "Captain Ulysses S. Grant arrives at Columbia (later Vancouver) Barracks on September 20, 1852." HistoryLink.org Essay 5255. http://www.historylink.org/File/5255 Posted Feb. 20, 2003.

The Oregon Spectator, May 18, 1848.

The Oregon Spectator, May 4, 1848.

The Oregon Spectator, Oregon City, Oregon. July 8, 1847.

The Oregon Trail: Fort Hall. http://oregontrail101.com/fthall.html

The Oregonian, September 20, 1851, and *The Oregon Spectator* September 23, 1851.

The Pacific Tribune, Olympia, Washington. April 1, 1874.

The Pacific Tribune, Olympia, Washington. January 21, 1865.

Panic of 1837. Ohio History Central. http://www.ohiohistorycentral.org/w/Panic_of_1837 and Panic of 1837 http://lehrmaninstitute.org/history/Andrew-Jackson-1837.html

Pathways of Pioneers. "Old Fort Boise." http://idahoptv.org/outdoors/shows/pathwaysofpioneers/oldfortboise.cfm

Pathways of Pioneers. "Soda Springs." http://idahoptv.org/outdoors/shows/pathwaysofpioneers/oldfortboise.cfm

The Pioneer and Democrat, June 5, 1857.

Plamondon, George F. "First settlers from Cowlitz Prairie to Tumwater." Cowlitz County Historical Society. November 1959.

Quick, Cindy, and Julie McDonald Zander, eds. *The Toledo Community Story, 1800–2008*. Chapters of Life. Originally published in 1953. Updated in 1976 and 2008.

Ramsey, Guy Reed. *Postmarked Washington: Lewis and Cowlitz Counties*. The Lewis County Historical Society. 1978.

Receipt for John Koontz dated December 9, 1872. Archived in the Jackson, Koontz, Glover family papers. Washington State Library.

Receipt for John Koontz's work on highways dated July 25, 1880. Archived in the Jackson, Koontz, Glover family papers. Washington State Library.

Receipt from John R. Jackson to Horace H. Pinto dated December 29, 1866. Archived in the Jackson, Koontz, Glover family papers. Washington State Library.

Receipt from L.L. Dubeau to John R. Jackson dated January 14, 1872. Archived in the Jackson, Koontz, Glover family papers. Washington State Library.

Receipt from L.L. Dubeau to John R. Jackson dated January 21, 1871. Archived in the Jackson, Koontz, Glover family papers. Washington State Library.

Receipt from Simon Plamondon, the treasurer, accepted by John R. Jackson, Clerk of Probate, January 10, 1851. Archived in the Jackson, Koontz, Glover family papers. Washington State Library.

Receipt in the Jackson, Koontz, Glover family papers. Washington State Library.

Receipts and accounts. 1868 and 1869. Archived in the Jackson, Koontz, Glover family papers. Washington State Library.

Rector, Elaine. "Looking Back In Order to Move Forward An Often Untold History Affecting Oregon's Past, Present and Future Timeline of Oregon and U.S. Racial, Immigration and Education History." Timeline of Oregon's Racial and Education History—The City of Portland. https://www.portlandoregon.gov/bps/article/412697 May 16, 2010.

Roberts, George B. Letters to Mrs. F.F. Victor, 1878–83. *Oregon Historical Quarterly,* Vol. 63, No. 2/3 (June–September 1962) pp. 175–236 (62 pages).

Root, Mabel Clarissa Glover. Family history of the Oregon pioneer families of Philip Glover and John H. Palmer. Portland, Ore.: M.G. Root. 1966. Archived at the Oregon Historical Society's Research Library.

Scott, Leslie M. "Oregon's Provisional Government, 1843–49." *Oregon Historical Quarterly.* Vol. 30, No. 3. September 1929.

The Seattle Post-Intelligencer, Seattle, Washington. May 24, 1899.

Secretary of State. Washington State Digital Archives. Title Info: 1847, Lewis County Heads of Family Census, Lewis County Territorial Auditor. https://www.digitalarchives.wa.gov/Collections/TitleInfo/405

Shine, Gregory P. "Hudson's Bay Company." The Oregon Encyclopedia. https://oregonencyclopedia.org/articles/hudson_s_bay_company/#.XDFtnlxKiUk

Simmons, Christopher Columbus. Ancestors and descendants of Christopher Columbus Simmons and Asenath Ann Kennedy Simmons, Washington State pioneers, [198-] / compiled by their granddaughter, Margaret Moore Keck. Washington State Library Northwest Genealogy.

Slip of paper listing books in the cabin. Dated April 9, 1959, in the Jackson file at the Lewis County Historical Museum.

Smith, Frederic A., Dutchess County clerk. Letter from the Office of the County Clerk of Dutchess County, Poughkeepsie, New York, March 28, 1952, to Walter Twiss, and note from Twiss to Anna Koontz, Matilda's granddaughter.

Soderland, Karin, guest columnist for Mrs. Betsy Hemenway. "Between Us Neighbors." *The Daily Chronicle.* April 4, 1959.

St. Charles County Place Names. The State Historical Society of Missouri. https://shsmo.org/manuscripts/ramsay/ramsay_saint_charles

Staeger, Carl P. "Rambling Around Lewis County: Two Chehalis Girls Tie In With History Of Lewis County 105 Years Ago." *The People's Advocate,* May 18, 1950.

Staeger, Carl P. "Rambling Lewis County: Lewis County Schools 100 Years Ago." *The Chehalis Advocate.* July 7, 1949.

Staeger, Carl P. "Sixty-five years ago in 1885." *The Chehalis Advocate.* November 9, 1950.

Steam Navigation Company Formed. Olympia's *Washington Democrat,* January 7, 1865.

Stevens, Governor Isaac, and Superintendent of Indian Affairs. Circular from Olympia dated July 1856. Archived with the Jackson, Koontz, Glover family papers. Washington State Library.

Stevens, Hazard. "Canoeing Up the Cowlitz," *The Life of Isaac Ingalls Stevens, Volume 1.* Boston and New York: Houghton, Mifflin and Company. 1901.

Stock certificate dated October 11, 1867, for shares in Cowlitz Steam Navigation Company. Another stock certificate dated July 20, 1867, lists one hundred shares at one hundred dollars each for $10,000. Archived in the Jackson, Koontz, Glover family papers. Washington State Library.

Stueve, Nathan. "Steamboats on the Cowlitz." *Cowlitz Historical Quarterly.* January 8, 2010. Jim LeMonds. http://writeteknorthwest.com/archives/14831/steamboats-on-the-cowlitz.

The Tacoma News Tribune, Tacoma, Washington. February 26, 1936.

Tate, Cassandra. "Cayuse attack mission, in what becomes known as the Whitman Massacre, on November 29, 1847." HistoryLink.org Essay 5192. http://www.historylink.org/File/5192 Posted September 24, 2014.

Tate, Cassandra. "Trial of five Cayuse accused of Whitman murder begins on May 21, 1850." HistoryLink.org Essay 9401. http://historylink.org/File/9401 Posted April 16, 2010.

Bibliography

Tax receipt for Widow Matilda Jackson. 1874. Archived in the Jackson, Koontz, Glover family papers. Washington State Library.

The Washington Standard, June 7, 1873.

The Washington Standard, Olympia, Washington. May 28, 1909.

The Washington State Constitution–1889. Washington Secretary of State Office. Legacy Washington. https://www.sos.wa.gov/legacy/constitution.aspx.

Third assistant postmaster. Letter to John R. Jackson, postmaster, Highland, dated December 10, 1862. Archived in the Jackson, Koontz, Glover family papers. Washington State Library.

Tisdale, Donna. "Chapter XV: The Elkanah Mills Family." First marriage at courthouse. *The Daily Chronicle*, Centralia, Washington. Sept. 8, 1941.

Tompkins, Professor Jim. "Mileposts along the Oregon Trail." http://www.oregonpioneers.com/Milepost4.htm

Tuberculosis. Wikipedia. https://en.wikipedia.org/wiki/Tuberculosis

Undated note to Matilda Jackson. Archived in the Jackson, Koontz, Glover family papers. Washington State Library.

Ware, Louisa (Jackson). Letter from Seattle, Washington Territory, to brother Barton Koontz dated February 28, 1875. Archived in the Jackson, Koontz, Glover family papers. Washington State Library.

Ware, Louisa Jackson, 1853–1938. Diary/daily journal 1865. MS 0078, Box 1, Folder 7—Part of the Jackson, Koontz, Glover family papers. Washington State Library.

Ware, Louisa Jackson. Handwritten note describing her mother hearing Marcus Whitman preach. Washington State Library.

Ware, Louisa. Handwritten notes regarding Pony Express, courthouse, etc. Washington State Library.

Washington State Centennial Booklet. Washington State Department of Conservation and Development in conjunction with the Washington Centennial association, the Chambers of Commerce of Olympia and Chehalis, the Washington Historical Society, and the State Capital Historical Association.

Webber, Bert and Margie. *Oregon City (By Way of the Barlow Road) At the End of the National Historic Oregon Trail*. Webb Research Group. Publishers of Books about the Oregon Country. Medford, Oregon. 1993.

Wilma, David. "Settlers of North Oregon convene a convention at Cowlitz Landing to form a separate territory on August 29, 1851." HistoryLink.org Essay 5560. http://www.historylink.org/File/5560 Posted Oct. 3, 2003.

Winkler, Pat. "Famed Jackson Flag Presented to State Museum: Patriotism Woven Deep in Fabric of Century-Old 4th of July Flag." *The Tacoma News Tribune*. July 4, 1958.

Young, John Quincy Adams. "Recollections." Typescript. Oregon Historical Society, Portland.

Zander, Julie McDonald. *Chapters of Life in 1915 Chehalis. The Chehalis Bee-Nugget Historical Souvenir Edition, May 14, 1915. Illustrated and Republished.* Chapters of Life. 2011.

Zander, Julie McDonald. *Images of America: Chehalis*. Arcadia Publishing. September 5, 2011.

Zimmerman, Jim. "Re: John, Jacob & Nicholas Coonce, St. Chas. MO." https://www.genealogy.com/forum/surnames/topics/coonce/36/

Index

A

Abernethy, George 81, 83, 105
Ackerman, James 59
Adna 134
Alaska (Russian) 20, 101, 105
Alexander, John 228, 252
Alexander, Mrs. Margaret (Urquhart) 228
Alexander, John W. 319
Alexander, Gerry L. (Washington State Supreme Court Justice) 321
American 5, 9, 14, 21, 95, 99, 101, 103, 105, 109, 110, 111, 128, 131, 134, 156, 162, 207, 219, 228, 306, 308, 317, 319, 322, 325, 326, 330, 331, 332, 334, 336, 338, 343, 344, 345, 346, 348
American Falls 64
American Fur Company 47
Americans 20, 55, 64, 79, 83, 100, 133, 134, 189, 243
Ammuns, Ammund 252
Anderson, J. Patton 199, 200
Anderson, Mrs. 200
Armstrong, Lewis 112
Ash Hollow 44
Astoria, Oregon 138, 268
Atlantic 58

B

Bainbridge, Mrs. 148
Baldwin, David 96
Baltimore, Lord 9, 325, 348
Barbé-Marbois, François 12
Barlow Road 54, 75, 330, 352
Barnett, Mr. 100
Barton, J. 184
Barton, M. 266
Bear River 61, 65
Bear River Mountains 61
Bear River Valley 61
Beireis, Mrs. Nettie (Koontz) 5, 237, 283, 316, 317, 342
Bellingham 121, 304
Benson, Adam 144
Benton County, Missouri 182
Bercier, Peter 104, 106, 132
Bernier 106, 225, 227, 256, 268, 290, 291, 338, 349
Bernier, Frances 225
Bernier, Frank 160, 229
Bernier, Julien 111, 231, 268, 338, 349
Bernier, Marcel 102, 104, 120, 130, 132, 225, 228, 229, 231, 256, 260, 267
Bernier, Cecelia 225
Bernier, Peter 160, 229, 231, 290
Bernier, Isadore 231
Berniers 229
Bersia, Baryeal 231
Bewley, Captain John William 76
Bible 28, 33, 76, 126, 159, 163, 204, 214, 247, 250, 316
Bigelow, Mrs. A.E. 311
Birnie, James 105
Bishop, Charles 251
Bishop, Mrs. C. 262
Bitter Fork 49
Blacks Fork 58
Blacks Fork of the Green River 58
Blanchet, Bishop Augustin Magloire Alexandre 34, 35, 40, 46
Blanchet, Bishop Francis Norbert 127, 326, 327, 328, 343
Blanchette, Louis 14
Blomdahl, George 320
Blue Mountains 41, 47, 67, 73, 74, 75
Blue River 34, 36, 37
Boise River 73
Boistfort 134, 139, 167, 199, 333, 344
Bonney, William P. 156, 307, 308, 332, 334, 343
Boone, A.D. 319
Boone, Daniel 13, 325, 343
Boone, John W. 319
Boone, Nellie 250
Boone's Lick Road 14
The Boon's Lick Times 18, 343
Boring, Morrison 95
Borst blockhouse 184, 186, 188
Borst, Joseph 105, 141
Borst, Mrs. Mary 184
Boston 111, 140, 190, 335, 351
Bostons 288
Bosworth 191
Bouchard, Jean Baptiste 132
Bouchards 219
Bower, John 254, 266
Bowlt, Sam 263
Bowseth, Mr. 169
Boy Scouts 323
Bradley, John 120, 144
Brashears, Israel 122
Brashears, Joseph 144
Bridger, James "Jim" 55, 59
Brill, George 120
Brock, R. 105
Bronk, George 98
Brooks, Honorable Quincy A. 157, 158
Brown, Dr. O. Phelps 187
Brown, J. 42
Brown, John 207, 209
Brown, Robert W. 137, 156
Brown, Sally 95
Brown, Sara 42
Brownfield, Daniel F. 141, 144
Browning, John 263
Browns 95
Brulez, Joseph 132
Brunk, William 116
Brushas, John 231
Bryant, Chief Justice William P. 120
Bryant, Hon. William P. 313
Budd, Sarah 32, 41
buffalo 23, 40, 47, 49, 53
buffalo chips 38, 44, 65
Burbee, Jonathan 120, 121, 139, 140, 141
Buren, President Martin Van 17
Buriess, Clarissa 116
Burney, James 139
Burnt River 73
Burress, Mr. 148
Busey, W.B. 184
Bush 42, 106, 274, 332, 333, 334, 335, 336, 337, 338, 344
Bush Prairie 104
Bush, Dan 247
Bush, Ethel M. 303, 308
Bush, George 104, 290
Bush, Judd C. 154, 163, 164, 165, 274
Buxton, J.R. 301
Bydenhour wagon 56
Bydenhours 58

C

Cain, J. 186
Calhound, Mr. 260
California 20, 21, 22, 54, 55, 61, 64, 87, 100, 162, 189, 197, 202, 207, 220, 244, 250, 326, 331, 341, 344, 346
Camas Mountain 65
Campbell, Kathy 2
Canada 20, 40, 133, 268
Canadians 61, 64, 109,

111, 132, 219
Canemah, Oregon 82
Cannon, James 116
Cape Horn 159
Carrie, a steamer 235
Carrier, Isam 120
Carruthers, Phineas 31
Carsons, Mr. 236
Carter, T.J. 184
Carter, Thomas 167
Cascade mountains 75, 99
Cascades 78, 99, 331, 332, 344
Case, Mrs. 262
Casnon, James 148
Castle Rock 44, 184, 225
Cathlamet 135, 139, 143, 147, 333, 344
Catlin, Seth 122, 139
Catman, Xavier 132
Cayuse 74, 75, 76, 84, 85, 87, 114, 158, 207, 330, 351
  Walla Walla Indians 74
Cayuse War of 1848 to 1850 85, 87, 207
Celilo Falls 78, 79, 329, 343
Centralia 2, 5, 99, 114, 134, 142, 156, 184, 185, 225, 259, 301, 319, 331, 333, 334, 335, 338, 339, 341, 342, 344, 345, 346, 348, 349, 351
Chable, F. 171, 252
Chambers, David 120, 141, 254
Chambers Prairie 251
Chambers, Thomas M. 120, 141
Champoeg 89
Champs, Wm. 269
Chapman, John B. 139, 140, 141, 142, 143, 144, 156, 266, 267, 344
Chapmans 274
Chappellier & Daulne 214
Chappellier, Marcell 225, 232, 233, 235
Chappelliers 219
Charles County, Maryland 15
Charloafter, John Batise 120
Chaulifoux, Jean 132
Chehalis 93, 99, 109, 118, 121, 123, 129, 130, 132, 134, 142, 159, 166, 167, 177, 184, 211, 212, 213, 215, 216, 225, 250, 251, 285, 287, 293, 299, 302, 305, 317, 319, 320, 331
The Chehalis Advocate 137, 237, 283, 333, 338, 341, 342, 343, 351
The Chehalis Bee-Nugget 128, 133, 154, 163, 165, 199, 219, 247, 274, 294, 296, 297, 300, 301, 303, 304, 306, 307, 316, 318, 326, 330, 332, 333, 334, 335, 336, 337, 338, 339, 341, 342, 343, 344, 347, 348, 349, 352
Chehalis Indians 118
Chehalis River 109, 123, 184, 186, 266, 296, 317
Chehalis tribe 159
Chehalis Women's club 320
Chicago 87, 208, 332, 343
Chimney Rock 45, 46
Chinook jargon 102, 159
Chinook precinct 139
Chittenden, Rev. A.H. 302
cholera 19, 35, 41, 98, 321, 326, 345
Christmas 112, 227
Civil Air Patrol 320
Civil War 162, 189, 207, 220
Civilian Conservation Corps 315
Clackamas Bottom 101
Clackamas County 178, 191, 336, 346
Clair, Mr. 221, 228
Clammoths 90
Claquato 134, 156, 166, 186, 199, 215, 222, 229, 256, 258, 263, 264, 287, 291
Claquato Academy 250
Claquato Landmarks 5, 133, 237, 326, 330, 332, 335, 337, 344
Clark County 121
Clark, Charles 252
Clark, F.A. 157
Clark, General William 13
Clark, Captain William 13
Clatsop County, Oregon 127
Clay County, Missouri 104
Clendenin, T.S. 169
Clinger, J.D. 228, 231, 252, 338, 348
Clyman, James 98, 100, 331, 344
Cochran, James 138, 156, 157
Coffman, Noah B. 5, 76, 133, 237
Coleman, Mrs. 315
Collins, L.M. 144
Columbia 31, 46, 75, 101, 102, 158, 162, 228, 262, 268, 280, 287, 290, 310, 314, 322, 345, 349
Columbia River 20, 21, 67, 68, 78, 80, 100, 103, 104, 105, 108, 109, 123, 138, 140, 157, 171, 189, 224, 308, 312, 317, 334
The Columbian 160, 334, 342
Colville 187
Common Prayer Book 214
Congress 12, 15, 17, 20, 66, 85, 105, 114, 133, 140, 144, 157, 158, 164, 199, 286, 313, 319, 334, 342
Connaires 219
Conover, C.T. 268
Coonc, David M. 78
Coonc, Elizabeth (Fenn) 78
Coonse baby 74
Coonse, Alonzo Barton (aka Coonce; see also Koontz) 16, 72, 73, 111, 126, 127, 135, 166, 169, 170, 171, 176, 184, 202, 209, 212, 214, 221, 222, 224, 225, 227, 228, 229, 230, 231, 236, 237, 238, 247, 251, 252, 254, 256, 258, 259, 260, 262, 264, 266, 267, 269, 270, 273, 274, 276, 278, 279, 280, 283, 285, 288, 289, 291, 292, 294, 296, 297, 300, 301, 302, 306, 315, 332, 334, 335, 336, 337, 338, 339, 342, 343, 344, 345, 348, 349, 351
Coonse boys 73
Coonse family 17, 32, 33, 40
Coontz, Abraham 13
Coontz, Felix (Nicholas's brother) 13
Coonse, Felix "Grundy" (aka Coons; see also Koontz) 16, 37, 72, 73, 89, 111, 174, 176, 187, 188, 203, 220, 288, 297
Coonse, Henry M. (aka Coonce; see also Koontz) 73, 169, 184, 203, 335, 336, 345
Coonse, John 72, 73, 111, 212, 221, 222, 224, 225, 227, 228, 229, 231, 256, 267, 288, 289
Coontz, Maria 13
Coonse, Mrs. Matilda N. (Glover) (aka Coons; see also Koontz) 10, 17, 107, 108, 111, 114, 187, 310, 325, 332, 346
Coonse, Nicholas 7, 10, 11, 13, 15, 16, 17, 19, 20, 21, 23, 24, 25, 27, 29, 30, 31, 32, 33, 40, 44, 49, 51, 53, 54, 58, 61, 68, 71, 74, 78, 83, 84, 87, 89, 147, 148, 151, 159, 164, 202, 207, 212, 288, 293, 297, 305, 317, 321, 322, 325, 326, 345, 349, 352
Coonse, Sarah "Sally" (see also Mrs. Philip Glover) 15
Coonse wagon 31, 37, 63

Index

Coonses 28, 31, 34, 39, 51, 55, 58, 68, 70, 98, 194
Coontz 10, 14, 25, 115, 231, 232, 337, 346, 349
Coontz family 7, 11, 13, 15, 325
Coontz Fort (aka Kountz Fort) 13
Coontz, Jacob 11
Coontz, Colonel John 11, 13, 14
Coontz, Nicholas Sr. 11, 13, 16
Coontz, Rebecca 13
Coontz, Sarah "Sally" (Nicholas's sister) 13, 15
Coontz, William 13
Corp, James M. 301
Corps of Discovery 13
Cottleville 13
Cottonier 132
Cottonier, Isabel 214
Cottonier, Michel 120
Coughenour, James 96
Coughenour, John 96
Coughenour, Peter L. 96
Coulter, Sam 263
Council Bluffs 35
Count, John 264
Courthouse Rock (aka Castle Rock) 44, 45
Castle Rock (aka Courthouse Rock) 44
Cow [Kaw or Kansas River] river. 31
Cowlitz Convention 140, 158, 313, 333, 334, 343, 349
Cowlitz County 221, 331, 350
Cowlitz Farm(s) 102, 103, 105, 106, 111, 128, 130, 132, 134, 135, 138, 162, 172, 190, 224, 228, 347
Cowlitz Hotel 167, 168
Cowlitz Indian(s) 102, 111, 118, 127, 138, 221
Cowlitz Landing 102, 103, 104, 106, 110, 121, 126, 132, 138, 139, 140, 141, 156, 157, 158, 159, 160, 163, 167, 168, 169, 170, 172, 177, 184, 187, 203, 220, 224, 225, 227, 228, 230, 232, 233, 256, 258, 259, 260, 262, 263, 264, 269, 276, 310, 322, 333, 344, 352
Cowlitz Mission 111, 131
Cowlitz tribe 159
Cowlitz Post Office 171, 220, 285
Cowlitz Prairie 101, 104, 120, 126, 132, 138, 160, 171, 214, 225, 280, 331, 350
Cowlitz River 93, 102, 105, 108, 109, 110, 120, 121, 138, 139, 143, 145, 147, 157, 158, 164, 184, 199, 203, 204, 214, 230, 242, 246
Cowlitz Road 167
Cowlitz Steam Navigation Co. 234
Cowlitz Steam Navigation Company 232, 233, 337, 351
Cowlitz to Klickitat prairie 185
Cowlitz township 121, 122, 167
Cowlitz Trail 103, 110, 123, 162, 199, 242
Cowlitz Prairie 99
Craig, William 120
Cravens, James I. 148
Crockett, Samuel B. "Sam" 104, 105, 106, 122
Crowell, Sandra 5
Cumberland Road 9, 10
Cunningham, Thomas 111
Curry, George Law 108
Cussass (see also Kussass)119, 120
Cutting, J.B. 138, 214

D

D.A.R. 316
The Daily Chronicle 5, 320, 331, 333, 334, 335, 336, 341, 343, 345, 346, 351
Dardenne Township 13
Daugherty, William P. 141, 142, 144, 156
Daughters of the American Revolution 14, 306
Daughters of the Pioneers of Washington (also Daughters of Washington Pioneers) 319, 320
Davis 156, 157, 168, 215, 287, 291
Davis, A.L. 266
Davis, Col. 199
Davis, J.C. 167, 177, 178
Davis, Lewis H. 216, 222
Davis, M. 156
Davis, Senator W.S. 308
Davis, Thomas 184
Decker, Mr. and Mrs. 222
Declaration of Independence 53, 54, 162
Delameter Creek 221
Delling, A.B. 214
Dement, John D. 283, 285
Deschutes River 101, 104
Dickson, Rev. 300
Dillenbaugh, Sheriff A.B. 157, 167, 168, 225, 231
District Court 127, 130, 139, 143, 144, 254, 276, 312, 333, 344
Dodge, Daniel 159, 225
Donahoe, Augustine 303, 304, 306, 314
Donahoe, Francis 297
Donation Land Claim Act of 1850 (also Donation Land Claim) 128, 130, 132, 133, 134, 138, 280, 291, 296, 299, 333, 342, 344, 345
Donner party 54, 55
Drew, Captain George 132, 137, 139, 160, 164
Drew's Creek 106
Drew's mill 164, 167
Drew's Prairie 111, 231, 280
Drew's Station 138
Dubeau, Louis L. (also L.L.) 214, 219, 228, 231, 235, 258, 265, 266, 268, 276, 278, 336, 338, 345, 348, 350
Duffany, Oliver 120
Duncan 112, 335, 345
Duncan, Hiram 112, 116, 118, 147, 178, 179, 182
Duncan, Janette "Jane" (Glover) (aka Jenett) 118, 147, 151, 152, 178, 179, 182
Dunlap, Smith 53
Mr. Durgons Saloon 218
Durham County, England 93, 202, 308, 317
Dutchess County, Poughkeepsie, New York 94, 95
Dutton, James 112
Dutton, John 152
Duwamish River 139, 144
Duwamish township 156

E

Eagle Creek 115
Eaton, Captain Charles 189, 256
Eaton's Rangers 189
Ebey, Honorable Isaac N. 115, 121, 138
Edding 263
Eden Prairie 177
Edgar, John 121
Eggers, Doctor 218
Elder, Mr. 216
Ellenberge, John 120
Elson, Thomas T. 116
Elton, Thomas 113, 180
Emigrant Bottom 80
The Emigrants' Guide to Oregon and California 21
Emma R. Hunt 138
England 9, 40, 93, 95,

101, 130, 138, 219, 252, 308, 336, 345
Ensign, Mr. 254
Ethel 134, 138, 230, 303, 308
Evans, David 197
The Evening Statesman 301, 339, 345

F
Farewell Bend 73
Father Richard 231
Fayette, Missouri 18, 326, 343
Federal District Court (aka Federal Court, District Court) 127, 143, 147, 312, 319
Fenn, Elizabeth Ann 76, 329, 345
Ferguson, Jesse 104
Fern Hill Cemetery 93, 212, 213, 274, 275, 297, 307, 336, 347
Ferry, Elisha P. 313
Fillmore, President Millard 158
Finch, J.L. 135
Fine, Thomas 90, 197, 202
Fishers 34, 39
Fissel, E.D. 302
Florida 133
Floyd, Representative John 133
Ford, Judge Sidney S. (aka Senator) 114, 120, 121, 134, 138, 139, 141, 142, 144, 156, 183, 185, 186, 225, 311, 312
Ford, Maskeefe (Tom's wife) 185
Ford, Mrs. 138
Ford, Nathaniel 98, 99
Ford, Tom "Tommy" 185, 186
Ford's company 98, 99
Ford's home 142, 143, 144, 147, 311
Ford's Prairie 114, 333, 344
Forrester, T. 236
Fort Arkansas, (Castle Rock blockhouse) 184
Fort Boise 67, 73, 329, 350
Fort Borst Park 184
Fort Bridger 59, 60, 61, 64, 328, 343
Fort Bridger State Historic Site and Museum 59, 60
Fort Hall 34, 64, 73, 328, 349
Fort Henness 184, 185, 186
Fort Humboldt 162
Fort John 47, 50
Fort Laramie 37, 46, 47, 48, 50, 54, 55, 61, 100, 327, 341, 346
Fort Nisqually 103, 107, 110, 118, 132, 162
Fort Osage 13
Fort Redding 189
Fort Steilacoom 119, 120, 123, 133, 139, 190, 227, 288, 294, 312, 319
Fort Vancouver 80, 81, 100, 101, 103, 123, 130, 162, 288, 294, 319
Fort Walla Walla 76, 77, 78, 288, 291, 293, 329, 346
Fort William 47
Foster, John H. 196, 227
Fourth of July 53, 56, 114, 160, 170, 227, 258
Fox Island 189
Fraser River Gold Rush 171
Fraser, William L. 122
French-Canadian 34, 102, 111, 126
Fulkerson, Fred Rich 56
Fund, Lewis County Commissioner Edna 5

G
Galloway, James 135, 191
Galvin, George J. 319
Gangloff, Gus 166, 219, 222
Garrison 258
Garrison, Erastus 231
Garrison, G. 263
Garrison, Kelly 263
Garrison, R. 263
Gates, Old Mr. 191

Germany 209
Gibbs 199
Gibson, Bardolph 197
Gibson, Humphrey 31
Gibson, James 31
Gibson, Joseph 196
Gibson, Mrs. 197
Giddings, Annie 218
Giddings, Edward 215, 216, 218
Giddings, Mrs. 216, 218
Gill, Commissioner Simon (aka Judge) 120, 121, 139, 141
Gill, G. 138
Gilliam, Cornelius 99
Glasgow, Thomas 143
Glen, Mr. 169
Glenn, William K. 320
Glenns Ferry, Idaho 68
Glover, Dely ann 148
Glover, Elton 148
Glover, Elvira 148
Glover, Elizaann 89
Glover, James 113, 116, 178, 180, 182
Glover, James (cousin) 196
Glover, Jane 25, 70, 72, 87, 89, 90, 96, 113, 194, 196, 197, 201, 336, 346
Glover, John P. 113, 115, 179, 191, 194, 195, 196, 202, 276, 335, 345
Glover, John Philpott 9, 16, 343
Glover, John T. 178
Glover, M. 152
Glover, Matilda 15, 118, 149, 150, 152
Glover, Matilda (Nettle) 9, 16, 20
Glover, Joe 127
Glover, Matthew D. 16, 88, 89, 111, 114. 116
Glover, Philip 10, 15, 16, 24, 25, 112, 115, 153, 325, 326, 335, 345, 350
Glover, Samuel (Matilda's nephew) 148, 263
Glover, Sarah "Sally" (Coontz, aka Koontz) 16, 24, 25, 115
Glover, Thomas 148
Glover, William 25, 70, 87, 89, 91, 113, 148, 194, 197, 198, 201, 202, 336, 346
Glovers 7, 9, 10, 15, 25, 28, 112, 178, 325
Goff, Captain John H. 186, 252, 297
Gold Rush 20, 171
Goldsborough, Hugh A. 122, 141, 211
Goodell, Reverend J.W. 162
Gordon, Benjamin 143
Gordon, John P. 98
Gordon, Rev. Herbert E. 319
Gosnell 233, 256, 260, 264, 266
Gosnell, Mr. 229, 231
Gosnell, Wesley B. 225, 264, 266
Grainger, Charles 190, 224
Grainger, Mrs. 219
Grand Mound Prairie 184, 185
Grand Ronde River 74
Grand Ronde Valley 74
Grandma Jackson (aka Grandmother) 250, 291, 294, 297, 308, 325, 335, 336, 344, 348
Grange, Johnnie 278
Grant County 207
Grant, Esther (Brown) 137, 183
Grant, General Ulysses S. "U.S." (aka Captain) 10, 64, 123, 162, 166, 294, 319, 322, 349
Grants 58, 134
Gray's Harbor 109
Great Britain 100, 133
Great Salt Lake Valley 61
Green River 57, 58, 61, 99
Green, Mr. 227
Greer, Ralph C. 58
Gregg, Charles C. 248, 252

Index

Gregg, Dr. Kate L. 5, 76, 99, 249, 252, 319
Griffith, Richard 252
Griggsville, Pike County, Illinois 95, 96, 97, 98

H

H.J. Miller Lumber Company 315
Hall, James 144
Hall, Sheriff Javan 216, 336, 347
Haller, Major Granville O. 189
Halls 219
Hamlin, Nathaniel 120
Hancock, Eliza Laura 118, 152
Hancock, Samuel 120
Hancock, Sarahann 112
Hancock, Thomas D. 148
Hannon, Trudy R. 5, 111
Harmon, Alexandra 190
Harris, Major Moses (Black) 99
Harrison, President Benjamin 286
Hartford, Edward 177
Hastings, Lansford W. 21, 22, 23, 24, 26, 326, 346
Hemenway, Lewis County Commissioner Carl 321
Hennessey, Captain Patrick 160, 186, 225
Hennesseys 227
Henrietta Maria (queen consort) 9
Henriot, Abel P. 285
Henriots 219
Hewitt, Judge C.C. 135
Highland 140, 172, 210, 211, 212, 226, 236, 254, 274, 308, 310, 314, 336, 351
Highland Farm 7, 103, 108, 110, 114, 123, 141, 153, 154, 155, 157, 161, 163, 165, 167, 171, 245, 317, 334

Highland Farm 106, 242, 251
Highland Post Office 171, 199, 215, 220
Highland Prairie 103, 104, 164
The Highlands 103, 123, 153, 162, 184, 212, 214, 280
Highway 99 305
Hill, Captain Bennett H. 119
Hinman, Gaffne 87
Hinman, Mr. [Alanson] 85
Historical Sites Advisory Board 320
Historylink.org 286, 330, 333, 334, 335, 338, 343, 345, 348, 349, 351, 352
Hitchcock, Lorenzo 95
Hobart, Colonel Charles W. 287, 290, 291, 339, 346
Hockett, William A. 39
Holland, John 233
Holmes, Azro 180
Holmes, James 256
Hopkinson, Judge Joseph 314
Horse Creek 46
Howe, Horace 135
Howes 219
Hudson's Bay Company 64, 78, 80, 81, 100, 102, 103, 105, 106, 111, 119, 128, 129, 130, 132, 135, 138, 154, 219, 224, 228, 288, 290, 333, 350
Huggins, Edward 128, 129, 130, 131, 132, 133, 166, 288, 333, 344, 347
Huggins, Mrs. 166
Huntington, Henry D. 139
hymns 28, 186, 214, 246, 316

I

Idaho 61, 63, 68, 127, 288, 293, 328, 342, 349
Idaho Department of Parks and Recreation 69
Illinois 10, 19, 35, 41, 95, 96, 97, 166, 285, 308, 317
Independence 9, 20, 24, 27, 28, 31, 38, 40, 46, 56, 58, 162, 170, 227, 258, 315
Independence Day 53, 55, 160, 162, 227, 258
Independence Rock 53, 55, 58
Indian Wars 7, 183, 185, 186, 187, 188, 189, 191, 193, 195, 197, 199, 207, 251, 335
Internal Revenue Service 211
Iowa 33, 35, 287
Iroquois 102

J

Jackson Courthouse (aka Jackson's Courthouse) 122, 130, 138, 139, 141, 143, 147, 156, 161, 189, 292, 303, 305, 307, 315, 320, 321, 322, 323, 324, 332, 339, 341, 343, 345, 349
Jackson farm 212
Jackson Highway 305, 322
Jackson House 165, 219, 314, 320, 321, 322, 341
Jackson Prairie (aka Jackson's Prairie) 99, 157, 251, 274, 287, 288, 290, 291, 294, 296, 299, 301, 302, 304, 306, 307, 315, 317, 320, 322, 332, 335, 336, 339, 341, 342, 343, 344
Jackson, President Andrew 17, 247
Jackson, Andrew M. 137, 159, 212, 213, 343
Jackson, Anne 93
Jackson, Anthony Calvert 93
Jackson, Catherine 93
Jackson, John H.P. 100
Jackson, Captain John Robinson "J.R." 5, 93, 94, 96, 97, 98, 100, 104, 105, 107, 108, 110, 111, 115, 118, 120, 121, 122, 123, 130, 131, 134, 135, 137, 139, 141, 142, 145, 152, 155, 157, 163, 164, 174, 175, 176, 177, 178, 184, 194, 197, 199, 203, 211, 216, 220, 221, 222, 226, 228, 229, 230, 231, 232, 233, 235, 241, 244, 247, 248, 251, 252, 254, 255, 259, 261, 262, 265, 266, 268, 271, 271, 274, 275, 276, 277, 280, 283, 287, 288, 290, 291, 293, 294, 296, 297, 299, 301, 302, 304, 306, 308, 310, 311, 312, 313, 314, 316, 317, 320, 321, 322, 325, 326, 330, 331, 332, 333, 334, 336, 337, 338, 341, 342, 343, 344, 345, 346, 348, 349, 350, 351
Jackson, John Roberson 317
Jackson, Louisa Matilda "Lulie" (see also Louisa (Jackson) Ware) 5, 159, 160, 163, 165, 166, 204, 206, 209, 212, 216, 217, 220, 221, 222, 223, 224, 225, 227, 228, 229, 230, 231, 239, 247, 250, 251, 254, 256, 258, 259, 260, 263, 264, 266, 267, 269, 270, 279, 285, 296, 297, 300, 302, 304, 305, 306, 314, 316, 317, 319, 324, 329, 331, 334, 337, 338, 339, 341, 342, 345, 348, 349, 351
Jackson, Martha 96
Jackson, Mary (John R. Jackson's sister) 93
Jackson, Mary Elizabeth (see also Mary (Jackson) Phillips) 115, 159, 166, 212, 216, 218, 225, 227, 228, 229, 251, 252, 253, 283, 299, 302, 337, 338, 348
Jackson, Matilda Ann Nettle (Glover) Koontz (also Coonse) 1, 5, 115, 123, 131, 138, 152, 159, 160, 161, 163, 164, 165,

191, 192, 200, 215, 213, 220, 222, 229, 232, 233, 237, 239, 240, 241, 244, 245, 246, 247, 251, 282, 283, 285, 287, 288, 290, 291, 292, 293, 294, 295, 296, 298, 303, 304, 305, 306, 308, 309, 310, 316, 319, 320, 321, 322, 324, 326, 330, 332, 333, 334, 335, 336, 337, 338, 339, 341, 342, 343, 345, 346, 347, 349, 351
Jackson, Michael 93
Jackson, Mrs. (Not Matilda) 222
Jackson Prairie 99
Jackson, Susannah 93
Jackson, William 93
Jackson, Widow 278, 282, 283
Jacksons, the 118, 137, 138, 140, 159, 165, 167, 169, 170, 171, 172, 189, 199, 211, 212, 214, 215, 219, 221, 224, 227, 229, 230, 250, 256, 258, 259, 263, 264, 269, 274, 280, 290, 305, 314
James, Mr. 229, 254
John, Rev. H. 310
Johnson, Karen L. 220, 225
Johnson, Reverend Hezekiah 108
Johnson, Serene A. 220, 225
Jones, Gabriel 120, 227, 256
Joneses 104
Jory, James Jr. 32, 35, 40, 41, 47, 57, 68, 70, 73, 74, 75, 76, 80, 326, 327, 328, 329, 348
Jory, Phoebe 73
Jory, Mrs. James Sarah (Budd) 32, 35, 73
Jorys 40, 55, 68, 76
Judson, Ann 219
July Fourth 140

K

Kamiakin, Chief 189
Kane, Paul 77, 106, 332, 344
Kansas City 28

Keeney Pass 73
Kelly, Mr. 262
Kentucky 10, 13, 103
Kerins, John T. 232
Keyes, Mrs. Sara 34
Keyser, Mrs. 174, 176
Kiltze, Mrs 278
Kimball, Omar J. 73
Kindred, David 120
Kindreds 104
King Charles I 9
Kiser, Louise E. 316
Klallam Indian 102
Klickitats 183
Klickitat warriors 189
Knighton, Mrs. 44
Knighten, Sagarlin Columbia 46
Koontz, Anna 5, 76, 94, 97, 127, 138, 163, 187, 206, 223, 247, 250, 283, 297, 303, 305, 307, 308, 309, 310, 315, 317, 319, 320, 325, 330, 339, 346, 349, 351
Koontz, Barton (aka Coonse, Coonce, Koons) 171, 222, 231, 247, 252, 280, 289, 291, 292, 294, 296, 297, 300, 301, 302, 306, 315, 335, 336, 338, 339, 342, 343, 344, 348, 351
Koontz, Charlotte (Simmons) 10, 231, 232, 237, 250, 252, 283, 290, 299, 314
Koontz, Felix Grundy 187, 188
Koontz, Henry M. 205, 206
Koontz, Jessie 283, 297, 305, 307, 317
Koontz, John Nicholas "Johny" (aka Coonse, Coontz) 16, 222, 225, 227, 229, 231, 237, 252, 260, 263, 268, 280, 281, 282, 283, 288, 291, 294, 296, 297, 314, 338, 341, 345, 350
Koontz, Mrs. Matilda Nettle (Glover) 288, 293, 299, 310, 317
Koontz, Mattie (daughter of John and

Charlotte) 250
Koontz, Nettie (aka Mrs. George Beireis) 5, 237, 247, 283, 297, 305, 307, 314, 316, 326, 330, 332, 337, 342, 343, 348
Koontz, Nicholas 288, 293, 297, 305, 317
Kountz Fort (aka Coontz Fort) 14, 325, 343, 346
Kucera, Vic 5
Kussass (see also Cussass), Skykomish chief 120, 313

L

L.L. Dubeau & Co. 214, 336, 348
Lacamas Creek 103
Ladu, Crumlin 170
LaDue, Louis Ledo 221, 224—225
Lahalet 118, 119
Lane, Governor Joseph 114, 119, 158
Lane, Mrs. 256
Lanes 227
Lansdale, Dr. Richard H. 144, 156
LaRamer, Benjamin 120
Laramie Mountain (aka Ice Peak) 49
Laramie River 46, 48
Larrabee estate 304
Laughlin, James "Jim" (aka Jim Loflin) 33, 51
Lavelatla 103
Layton, Charles 184
Laytons 227
Ledo, Mr. 221, 225
Lee, Jason 133
Lee, Senator Virgil R. 320
Legard, Joseph 132
Leheat, Dr. Wilmot Jessy 197
Lerby, Lewis 209
Lerby, Lewis Jr. 209
Leschi, Nisqually Chief 183, 189, 190, 224, 335, 345
Levitt, Andrew 169, 335, 336, 345
Lewis County 93, 99, 105, 106, 108, 114, 119,

121, 134, 137, 142, 146, 156, 163, 167, 168, 171, 174, 177, 184, 206, 215, 219, 228, 231, 252, 264, 266, 268, 274, 276, 278, 280, 283, 287, 294, 297, 299, 301, 302, 304, 305, 306, 310, 311, 312, 317, 321, 326, 329, 330, 332, 333, 334, 335, 336, 337, 338, 339, 341, 342, 343, 344, 347, 348, 349, 350, 351
The Lewis County Advocate 299, 302, 303, 339, 341, 342
Lewis, Meriwether 13, 65, 105
Limpkin, Thomas 95
Lincoln County, Missouri 115, 147, 178, 335, 345, 346
Lincoln, President Abraham 162, 220, 313
Lindenwood University 13
Linn, Senator Lewis F. 133
Lister, Governor 304
Liverpool 252
Livingston, Robert 12
London 19, 138, 331, 336, 345
Long, Senator J.H. 287
Longmire, James 99
Longview 120, 157, 219, 224, 235
Loowit (fire mountain) 103
Louisiana Purchase 12
Lovejoy, A.L. 105
Lowe, Thomas 139
Lucas, Flossie 320
Lucas, Henry 319, 320
Luelling, Henderson 33, 326, 341

M

MacDonald, John M. 160, 228
MacDonald, Mary J. 228
MacDonald, Martha Harriet 228
MacDonalds 219, 227
Magone Lake 207
Magone Park 207

Index

Magone, Captain Joseph 28, 31, 33, 34, 35, 36, 37, 38, 39, 40, 41, 42, 44, 47, 49, 50, 54, 55, 58, 65, 67, 68, 70, 72, 73, 74, 76, 80, 83, 85, 86, 87, 90, 202, 207, 208, 326, 330, 336, 348, 349
Malad River 65
Malheur River, 73
Mannen, J.P. 184, 260
Mannen, Mrs. 260
Manning, Emmy 263
Manning, G. 263
Manning, Joseph P. 127, 167, 178
Manning, Mr. 222, 229, 263
Mannings 264
Marcum, Mr. 72
Marion College, Alabama 16
Marion County 178, 194, 201, 202, 276, 336, 346
Martin, John 5
Mary's Corner 305
Maryland 9, 10, 15, 288, 293, 296, 316, 317, 325, 348
Maskeefe, Tom [Ford]'s wife 185
Mason, Washington Territory's Acting Governor Charles H. 184
Matilda Jackson State Park 320, 322
Maynard, David S. 139, 141
Maynard, Mrs. 278
McAllister, James 141, 143
McAllisters 104
McBean, Mr. 78
McCallister, John 96, 98
McClellan, General George B. 10, 123, 162, 165, 294, 319, 322
McConnell, John M. 96
McConnell, Rebecca 11

McCormick, John 184
McDonald, John 269
McDonald, Mrs. 262
McDonald, Nora Charline (Sheehan) 3
McDonald Zander, Julie 2
McDonalds 256
McFadden Addition 297
McFadden, Honorable Judge O.B. 225, 256
McGuffey Fourth Reader 214
McIlroy, John 225
McKinney 28
McKinney, Captain John 31
McKinney, Rev. John 83, 85, 87
McKinney, Matilda 83
McKinney, William 83
McKinneys 83
McLoughlin, Dr. John 81, 83, 100, 101, 103, 107, 134
McMillan, Mr. 83
McTavish, John G. 268
Meany, Professor Edmond S. 103, 154, 156, 308, 317, 331, 333, 334, 349
Meek, Helen Mar 85, 114
Meek, Joseph "Joe" 85, 114, 120, 313
Meeker, Ezra 26, 190, 306
Meeker, Eliza Jane 306
Meeker, Marion 306
Metcalf, William 177, 178
Mexico 113
Michele, J.L. 178
Michigan 299
Miles, Charles 5, 133, 237, 326, 330, 332, 335, 337, 344
Miles, Henry 177, 225, 228
Military Road 197, 199, 211, 244, 294
Miller, A.I. 256
Miller, Joseph 189

Miller, Mabel J. 316
Miller, Mr. 221, 228
Miller, W.W. 216
Mills family 183, 185, 334, 335, 351
Mills, Cain 137
Mills, Elkanah 141, 156, 183, 184, 185, 334, 335, 351
Mills, Mary Jane 137, 156
Mills, Vianna Lorinda (Wisdom) 183
Mills, William (Elkanah's son) 183
Milwaukie 196
Minear, Jane 321
Mississippi Valley 68
Missouri 7, 10, 11, 12, 13, 14, 15, 16, 17, 18, 19, 20, 31, 33, 35, 41, 57, 58, 63, 70, 81, 87, 89, 91, 96, 98, 103, 104, 108, 111, 113, 115, 133, 140, 147, 157, 163, 178, 182, 189, 197, 202, 288, 293, 306, 308, 319, 320, 321, 325, 326, 327, 328, 330, 332, 335, 342, 343, 345, 346, 349, 351
Mitchel, J.L. 184
Mitchele, Sheriff J.L. 177
Mitchell, Ben 267
Mitchell, C.R. 319
Mitchell, M. 263
Mitchell, Miss 285
Mitchell, Mr. 256, 270, 273
Mitchell, Mrs. 264, 278
Mitchell, T.B. 252, 297
Mittge, Brian 5
Monfort, Rev. 297
Monroe, James 12
Monroe, Judge 200
Montana 127, 286
Montgomery County 111, 330, 332, 346
Montgomery, Mrs. 203
Monticello 120, 197, 214, 219, 224, 233, 235, 263, 264, 311, 333, 334, 342, 344, 345

Monticello Convention 157, 158, 160, 313
Montreal 102, 326, 327, 328, 343
Moore, John 168
Moore, Mrs. Mary 231
Moore, Paul 106
Moore, Philip D. 211
Moore, Sarah Jane 251
Moores 160
Mormon Ferry 54
The Morning Oregonian 274, 295, 296, 338, 339, 341, 342, 349
Moses, Abram Benton 189, 221
Mossyrock 134, 263
Mount Hood 80
Mount Rainier 103, 132
Mount St. Helens 103, 104, 106, 132, 331, 332, 344
Mourning, Susan 179
Muckleshoot(s) 183, 189
Muddy Creek 61
Munro, Washington Secretary of State Ralph 321, 322, 323
Myres, J.H. 236, 254

N

Napavine 134, 138, 199, 214, 290, 294, 336, 341, 345, 349
National Parks Service 315
National Register of Historic Places 320, 321
Nebraska 37, 42, 43
Nelson wagon 74
Nelson, Mr. 274
Nettle, Edith Dutton 9
New Jersey 162
New Market 104, 106, 109, 110, 231
New Testament 204, 247
New Year 202, 227, 230
New York 11, 28, 40, 95, 157, 202, 208, 224, 251, 252, 299, 308, 317,

359

330, 335, 351
New York City 95, 251
Newaukum 184, 224, 225, 258, 259, 260, 269, 270
Newaukum Prairie 99, 111, 138, 159, 160, 268
Newaukum River 103, 130, 168, 186, 266, 317
Newaukum township 141
Newland, John T. 297
Nez Perce 64, 74, 75
Niagara County, New York 299
Nichols, Jane 96
Nisqually 103, 105, 106, 107, 118, 121, 128, 132, 134, 139, 141, 143, 162, 183, 189, 335, 345, 347
Nisqually bottom 110
Nisqually River Flats 99
North Dakota 286
Northern Pacific Railroad 216, 264
Northwest Trading Company 102

O

Obrits, Charles 121
Ogden, William S. 232, 233
Ogdensburg 208
Olympia 99, 115, 139, 140, 143, 144, 147, 158, 160, 163, 164, 166, 167, 170, 174, 176, 183, 186, 203, 204, 211, 214, 216, 220, 224, 225, 227, 229, 251, 256, 258, 260, 263, 264, 266, 274, 276, 283, 286, 310, 311, 312, 314, 333, 334, 335, 336, 338, 339, 341, 342, 344, 346, 349, 350, 351, 352
Olympia township 121, 122, 141
Orbit (freighter)115
Oregon City 7, 54, 72, 76, 78, 81, 83, 84, 85, 87, 88, 89, 91, 92, 93, 100, 103, 106, 107, 108, 110, 114, 119, 134, 140, 151, 202, 236, 288, 291, 293, 297, 299, 310, 317,
322, 326, 330, 332, 345, 349, 352
Oregon Country 13, 133, 330, 331, 343, 352
Oregon Provisional Government 83, 104, 105, 133, 276
The Oregon Spectator 87, 106, 108, 114, 140, 144, 310, 332, 333, 349, 350
Oregon State Library 127
Oregon Steam Navigation Company 235
Oregon Territory 10, 20, 21, 23, 34, 35, 41, 47, 56, 57, 64, 72, 83, 84, 87, 103, 111, 114, 127, 128, 130, 133, 136, 140, 147, 156, 157, 178, 189, 191, 194, 201, 326, 327, 328, 329, 330, 332, 336, 343, 344, 346, 348
Oregon Trail 20, 21, 26, 27, 32, 33, 36, 55, 57, 59, 61, 62, 63, 73, 75, 81, 84, 87, 115, 124, 159, 178, 194, 207, 219, 231, 291, 306, 308, 314, 322, 326, 327, 328, 330, 341, 342, 343, 345, 346, 347, 349, 351, 352
The Oregonian 128, 140, 143, 291, 333, 341, 344, 347, 350
The Oregonian Statesman 143, 344
Orton, Nathan 221, 222, 224, 227
O'Sullivan, Timothy H. 66

P

Pacific City precinct 139
Pacific County 121, 174
Pacific Hotel 258
Pacific Northwest 10, 128, 134, 207, 274, 335, 336, 345
Pacific Ocean 58, 121, 312
Pacific Realty
Company 304
Packwood Saddle 99
Packwood, Mrs. Rhoda Bell (Prothro) 99
Packwood(town) 99
Packwood, William 99, 141, 143
Pagett, C.C. 167, 177, 178, 184, 231, 232
Park Rose 85
Parkman, Francis 21
Patkanim, Chief 119, 120, 313
Patrick County, Virginia 99
Patterson, Captain Elijah 31
Pe Ell 134
Pearson, Thomas M. 135, 184, 224
Peerson, John 98
Pell, Louise Henriette 126
Perkins, Henry 80
Phile, Philip 314
Philips, Andrew 98
Phillips family 258, 259, 263, 269, 273
Phillips, Edward "Eddie" 249, 250, 251, 252, 259
Phillips, James T. 225, 263
Phillips, Mrs. Mary Elizabeth (Jackson) 239, 248, 250, 251, 252, 258, 259, 263, 264, 267, 269, 273, 294, 296, 297, 299, 301, 302, 319, 339, 342, 349
Phillips, Mary Adelia "Mollie" (daughter of Sylvanus "Vean" A.) 249, 250, 251, 258
Phillips, Sylvanus A. "Vean" 239, 251, 252, 253, 254, 256, 258, 259, 260, 262, 263, 264, 267, 269, 270, 273, 276, 282, 283, 285, 296, 297, 299, 301, 302
Pickering, Washington Territorial Governor William 220
Pierce County 128, 129, 174, 332, 343
Piercy, Frederick 59
Pike County 95
Pike, General Zebulon 13
Pinnix, Cleve 321
Pinto, Horace H. 230, 231, 233, 256, 285, 337, 350
Pintos 219
Pioneer and Democrat 203, 204, 336, 350
Pittsfield, Pike County, Illinois 95
Plamondon, Simon Bonaparte 101, 102, 104, 106, 111, 120, 121, 122, 126, 132, 136, 137, 139, 140, 141, 156, 186, 214, 228, 280, 331, 333, 335, 344, 350
Plamondon's Landing 121, 139, 141
Plant, Salim 252
Platte River 7, 36, 37, 38, 39, 40, 41, 42, 43, 45, 46, 47, 49, 51, 53, 54, 321, 327
Plomondon 136
Plum Creek 39
Poe, Alonzo M. 105, 121, 140, 141, 144, 156, 157
Polk, President James Knox 20, 114
Polyglott Bible 214
Poplisteth 170
Port Townsend 157
Porter, James 120
Portland 130, 189, 191, 220, 232, 233, 235, 236, 254, 256, 258, 264, 266, 283, 293, 306, 316, 326, 327, 328, 329, 331, 337, 338, 339, 341, 342, 345, 346, 350, 352
Portneuf Range 64
Portneuf River 64
Poughkeepsie, Dutchess County, New York 95
Powel, Mr. 194
Powell, W. 58
Pre-Emption Act of 1841 20
Prince, Levi 252
Prudhomme, Martin S. 177

Index

Puget Sound 99, 104, 108, 109, 110, 119, 120, 121, 123, 130, 139, 140, 141, 162, 169, 207, 211, 264, 268, 276, 308, 317, 333, 334, 342, 344
Puget Sound Agricultural Company 102, 105, 128, 134, 135, 154, 156, 347
Puget Sound War 183, 189
Pumphrey, William 263
Pumphrey's 263, 264
Pumphrey'sLanding 214
Puyallup River 184
Puyallups 183
Pyett, Joseph 252

Q
Quaker 33, 34
Quallahworst 313
Quallahwowt (aka Quallawowt) 120
Quebec 101

R
Rabbeson, Antonio B. 114, 120
Raft Creek 64
Rainier, Oregon 138, 233
Rainier, a steamboat 233
Rains, Major Gabriel J. 189
Ray, D. 98
Rayton, John 252
Real, J. Batise 120
Register Cliff 49, 52, 62
Rice, Richard D. 264
Riches, Mrs. Jane E. 300
Richmond, Dr. J.P. 103
Ridgeway, William 95
Ring (Magone's dog) 35
Riverside Park 184
Roberts, George B. 103, 106, 111, 122, 130, 132, 134, 135, 138, 139, 141, 157, 159, 160, 167, 168, 184, 190, 222, 224, 225, 227, 228, 229, 231, 263, 264, 269, 270, 273, 274, 333, 335, 350
Roberts, J.B. 184
Robertson, Richard C. 96
Robinson, Mary 93
Robinson, R.S. 162, 169
Rockies 100
Rocky Mountains 7, 21, 63, 65, 100, 312, 321, 328
Rogers, John 269, 270
Roman Catholic 34, 131
Root, Mabel Glover 5, 316
Ross, Colonel 264
Ross, Walter 118, 119
Roundtree, Andrew J. 184
Roundtree, Mrs. J.H. 184
Roundtree, P.O. 184
Rowland, Mr. 258
Russ house 264
Russells 219

S
S'Geass 119
Sabbath 53, 170, 203, 216, 221, 227, 229, 230, 259
Sacks, Louis 184
Sager children 100
Sager, Louise 85
Sager, Henry 99
Saint Joseph Mission 189
Salem 89, 115, 127, 328, 332, 346, 348
Salish tribe 102
Salmon Falls 67
Salomon, Territorial Governor Edward Selig 256
San Francisco 115, 138, 160, 191, 251, 252, 314, 319, 321
Sandwich Islands [now the Hawaiian Islands] 101
Sandy River 35
Sandy River (Wyoming) 58
Sareault, Elie 132
Sareaults 219
Saunders Bottom 128, 141, 225
Saunders School Reader 214
Saunders, Eliza 84, 118, 128, 129, 148, 152, 186, 212, 306
Saunders, Schuyler S. 123, 128, 129, 139, 147, 167, 184, 186, 211, 212
Saundersville 167, 211, 215, 225
Scanewa, Chief 102
Schalle, Peter 121
Scotland 93, 166, 219
Scottish 166, 222
Scotts Bluff 40, 45, 46
Seaside, Oregon 137, 333, 343, 346
Seattle 121, 137, 169, 189, 250, 268, 278, 283, 291, 302, 311, 315, 317, 329, 331, 332, 333, 334, 335, 338, 339, 345, 347, 349, 350, 351
The Seattle Post-Intelligencer 291, 331, 334, 339, 345, 347, 349, 350
Seattle Preparatory School 250
The Seattle Times 169, 268, 332, 333, 335, 345, 349
Serl, Kerry MacGregor 5
Seward, Mr. 220
Sexton, John 120
Shad, Usler 96
Shaw, Captain 99
Shazeer, George 143
Sheridan, General Philip H. (aka Second Lieutenant) 10, 123, 294, 319
Shoshone Falls 66
Simmons, Sheriff Andrew Jackson "A.J." 120, 121, 122, 137, 138, 139, 140, 141, 143, 144, 147, 156, 157, 254, 256
Simmons, Benjamin 231
Simmons, Catherine 231
Simmons, Charles Mason 231
Simmons, Charlotte E. 231, 283, 299
Simmons, Christopher Columbus 104, 231
Simmons, David K. 231
Simmons, Douglas Woodbury 231
Simmons, Mrs. Elizabeth (Kindred) 231, 232, 278
Simmons, Enos F. M.D. 231
Simmons, George W. 231
Simmons, Jack 273
Simmons, Macdonald 231
Simmons, Mary 231
Simmons, Colonel Michael Trout "M.T." 99, 103, 106, 115, 120, 121, 134, 139, 141, 143, 144, 156, 228, 231, 290, 299, 320
Simmons, Michael T. 231
Simonton, Nellie Boone 250
Simpson, Sir George 268
Sioux 47, 49
Skagit 139
Skinner, District Attorney Alonzo A. 120
Skookumchuck 137, 224, 225, 259
Skookumchuck River 104, 121, 142, 184, 186, 188
Smith, David 139
Smith, Elizabeth Dixon 49, 72, 327, 328, 329, 346
Smith, Hiram 236
Smith, L.P. 139
Smith, Matilda (Koontz) (aka Mrs. John Smith) 283, 297, 305, 307, 317
Smith, John U. 283
Smith, Peter 227, 252,

361

260, 262, 263, 267
Snake River 7, 64, 65, 66, 67, 68, 69, 71, 72, 73, 75, 77, 79, 89, 107, 115, 203, 204, 288, 291, 293, 299, 304, 305, 317, 322, 328, 329, 349
Snake River Valley 47, 72
Snohomas river 110
Snoqualmie 107, 118, 119, 120, 313
Snoqualmie Indians 107, 118
Snoqualmies 119
Snow, John 19
Soda Springs 61, 63, 64, 328, 342, 350
Sons of the American Revolution 306
South Dakota 286
South Pass 47, 58, 100
South, Rebecca 96
Southerland, John 184
Spaulding, Eliza 84
Spencer, John 17
Spencers 219
St. Charles, Missouri 11, 13, 14, 15, 16, 17, 18, 25, 28, 81, 319, 325, 341, 342, 346, 351
St. Germain, Joseph St. 168, 230
St. Helens Club 303, 304, 306, 308, 309, 319, 320, 321
St. Joseph, Missouri 35
St. Louis 11, 13, 18, 19, 41, 61, 112, 140, 348
St. Peters 278
St. Urban 199
Staeger, Carl P. 283
Stafford 176, 191
Staindrop parish, Durham County, England 93, 308
Stannard, Reverend F.C. 308
Stark, James V. 184
Steamboat Springs 63
Stearns, Henry Sr. 250
Steilacoom 106, 107, 119, 120, 123, 129, 133, 139, 141, 142, 143, 144,
147, 163, 171, 190, 199, 227, 280, 288, 294, 312, 313, 319
Stevens, Washington Territorial Governor Isaac 158, 165, 166, 170, 172, 183, 190, 266, 269, 273, 310, 314, 322
Stevens, Mrs. 172, 310
Stillman, Henry R. 177, 178
Stoep, J.A. Vander 320
Stone, David 120
Strait of Juan de Fuca 121
Strong, James C. (brother to Judge Strong) 128, 139, 143, 156
Strong, Judge William 127, 128, 130, 135, 143, 144, 147, 156
Stuart, Hiram 120
Stuart, Peter G. 120
Stueve, Nathan 233, 235, 337, 351
Sublette, William 47
Summatah 132
Sumner, Clements 139
The Sunday Oregonian 315, 342
Suquamish Indians 107
Sutherland, John 128
Swan, John M. 141, 143
Sweetwater River 54, 55, 57, 100
Sylvester, Edmund 142, 143

T

Tacoma 121, 133, 156, 160, 189, 287, 298, 308, 315, 331, 334, 339, 342, 343, 346, 351, 352
Tacoma Daily Ledger 287, 339, 346
The Tacoma News Tribune 160, 315, 334, 339, 342, 351, 352
Taylor, Patsey 96
Taylor, President Zachary (aka Old General) 113, 127
Tennessee 13, 20
Territorial Legislature 15, 99, 156, 170, 174,
175, 190, 276, 290, 313, 317
Territory of Columbia 140, 157
Texas 5, 20, 148
Thackery, William Makepeace 214
Thasemuth, baptized as Veronica (chief Scanewa's daughter) 102
The Dalles 75, 76, 80, 82, 83, 100, 187
The Dalles Dam 79
Thompson, Mariah 96
Thons, Mr. 269
Thorp, John 99
Thornhill, Polly 197
Three Island Crossing 68, 69, 71, 74, 107, 329, 349
Thurston 130, 158
Thurston County 146, 147, 156, 184, 290, 329, 333, 344, 345
Tilaukait, Cayuse Chief 85
Tisdale, Donna 156, 183
Toledo 2, 102, 128, 134, 147, 163, 172, 184, 203, 225, 230, 242, 285, 297, 322, 331, 332, 333, 347, 349, 350
Tolmie, Hudson Bay Company Chief Factor Dr. William F. 105, 106, 119, 134, 166
Tom, a Cowlitz Indian 221, 258, 269
Tompkins 85, 351
Toppenish Creek 189
Traver, Mr. 266
Treaty of Medicine Creek 183
Troy, Missouri 16
Trullinger, G 236
Tucker, Mr. 227
Tuckers 227
Tullis, James 252, 266
Tumwater 104, 118, 119, 147, 220, 228, 230, 231, 260, 263, 331, 350
Tumwater Falls 101, 290
Turner, Mrs. 196, 197
Turner, Friend 196
Turner, Mary Jane 196
Turner, Elizabeth 196
Twiss, Charles P. 280
Twiss, Mr. 273
Twiss, Walter H. 94, 95, 330, 351
Tyling, Tom 264

U

U.S. District Court 276
Umatilla Indians 85
Umatilla River 74, 75
Umatilla Valley 74
Union Army 162
Union Gap 189
United States 12, 13, 15, 17, 20, 105, 114, 131, 133, 134, 135, 138, 154, 160, 162, 171, 207, 228, 231, 252, 266, 286, 308, 312, 313, 334, 337, 338, 344, 348
United States Internal Revenue 211
University of Washington 103, 154, 308, 317, 319, 331, 333, 334, 335, 336, 345, 349
Unruh, John D. Jr 20
Urquhart, Alee 222
Urquhart, Andrew 222
Urquhart Cemetery 274, 296, 297
Urquhart, David 222
Urquhart, Ellen 222, 274
Urquhart, James 228, 252, 254, 256, 267, 270
Urquhart, James Jr. 222
Urquhart, Jimmy 274
Urquhart, John 222
Urquhart, Margaret 222, 228
Urquhart, Mr. 225
Urquhart, Noble 222
Urquhart, Robb 222
Urquhart, William M. 222, 297
Urquharts 160, 219

V

Vale 73
Vancouver 80, 81, 100, 101, 103, 123, 127, 130, 162, 163, 199, 288, 294, 319, 349

Index

Vancouver district 105
Victor, Mrs. F.F. 134, 333, 335, 350
Victoria, British Columbia 105, 228
Virginia 99, 133, 157, 207

W

Waiilatpu 76, 77, 84, 99, 100
Walla Walla 34, 54, 57, 74, 76, 78, 84, 99, 140, 189, 286, 288, 291, 293, 301, 317, 326, 327, 328, 329, 339, 343, 345, 346
Wallace, Leander C. 107, 111, 118, 310, 313, 332, 343
Wallace, Leander G. 313
Wallace, William 120
Wallace, Mr. 87, 164
Waller, Methodist Reverend Alvin F. 81
Walmito, W. 235
Warbass, Captain Edward D. 132, 139, 140, 157, 171, 177, 178, 184
Warbassport 132
Ware, Josiah "Joe" Greenbury 285, 300, 301, 317
Ware, Mrs. Louisa Matilda (Jackson) 5, 160, 165, 223, 239, 296, 297, 301, 302, 304, 305, 306, 307, 314, 316, 324, 339, 341, 342
Warre, Lieutenant Henry 101
Wascopam Mission 75, 80, 82, 329, 343
Washington City 158, 199, 200, 266
The Washington Democrat 225
Washington Heritage Register 321
The Washington Standard 268, 276, 301, 338, 339, 349, 351
Washington State Historical Society 156, 287, 298, 303, 307, 308, 309, 314, 316, 319, 321, 326, 330, 331, 332, 334, 337, 343
Washington State Library 5, 29, 30, 86, 88, 91, 94, 97, 117, 136, 149, 150, 155, 175, 192, 198, 210, 211, 217, 220, 223, 226, 230, 234, 235, 253, 255, 257, 261, 262, 265, 271, 272, 281, 282, 284, 289, 312, 325, 326, 329, 330, 331, 332, 333, 334, 335, 336, 337, 338, 339, 343, 344, 345, 346, 347, 348, 349, 350, 351
Washington State Parks and Recreation Commission 320, 321
Washington State Parks and Recreation Department 321
Washington Territorial Legislature 99, 156, 174, 190
Washington Territorial Volunteers 183, 189
Washington Township 122, 139, 141
Washington, George (founder of Centralia) 156, 184, 314
Washougal 103, 104
Washougal River 103
Waterbury, Thomas 278
Watson School Reader 214
Watts, Dr. 316
Watts, Mrs. 65
Waunch, German native George 104, 105, 106
Webfoot, Esqr. Clinger. 256
Welch, Keziah 96
Welsh, Jimmy 262
West Indies 209
West Linn, Oregon 207
West, William 219, 252, 297
Western Union Telegraph 233, 235, 337, 344
Westminster Presbyterian Church 320
Westover, Justice W. A. 300
Westport 169
Whatcom County 171
Whay-guaylalkit, Chief 120
Wherry, Lt. William Mackey 13
Whidbey Island (aka Whitby's Island) 110, 120
Whit, Mr. 278
White Pass 99
White River Massacre 189
White, Clerk 157
White, Richard J. 156
Whitman Mission 7, 75, 76, 77, 80, 81, 83, 85, 87, 89, 91, 100, 330
Whitman, Doctor Marcus 57, 75, 76, 77, 78, 82, 84, 85, 99, 207, 288, 291, 293, 317, 329, 351
Whitman, Narcissa (Prentiss) 7, 84, 85, 99, 207
Whitmans 76, 84, 85, 99, 114
White River 184
Whitson, Mrs. 278
Whitworth, Mr. 216
Whyesk (Whyerk) 120
Wilcox family 35, 56
Wiley, Mr. 270, 274
Wilkins, Pam 321, 323
Willamette 80, 232, 234, 310, 322
Willamette Falls 81, 82
Willamette Iron Works Company 232, 234
Willamette Valley 20, 21, 27, 28, 61, 65, 67, 288, 293, 308
Willapa Bay 169
Wilson, W.H. 85, 103
Windsor, John A. 98
Windsor, Richard 98
Winkler, Pat 160
Winlock 134, 339, 341
The Winlock Pilot 291
Winsor, Henry 225, 258, 262
Winsor, Mrs. 262
Winston, Timothy R. 225
Wood, Richard 231
Wooley, Jacob 105
Wright, John 256
Wyam 78
Wylie, Dr. 191
Wyoming 58, 62, 327, 328, 341, 343, 346

Y

Yakama 187, 189, 207, 335, 343
Yakama War 183, 189
Yakamas 183
Yakima River 189
Yamhill County, Oregon, 99
Yantis, Mr. 222
Yates, Edward 163, 164, 222, 231, 258, 274, 334, 337, 338, 344
Yelm 143
Yorkshire 130, 131, 135
Young, J.Q.A. 76
Young, John 319
Young, R. 35

Z

Zander, Larry 5
Zander, Paul 5
Zander, Nora 5

www.ingramcontent.com/pod-product-compliance
Lightning Source LLC
Chambersburg PA
CBHW071313150426
43191CB00007B/611